For the best interactive guide to cooking,
nutrition, weight loss, and fitness,
visit our Web site at **http://www.healthyideas.com**

INTRODUCTION

❧ ❧ ❧

When the family comes home from a day at work, school or weekend play, it isn't carrot sticks or a bowl of broth they'll be clamoring for. They'll want real food, hearty food—preferably familiar dishes that they've come to love over the years. Can you fulfill this hunger for homestyle cooking without serving up too much fat, cholesterol and salt—and without spending hours in the kitchen cooking and cleaning up?

With *Prevention's Ultimate Quick and Healthy Cookbook*, you can. This book shows you how to trim down those family favorites and also introduces some new homestyle meals that will fit perfectly—and deliciously—into the busy schedules of today's families.

Perhaps the most important concept in reducing the fat content of a classic dish lies in shifting the focus so that more calories come from carbohydrates, especially complex carbohydrates (starches) and protein, than from fat. Take that universal favorite, macaroni and cheese, as an example. A standard recipe to serve four people calls for equal amounts of pasta and cheese, plus eggs, whole milk, and a topping of buttered bread crumbs and grated cheese. This casserole comes laden with more than 30 grams of fat per serving. To lighten the recipe, use more protein and less cheese, and add some vegetables to the dish. The recipe for Macaroni 'n' Cheese with Chicken (page 74), created along these lines, boasts a creamy sauce made from low-fat milk and a small amount of Cheddar and Romano cheeses. Smoked chicken, fresh herbs, and Dijon mustard pump up the flavor, and spinach is stirred into the sauce before the pasta is baked. The result is an undeniably delicious dish with just over 11 grams of fat per serving.

The same "tipping the balance" theory can be applied to stews (use less beef and more potatoes and carrots), steak dinners (pair sliced sirloin with lots of colorful sautéed bell peppers) and even desserts (top an abundant serving of fruit with frozen yogurt rather than garnishing a bowl of premium ice cream with a single cherry). And these aren't just theoretical cases: You'll find the recipes for these very "makeovers" in the pages of this book.

The substitution of low-fat ingredients is another route to healthier meals. Leaner cuts of meat, low-fat dairy products and egg whites instead of whole eggs can be introduced in standard recipes, although it may take a bit of experimentation. When lightening your own recipes, start by removing (or replacing) high-fat ingredients a little at a time until you find out how much alteration the dish can tolerate.

Of course, there will be times when you want to go all-out—to serve a lavishly frosted layer cake for a birthday party or share your great-grandmother's old-world lasagna at a family reunion. If your everyday meals are as wholesome as those you'll find within these pages, there's no reason not to enjoy the occasional splurge.

The next few pages of this book present healthy transformations of some of America's best-loved foods, including brownies and pizza. These recipes demonstrate some principles of healthier cooking that you can apply to your own favorite recipes: Bake rather than fry; use turkey or chicken instead of red meat; substitute yogurt for mayonnaise and sour cream; replace some of the fat in cookies and cakes with applesauce or yogurt.

On pages 8 and 9, you'll find a glossary of equipment that can help you minimize the fat in your diet while maximizing the flavor in your meals. You may already have some of these tools in your kitchen; if not, they're a small but worthwhile investment in your family's health and eating pleasure.

OVEN-FRIED CHICKEN

❧ ❧ ❧

Instead of frying chicken in several cups of fat, you can bake these slightly spicy, crisp-crusted chicken parts using only 2 teaspoons of oil.

- 1 cup unseasoned dry bread crumbs
- ½ cup plain nonfat yogurt
- 2 garlic cloves, crushed
- 2 teaspoons cider vinegar
- ½ teaspoon hot-pepper sauce
- 1½ pounds skinned chicken legs, drumsticks and thighs cut apart
- 2 teaspoons canola oil

1 Preheat the oven to 450°. Spray a jelly-roll pan with no-stick spray. Spread the breadcrumbs in a shallow plate.

2 In a large bowl, stir together the yogurt, garlic, vinegar and hot-pepper sauce. Add the chicken pieces and toss to coat well. One piece at time, transfer the chicken pieces to the plate of breadcrumbs and dredge them in the crumbs to coat evenly. Arrange the chicken in a single layer on the prepared pan.

3 Drizzle the oil over the chicken and bake for 30 to 35 minutes, or until the chicken is browned and no longer pink near the bone.

Per serving 286 calories, 8.4 g. fat, 1.7 g. saturated fat, 93 mg. cholesterol, 370 mg. sodium **Serves 4**

TUNA SALAD

❧ ❧ ❧

You don't have to "hold the mayo"—just use a combination of reduced-calorie mayonnaise and nonfat yogurt. Add lots of diced vegetables and chick-peas to yield truly bountiful portions.

2 cans (6⅛ ounces each) water-packed tuna

1 can (10½ ounces) chick-peas

1 large red bell pepper, diced

½ cup peeled, diced cucumber

1 medium tomato, diced

¼ cup sliced scallions

⅓ cup plain nonfat yogurt

3 tablespoons snipped fresh dill

2 tablespoons reduced-calorie mayonnaise

2 tablespoons fresh lemon juice

½ teaspoon freshly ground black pepper

½ teaspoon dry mustard

1 Drain the tuna, break it into chunks and place it in a strainer; rinse it under cold running water and drain again. Transfer the tuna to a serving bowl.

2 To the tuna, add the chick-peas, bell peppers, cucumbers, tomatoes and scallions, and toss gently. Add the yogurt, dill, mayonnaise, lemon juice, ground pepper and mustard, and stir until well mixed.

Per serving 243 calories, 3.5 g. fat, 0.7 g. saturated fat, 35 mg. cholesterol, 559 mg. sodium **Serves 4**

SPINACH PIZZA

❧ ❧ ❧

Easy on the cheese, generous with the vegetables—that's the way to make a guilt-free pizza. This one has a chewy herbed crust, a garlicky spinach topping and the rich flavor of sun-dried tomatoes.

1½ teaspoons active dry yeast

½ teaspoon granulated sugar

¾ cup lukewarm water (105° to 115°)

1¾ cups all-purpose flour

2 tablespoons grated Parmesan cheese

½ teaspoon dried oregano, crumbled

¼ teaspoon fennel seeds

½ teaspoon freshly ground black pepper

¼ teaspoon salt

2 ounces sun-dried tomatoes (not oil-packed)

1 cup boiling water

3 garlic cloves, thinly sliced

1 teaspoon extra-virgin olive oil

8 cups trimmed, loosely packed fresh spinach

1 can (8 ounces) no-salt-added tomato sauce

3 ounces shredded part-skim mozzarella cheese

⅛ teaspoon crushed red pepper flakes

1 In a small bowl, sprinkle the yeast and sugar over ¼ cup of the lukewarm water; stir until dissolved. Cover with plastic wrap and let stand for 5 to 10 minutes (the mixture should foam up).

2 Meanwhile, in a large bowl, mix the flour, 1 table-spoon of the Parmesan, the oregano, fennel seeds, ¼ teaspoon of the pepper and ⅛ teaspoon of the salt. Add the yeast mixture and the remaining ½ cup lukewarm water, and stir until a soft dough forms.

3 Gather the dough into a ball and knead on a lightly floured surface for 5 minutes, or until smooth and elastic. Spray a medium bowl with no-stick spray; place the dough in the bowl and turn to coat the dough with the spray. Cover the bowl with plastic wrap and let the dough rise in a warm place for 45 minutes, or until it is doubled in bulk.

4 Meanwhile, halve the sun-dried tomatoes. Place them in a small heatproof bowl and pour the boiling water over them. Let the tomatoes stand for 10 minutes, or until softened; drain and pat dry.

5 In a large no-stick skillet, mix the garlic cloves and oil. Place the skillet over high heat and sauté, stirring constantly, for 2 to 3 minutes, or until the garlic is lightly browned; transfer to a small plate.

6 Add half of the spinach to the skillet and stir-fry over high heat for 1 minute. Add the remaining spinach and stir-fry for 1 minute, or until wilted. Remove the skillet from the heat; stir in the remaining ¼ teaspoon pepper and remaining ⅛ teaspoon salt.

7 Preheat the oven to 500°. Spray a large baking sheet or a 12-inch pizza pan with no-stick spray. On a floured surface, using a floured rolling pin, roll the dough out to a 12-inch circle. Transfer the dough to the prepared sheet or pan. (If using a baking sheet, roll and pinch the edge of the dough into a raised border; if using a pizza pan, press the dough up the sides.) Spread the tomato sauce over the dough and bake for 8 to 10 minutes, or until the crust is lightly browned and the sauce is bubbly.

8 Remove the pizza from the oven and top with the spinach mixture. Sprinkle with the sautéed garlic and place the sun-dried tomatoes on top. Scatter the mozzarella over the pizza, then sprinkle with the remaining 1 tablespoon Parmesan and the red pepper. Bake for another 10 minutes, or until the cheese is bubbly and the crust is golden. Cut the pizza into wedges to serve.

Per serving 382 calories, 7.4 g. fat, 3.2 g. saturated fat, 15 mg. cholesterol, 427 mg. sodium **Serves 4**

HERBED OVEN FRIES

❧ ❧ ❧

The next time you're tempted by fast-food french fries, consider baking a batch of these herbed potatoes instead: A medium portion of fast-food fries may be laden with as much as 20 grams of fat.

1 **pound russet potatoes**

1 **tablespoon chopped fresh Italian parsley**

1½ **teaspoons olive oil**

½ **teaspoon dried thyme, crumbled**

¼ **teaspoon freshly ground black pepper**

⅛ **teaspoon salt**

1 Preheat the oven to 450°. Spray a heavy baking sheet or jelly-roll pan with no-stick spray.

2 Scrub the potatoes and cut them into ½-inch-thick matchsticks. Pile the potato sticks in the center of the prepared baking sheet and sprinkle with the parsley, oil, thyme, pepper and salt. Toss to coat well, then spread the potatoes in an even layer.

3 Bake the potatoes, turning them several times, for 20 to 25 minutes, or until crisp and browned.

Per serving 110 calories, 2.2 g. fat, 0.2 g. saturated fat, 0 mg. cholesterol, 78 mg. sodium **Serves 4**

¼ cup plain nonfat yogurt

¼ cup frozen apple juice concentrate

1 large egg plus 2 large egg whites

2 tablespoons vegetable oil

2 teaspoons vanilla extract

1 square (1 ounce) semisweet chocolate, melted

⅛ teaspoon salt

BROWNIES

✣ ✣ ✣

Serious chocolate lovers—especially those who half-jokingly refer to themselves as "chocolate addicts"—find their favorite high-fat treat all but impossible to forgo. These cakelike brownies will fill the "chocolate gap" nicely, with a minimum of fat.

1 cup all-purpose flour

⅓ cup unsweetened cocoa powder

¾ teaspoon baking powder

¼ teaspoon baking soda

⅔ cup unsweetened applesauce

½ cup granulated sugar

1 Preheat the oven to 350°. Spray an 8 x 8-inch baking pan with no-stick spray.

2 In a large bowl, combine the flour, cocoa, baking powder and baking soda, and stir until well mixed; set aside.

3 In a medium bowl, whisk together the applesauce, sugar, yogurt, apple juice concentrate, whole egg, oil and vanilla, then whisk in the melted chocolate; set aside.

4 In another large bowl, using an electric mixer on high speed, beat the egg whites and salt just until stiff, glossy (but not dry) peaks form.

5 Stir the chocolate mixture into the flour mixture, then, using a rubber spatula, fold in the beaten egg whites. Scrape the mixture into the prepared pan and bake for 25 minutes, or until a toothpick inserted in the center comes out clean.

6 Cool the brownies in the pan on a wire rack, then cut into 9 squares.

Per serving 183 calories, 5.2 g. fat, 1.4 g. saturated fat, 24 mg. cholesterol, 133 mg. sodium **Serves 9**

THE SMART COOK'S TOOLS

❧ ❧ ❧

Dependable recipes and high-quality ingredients are just two components of healthy home cooking. A third factor is the right kitchen tools, which can spell the difference between success and failure, efficiency and waste. Some of the equipment described here makes the preparation of healthful foods, such as fruits and vegetables, less of a chore, while some of the implements actually enable you to reduce the fat content of the dishes you prepare.

STEAMER Steaming is hard to beat as a healthful cooking method, especially for vegetables. Because the food does not directly contact the water, most nutrients are conserved. And because food is not likely to stick, there's no need for added fat. Steaming works very well for fish fillets and chicken cutlets. The familiar (and inexpensive) collapsible vegetable steamer, set into a pot with a tight-fitting lid, is fine for small quantities of food; steamers with multiple stacking inserts—either the Chinese bamboo type or stainless steel ver-

sions—let you cook an entire meal at once. Specialized electric rice steamers turn out perfect rice (and vegetables, too). You can improvise your own steamer by crossing a pair of wooden chopsticks in the bottom of a deep pan or wok and setting a plate on top of them; a wire cake-cooling rack can be used in the same way.

YOGURT FUNNEL If you've been trying to reduce the fat in your diet, you're probably eating less whipped cream, cream cheese, sour cream and mayonnaise. It's possible, however, to make sauces, dips, spreads—even cheesecake—with yogurt: not yogurt spooned straight from the container, but yogurt that's been thickened by draining off the whey (the liquid part). This can be

done by placing the yogurt in an inexpensive mesh yogurt funnel, or you can improvise with a strainer lined with cheesecloth or a drip-style coffee filter fitted with a paper liner. Use low-fat or nonfat plain yogurt—or a "smooth" yogurt flavor

such as coffee, vanilla or lemon. After draining for an hour or two, plain yogurt is ready to stand in for sour cream; if you're making a spread, dip or creamy dessert, drain the yogurt overnight. Sweeten or season the yogurt as you like after draining. Refrigerate the yogurt-draining setup if you're letting it stand for more than a few minutes.

GRAVY STRAINER It's hard to do a thorough job of skimming the fat from a pot of gravy, soup or sauce. The easy way out is to use a gravy strainer or a fat-removing ladle. A gravy strainer looks like a plastic measuring cup with a spout that originates near the bottom of the cup: When you pour in liquid, any fat rises to the top, and the defatted liquid can be poured off from the bottom through the spout. A strainer ladle accomplishes the same thing in a different way, acting as a skimmer to collect the fat from the top of the soup or stew while letting the defatted liquid flow back into the pot through the ladle's slotted edge.

SALAD SPINNER The process of cleansing greens—especially sandy ones like spinach—is

enough to put some people off eating salads. A big salad spinner makes quick work of cleaning lettuce, spinach and similar greens; small spinners are just the thing for washing herbs. You place the greens in the slotted interior basket and rinse them under the faucet, then slip the basket into an outer bowl. A crank or a pull cord spins the basket inside the bowl, "centrifuging" the leaves dry without splashing a drop. Store the greens in the spinner until mealtime.

MEASURING CUPS AND SPOONS Careful measuring of ingredients ensures that recipes will come out right (especially in baking, where the recipe is, in a sense, a chemical formula); and a measuring spoon or cup can give you a better idea  of portion sizes. Dry measuring cups come in graduated sizes: For accuracy, overfill the cup a bit, then level the contents with a knife. Clear measures for liquids come in 1-, 2- cup and larger sizes. Pour in the liquid, then check the measurement at eye level (by bending over rather than by lifting the cup). Dry measuring cups and measuring spoons should be deep, with smooth, flat rims for leveling.

SCALE Like measuring cups and spoons, a scale can help you learn to gauge portion sizes for high-fat foods such as meat, cheese and nuts: Once you have an idea of what a 4-ounce burger looks like, you no longer need to weigh the food each time. A scale will help you measure accurately for recipes that call for ingredients by weight, whether you need a 4-ounce fish fillet or a half-pound of potatoes. The best scales have a "tare" setting, which allows you to place a bowl on the platform and then reset to zero before adding the ingredient to be weighed. This function also lets you add one ingredient at a time, weighing each in turn as it goes into the bowl.

NO-STICK POTS AND PANS No-stick cook-ware—greatly improved since its introduction in the 1960s—is an indispensable tool for low-fat cooking. Today's no-stick surfaces, far more durable than the original, can withstand higher temperatures, and some can be used with metal kitchen utensils (although nylon or wooden tools are kinder to the coating). No-stick finishes are now available on bakeware, broiler pans, woks and appliances such as electric griddles and waffle irons. No-stick cookware may be made of steel, aluminum or even cast-iron, and it pays to invest in good-quality, heavyweight pots and pans, which distribute heat evenly to prevent scorching. A double or triple coating also ensures longer life for the no-stick surface. Even in a no-stick pan, a misting with no-stick spray makes it easier to cook foods that tend to break apart, such as fish fillets or pancakes, but you'll still be using a tiny of fraction of the fat you'd need in a regular pan.

CHEESE GRATER Surveys have shown that people trying to cut down on fat have a very hard time cutting down on cheese. Whether your favorite is Cheddar, Parmesan or Swiss, it helps to know that the more finely cheese is grated, the further it goes in a recipe or a sandwich—and the more flavor it releases on your tongue, so  you can use less cheese in your favorite dishes. A rotary grater produces very fine shreds of cheese, and works best when the cheese is well chilled.

SHARP KNIVES Literally "cutting the fat" from meat and poultry is much easier when you equip your kitchen with a few good basic knives. The vegetables and fruits that go into healthful meals also need to be sliced, diced and chopped, and good knives speed the job. A chef's knife, with a large, wedge-shaped blade, is a must, as is a small paring knife. Specialized knives for slicing bread, tomatoes or cheese, or for carving, are optional. Fine-quality knives of high-carbon steel (regular or stainless) hold an edge longer and take well to re-sharpening; ingeniously constructed sharpeners make sharpening nearly foolproof. You can also buy state-of-the-art knives that never need sharpening.

Soups &
Stews

❧ ❧ ❧

WARMING ONE-DISH MEALS

TO WELCOME THE FAMILY HOME

ON CHILLY NIGHTS

SCALLOP AND POTATO CHOWDER

3 large all-purpose potatoes, peeled and cut into ½-inch chunks

1¾ cups defatted reduced-sodium chicken broth

1 medium onion, diced (about 1 cup)

2 large celery stalks with leaves, thinly sliced (about 1 cup)

½ cup water

1 bay leaf

½ teaspoon freshly ground white pepper

¼ teaspoon dried thyme, crumbled

1 cup 1% low-fat milk

8 ounces sea scallops, rinsed and cut into ½-inch chunks

¼ teaspoon salt

1 tablespoon snipped fresh chives or thinly sliced scallion greens

¼ cup minced red bell peppers for garnish, optional

The word "chowder," usually applied to rich seafood soups, comes from the French word *chaudière*, meaning a large stew pot or caldron. But you don't need a special pot—or any other exotic equipment or ingredients—for this soothing, subtly herbed chowder: A saucepan and a spoon, some fresh vegetables, milk and a half-pound of sea scallops are just about all that's required for a delicious, light dinner that's ready in under an hour.

1 In a large, heavy saucepan, combine the potatoes, broth, onions, celery, water, bay leaf, white pepper and thyme; cover and bring to a boil over high heat. Reduce the heat to medium-low and simmer for 10 minutes, or until the potatoes are fork-tender.

2 Remove the pan from the heat and mash the potatoes slightly to thicken the soup. Stir in the milk.

3 Place the pan of soup over medium heat and bring to a simmer, stirring occasionally. Add the scallops and salt; cook, stirring occasionally, for 3 to 4 minutes, or until the scallops are just firm. Remove from the heat and stir in the chives or scallions. Top the chowder with the red bell peppers, if desired.

Preparation time 20 minutes • **Total time** 40 minutes • **Per serving** 208 calories, 1.8 g. fat (8% of calories), 0.5 g. saturated fat, 21 mg. cholesterol, 572 mg. sodium, 3.2 g. dietary fiber, 124 mg. calcium, 2 mg. iron, 31 mg. vitamin C, 0.1 mg. beta-carotene • **Serves 4**

❧   ❧   ❧

The freshest chives are those you grow yourself. Potted chives flourish in a sunny window; just snip off the tops as needed.

ON THE MENU
Crackers are traditional with chowder, but warm rolls make for an even more inviting meal. Another option: Serve thick slices of bread—perhaps a homemade quick bread flavored with dill and Cheddar.

FOOD FACT
When you're trimming celery stalks, don't toss out the leaves—they are the most flavorful part of the vegetable: This recipe

calls for celery stalks with their leaves for just that reason. The leaves add a fresh celery taste to soups and stews (highly preferable to bottled celery powder or celery salt). Crisp celery leaves make a refreshing difference in salads and can also serve as a pretty, edible garnish for a plate or platter. When you do need just the stalks, cut off the tops, wrap them tightly in plastic wrap and freeze them for future use as a seasoning.

MUSHROOM-BARLEY SOUP

- 1 **ounce dried mushrooms, such as porcini**
- 1 **cup boiling water**
- 2 **teaspoons olive oil**
- 12 **ounces fresh mushrooms, sliced (about 4 cups)**
- 1 **medium onion, chopped**
- ¾ **cup thinly sliced carrots**
- ⅓ **cup thinly sliced shallots or scallions (white parts only)**
- 2 **garlic cloves, minced**
- 1¾ **cups defatted reduced-sodium beef broth**
- ⅓ **cup quick-cooking barley (1½ ounces)**
- 1 **bay leaf**
- ¼ **teaspoon freshly ground black pepper**
- ¼ **teaspoon dill seeds**
- 1 **tablespoon snipped fresh dill**

One of the first crops cultivated by humankind, barley is still an important grain, although American diets are based much more on wheat and rice. Eastern Europeans, on the other hand, have long enjoyed thick barley soups like this one, made with dried mushrooms and dill. For a touch of richness, top each portion of soup with a spoonful of plain yogurt or light sour cream.

1 Place the dried mushrooms in a medium heatproof bowl and pour the boiling water over them. Set aside for 5 minutes, or until the mushrooms have softened.

2 Using a slotted spoon, lift the mushrooms from the liquid, reserving the liquid. Set the mushrooms aside to cool. Strain the reserved liquid through a cheesecloth-lined strainer into a small bowl, leaving behind any sediment. Coarsely chop the softened mushrooms.

3 In a large, heavy saucepan, warm the oil over high heat. Add the dried and fresh mushrooms, the onions, carrots, shallots or scallions and garlic; stir well to coat the vegetables with oil. Reduce the heat to medium-high, cover and cook, stirring occasionally, for 4 to 5 minutes, or until the fresh mushrooms begin to release their liquid.

4 Stir in the reserved mushroom soaking liquid, the broth, barley, bay leaf, black pepper and dill seeds; cover and bring to a boil over high heat. Reduce the heat to medium-low and simmer for 10 to 15 minutes, or until the barley is tender. Just before serving, stir in the fresh dill.

Preparation time 20 minutes • **Total time** 45 minutes • **Per serving** 143 calories, 2.9 g. fat (18% of calories), 0.4 g. saturated fat, 0 mg. cholesterol, 292 mg. sodium, 3.6 g. dietary fiber, 40 mg. calcium, 3 mg. iron, 9 mg. vitamin C, 2 mg. beta-carotene
Serves 4

Barley is wonderful in soups; you can also cook this flavorful grain as you would rice—steam it, bake it or prepare it as a pilaf—and serve the barley as a side dish or a main-dish casserole.

ON THE MENU
A light meal in itself, the soup also makes a good partner for sandwiches, such as turkey breast on peasant bread with honey-mustard and Romaine lettuce. Offer apples and gingersnaps for dessert.

MARKET AND PANTRY
Shallot heads are formed like garlic, with several cloves individually covered with a thin skin. Their flavor is about midway between onions and garlic. Choose firm, dry shallots free of soft spots or sprouts.

CHICKEN CHILI

1 can (14½ ounces) tomatoes
with juice

2 fresh medium tomatoes

1 can (8 ounces) no-salt-added
tomato sauce

8 ounces boneless, skinless
chicken breasts, cut into chunks

1 large onion, chopped

1 small red bell pepper, diced

1 small green bell pepper, diced

3 tablespoons chili powder

2 garlic cloves, minced

¾ teaspoon ground cumin

½ teaspoon freshly ground black
pepper

4 teaspoons olive oil

1 can (16 ounces) red kidney
beans, rinsed and drained

1 cup frozen corn kernels

½ cup medium or mild low-
sodium salsa

Hot-pepper sauce to taste
(optional)

¼ cup chopped fresh cilantro

There are as many ways to make chili as there are chili lovers: with beans, without beans, with chopped meat, with ground meat and with no meat at all. Here is a good basic recipe that you can tailor to your own tastes, adjusting the amounts of chili powder, garlic, salsa and hot-pepper sauce as you like.

1 Coarsely chop the undrained canned tomatoes and the fresh tomatoes in a food processor or by hand; transfer the tomatoes to a large bowl and stir in the tomato sauce.

2 Process the chicken in the food processor until finely chopped. Add the onions, bell peppers, chili powder, garlic, cumin and black pepper, and pulse just until mixed; set aside.

3 In a large, heavy saucepan, warm the oil over high heat until very hot. Add the chicken mixture and sauté for 3 to 4 minutes, or until the chicken turns white.

4 Stir in the tomato mixture, the beans, corn and salsa, and bring the mixture to a boil. Reduce the heat to medium-low, cover the pan and simmer for 10 minutes, or until the flavors are blended. Uncover the pan and simmer for 5 minutes longer.

5 Season the chili with hot-pepper sauce, if using. Ladle the chili into bowls and sprinkle with the cilantro.

Preparation time 20 minutes • **Total time** 40 minutes • **Per serving** 329 calories, 8 g. fat (22% of calories), 0.9 g. saturated fat, 33 mg. cholesterol, 426 mg. sodium, 11.2 g. dietary fiber, 101 mg. calcium, 4 mg. iron, 88 mg. vitamin C, 3 mg. beta-carotene • **Serves 4**

❧   ❧   ❧

MARKET AND PANTRY
Buying tomatoes out of season can be a risky proposition. Most are picked green so they'll survive shipping, and of these, the majority will ripen, but some—picked a bit too early—will never soften, turn red or develop any flavor. With that in mind, your best bet is to choose the reddest (or pinkest) tomatoes available and to look for heavy specimens that yield slightly when pressed between your hands. Ripen the tomatoes at room temperature for a few days; placing them in a paper bag with an apple will speed the natural ripening process. Never refrigerate tomatoes—it destroys both their flavor and texture.

NEW-FASHIONED BEEF STEW

4 small red potatoes

1 medium turnip

1 medium parsnip

1 cup peeled pearl onions

3 medium carrots

1 cup drained canned tomatoes

1¾ cups defatted reduced-sodium beef broth

1 tablespoon red wine vinegar

2 garlic cloves, crushed

1 bay leaf

½ teaspoon dried thyme, crumbled

½ teaspoon freshly ground black pepper

12 ounces lean, trimmed beef top round or sirloin, cut into ½-inch cubes

1 tablespoon all-purpose flour

1 tablespoon olive oil

Heating up a can of beef stew is one way of putting a quick hot meal on the table, but it's not the only alternative—and certainly not the best one—to spending hours over the stove. This chunky beef-and-vegetable stew is prepared in a streamlined fashion—the meat is quickly sautéed, then added to the already cooked vegetables.

1 Cut each potato into 6 wedges. Peel the turnip and cut it into chunks. Peel the parsnip and cut it into chunks. Peel the onions. Peel the carrots and cut them into chunks.

2 In a large, heavy saucepan, combine the potatoes, turnips, parsnips, onions, carrots, tomatoes, broth, vinegar, half the garlic, the bay leaf, ¼ teaspoon of the thyme and ¼ teaspoon of the black pepper. Break up the tomatoes with the edge of a spoon. Cover and bring to a boil over high heat. Reduce the heat to medium and simmer for 25 minutes, or until the vegetables are just tender.

3 Meanwhile, toss the beef cubes with the remaining garlic and the remaining ¼ teaspoon each thyme and black pepper. Dredge the seasoned beef cubes with the flour.

4 In a large, heavy skillet, warm the oil over high heat until very hot but not smoking. Add the beef and sauté for 5 minutes, or until the beef is browned on the outside and medium-rare on the inside.

5 Add the beef to the vegetables, reduce the heat to medium-low and simmer for 5 minutes, or until the vegetables are fully tender and the flavors are blended.

Preparation time 20 minutes • **Total time** 45 minutes • **Per serving** 335 calories, 6.9 g. fat (18% of calories), 1.5 g. saturated fat, 49 mg. cholesterol, 469 mg. sodium, 6.9 g. dietary fiber, 72 mg. calcium, 4 mg. iron, 47 mg. vitamin C, 9 mg. beta-carotene
Serves 4

Carrot-size parsnips (8 to 9 inches long) are likely to be tender throughout. Larger parsnips, which may be overmature, tend to have tough, woody cores that will need to be removed.

BLACK BEAN SOUP

2 cans (19 ounces each) black beans, rinsed and drained

1¾ cups defatted low-sodium chicken broth

1 cup water

1 teaspoon ground cumin

¼ teaspoon dried oregano

¼ teaspoon freshly ground black pepper

Large pinch of ground red pepper

1 teaspoon olive oil

½ large red bell pepper, slivered

½ large green bell pepper, slivered

½ teaspoon grated lemon zest

Bean soups, from sustaining Yankee bean to savory Italian mine-strone, find favor all over the world. If you'd like to make this soup with dried black beans, place 1 pound of beans in a large pot with cold water to cover; refrigerate overnight. Drain the beans, cover with fresh water, and simmer for 1¼ hours, or until tender. You'll have enough for this recipe, plus leftovers for other dishes.

1 In a large, heavy saucepan, combine the beans, broth, water, cumin, oregano, black pepper and ground red pepper. Cover and bring to a boil over high heat. Reduce the heat to low and simmer, stirring once or twice, for 15 minutes, or until the flavors are blended.

2 Meanwhile, in a small no-stick skillet, warm the oil over medium-high heat. Add the bell peppers, reduce the heat to medium and sauté for 4 to 6 minutes, or until tender.

3 Ladle half of the soup into a food processor or blender and process until puréed (work in batches if necessary). Return the purée to the pan; add the lemon zest.

4 Ladle the soup into bowls and top each serving with some of the sautéed bell peppers.

Preparation time 15 minutes • **Total time** 35 minutes • **Per serving** 182 calories, 3.1 g. fat (15% of calories), 0.4 g. saturated fat, 0 mg. cholesterol, 460 mg. sodium, 7.8 g. dietary fiber, 62 mg. calcium, 4 mg. iron, 38 mg. vitamin C, 0.3 mg. beta-carotene • **Serves 4**

To soak dried beans, place them in a pot or bowl and add cold water to cover.

After soaking, simmer the beans in fresh water, skimming the foam as they cook.

HEARTY CHICKEN AND GREENS SOUP

1 medium leek

2 cups water

1¾ cups defatted reduced-sodium chicken broth

8 ounces boneless, skinless chicken breasts, cut crosswise into ½-inch-thick strips

1 cup frozen chopped leaf spinach

2 large carrots, sliced

2 garlic cloves, minced

½ teaspoon dried thyme, crumbled

¼ teaspoon salt

¼ teaspoon freshly ground black pepper

3 ounces thin egg noodles

2 tablespoons chopped fresh Italian parsley

Chicken soup may really be good for a cold (scientific research has shown that its steamy heat does help clear your head). Medicinal properties aside, however, a bowl of this home-made soup, brimming with chunks of chicken, vegetables and egg noodles, seems to make everyone feel better, especially on a chilly autumn or winter evening.

1 Halve the leek lengthwise and rinse each half well under cold running water. Cut the leek halves crosswise into ½-inch pieces.

2 In a large, heavy saucepan, combine the leeks, water, broth, chicken strips, spinach, carrots, garlic, thyme, salt and black pepper. Cover and bring to a boil over high heat. Reduce the heat to low and simmer for 8 minutes.

3 Stir in the noodles, increase the heat to medium-high and return to a boil. Reduce the heat to medium-low, cover and simmer, stirring occasionally, for 4 to 6 minutes, or until the noodles, vegetables and chicken are tender.

4 Remove the pan from the heat and stir in the parsley.

Preparation time 10 minutes • **Total time** 35 minutes • **Per serving** 217 calories, 2.5 g. fat (10% of calories), 0.4 g. saturated fat, 53 mg. cholesterol, 523 mg. sodium, 3.9 g. dietary fiber, 121 mg. calcium, 4 mg. iron, 26 mg. vitamin C, 11 mg. beta-carotene • **Serves 4**

To clean leeks, first cut off the coarse parts of the green tops (leave on the tender green parts for this recipe).

Sand can get caught between the layers of the leek; splitting the leek lengthwise makes it easier to wash the sand away.

Hold the split leeks under cold running water, fanning the layers to release any dirt. Wash the leaves separately.

LAMB AND POTATO STEW WITH PEAS

1½ **pounds new red potatoes, thinly sliced**

1¾ **cups defatted reduced-sodium chicken broth**

1 **large onion, halved and thinly sliced**

3 **garlic cloves, crushed**

½ **teaspoon freshly ground black pepper**

½ **teaspoon dried rosemary, crushed**

12 **ounces lean, boneless trimmed lamb steak, cut into ½-inch cubes**

⅛ **teaspoon salt**

1 **tablespoon all-purpose flour**

1 **tablespoon olive oil**

1 **cup frozen peas**

2 **tablespoons chopped fresh Italian parsley**

Hearty Irish stew, a classic of country cooking, relies on starchy potatoes to thicken the mixture as it cooks. The French equivalent, *navarin printanier,* is somewhat more delicate, made with spring vegetables and new potatoes that have been painstakingly trimmed into uniform ovals. This version is on the lighter side: The sliced new potatoes hold their shape rather than falling apart, and green peas and parsley add a note of spring freshness.

1 In a large, heavy saucepan, combine the potatoes, broth, onions, half of the garlic, ¼ teaspoon of the black pepper and ¼ teaspoon of the rosemary. Cover and bring to a boil over high heat. Reduce the heat to medium-low and simmer, stirring occasionally, for 15 minutes, or until the potatoes are fork-tender.

2 While the potatoes are cooking, place the lamb cubes in a medium bowl. Add the remaining garlic, black pepper and rosemary, and the salt, and toss until the lamb is coated with the seasonings. Sprinkle in the flour and toss the lamb cubes until they are coated with flour.

3 In a large, heavy no-stick skillet, warm the oil over high heat until very hot. Add the lamb cubes and sauté for 5 minutes, or until the lamb is medium-rare.

4 Add the lamb to the potato mixture, then stir in the peas, cover, and simmer for 2 to 3 minutes longer, or until the peas are heated through. Sprinkle the stew with the parsley and serve.

Preparation time 15 minutes • **Total time** 45 minutes • **Per serving** 361 calories, 10.2 g. fat (25% of calories), 2.5 g. saturated fat, 56 mg. cholesterol, 465 mg. sodium, 5.3 g. dietary fiber, 42 mg. calcium, 4 mg. iron, 39 mg. vitamin C, 0.2 mg. beta-carotene • **Serves 4**

New potatoes—freshly harvested ones that have not been stored—have a lower starch content than mature potatoes. They cook quickly and have a slightly sweet flavor.

MARKET AND PANTRY
Look for unusual potato varieties at gourmet groceries and farmers' markets. The small, pink Rose Fir has joined the Red LaSoda and Red Pontiac as a favorite red potato. Yukon Gold and Finnish Yellow Wax potatoes are deep yellow within: The butter-hued flesh of these varieties can be a healthful palate-fooler, convincing people to skip the butter they would otherwise add. Among the most novel potatoes are the Blue Carib and the All Blue; their purple-blue skin and dark blue flesh add a jolt of color to the dinner plate.

Milanese Pork Stew with Gremolata

Pork Stew

2 cups water

1 cup long-grain white rice

Pinch of dried saffron

12 ounces lean, boneless pork loin, cut into ¾-inch cubes

½ teaspoon salt

¼ teaspoon freshly ground black pepper

1 tablespoon plus 1 teaspoon olive oil

1 medium onion, chopped

2 medium carrots, chopped

2 celery stalks, chopped

2 garlic cloves, minced

½ teaspoon dried basil

½ teaspoon dried thyme

1 bay leaf, preferably imported

½ cup white wine

1 strip (3 inches long) lemon zest

1 can (16 ounces) whole tomatoes in purée

½ cup defatted reduced-sodium chicken broth

8 ounces small white mushrooms, quartered

1 cup frozen peas

Gremolata

¼ cup chopped Italian parsley

1 tablespoon zest shaved with a vegetable peeler and cut into thin strips or 1 tablespoon grated zest

2 small garlic cloves, minced

An Italian creation, *gremolata* is a delicious, fresh seasoning mixture made from citrus zest, garlic and parsley. It's most commonly used on osso buco (braised veal shanks) but is an equally fine complement to this rich-tasting pork stew.

1 In a medium saucepan, bring the water to a boil over high heat. Stir in the rice and saffron, and reduce the heat to medium-low; cover and simmer for 20 minutes, or until the rice is tender and the liquid is absorbed. Remove the rice from the heat and set aside, covered.

2 While the rice cooks, in a medium bowl, toss the pork with ¼ teaspoon of the salt and the black pepper. In a large, heavy saucepan, warm 2 teaspoons of the oil over medium-high heat until very hot but not smoking. Add the pork and sauté for 2 minutes, or until browned. With a slotted spoon, transfer the pork to a plate.

3 Add the remaining 2 teaspoons oil to the saucepan and warm over medium heat. Stir in the onions, carrots and celery; cover and cook, stirring occasionally, for 5 minutes, or until the vegetables begin to soften. Stir in the garlic, basil, thyme and bay leaf, and cook for 30 seconds. Add the wine and strip of lemon zest, and cook for 2 minutes, scraping up any browned bits from the bottom of the pan.

4 Add the tomatoes, broth and remaining ¼ teaspoon salt. Reduce the heat to medium-low and simmer, covered, for 20 minutes.

5 Stir in the mushrooms and simmer, uncovered, for 5 minutes. Stir in the peas and simmer for 5 minutes, or until the pork is cooked through.

6 Meanwhile, prepare the gremolata. In a small bowl, combine the parsley, lemon zest and garlic.

7 Divide the rice among 4 bowls or plates and top with the stew. Sprinkle some gremolata over each portion.

Preparation time 35 minutes • **Total time** 1 hour • **Per serving** 449 calories, 10.1 g. fat (20% of calories), 2.4 g. saturated fat, 50 mg. cholesterol, 658 mg. sodium, 4.9 g. dietary fiber, 131 mg. calcium, 5 mg. iron, 41 mg. vitamin C, 6.8 mg. beta-carotene • **Serves 4**

Asian Chicken Noodle Soup

1 tablespoon plus 1 teaspoon vegetable oil

12 ounces skinless, boneless chicken breast halves, thinly sliced

4 scallions, thinly sliced on the diagonal

2 garlic cloves, minced

1 teaspoon grated fresh ginger

2 cups thinly sliced small white mushrooms

3 cups defatted reduced-sodium chicken broth

2½ cups water

½ cup canned sliced bamboo shoots, rinsed and drained

¼ teaspoon crushed red pepper flakes

4 ounces fresh cappellini pasta

4 cups packed fresh spinach leaves, coarsely chopped

1 tablespoon balsamic vinegar

2 tablespoons reduced-sodium soy sauce

2 large egg whites, lightly beaten

½ teaspoon dark sesame oil

1 medium carrot, shredded

¼ cup chopped fresh cilantro

This bountiful soup is made with cappellini (angel-hair pasta) instead of Asian noodles. If you can get Chinese or Japanese noodles (shown below), try them in this soup; cook the noodles according to the package directions.

1 In a large saucepan, warm the vegetable oil over medium-high heat until very hot but not smoking. Add the chicken and stir-fry for 2 minutes, or until opaque. Add the scallions, garlic and ginger, and stir-fry for 30 seconds, or until fragrant. Add the mushrooms and stir-fry for 1 minute, or until tender.

2 Add the broth, water, bamboo shoots and red pepper flakes, and bring to a boil over high heat. Stir in the pasta and spinach, and cook for 1 minute, or until the pasta is tender and the spinach is just wilted. Reduce the heat to medium and stir in the vinegar and soy sauce. Stir in the beaten egg whites and simmer, stirring, for 1 minute. Stir in the sesame oil.

3 Ladle the soup into 4 bowls and top with the carrots and cilantro.

Preparation time 20 minutes • **Total time** 35 minutes • **Per serving** 293 calories, 7.3 g. fat (23% of calories), 1.1 g. saturated fat, 70 mg. cholesterol, 952 mg. sodium, 4.2 g. dietary fiber, 122 mg. calcium, 5 mg. iron, 31 mg. vitamin C, 6.5 mg. beta-carotene • **Serves 4**

Japanese dried noodles: *tomoshiraga somen* (fine wheat noodles), *soba* (buckwheat noodles) and *udon* (wheat noodles).

Two types of quick-cooking Chinese dried egg noodles, or *dan mian*. Those on the right are made with wheat flour.

GULF COAST SEAFOOD GUMBO WITH RICE

2¾ cups water

1 cup long-grain white rice

1 tablespoon plus 1 teaspoon olive oil

2 ounces trimmed Canadian bacon, diced

2 tablespoons all-purpose flour

1 medium onion, chopped

1 medium green bell pepper, diced

1 medium red bell pepper, diced

1 celery stalk, diced

3 garlic cloves, minced

½ teaspoon dried thyme or 1 teaspoon fresh thyme

½ teaspoon freshly ground black pepper

¼ teaspoon salt

1 cup defatted reduced-sodium chicken broth

1 cup sliced frozen okra

1 cup drained canned whole tomatoes, coarsely chopped, with juice reserved

1 bay leaf, preferably imported

½ teaspoon hot-pepper sauce

8 ounces skinned red snapper fillet, cut into 1½-inch pieces

8 ounces medium shrimp, peeled and deveined, with tails attached

2 scallions, chopped

Fresh thyme sprigs, for garnish (optional)

Gumbo, like so many of Lousiana's beloved dishes, combines French and African ingredients and methods with the bounty of local produce, seafood and meats. It is based on a browned flour mixture called a *roux* and contains crisp sliced okra, a vegetable that was brought to America by African slaves. Tomatoes, bell peppers, onions and celery go into most gumbos; in addition to the fish and shrimp used here, some Louisiana cooks incorporate crabmeat, oysters, ham or sausage, chicken or duck.

1 In a medium saucepan, bring 2 cups of the water to a boil over high heat. Stir in the rice and reduce the heat to medium-low; cover and simmer for 20 minutes, or until all the liquid is absorbed. Remove the pan from the heat; set aside, covered, until the gumbo is ready.

2 While the rice is cooking, in a large, heavy saucepan, warm the oil over medium heat. Add the bacon and cook for 2 minutes, or until golden and crisp. With a slotted spoon, transfer the bacon to a small bowl and set aside.

3 Reduce the heat to medium-low and stir the flour into the pan. Cook, stirring frequently, for 3 to 4 minutes, or until the flour mixture turns a deep golden brown. (Be careful not to scorch the flour.)

4 Stir in the onions, bell peppers, celery, garlic, thyme, black pepper and salt. Cover and cook, stirring occasionally, for 5 minutes.

5 Stir in the remaining ¾ cup water, the broth, okra, tomatoes and their juice, bay leaf and hot-pepper sauce. Return to a simmer, cover and cook for 10 minutes, or until the mixture thickens and the vegetables are tender. Stir in the snapper and shrimp, and cook for 5 minutes, or until the seafood is opaque. Return the bacon to the pan.

6 Divide the rice among 4 bowls. Serve the gumbo over the rice, and sprinkle with the scallions. Garnish with fresh thyme sprigs, if desired.

Preparation time 25 minutes • **Total time** 40 minutes • **Per serving** 418 calories, 7.8 g. fat (17% of calories), 1.4 g. saturated fat, 98 mg. cholesterol, 731 mg. sodium, 4.4 g. dietary fiber, 147 mg. calcium, 5 mg. iron, 76 mg. vitamin C, 1.1 mg. beta-carotene • **Serves 4**

CHICKEN PRIMAVERA STEW

1 small chicken (2½ to 3 pounds), skinned and cut into 8 pieces

2½ cups water

1½ cups defatted reduced-sodium chicken broth

¾ teaspoon salt

1 garlic clove, crushed

1 bay leaf, preferably imported

8 ounces small red potatoes, quartered

2 medium carrots, cut into ½-inch-thick slices

1 medium yellow bell pepper, diced

1 medium zucchini, diced

4 ounces fresh asparagus spears, diagonally sliced into 1-inch pieces

2 tablespoons cornstarch

¼ cup 1% low-fat milk

½ teaspoon dried tarragon

¼ teaspoon freshly ground black pepper

2 tablespoons chopped Italian parsley

½ teaspoon grated lemon zest

2 scallions, thinly sliced

The most delicate stews in French cuisine are called *blanquettes*, which means that the meat (usually veal or chicken) is not browned, but simply simmered in a light stock that is later enriched with eggs and cream. This stew has the pale delicacy of a blanquette, but the high-fat finishing touches are omitted.

1 In a large saucepan, combine the chicken, water, broth, ¼ teaspoon of the salt, the garlic and bay leaf, and bring to a boil over high heat. Reduce the heat to medium and simmer, uncovered, for 20 minutes, or until the chicken is just tender, skimming off the surface foam occasionally. With a slotted spoon, transfer the chicken to a medium bowl and cover loosely to keep warm.

2 Increase the heat to high and return the broth to a boil. Add the potatoes and carrots, and cook for 7 minutes. Add the bell peppers, zucchini and asparagus, and cook for 2 minutes, or until the vegetables are just tender. With a slotted spoon, transfer the vegetables to the bowl with the chicken; let the broth continue to boil.

3 In a small bowl, whisk together the cornstarch and milk. Whisk the milk mixture into the broth. Add the tarragon, black pepper and remaining ½ teaspoon salt, and return to a boil. Reduce the heat to medium-low and simmer for 1 minute.

4 Return the chicken and vegetables to the saucepan. Add the parsley and lemon zest, and stir to combine. Simmer for 2 minutes, or until heated through. Sprinkle the scallions over the stew and serve.

Preparation time 30 minutes • **Total time** 40 minutes • **Per serving** 291 calories, 5.1 g. fat (16% of calories), 1.3 g. saturated fat, 105 mg. cholesterol, 798 mg. sodium, 3.2 g. dietary fiber, 78 mg. calcium, 3 mg. iron, 49 mg. vitamin C, 6.5 mg. beta-carotene • **Serves 4**

SUBSTITUTION
If dark meat doesn't find favor with your family, use bone-in chicken breast halves instead of a cut-up whole chicken. Cut the breasts in half crosswise for easy-to-serve pieces.

ON THE MENU
Start off the meal with a salad of dark, flavorful greens, such as arugula or watercress, tossed with a lively mustard vinaigrette. Complete the meal with juicy peaches and crisp rolled wafer cookies.

Basil Minestrone

1 tablespoon olive oil

2 cups peeled, diced all-purpose potatoes

2 cups diced celery

1 medium onion, chopped

2 garlic cloves, minced

2 cups diced carrots

1½ cups defatted reduced-sodium chicken broth

1½ cups water

1 strip (2 inches long) lemon zest

1 bay leaf, preferably imported

½ teaspoon dried rosemary

½ teaspoon dried thyme

¼ teaspoon salt

¼ teaspoon freshly ground black pepper

1 cup diced zucchini

4 ounces green beans, cut into ½-inch pieces

1 can (14½ ounces) diced tomatoes with juice

1 can (10 ounces) cannellini beans, rinsed and drained

½ cup loosely packed fresh basil leaves, slivered

1 ounce Parmesan cheese, coarsely grated (optional)

Minestrone means "big soup," which suggests that all kinds of good things can go into this Italian favorite. The basics are dried beans, vegetables and pasta or rice—a combination that makes for hearty eating.

1 In a large saucepan, warm the oil over medium heat. Add the potatoes, celery and onions, and cook, stirring occasionally, for 5 minutes, or until the vegetables begin to soften. Stir in the garlic and cook for 30 seconds, or until fragrant.

2 Add the carrots, broth, water, lemon zest, bay leaf, rosemary, thyme, salt and black pepper; increase the heat to high and bring to a boil. Reduce the heat to medium-low and simmer, uncovered, for 10 minutes, or until the vegetables are tender. Stir in the zucchini and green beans, and cook for 5 minutes longer.

3 Stir in the tomatoes and their juice and the cannellini beans, and return to a boil over high heat. Reduce the heat to medium-low and simmer for 5 minutes. Stir in ¼ cup of the basil. Ladle the soup into 4 bowls and sprinkle with the remaining ¼ cup basil, and the Parmesan, if desired.

Preparation time 30 minutes • **Total time** 50 minutes • **Per serving** 242 calories, 4.6 g. fat (17% of calories), 0.6 g. saturated fat, 0 mg. cholesterol, 714 mg. sodium, 9 g. dietary fiber, 193 mg. calcium, 5 mg. iron, 54 mg. vitamin C, 10.1 mg. beta-carotene • **Serves 4**

To sliver the basil leaves, first stack them, then roll them together.

Holding the roll of leaves, slice them crosswise so the leaves fall into slivers.

HEARTY BORSCHT WITH CHICKEN

- 2 teaspoons olive oil
- 12 ounces skinless, boneless chicken thighs
- 3 medium carrots, sliced
- 1 large onion, diced
- 2 celery stalks, diced
- 2 garlic cloves, minced
- 2½ cups water
- 1 can (14½ ounces) diced tomatoes with juice
- 1 cup defatted reduced-sodium chicken broth
- 1 bay leaf, preferably imported
- 2 whole cloves
- ¼ teaspoon salt
- ¼ teaspoon freshly ground black pepper
- 2 cups diced red cabbage
- 2 cans (14½ ounces each) sliced beets, drained and cut into ½-inch-wide pieces
- 8 ounces all-purpose potatoes, diced
- 2 tablespoons red wine vinegar
- ¼ cup chopped fresh dill
- ½ cup reduced-fat sour cream or low-fat yogurt

Most Americans know borscht as a summery chilled beet soup they can buy in a jar. But in Eastern Europe, where borscht originated, it's more often a sustaining winter dish in which the beets are accompanied by a number of other vegetables and often pork and sausage. Potatoes, tomatoes, cabbage, carrots and chicken make this version a filling but low-fat meal-in-a-bowl.

1 In a large, heavy saucepan, warm the oil over medium-high heat until very hot but not smoking. Sauté the chicken for 4 minutes, or until browned on all sides. Reduce the heat to medium.

2 Stir in the carrots, onions, celery and garlic. Cover and cook for 5 minutes, or until the vegetables are just tender. Stir in the water, tomatoes and their juice, broth, bay leaf, cloves, salt and black pepper; increase the heat to high and bring the soup to a boil.

3 Stir in the cabbage, beets and potatoes. Reduce the heat to medium-low, cover and simmer for 20 minutes, or until the vegetables are tender. Stir in the vinegar and 2 tablespoons of the dill; remove the soup from the heat.

4 With tongs, remove the chicken from the soup and transfer to a plate. Allow the chicken to cool for about 5 minutes, then tear it into bite-size pieces and return to the pan.

5 Ladle the soup into 4 bowls and serve topped with the sour cream or yogurt and the remaining 2 tablespoons dill.

Preparation time 25 minutes • **Total time** 45 minutes • **Per serving** 346 calories, 10.4 g. fat (27% of calories), 3.3 g. saturated fat, 81 mg. cholesterol, 915 mg. sodium, 7.7 g. dietary fiber, 137 mg. calcium, 6 mg. iron, 64 mg. vitamin C, 9.6 mg. beta-carotene • **Serves 4**

MAKE AHEAD
You can prepare the soup ahead of time through Step 4, then cover and refrigerate it. Remove any fat that has congealed at the top, reheat the soup and top with sour cream or yogurt and dill.

MARKET NOTE
Unlike some canned vegetables, canned beets retain most of the flavor and nutritional value of the fresh cooked vegetable. They do, however, lose some of their vitamin C and folacin in processing.

EIGHT-VEGETABLE CURRY

1 tablespoon plus 1 teaspoon olive oil

1 tablespoon curry powder

2 teaspoons ground cumin

1 teaspoon ground coriander

1 large onion, chopped

3 medium carrots, cut into 1-inch pieces

2 celery stalks, cut into 1-inch pieces

3 medium all-purpose potatoes, cut into 1-inch chunks

12 ounces butternut squash, peeled and cut into 1-inch chunks

2 garlic cloves, minced

1 large fresh jalapeño pepper, seeded and minced

1 bay leaf, preferably imported

¼ teaspoon salt

1½ cups defatted reduced-sodium chicken broth

1 cup water

2 cups small cauliflower florets

1 cup frozen peas

1 cup plain low-fat yogurt

¼ cup chopped fresh cilantro

Pinch of ground red pepper

J ust about any vegetable you can think of could go into a curry, but a meatless curry tastes better made with dense, starchy vegetables. Potatoes, carrots and winter squash give this dish satisfying depth, and they absorb the seasonings beautifully. Acorn squash or pumpkin could stand in for the butternut squash; however, butternut is the easiest to peel and cut up.

1 In a large, heavy saucepan, warm the oil over medium-low heat. Add the curry powder, cumin and coriander, and cook, stirring, for 30 seconds, or until fragrant. Add the onions, carrots and celery; cover and cook for 10 minutes, stirring occasionally, until the vegetables begin to brown. Add the potatoes and cook, covered, for 5 minutes. Add the squash, garlic, jalapeño, bay leaf and salt, and cook, covered, for 5 minutes longer.

2 Stir the broth and water into the vegetable mixture; increase the heat to high and bring to a boil. Reduce the heat to medium and simmer, uncovered, for 10 minutes.

3 Add the cauliflower and simmer, uncovered, for 5 minutes. Add the peas and cook for 3 minutes longer, or until all the vegetables are tender.

4 Meanwhile, in a small bowl, whisk together the yogurt, cilantro and ground red pepper.

5 Ladle the curry into 4 bowls and top with the yogurt mixture.

Preparation time 35 minutes • **Total time** 55 minutes • **Per serving** 317 calories, 6.4 g. fat (18% of calories), 1.3 g. saturated fat, 3 mg. cholesterol, 516 mg. sodium, 9.4 g. dietary fiber, 229 mg. calcium, 4 mg. iron, 106 mg. vitamin C, 12.7 mg. beta-carotene • **Serves 4**

ON THE MENU
Indian basmati rice is the perfect complement to any curry. This fragrant long-grain rice has a deliciously nutlike fragrance and flavor. As an alternative, try Texmati and Calmati, American rice varieties that taste similar to basmati but are grown in Texas and California, respectively. After opening the package, transfer basmati rice to an airtight container.

SEAFOOD CHOWDER WITH GARLIC TOASTS

1 tablespoon olive oil

1 medium onion, chopped

2 celery stalks, diced

¼ cup chopped shallots or onion

1 bay leaf, preferably imported

¼ teaspoon fennel seeds, crushed

2 tablespoons all-purpose flour

½ cup white wine

12 ounces small red potatoes, diced

1½ cups sliced carrots, cut ½-inch thick

1½ cups defatted reduced-sodium chicken broth

1½ cups water

½ cup 1% low-fat milk

½ teaspoon dried thyme

¼ teaspoon salt

¼ teaspoon freshly ground black pepper

8 slices crusty French bread, cut ½-inch thick (about 4 ounces total)

1 garlic clove, halved

8 ounces cod fillet, cut into chunks

4 ounces medium shrimp, peeled and deveined, with tails attached

¼ cup chopped Italian parsley

Because seafood cooks in so little time (and you don't have to brown fish or shellfish before simmering it), chowders are quicker to make than meat stews. This chowder calls for cod and shrimp, readily available everywhere in the country. A touch of anise flavor, in the form of crushed fennel seeds, is reminiscent of French bouillabaisse, which often contains anise liqueur. The garlicky toasts served with the chowder are another classic French touch.

1 In a large saucepan, warm the oil over medium-low heat. Add the onions, celery, shallots or onions, bay leaf and fennel seeds; cover and cook, stirring occasionally, for about 5 minutes, or until the vegetables begin to soften.

2 Add the flour and cook, stirring, for 2 minutes. Stir in the wine, increase the heat to high and bring to a boil. Boil for 1 minute.

3 Add the potatoes, carrots, broth, water, milk, thyme, salt and black pepper, and bring to a boil. Reduce the heat to medium-low, cover and simmer for 15 minutes, or until the vegetables are tender.

4 Meanwhile, preheat the broiler. Toast the bread 5 to 6 inches from the heat for about 1 minute per side, or until lightly browned. Rub the toasted bread with the cut sides of the garlic clove; set aside.

5 Add the cod and shrimp to the soup. Cover and simmer for 4 to 5 minutes, or until the seafood turns opaque.

6 Ladle the soup into 4 bowls and serve each with 2 pieces of toasted bread. Sprinkle with the parsley.

Preparation time 35 minutes • **Total time** 45 minutes • **Per serving** 349 calories, 5.7 g. fat (15% of calories), 1 g. saturated fat, 61 mg. cholesterol, 674 mg. sodium, 4.9 g. dietary fiber, 129 mg. calcium, 3 mg. iron, 26 mg. vitamin C, 7.2 mg. beta-carotene • **Serves 4**

SUBSTITUTION
As with many fish recipes, it's possible to replace the cod with another similarly textured fish, such as pollack or haddock.

MARKET AND PANTRY
French bread should be kept in a paper bag; if stored in a plastic bag, its crust will become soggy and tough.

MOROCCAN LENTIL AND CHICK-PEA SOUP

1 tablespoon plus 1 teaspoon olive oil

1 cup finely chopped onions

4 medium carrots, finely chopped

2 celery stalks, finely chopped

3 garlic cloves, minced

2 teaspoons grated fresh ginger

2 teaspoons ground cumin

½ teaspoon dried thyme

½ teaspoon ground turmeric

Pinch of ground cloves

8 ounces lentils, picked over and rinsed

2 cups defatted reduced-sodium chicken broth

1 can (14½ ounces) diced tomatoes with juice

3 cups water

1 bay leaf, preferably imported

½ teaspoon freshly ground black pepper

¼ teaspoon salt

1 can (10 ounces) chick-peas, rinsed and drained

¼ cup chopped fresh cilantro

Some culinary historians hold that highly spiced cuisines develop in hot climates because heat deadens hunger; spicy food, which piques the appetite, thus becomes almost a necessity for survival. Moroccan cuisine is often spicy, combining seasonings we think of as "sweet"—cloves, cinnamon and nutmeg, for instance—with savory garlic and herbs, meats, grains and legumes.

1 In a large, heavy saucepan, warm the oil over medium-high heat. Add the onions, carrots and celery; cover and cook, stirring frequently, for 5 minutes, or until the vegetables are tender. Stir in the garlic, ginger, cumin, thyme, turmeric and cloves, and cook for 30 seconds, or until fragrant.

2 Add the lentils, broth, tomatoes and their juice, water, bay leaf, black pepper and salt. Increase the heat to high and bring to a boil. Reduce the heat to medium, cover and simmer for 30 to 40 minutes, or until the lentils are tender.

3 Stir in the the chick-peas and simmer for 2 minutes, or until heated through. Just before serving, stir in the cilantro.

Preparation time 30 minutes • **Total time** 1 hour 10 minutes • **Per serving** 369 calories, 6.9 g. fat (17% of calories), 0.8 g. saturated fat, 0 mg. cholesterol, 755 mg. sodium, 12.5 g. dietary fiber, 128 mg. calcium, 8 mg. iron, 31 mg. vitamin C, 12.6 mg. beta-carotene • **Serves 4**

Brownish green lentils are those most commonly found in supermarkets. Like all lentils, they need no presoaking. This type cooks in 30 to 40 minutes.

Red lentils, sold in health-food stores and gourmet shops, cook more quickly—in 20 to 30 minutes. Use them in this recipe if you prefer.

Cincinnati Turkey Chili

1 tablespoon plus 1 teaspoon vegetable oil

12 ounces skinless, boneless turkey breast, cut into 1-inch cubes

1 medium yellow onion, finely chopped

1 medium green bell pepper, diced

3 garlic cloves, minced

4 teaspoons chili powder

2 teaspoons ground cumin

1 teaspoon dried oregano

½ teaspoon ground cinnamon

1 can (28 ounces) crushed tomatoes with juice

¾ cup defatted reduced-sodium chicken broth

2 cans (19 ounces each) red kidney beans, rinsed and drained

1 teaspoon red wine vinegar

½ teaspoon Worcestershire sauce

6 ounces spaghetti

¼ cup finely chopped red onion

2 ounces reduced-fat sharp Cheddar cheese, finely grated

½ cup oyster crackers (optional)

Cincinnati's famed chili is in a class by itself. Its seasonings, including cinnamon and cloves, support the theory that the dish was devised by Greek immigrants. Served atop a mound of spaghetti, this chili may have been the first "have it your way" food. In a code peculiar to the dish, you order it "three-way" (the spaghetti and chili topped with shredded Cheddar); "four-way" (with cheese plus chopped raw onions); or "five-way" (crowned with Cheddar, onions and kidney beans). This five-way turkey chili—here the beans are cooked right in the chili—is served with oyster crackers, a traditional, if surprising, accompaniment.

1 Bring a large covered pot of water to a boil over high heat.

2 Meanwhile, in a large, heavy saucepan, warm the oil over medium-high heat until very hot but not smoking. Sauté the turkey for 2 to 3 minutes, or until browned; transfer the turkey to a plate.

3 Add the yellow onions and bell peppers to the pan. Reduce the heat to medium, cover and cook, stirring occasionally, for 5 minutes, or until the vegetables are tender. Add the garlic, chili powder, cumin, oregano and cinnamon, and stir for 30 seconds, or until fragrant.

4 Add the tomatoes and their juice, and the broth, and bring to a boil. Add the beans, vinegar and Worcestershire, and bring to a boil. Reduce the heat to medium-low, cover and simmer for 10 minutes. Add the turkey and simmer for 5 minutes longer.

5 While the chili is simmering, add the spaghetti to the boiling water, return to a boil and cook for 10 to 12 minutes, or according to package directions until al dente. Drain the spaghetti in a colander.

6 Divide the spaghetti among 4 bowls. Ladle the chili over the spaghetti and top with the red onions and Cheddar. Serve with oyster crackers, if desired.

Preparation time 25 minutes • **Total time** 40 minutes • **Per serving** 608 calories, 11 g. fat (16% of calories), 2.8 g. saturated fat, 63 mg. cholesterol, 971 mg. sodium, 15.4 g. dietary fiber, 295 mg. calcium, 8 mg. iron, 55 mg. vitamin C, 1.4 mg. beta-carotene • **Serves 4**

MEXICAN TURKEY MEATBALL SOUP

- 3 garlic cloves, crushed
- 1 large fresh jalapeño pepper, seeded and coarsely chopped
- 12 ounces skinless, boneless turkey breast, cut into chunks
- 1 cup fresh breadcrumbs
- 2 large egg whites, lightly beaten
- ¼ cup chopped fresh cilantro
- 1½ teaspoons ground cumin
- ¼ teaspoon salt
- 1 tablespoon vegetable oil
- 1 medium onion, finely chopped
- 2 medium carrots, thinly sliced
- 2 celery stalks, finely chopped
- 8 ounces medium white mushrooms, sliced
- 1 can (35 ounces) whole Italian tomatoes, drained and coarsely chopped, with juice reserved
- 1½ cups defatted reduced-sodium chicken broth
- 1½ cups water
- ½ teaspoon freshly ground black pepper
- 1 cup frozen corn kernels
- ½ medium avocado, diced
- Cilantro leaves, for garnish (optional)

*S*opa de albóndigas—that's the Mexican term for meatball soup. Garlic, jalapeño, cilantro and cumin give the low-fat turkey meatballs real Mexican flavor; the corn in the soup and the avocado garnish are also south-of-the-border touches.

1 In a food processor, combine the garlic and jalapeño, and process just until minced; transfer 1 tablespoon of the mixture to a cup.

2 Add the turkey to the processor and process until finely ground.

3 Add the breadcrumbs, egg whites, chopped cilantro, cumin and ⅛ teaspoon of the salt, and pulse just until blended. Shape the mixture into twelve to sixteen 1½- to 2-inch meatballs; set aside.

4 In a large saucepan, warm the oil over medium heat. Add the onions, carrots, celery and reserved 1 tablespoon jalapeño-garlic mixture; cover and cook for 4 to 5 minutes, or until the vegetables begin to soften. Stir in the mushrooms and cook for 2 minutes longer.

5 Stir in the tomatoes and their juice, the broth, water, black pepper and remaining ⅛ teaspoon salt. Increase the heat to high and bring to a boil. Add the meatballs and return to a boil. Reduce the heat to medium-low, cover and simmer the soup for 10 minutes.

6 Add the corn and simmer for 2 minutes longer. Spoon the meatball soup into 4 bowls and top each portion with some diced avocado. Garnish with cilantro leaves, if desired.

Preparation time 35 minutes • **Total time** 50 minutes • **Per serving** 354 calories, 9.7 g. fat (25% of calories), 1.5 g. saturated fat, 53 mg. cholesterol, 946 mg. sodium, 6.6 g. dietary fiber, 135 mg. calcium, 5 mg. iron, 64 mg. vitamin C, 7.2 mg. beta-carotene • **Serves 4**

FOR A CHANGE
When fresh corn is plentiful, you can slice the kernels off a few cobs to use instead of the frozen corn.

NUTRITION NOTE
Smooth-skinned green Florida avocados contain about half the fat of California's black-skinned Haas and Fuerte avocados.

LAMB AND VEGETABLE STEW

12 ounces lean, well-trimmed
boneless leg of lamb, cut into
¾-inch chunks

½ teaspoon salt

¼ teaspoon freshly ground black
pepper

1 tablespoon plus 1 teaspoon
olive oil

1 medium onion, chopped

2 celery stalks, diced

3 garlic cloves, minced

2 teaspoons ground coriander

2 teaspoons ground cumin

1 teaspoon dried oregano

½ teaspoon dried thyme

1 bay leaf, preferably imported

1 can (35 ounces) whole
tomatoes, drained and chopped,
with juice reserved

½ cup defatted reduced-sodium
chicken broth

1 pound all-purpose potatoes,
peeled and cut into 2 x ½-inch
pieces

½ pound carrots, cut into 2 x ½-
inch pieces

1 cup frozen lima beans

¼ cup chopped Italian parsley

For a bit of a change—and to cut a traditionally long cooking time—the carrots and potatoes that go into this stew are cut into thick sticks rather than cubes. Thin-skinned long white potatoes (one variety is called White Rose) are best for this recipe; starchy baking potatoes such as Russets will fall apart if cooked in this fashion.

1 In a medium bowl, toss the lamb with ¼ teaspoon of the salt and the black pepper. In a large, heavy saucepan, warm the oil over medium-high heat until very hot but not smoking. Sauté the lamb for 2 minutes, or until browned on all sides.

2 Reduce the heat to medium and stir in the onions and celery. Cover and cook, stirring occasionally, for 5 minutes, or until the vegetables begin to soften. Stir in the garlic, coriander, cumin, oregano, thyme and bay leaf, and cook for 30 seconds, or until fragrant. Add the tomatoes and their juice, the broth and remaining ¼ teaspoon salt. Reduce the heat to medium-low and simmer, covered, for 20 minutes.

3 Stir in the potatoes, carrots and lima beans, and simmer, uncovered, for 20 minutes longer, or until the meat and vegetables are tender. Just before serving, sprinkle with the parsley.

Preparation time 20 minutes • **Total time** 1 hour 10 minutes • **Per serving**
365 calories, 9.6 g. fat (24% of calories), 2.1 g. saturated fat, 54 mg. cholesterol, 882 mg. sodium, 8.7 g. dietary fiber, 150 mg. calcium, 6 mg. iron, 76 mg. vitamin C, 10.7 mg. beta-carotene • **Serves 4**

HEAD START
Chop and dice the onion and celery, and combine them in a tightly sealed bag; cut up the potatoes and carrots, and combine them in a second bag; measure out the coriander, cumin, oregano and thyme, and seal the mixture in a twist of foil.

MAKE AHEAD
You can cook the stew a day ahead of time, then reheat it before serving. Add the parsley at the last minute. You can also freeze the stew (in individual portions for convenience, if you like), but the potatoes may be a bit mushy when you thaw and reheat it.

NUTRITION NOTE
Lima beans, like most legumes, are an excellent low-fat source of protein, iron and dietary fiber. Use either baby limas or meaty Fordhooks for this recipe.

Satisfying Oven Dinners

❧ ❧ ❧

CASSEROLES, PASTAS AND POT PIE—

OLD FAVORITES AND

NEW DELIGHTS

FROM THE OVEN

TEX-MEX ARROZ CON POLLO

2 teaspoons olive oil

1 large red bell pepper, diced

1 medium onion, diced

2 celery stalks, diced

3 garlic cloves, minced

1 bay leaf, preferably imported

12 ounces skinless, boneless chicken thighs, cut into 2-inch chunks

¾ cup long-grain white rice

2 teaspoons chili powder

2 teaspoons ground cumin

1 teaspoon dried oregano

½ teaspoon ground turmeric

⅛ teaspoon ground red pepper

1 cup defatted reduced-sodium chicken broth

½ cup water

1 can (4 ounces) chopped green chilies, drained

1 can (15 ounces) black beans, rinsed and drained

½ cup diced tomato

Fresh cilantro or parsley sprigs and lemon slices, for garnish (optional)

S panish in origin, *arroz con pollo* (literally "chicken with rice") is a down-to-earth version of the lavish party dish called *paella* (saffron-tinted rice with shellfish, sausage, chicken and vegetables). Simpler but no less delicious, this Mexican-influenced arroz con pollo is made with hearty black beans—*frijoles negros*—and green chilies; the typically Tex-Mex seasonings include chili powder, garlic, cumin and oregano.

1 Preheat the oven to 375°.

2 In a Dutch oven or large ovenproof saucepan, warm the oil over medium-high heat. Add the bell peppers, onions, celery, garlic and bay leaf, and sauté for 2 to 3 minutes, or until the vegetables begin to soften. Add the chicken, reduce the heat to medium and sauté for 3 minutes, or until the chicken is lightly browned. Stir in the rice, chili powder, cumin, oregano, turmeric and ground red pepper, and cook for 1 minute, or until the spices are fragrant.

3 Stir in the broth, water and green chilies, and bring to a boil over medium-high heat. Cover the pan tightly and bake for 20 minutes.

4 Uncover the pan and stir in the black beans and tomatoes. Bake, uncovered, for 5 minutes longer, or until the beans are heated through. Garnish with cilantro or parsley sprigs and lemon slices, if desired.

Preparation time 20 minutes • **Total time** 1 hour • **Per serving** 363 calories, 7 g. fat (17% of calories), 1.3 g. saturated fat, 71 mg. cholesterol, 617 mg. sodium, 5.7 g. dietary fiber, 86 mg. calcium, 5 mg. iron, 81 mg. vitamin C, 1.4 mg. beta-carotene • **Serves 4**

FOOD FACT
The orangy-yellow spice turmeric gives the rice in this recipe a golden color (saffron, which costs much more than turmeric, is often used for this purpose in Spanish dishes). Ground turmeric is produced by drying and then grinding a root-like rhizome that resembles gingerroot. Turmeric is found in curry powder and in prepared mustard.

SPICE-RUBBED COD WITH VEGETABLES

1½ **pounds cod fillet, in one piece (1 inch thick)**

1 **teaspoon ground cumin**

½ **teaspoon ground ginger**

½ **teaspoon salt**

¼ **teaspoon paprika**

Pinch of ground red pepper

1 **tablespoon plus 1 teaspoon extra-virgin olive oil**

1½ **pounds small red potatoes, quartered**

4 **medium carrots, cut diagonally into ¼-inch-thick slices**

12 **ounces green beans, trimmed**

12 **ounces yellow squash, cut diagonally into ¼-inch-thick slices**

¼ **teaspoon freshly ground black pepper**

¼ **cup chopped fresh cilantro**

2 **scallions, thinly sliced**

You know how to roast turkey and chicken, beef and pork—now try roasting a thick fish fillet. Here cod fillet is rubbed with a cumin-based spice mixture and roasted on a bed of potatoes, carrots, summer squash and green beans. Because the fish cooks in such a short time, some of the vegetables are briefly parboiled so that they will be done as quickly as the cod.

1 Preheat the oven to 425°.

2 Line a baking sheet with foil. Place the fish on the prepared baking sheet. In a small bowl, combine the cumin, ginger, ¼ teaspoon of the salt, the paprika and ground red pepper. Stir in 2 teaspoons of the oil. Brush both sides of the fish with the seasoned oil. Cover the fish loosely and refrigerate while you prepare the vegetables.

3 Place the potatoes in a large saucepan and add water to cover; bring to a boil over high heat. Reduce the heat to medium, cover and simmer for 5 minutes. Add the carrots, cover and cook for 2 minutes. Add the green beans and cook, uncovered, for 1 minute. Drain the vegetables in a colander.

4 Transfer the drained vegetables to a large bowl and add the squash, black pepper and the remaining 2 teaspoons oil and ¼ teaspoon salt; toss to combine. Spread the vegetables out in a single layer in a jelly-roll pan and bake for 15 minutes.

5 Place the fish on top of the vegetables and bake for 10 to 15 minutes longer, or until the fish just flakes when tested with a knife and the vegetables are tender. Transfer the fish and vegetables to a warmed platter and scatter the cilantro and scallions over the fish and vegetables.

Preparation time 20 minutes • **Total time** 1 hour • **Per serving** 393 calories, 6.7 g. fat (15% of calories), 1 g. saturated fat, 73 mg. cholesterol, 412 mg. sodium, 7.6 g. dietary fiber, 106 mg. calcium, 4 mg. iron, 56 mg. vitamin C, 12.8 mg. beta-carotene • **Serves 4**

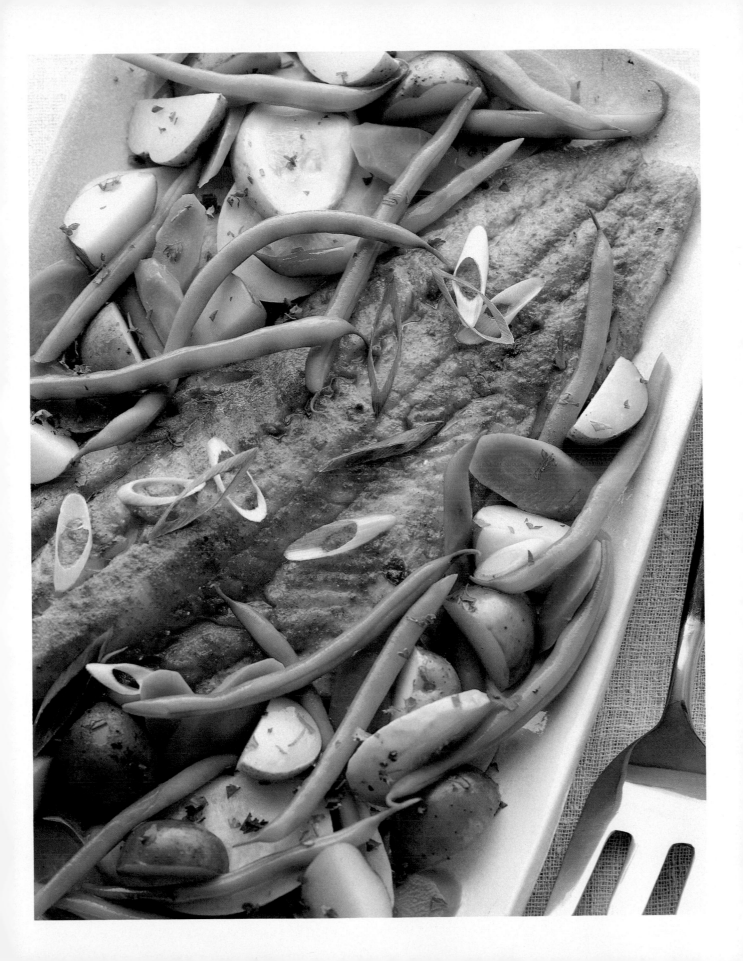

MEDITERRANEAN SHRIMP WITH FETA

- 1 pound all-purpose potatoes, peeled and thinly sliced
- 8 ounces green beans, trimmed and halved diagonally
- 1 medium zucchini, halved lengthwise and thinly sliced
- 2 teaspoons olive oil
- 1 medium onion, thinly sliced
- 1 red bell pepper, coarsely chopped
- 2 garlic cloves, minced
- 1 can (28 ounces) crushed tomatoes with juice
- 1 pound medium shrimp, peeled and deveined, with tails attached
- ¼ cup dry white wine
- ½ teaspoon dried oregano
- ½ teaspoon salt
- ¼ teaspoon freshly ground black pepper
- 2 ounces feta cheese, crumbled
- 3 tablespoons chopped Italian parsley

The Greek islands are, naturally enough, the home of some exceptional seafood cookery. This is a favorite Greek way of preparing shrimp—the shellfish Americans love best. The potatoes are not a traditional component of this dish, but they make substantial fare of what might otherwise be a very light meal.

1 Preheat the oven to 375°.

2 Place the potatoes in a large saucepan and add water to cover. Bring to a boil and cook for 7 minutes. Add the green beans and zucchini, and cook for 3 minutes longer. Drain the vegetables in a colander and transfer to a large bowl.

3 Meanwhile, in a medium no-stick skillet, warm the oil over medium heat. Add the onions, bell peppers and garlic, and cook for 3 minutes, or until softened. Add the onion mixture to the bowl with the other vegetables.

4 Add the tomatoes and their juice, the shrimp, wine, oregano, salt and black pepper to the vegetables, and toss to combine. Transfer the mixture to an 11 x 7-inch baking dish, cover with foil and bake for 25 minutes.

5 Uncover the dish and sprinkle the feta on top. Bake, uncovered, for 3 minutes longer.

6 Remove the dish from the oven and sprinkle with the parsley.

Preparation time 15 minutes • **Total time** 1 hour • **Per serving** 309 calories, 7.6 g. fat (22% of calories), 2.8 g. saturated fat, 152 mg. cholesterol, 904 mg. sodium, 5.2 g. dietary fiber, 223 mg. calcium, 5 mg. iron, 100 mg. vitamin C, 1.7 mg. beta-carotene • **Serves 4**

MARKET AND PANTRY
If you prefer to purchase shelled shrimp, buy about 8 ounces instead of 1 pound of unshelled shrimp. Either way, you should get 30 to 35 medium shrimp.

ON THE MENU
Offer French or Italian bread—or warm pita pockets—with the shrimp. Finish with a fruit salad sweetened with honey and sprinkled lightly with cinnamon.

Turkey and Rice Stuffed Peppers

4 large red bell peppers plus
  1 small red bell pepper, or a
  mix of red and yellow peppers

2 cups water

½ cup long-grain white rice

¾ teaspoon salt

2 teaspoons olive oil

1 pound lean ground turkey

1 medium onion, chopped

2 garlic cloves, minced

1½ teaspoons dried thyme or
  1 teaspoon chopped fresh
  thyme

¼ teaspoon freshly ground black
  pepper

1 pound fresh spinach, stemmed
  and coarsely chopped

½ cup dried currants

¼ cup chopped parsley

To make sure the peppers stand upright in the pan, shave a thin slice off the bottoms of the peppers before blanching them.

Food served in edible containers—zucchini boats, melon bowls or these striking red bell pepper cups—always makes a fun meal. When you've eaten the filling, be sure to polish off your "dish" as well: Red bell peppers are a good source of vitamin C.

1 Preheat the oven to 350°. Bring a large saucepan of water to a boil over high heat.

2 Meanwhile, cut off and discard the tops of the 4 large bell peppers. Seed the large peppers, being careful not to puncture them. Seed and dice the small bell pepper; set aside.

3 Blanch the whole peppers in the boiling water for 2 minutes, or until slightly softened. Drain the peppers on paper towels, then stand the peppers upright in an 8 x 8-inch baking dish; set aside.

4 In a medium saucepan, combine 1 cup of the water, the rice and ¼ teaspoon of the salt. Cover and bring to a boil over medium-high heat; reduce the heat to medium and cook, covered, for 15 to 17 minutes, or until the rice is tender and the liquid is absorbed.

5 Meanwhile, in a large no-stick skillet, warm the oil over medium-high heat until hot but not smoking. Add the turkey and sauté for about 3 minutes, breaking up any clumps with a spoon. Add the onions, garlic, thyme, black pepper and remaining ½ teaspoon salt, and cook for about 3 minutes, or until the onions are softened.

6 Add the diced bell peppers, spinach, currants and parsley; cover and cook for 3 minutes, or until the spinach is wilted. Remove the pan from the heat.

7 Fluff the cooked rice with a fork. Add the spinach mixture to the rice and stir to combine. Spoon the rice mixture into the bell peppers, pour the remaining 1 cup water into the baking dish around the peppers and bake for 15 minutes, or until the peppers and filling are hot.

Preparation time 15 minutes • **Total time** 1 hour • **Per serving** 386 calories, 11.5 g. fat (27% of calories), 2.7 g. saturated fat, 83 mg. cholesterol, 591 mg. sodium, 6 g. dietary fiber, 157 mg. calcium, 7 mg. iron, 246 mg. vitamin C, 7.3 mg. beta-carotene • **Serves 4**

GARDEN LASAGNA

1 teaspoon vegetable oil

8 ounces eggplant, diced

½ cup chopped onion

1 large garlic clove, minced

¼ cup plus 1 tablespoon chopped fresh basil

½ teaspoon salt

¼ teaspoon freshly ground black pepper

1 can (16 ounces) crushed tomatoes with juice

3 medium carrots, diced

1¼ cups water

1 cup part-skim ricotta cheese

1 tablespoon grated Parmesan cheese

1 large egg white

6 uncooked no-boil lasagna noodles

2 ounces part-skim mozzarella cheese, grated

The Italians use the term *alla giardiniera*—meaning lady-gardener-style—to describe a dish made with plenty of fresh vegetables. The sauce for this lasagna alla giardiniera contains eggplant, onions, carrots and basil along with the usual tomatoes. A busy gardener (or any busy person) will appreciate no-boil lasagna noodles: They go right from the package into the casserole (you don't have to precook them) and absorb liquid as they bake. To ensure that the noodles soften completely, see that they are completely covered with sauce.

1 Preheat the oven to 375°. Spray an 8 x 8-inch baking dish with no-stick spray.

2 In a large no-stick skillet, warm the oil over medium-high heat. Add the eggplant, onions, garlic, 1 tablespoon of the basil, ¼ teaspoon of the salt and the black pepper, and sauté for 3 minutes. Add the tomatoes and their juice, the carrots and 1 cup of the water, and simmer for 5 minutes, or until the eggplant is tender.

3 While the sauce is simmering, in a medium bowl, combine the ricotta, Parmesan, egg white, and remaining ¼ cup basil and ¼ teaspoon salt; set aside.

4 Spoon one-third of the tomato sauce into the prepared baking dish. Lay 2 lasagna noodles over the sauce, then top with half the cheese mixture and 2 more noodles. Repeat, using half the remaining sauce and all the remaining noodles and cheese mixture. Spoon the remaining sauce on top and sprinkle with the mozzarella. Pour the remaining ¼ cup water into the baking dish, around the edges.

5 Cover the lasagna with foil and bake for 15 minutes; uncover the dish and bake for another 15 minutes, or until bubbly.

Preparation time 20 minutes • **Total time** 1 hour • **Per serving** 298 calories, 9.4 g. fat (28% of calories), 4.9 g. saturated fat, 28 mg. cholesterol, 662 mg. sodium, 4.4 g. dietary fiber, 379 mg. calcium, 3 mg. iron, 25 mg. vitamin C, 9.8 mg. beta-carotene • **Serves 4**

PASTITSIO

1 cup 1% low-fat milk

½ cup defatted chicken broth

3 tablespoons all-purpose flour

3 tablespoons grated Parmesan cheese

¼ teaspoon nutmeg, preferably freshly grated

½ cup part-skim ricotta cheese

1 tablespoon chopped fresh dill

8 ounces fettuccine

12 ounces lean leg of lamb, cut into chunks

8 ounces eggplant, diced

8 ounces zucchini, diced

½ cup coarsely chopped onion

3 tablespoons chopped fresh mint

¼ teaspoon freshly ground black pepper

1 can (15 ounces) tomato sauce

A not-too-distant cousin of lasagna, *pastitsio* is a Greek pasta casserole with layers of macaroni, cheese sauce and meat. Rather than the traditional béchamel, this recipe is made with a ricotta-based sauce that's thick and rich-tasting, but low in fat. And, for a contemporary look, fettuccine is used instead of macaroni.

1 Preheat the oven to 375°. Bring a large covered pot of water to a boil over high heat.

2 Meanwhile, in a large no-stick skillet, whisk together the milk, broth, flour, 2 tablespoons of the Parmesan and the nutmeg over medium-high heat. Cook, whisking constantly, for 3 minutes, or until thickened. Whisk in the ricotta and dill, then transfer the mixture to a large bowl. Rinse and dry the skillet.

3 Add the noodles to the boiling water, return to a boil and cook for 6 to 7 minutes, or according to package directions until al dente. Drain the pasta in a colander, then add to the cheese mixture and toss well; set aside.

4 While the pasta is cooking, place the lamb chunks in a food processor and process until finely ground.

5 Place the lamb, eggplant, zucchini and onions in the large skillet, and cook over medium-high heat for 5 minutes, or until the vegetables are tender and the lamb is browned on all sides. Stir in the mint and black pepper. Stir in the tomato sauce and simmer, stirring occasionally, for 2 minutes. Remove the skillet from the heat.

6 Spray an 11 x 7-inch baking dish with no-stick spray. Spoon half of the pasta-cheese mixture into the bottom. Spoon the lamb mixture over the pasta and then top with the remaining pasta-cheese mixture. Bake for 10 minutes, then sprinkle with the remaining 1 tablespoon Parmesan. Bake for another 5 minutes, or until heated through.

Preparation time 20 minutes • **Total time** 1 hour • **Per serving** 501 calories, 11.3 g. fat (20% of calories), 4.6 g. saturated fat, 123 mg. cholesterol, 977 mg. sodium, 4.8 g. dietary fiber, 289 mg. calcium, 6 mg. iron, 23 mg. vitamin C, 1 mg. beta-carotene • **Serves 4**

❧ ❧ ❧

Moroccan Chicken Pot Pie

2 cups water

1 cinnamon stick

4 whole cloves

¼ teaspoon ground turmeric

½ teaspoon salt

¼ teaspoon freshly ground black pepper

1 pound skinless, boneless chicken breast halves, cut into 1-inch cubes

1 pound carrots, diced

12 ounces all-purpose potatoes, peeled and diced

8 ounces small pearl onions, peeled and halved

1 tablespoon cornstarch dissolved in 3 tablespoons cold water

1 cup frozen peas, thawed

½ cup golden raisins

¼ cup chopped Italian parsley

2 tablespoons honey

1 tablespoon vegetable oil

1 tablespoon hot water

6 sheets phyllo dough

Rather than a heavy crust, this very deep-dish pie is topped with a light, crisp layer of phyllo—paper-thin Greek pastry sheets. Phyllo (or filo) is sold in most supermarkets. Keep it wrapped or covered with a damp towel during preparation.

1 Preheat the oven to 400°. In a large skillet, combine the 2 cups of water, the cinnamon stick, cloves, turmeric, ¼ teaspoon of the salt and ⅛ teaspoon of the black pepper. Add the chicken to the skillet and bring to a simmer over medium-high heat. Poach the chicken for 5 to 7 minutes, or until cooked through. Using a slotted spoon, transfer the chicken to a large bowl. Discard the cinnamon stick and cloves.

2 Add the carrots, potatoes and onions to the skillet, and cook for about 8 minutes, or until the vegetables are tender. Using a slotted spoon, transfer the vegetables to the bowl with the chicken.

3 Pour off all but ¼ cup of the liquid from the skillet. Stir the cornstarch mixture to recombine it, then add it to the skillet. Cook, stirring, over medium-high heat for 1 minute, or until the sauce is slightly thickened. Pour the sauce over the chicken and vegetables, then add the peas, raisins, parsley, and remaining ¼ teaspoon salt and ⅛ teaspoon black pepper. Toss gently but thoroughly to combine. Spoon the chicken mixture into a 1½-quart soufflé dish or casserole; set aside.

4 In a small bowl, whisk together the honey, oil and hot water. Place the stacked sheets of phyllo on a work surface and cover with a damp towel. Remove 1 sheet from the stack and place it on the work surface; brush lightly with the honey mixture. Place a second sheet on top of the first and brush with the honey mixture. Continue in this manner for all 6 sheets (don't worry if the sheets stick together). Place the phyllo stack on top of the soufflé dish or casserole, tucking under the edges if necessary for fit. Brush the top with any remaining honey mixture.

5 Bake the pot pie for 15 minutes, or until the crust is golden.

Preparation time 20 minutes • **Total time** 1 hour • **Per serving** 485 calories, 7.1 g. fat (13% of calories), 1.1 g. saturated fat, 66 mg. cholesterol, 579 mg. sodium, 7.2 g. dietary fiber, 101 mg. calcium, 4 mg. iron, 40 mg. vitamin C, 19.5 mg. beta-carotene • **Serves 4**

❧ ❧ ❧

SALMON AND VEGETABLE PACKETS

1 tablespoon olive oil

2 medium carrots, cut into julienne strips

2 small leeks, white part only, well washed and sliced ¼ inch thick

2 small zucchini, halved and thinly sliced lengthwise

2 medium tomatoes, seeded and diced

⅓ cup minced shallots

2 tablespoons chopped Italian parsley

½ teaspoon grated fresh ginger

¼ teaspoon freshly ground black pepper

⅛ teaspoon salt

4 salmon fillets (4 ounces each), skinned

2 tablespoons dry sherry

2 tablespoons reduced-sodium soy sauce

1 teaspoon honey

6 ounces orzo pasta

Foil packets make it a snap to poach individual portions of salmon along with a medley of vegetables.

1 Preheat the oven to 425°. Bring a large covered pot of water and a large covered saucepan of water to a boil over high heat. Meanwhile, cut four 17 x 12-inch sheets of foil. Brush the sheets of foil lightly with the oil.

2 Add the carrots, leeks and zucchini to the saucepan of boiling water, and cook for 3 minutes. Drain the vegetables in a colander and rinse under cold running water; drain again. Transfer the vegetables to a medium bowl and toss with the tomatoes, shallots, parsley and ginger.

3 Spoon the vegetables evenly onto one end of each piece of foil; sprinkle with the pepper and salt. Place each fillet on top of a portion of vegetables.

4 In a small bowl, stir together the sherry, soy sauce and honey. Drizzle this mixture evenly over the fish and vegetables, then fold the foil over the contents, sealing the edges together with small folds.

5 Place the packets on a baking sheet and bake for 15 minutes, or until the fish just flakes when tested with a fork (open one packet to check).

6 While the fish is baking, add the pasta to the boiling water in the large pot, return to a boil and cook for 6 to 7 minutes, or according to package directions until al dente. Drain in a colander.

7 Divide the pasta among 4 plates. Open the packets, remove the fish and vegetables and arrange on top of each serving of pasta. Pour any cooking juices left in the packets over the fish and vegetables.

Preparation time 30 minutes • **Total time** 55 minutes • **Per serving** 441 calories, 11.7 g. fat (24% of calories), 1.7 g. saturated fat, 62 mg. cholesterol, 453 mg. sodium, 4 g. dietary fiber, 78 mg. calcium, 5 mg. iron, 28 mg. vitamin C, 6.5 mg. beta-carotene
Serves 4

VEGETARIAN SHEPHERD'S PIE

- 1½ pounds small unpeeled all-purpose potatoes, cut into 1-inch cubes
- 1 cup canned black beans, rinsed and drained
- 1 cup canned kidney beans, rinsed and drained
- 1 can (15 ounces) no-salt-added tomato sauce
- 1 cup chopped onion
- 2 garlic cloves, minced
- ½ teaspoon salt
- ½ teaspoon freshly ground black pepper
- ½ cup 1% low-fat milk
- 2 tablespoons unsalted butter or margarine
- 2 tablespoons chopped fresh cilantro
- 1 package (10 ounces) frozen corn kernels, thawed
- 1 ounce Cheddar cheese, grated

You can pipe the potatoes over the filling in a lattice pattern, using a plain or fluted wide tip or a large round tip.

Shepherd's pie, as the name suggests, is traditionally made with lamb or mutton (and sometimes with beef). This wonderfully warming rendition of the British favorite is quite different: It's a vegetarian dish, with a savory filling of potatoes and beans in tomato sauce, a layer of corn and a cheese-crowned mashed-potato crust. To dress the pie up a bit, you can pipe the potato topping through a pastry bag (see below), using a wide tip.

1 Preheat the oven to 375°.

2 Place the potatoes in a large saucepan and add water to cover. Cover the pan and bring to boil over high heat. Reduce the heat to medium, cover and simmer for 10 minutes, or until the potatoes are just tender.

3 Meanwhile, in a medium saucepan, combine the black beans, kidney beans, tomato sauce, onions, garlic and ¼ teaspoon each of the salt and black pepper. Bring to a boil over medium-high heat; reduce the heat to medium and simmer for 2 to 3 minutes, or just until heated through. Spread the bean mixture in an 11 x 7-inch baking dish and set aside.

4 When the potatoes are cooked, drain in a colander and return to the large pan. Add the milk, butter or margarine, cilantro and remaining ¼ teaspoon each salt and black pepper; mash with a potato masher until smooth.

5 Spread the corn over the bean mixture, then spread the mashed potatoes on top. Sprinkle with the Cheddar.

6 Bake the shepherd's pie for 20 minutes, or until the top is golden. Remove from the oven and place under the broiler for about 1 minute to brown the topping slightly.

Preparation time 15 minutes • **Total time** 50 minutes • **Per serving** 424 calories, 10.1 g. fat (21% of calories), 5.5 g. saturated fat, 24 mg. cholesterol, 716 mg. sodium, 11.8 g. dietary fiber, 175 mg. calcium, 5 mg. iron, 53 mg. vitamin C, 0.9 mg. beta-carotene • **Serves 4**

BAKED CHICKEN WITH ROOT VEGETABLES

¼ cup mixed fresh herbs (such as tarragon, basil, parsley and mint), minced

2 teaspoons grated lemon zest

2 garlic cloves, minced

1 broiler-fryer chicken (2¼ pounds), cut into 8 serving pieces

3 tablespoons fresh lemon juice

8 ounces small red potatoes, quartered

1 small fennel bulb, trimmed and quartered

2 medium turnips, peeled and cut into 1-inch pieces

3 medium carrots, cut into 2-inch pieces

3 shallots, quartered

½ cup defatted reduced-sodium chicken broth

½ teaspoon salt

¼ teaspoon freshly ground black pepper

Fresh thyme and tarragon sprigs, for garnish (optional)

Degreasing the pan juices is an important step in this recipe. The best tool for the job is a gravy separator, a clear cup with a spout that begins at the base (rather than the top). When you pour in fatty pan juices, soup or sauce, the fat rises to the top, allowing the defatted juices to be poured out through the spout.

1 Preheat the oven to 375°. Line a large roasting pan with foil.

2 In a small bowl, combine the herbs, lemon zest and garlic. Spread 2 tablespoons of this mixture under the skin of the chicken. Stir the lemon juice into the remaining herb mixture; set aside.

3 Arrange the chicken pieces on a rack at one end of the prepared roasting pan. Spread the potatoes, fennel, turnips, carrots and shallots on the rack at other end of the pan. Brush the chicken with half of the lemon-herb mixture. Drizzle the vegetables and chicken evenly with the broth, then sprinkle with the salt and black pepper.

4 Bake the chicken and vegetables for 15 minutes, then baste the chicken with the remaining lemon-herb mixture. Increase the oven temperature to 400° and continue to bake for another 25 minutes, or until the chicken is browned and cooked through.

5 Remove the pan from the oven and transfer the chicken and vegetables to a platter. Pour the juices remaining in the pan into a gravy separator. Pour the degreased pan juices over the chicken and vegetables. Garnish with thyme and tarragon sprigs, if desired. Remove the skin from the chicken before eating.

Preparation time 15 minutes • **Total time** 1 hour • **Per serving** 278 calories, 7 g. fat (23% of calories), 1.9 g. saturated fat, 81 mg. cholesterol, 537 mg. sodium, 4.4 g. dietary fiber, 80 mg. calcium, 3 mg. iron, 41 mg. vitamin C, 9.3 mg. beta-carotene • **Serves 4**

KITCHEN TIP
If you don't have a gravy separator, use this trick for skimming the fat with a spoon: Pour the pan juices into a tall container, such as a glass measuring cup, rather than trying to skim them in the pan. This way, the fat will rise to the top in a deep layer, which is easier to remove.

TURKEY PRIMAVERA IN PARCHMENT

16 ounces fresh asparagus spears, trimmed and cut diagonally into ½-inch slices

2 medium carrots, cut into julienne strips

1 medium yellow bell pepper, cut into julienne strips

8 ounces fusilli or penne pasta

4 turkey cutlets (4 ounces each), pounded thin

1 tablespoon chopped fresh tarragon or thyme

1 teaspoon grated lemon zest

½ teaspoon salt

¼ teaspoon freshly ground black pepper

¼ cup fresh lemon juice

2 teaspoons reduced-sodium soy sauce

1 tablespoon olive oil

1 medium tomato, finely diced

2 tablespoons minced fresh chives

Lemon zest and fresh thyme sprigs, for garnish (optional)

Starting at the rounded end, fold over and crimp the edges of the parchment in a series of small pleats. When you reach the point of the heart, twist the "tail" to finish.

Few food-presentation techniques are as impressive as a *papillote,* or parchment-paper packet. (The name, close to the French word for butterfly, may derive from the fact that when the folded paper is cut into a heart shape, it looks like butterfly wings.) Rolls of kitchen parchment are sold in cookware shops.

1 Preheat the oven to 350°. Cut four 17 x 12-inch pieces of parchment paper or foil. If using parchment, fold each piece in half and cut into a half-heart shape.

2 Bring a large covered pot of water to a boil over high heat. Add the asparagus, carrots and bell peppers, and blanch for 2 minutes. Using a strainer or slotted spoon, transfer the vegetables to a large bowl; keep the water boiling.

3 Add the pasta to the boiling water, return to a boil and cook for 8 minutes (the pasta will not be fully cooked). Drain the pasta in a colander.

4 If using the parchment, unfold. Place one-fourth of the pasta on one side of each piece of parchment or at one end of each piece of foil. Place a turkey cutlet on top of the pasta and sprinkle with the tarragon or thyme, lemon zest, salt and black pepper. Spoon one-fourth of the vegetables on top of each, then sprinkle with the lemon juice, soy sauce and oil. Close the parchment or foil packets, sealing the edges with small folds.

5 Place the packets on a baking sheet and bake for 20 minutes, or until the parchment is puffed (the foil will not puff) and the turkey is cooked through (open one packet to check).

6 Place the packets on 4 plates and cut open. Top each with some diced tomato and minced chives, and garnish with lemon zest and thyme sprigs, if desired.

Preparation time 20 minutes • **Total time** 1 hour • **Per serving** 414 calories, 5.3 g. fat (12% of calories), 0.9 g. saturated fat, 70 mg. cholesterol, 451 mg. sodium, 3.9 g. dietary fiber, 57 mg. calcium, 5 mg. iron, 54 mg. vitamin C, 6.7 mg. beta-carotene • **Serves 4**

Macaroni 'n' Cheese with Chicken

6 ounces macaroni, such as elbows

1 teaspoon olive oil

3 medium carrots, diced

½ cup chopped shallots

2 garlic cloves, minced

1 teaspoon chopped fresh thyme or ½ teaspoon dried thyme

½ teaspoon salt

¼ teaspoon freshly ground black pepper

⅛ teaspoon ground red pepper

1 tablespoon cornstarch

1½ cups 1% low-fat milk

2 ounces Cheddar cheese, shredded

2 tablespoons grated Romano cheese

1 tablespoon Dijon mustard

4 ounces skinless smoked chicken breast, diced

1 package (10 ounces) frozen chopped spinach, thawed and squeezed dry

½ cup unseasoned dry breadcrumbs

2 tablespoons chopped Italian parsley

D ear as your childhood memories may be of bright orange macaroni and cheese, now you'd probably prefer one of these individual gratins, filled with macaroni, chunks of smoked chicken and spinach in a sophisticated Cheddar-Romano sauce.

1 Preheat the oven to 375°. Spray four 1½-cup gratin dishes or an 11 x 7-inch baking dish with no-stick spray.

2 Bring a large covered pot of water to a boil over high heat. Add the macaroni to the boiling water, return to a boil and cook for 6 to 7 minutes, or according to package directions until al dente. Drain in a colander, rinse briefly under cold running water and drain again.

3 While the pasta is cooking, in a large saucepan, warm the oil over medium-high heat. Add the carrots, shallots and garlic, and sauté for 2 to 3 minutes, or until the vegetables are softened. Stir in the thyme, salt, black pepper and ground red pepper, and cook, stirring, for 30 seconds, or until fragrant.

4 In a small bowl, whisk the cornstarch with ½ cup of the milk. Add the cornstarch mixture to the saucepan along with the remaining 1 cup milk; increase the heat to high and bring to a boil, stirring constantly. Reduce the heat to medium and simmer for 1 minute.

5 Whisk in the Cheddar, Romano and mustard until smooth. Remove the pan from the heat and add the smoked chicken, spinach and drained macaroni; stir gently to combine. Spoon the mixture into the prepared gratin dishes or baking dish.

6 In a small bowl, combine the breadcrumbs and parsley. Sprinkle the breadcrumb mixture over the top of the macaroni. Bake for 20 to 25 minutes, or until hot and bubbly.

Preparation time 20 minutes • **Total time** 1 hour • **Per serving** 437 calories, 11.2 g. fat (23% of calories), 4.4 g. saturated fat, 33 mg. cholesterol, 987 mg. sodium, 5.1 g. dietary fiber, 393 mg. calcium, 5 mg. iron, 27 mg. vitamin C, 12.7 mg. beta-carotene • **Serves 4**

Stir-Fries & Other Skillet Meals

❧ ❧ ❧

POPULAR PAN DINNERS INSPIRED BY

THE WORLD'S GREAT CUISINES

DOUBLE ORANGE BEEF WITH VEGETABLES

2¼ cups plus ⅓ cup water

2 cups quick-cooking brown rice

⅓ cup fresh orange juice

2 tablespoons orange marmalade

2 tablespoons reduced-sodium soy sauce

1½ teaspoons cornstarch

¼ teaspoon crushed red pepper flakes

12 ounces lean, trimmed boneless beef sirloin or top round steak, thinly sliced

½ pound fresh asparagus spears, trimmed and diagonally sliced into 1-inch pieces

2 medium carrots, thinly sliced on the diagonal

2 teaspoons vegetable oil

1 medium red bell pepper, cut into thin strips

4 ounces shiitake or white mushrooms, sliced

3 large scallions, thinly sliced on the diagonal

2 garlic cloves, minced

½ teaspoon grated fresh ginger

Rice turns this stir-fry into a well-rounded meal, and quick-cooking brown rice, used here, is a great time-saver. Alternatively, you could cook regular brown rice the night before you plan to serve this dish, then reheat it while you stir-fry the vegetables and beef. Add a little water or broth to the rice before reheating in a covered pot over gentle heat.

1 In a medium saucepan, bring 2¼ cups of the water to a boil over high heat. Stir in the rice and reduce the heat to medium-low; cover and simmer for 10 minutes, or until the rice is tender and the liquid is absorbed. Remove the pan from the heat and set aside.

2 While the rice is cooking, in a medium bowl, combine the orange juice, marmalade, soy sauce, cornstarch and red pepper flakes, stirring until smooth. Stir in the beef and let stand while you prepare the vegetables.

3 In a large no-stick skillet, bring the remaining ⅓ cup of water to a boil over medium-high heat. Add the asparagus and carrots, cover and cook for 3 minutes, or until the vegetables are just tender. Drain the vegetables in a colander and transfer to a medium bowl. Wipe the skillet dry.

4 In the dry skillet, warm 1 teaspoon of the oil over medium-high heat. Add the bell peppers and mushrooms, and stir-fry for 2 minutes, or until the vegtables are tender. Add the scallions, garlic and ginger, and stir-fry for 30 seconds, or until fragrant. Transfer to the bowl with the other vegetables.

5 Add the remaining 1 teaspoon oil to the skillet. Add the beef and the marinade, and stir-fry for 3 to 4 minutes, or until the beef is cooked through. Add the vegetables and stir-fry for 1 minute, or until the vegetables are heated through. Fluff the rice with a fork and serve with the beef and vegetables.

Preparation time 25 minutes • **Total time** 35 minutes • **Per serving** 399 calories, 8.4 g. fat (18% of calories), 1.7 g. saturated fat, 52 mg. cholesterol, 395 mg. sodium, 4.8 g. dietary fiber, 51 mg. calcium, 4 mg. iron, 70 mg. vitamin C, 7.1 mg. beta-carotene • **Serves 4**

ॐ ॐ ॐ

Turkey-Vegetable Hash

2 pounds small red potatoes, quartered

½ teaspoon salt

1 cup diced carrots

1 tablespoon plus 1 teaspoon olive oil

1 medium green bell pepper, diced

1 medium onion, diced

2 garlic cloves, minced

½ cup defatted reduced-sodium chicken broth

¾ teaspoon dried thyme or 1 tablespoon fresh, chopped thyme

½ teaspoon dried sage or 1 tablespoon fresh sage

½ teaspoon freshly ground black pepper

12 ounces skinless roast turkey breast (in one piece), cut into ½-inch cubes

¼ cup chopped Italian parsley

Think of the best hash-browns you ever ate for breakfast. Now imagine those same crisp potatoes amplified with carrots, peppers and chunks of turkey and glorified with garlic and herbs. You'd have to agree it's a wonderfully homey idea for a simple supper.

1 Preheat the broiler. Place the potatoes in a medium saucepan with water to cover and ¼ teaspoon of the salt; cover the pan and bring to a boil over high heat. Boil for 2 minutes; add the carrots and boil for 4 minutes longer, or until tender. Drain the vegetables in a colander.

2 While the potatoes and carrots are cooking, in a large flameproof skillet, warm the oil over medium-high heat. Add the bell peppers, onions and garlic, and sauté for 2 to 3 minutes, or until tender.

3 Stir in the potatoes and carrots, the broth, thyme, sage, black pepper and remaining ¼ teaspoon salt. Cook, stirring frequently, for 7 minutes, or until the hash starts to brown. Reduce the heat to medium-low, stir in the turkey and parsley, and cook for 2 minutes.

4 Place the skillet under the broiler and broil the hash 4 to 5 inches from the heat for 2 minutes, or until the top is browned and crisp.

Preparation time 25 minutes • **Total time** 50 minutes • **Per serving** 378 calories, 5.8 g. fat (14% of calories), 0.9 g. saturated fat, 71 mg. cholesterol, 429 mg. sodium, 5.9 g. dietary fiber, 45 mg. calcium, 4 mg. iron, 61 mg. vitamin C, 4.8 mg. beta-carotene • **Serves 4**

Italian parsley has flat, deeply toothed leaves. It's considered superior in flavor to curly and is preferable for seasoning.

Curly parsley, with its frilled leaves, is a fine addition to salads and makes a pretty garnish for many main dishes.

GREEK SKILLET DINNER IN A PITA

1 tablespoon plus 1 teaspoon
olive oil

1 pound eggplant, cut into ¾-inch
cubes

¼ cup defatted reduced-sodium
chicken broth

12 ounces lean, well-trimmed
boneless leg of lamb or beef top
round, cut into ½-inch chunks

1 medium onion, chopped

2 celery stalks, diced

3 garlic cloves, minced

2 teaspoons ground cumin

½ teaspoon dried oregano

¼ teaspoon dried mint or
2 tablespoons fresh mint

¼ teaspoon salt

¼ teaspoon freshly ground black
pepper

1 can (14½ ounces) diced
tomatoes with juice

1 can (10 ounces) chick-peas,
rinsed and drained

4 pita breads (6-inch diameter),
halved

½ cup plain nonfat yogurt

4 cups shredded Romaine lettuce

1 cup peeled, sliced cucumbers

2 plum tomatoes, thinly sliced

Chopped fresh mint, for garnish
(optional)

Long before you could buy skillet-dinner mixes in a box, cooks were stirring up ground meat, vegetables and favorite seasonings to feed the family economically and well. Resembling an exotic street snack more than a traditional skillet dinner, this delicious lamb-and-eggplant mixture is served in pitas.

1 In a large, heavy skillet, warm 2 teaspoons of the oil over medium-high heat. Add the eggplant and sauté for 2 to 3 minutes, or until browned. Stir in the broth and bring to a boil; reduce the heat to medium and cook for about 4 minutes, or until the eggplant is tender and the liquid is absorbed. Transfer the eggplant to a large plate.

2 Meanwhile, process the lamb or beef in a food processor until coarsely ground.

3 In the large skillet, warm the remaining 2 teaspoons oil over medium-high heat. Add the onions, celery and garlic, and sauté for 2 to 3 minutes, or until the onions are tender. Crumble in the ground meat and cook, stirring, for 3 minutes, or until the meat is no longer pink. Stir in the cumin, oregano, mint, salt and black pepper; cook, stirring constantly, for 30 seconds.

4 Add the tomatoes and their juice, and bring to a boil. Stir in the chick-peas and the reserved eggplant. Reduce the heat to low and simmer, stirring occasionally, for 5 to 7 minutes to blend the flavors.

5 Spoon one-fourth of the lamb mixture into each pita. Serve with the yogurt, lettuce, cucumbers and tomatoes, and garnish with chopped fresh mint, if desired.

Preparation time 25 minutes • **Total time** 40 minutes • **Per serving** 475 calories, 11.1 g. fat (21% of calories), 2.2 g. saturated fat, 55 mg. cholesterol, 851 mg. sodium, 7.9 g. dietary fiber, 257 mg. calcium, 7 mg. iron, 45 mg. vitamin C, 1.5 mg. beta-carotene • **Serves 4**

FOR A CHANGE
Instead of spooning the lamb mixture into pitas, serve it over hot pasta, with a sprinkling of feta cheese.

MARKET AND PANTRY
With eggplants, think "handsome is as handsome does." The shiniest, plumpest, purplest and smoothest are those to buy.

SPICY VEGETABLE FRITTATA

2 teaspoons olive oil

1 pound small red potatoes, diced

1 cup diced red bell pepper

1 small onion, diced

¼ cup defatted reduced-sodium chicken broth

1 cup diced zucchini

½ cup sliced scallions

2 garlic cloves, minced

¾ teaspoon dried thyme

½ teaspoon dried oregano

½ teaspoon salt

¼ teaspoon freshly ground black pepper

⅛ teaspoon ground red pepper

3 large whole eggs

6 large egg whites

¼ cup 1% low-fat milk

1 ounce Parmesan cheese, coarsely grated

1 cup seeded, diced tomato

2 tablespoons chopped Italian parsley

French folded omelets are delicious to eat but tricky to make. It is much easier to put together an Italian frittata, in which the ingredients that would serve as the filling for a folded omelet are simply mixed with the beaten eggs. This frittata uses just three whole eggs for four servings (six additional egg whites add a fluffy lightness but contribute no fat or cholesterol). It's packed with potatoes, peppers and onions, and topped with fresh tomatoes for an instant "relish."

1 In a large no-stick skillet, warm the oil over medium-high heat. Add the potatoes, bell peppers and onions, and cook for 2 minutes, or until the vegetables begin to brown. Add the broth and cook, stirring occasionally, for about 5 minutes, or until the potatoes begin to soften. Stir in the zucchini, scallions, garlic, thyme, oregano, salt, black pepper and ground red pepper, and cook for 4 minutes, or until the vegetables are tender and golden.

2 Meanwhile, in a medium bowl, whisk together the whole eggs, egg whites, milk and Parmesan.

3 Pour the egg mixture all at once over the vegetables and reduce the heat to medium-low. Stir to combine the eggs and vegetables, then cook, without stirring, for 10 minutes, or until the mixture begins to set.

4 Cover the skillet and cook for 2 minutes longer, or until the eggs are set on top. Slide the frittata onto a serving plate and sprinkle with the tomatoes and parsley.

Preparation time 25 minutes • **Total time** 40 minutes • **Per serving** 268 calories, 8.6 g. fat (28% of calories), 2.8 g. saturated fat, 165 mg. cholesterol, 583 mg. sodium, 3.9 g. dietary fiber, 164 mg. calcium, 3 mg. iron, 83 mg. vitamin C, 1.4 mg. beta-carotene • **Serves 4**

KITCHEN TIP
Rather than separating an egg by dropping the yolk from one half shell to the other (you're all too likely to break a yolk and waste an egg), buy an inexpensive egg separator. This tool looks like a big spoon with a slotted bowl; when you break an egg into the center, the yolk is held in the inner bowl while the white flows out through the slots on the sides.

MEDITERRANEAN-STYLE TUNA AND PASTA

1 pint (8 ounces) cherry tomatoes, stemmed and halved

2 tablespoons rinsed and drained capers

2 tablespoons chopped fresh dill

2 garlic cloves, minced

2 teaspoons grated lemon zest

2 teaspoons olive oil

½ teaspoon salt

½ teaspoon freshly ground black pepper

8 ounces penne pasta

1½ pounds spinach, trimmed and chopped

8 ounces tuna steak, cut into 1-inch cubes

2 ounces feta cheese, crumbled

This meal is almost like a salad in a skillet—light and fresh and full of vegetables. In fact, you needn't rush to the table with the dish, as it would be delicious served warm, in the manner of many stylish dinner salads. The fresh tuna, tomatoes, herbs, garlic, olive oil and capers reflect its Mediterranean roots.

1 Bring a large covered pot of water to a boil over high heat.

2 In a large bowl, combine the cherry tomatoes, capers, dill, garlic, lemon zest, olive oil and ¼ teaspoon each of the salt and black pepper.

3 Add the penne to the boiling water, return to a boil and cook for 8 to 10 minutes, or according to package directions until al dente. During the last 1 minute of cooking, add the spinach. Drain the pasta and spinach together in a colander.

4 Add the pasta and spinach to the tomato mixture, and toss gently to combine.

5 Spray a large no-stick skillet with no-stick spray. Add the tuna and cook over medium-high heat for 3 to 5 minutes, or just until browned. Add the remaining ¼ teaspoon each salt and black pepper, and toss with the tuna.

6 Add the pasta and spinach mixture to the tuna in the skillet, then stir in the feta cheese; toss well. Cook for 1 minute to heat through.

The tiny, tight buds of "nonpareil" capers (on the left) are considered superior to the larger capers on the right. Nonpareils are slightly more expensive.

Preparation time 15 minutes • **Total time** 30 minutes • **Per serving** 395 calories, 9.8 g. fat (22% of calories), 3.3 g. saturated fat, 34 mg. cholesterol, 671 mg. sodium, 5.4 g. dietary fiber, 218 mg. calcium, 7 mg. iron, 47 mg. vitamin C, 5.9 mg. beta-carotene • **Serves 4**

FOR A CHANGE
Scallops are a delicious variation on this recipe. Use 8 ounces of sea scallops; halve any that are very large. Sauté the scallops for 4 to 5 minutes, or until opaque. You can vary the seasonings, too: Fresh dill is wonderful with fish and shellfish, but you could try other fresh herbs, such as tarragon or oregano, when available.

ON THE MENU
Serve lime sorbet with fresh or frozen raspberries for a pretty, refreshing finale.

CHICKEN SUCCOTASH

2 teaspoons olive oil

12 ounces skinless, boneless chicken breast halves, cut into ½-inch chunks

½ teaspoon dried thyme

½ teaspoon salt

¼ teaspoon freshly ground black pepper

Pinch of ground nutmeg

Pinch of ground red pepper

1 medium red bell pepper, diced

2 celery stalks, finely diced

½ cup chopped shallots or onion

6 ounces ditalini or other small pasta

1 package (10 ounces) frozen baby lima beans

1 cup defatted reduced-sodium chicken broth

1 cup frozen corn kernels

1 tablespoon cornstarch

¾ cup 1% low-fat milk

2 tablespoons chopped Italian parsley

Ascending from side-dish to main-dish status, this succotash takes on some new components; indeed, the Native Americans who introduced this sturdy fare to the Pilgrims would probably not recognize their creation. In addition to the traditional lima beans and corn, there are chicken chunks, pasta, peppers, shallots and celery in this tasty rendition of a longtime American favorite.

1 Bring a large covered pot of water to a boil over high heat.

2 In a large no-stick skillet, warm the oil over medium-high heat. Add the chicken, thyme, salt, black pepper, nutmeg and ground red pepper, and sauté for 3 minutes, or until the chicken turns golden. Stir in the bell peppers, celery and shallots or onions, and sauté for 3 minutes, or until the vegetables begin to soften.

3 Add the pasta to the boiling water, return to a boil and cook for 10 to 12 minutes, or according to package directions until al dente. Drain in a colander and return to the pot to keep warm.

4 While the pasta is cooking, add the lima beans and broth to the skillet and bring to a boil. Reduce the heat to medium-low and simmer for 10 minutes. Stir in the corn and simmer for 1 minute longer, or until heated through.

5 In a cup, whisk the cornstarch with ¼ cup of the milk. Stir the cornstarch mixture into the chicken mixture, then stir in the remaining ½ cup milk. Simmer for 1 minute, or until slightly thickened. Add the chicken to the pasta and toss to combine. Divide the succotash among 4 plates and sprinkle each serving with some chopped parsley.

Preparation time 20 minutes • **Total time** 40 minutes • **Per serving** 456 calories, 5.2 g. fat (10% of calories), 1.1 g. saturated fat, 51 mg. cholesterol, 575 mg. sodium, 5.9 g. dietary fiber, 125 mg. calcium, 5 mg. iron, 51 mg. vitamin C, 0.9 mg. beta-carotene • **Serves 4**

FOOD FACT
Ditalini are small pasta cuts shaped like open-ended thimbles (ditalini means "thimbles"). The pasta is close in size to the corn kernels and lima beans, giving the dish a pleasing texture. The small shell pasta called conchigliette, or even small elbow macaroni, could also be used.

SHRIMP WITH LEMON AND ALMONDS

¼ cup fresh lemon juice

2 tablespoons rice wine vinegar

1 tablespoon plus 1 teaspoon sugar

1 teaspoon grated lemon zest

⅛ teaspoon crushed red pepper flakes

1 tablespoon plus 1 teaspoon reduced-sodium soy sauce

1 tablespoon dry sherry

2 teaspoons cornstarch

12 ounces medium shrimp, peeled and deveined, with tails attached

¼ cup blanched slivered almonds

1 tablespoon plus 1 teaspoon vegetable oil

8 ounces sugar snap peas or snow peas, trimmed

1 medium red bell pepper, diced

1 medium yellow bell pepper, diced

1 small onion, diced

2 garlic cloves, minced

2 tablespoons water

½ cup sliced water chestnuts

2 tablespoons chopped Italian parsley

6 ounces fresh cappellini pasta

Here's an eclectic meal worthy of today's hot young chefs—who often label such dishes "fusion cuisine." While many of the ingredients (soy sauce, rice wine vinegar and water chestnuts) and techniques ("velvet-coating" the shrimp with a cornstarch mixture and stir-frying) are Asian, the stir-fried shrimp and vegetables are served over cappellini pasta in classic Italian style.

1 Bring a large covered pot of water to a boil over high heat. Meanwhile, in a small bowl, whisk together the lemon juice, vinegar, sugar, lemon zest and red pepper flakes until blended; set aside.

2 In a medium bowl, whisk together the soy sauce, sherry and cornstarch until smooth. Add the shrimp and toss to coat. Refrigerate for 15 minutes.

3 Meanwhile, in a large skillet over medium-high heat, toast the almonds, tossing frequently, for 2 to 3 minutes, or until golden. Transfer to a small bowl.

4 In the large skillet, warm 2 teaspoons of the oil over medium-high heat until very hot but not smoking. Add the peas, peppers, onions and garlic, and stir-fry for 1 minute. Add the water, cover and cook for 2 minutes, or until the vegetables are just tender. Transfer to a plate.

5 In the large skillet, warm the remaining 2 teaspoons oil over medium-high heat. Add the shrimp and the marinade, and stir-fry for 5 to 6 minutes, or just until the shrimp turn pink and opaque. Stir in the lemon-juice mixture, reduce the heat to medium and simmer for 1 minute. Stir in the vegetables, water chestnuts and parsley. Sprinkle with the toasted almonds and remove the pan from the heat.

6 Add the cappellini to the boiling water; return to a boil and cook for 30 to 45 seconds, or until the pasta is al dente. Drain in a colander. Divide the pasta among 4 plates and top with the shrimp mixture.

Preparation time 25 minutes • **Total time** 30 minutes • **Per serving** 391 calories, 11.3 g. fat (26% of calories), 1.4 g. saturated fat, 136 mg. cholesterol, 378 mg. sodium, 4.3 g. dietary fiber, 121 mg. calcium, 4 mg. iron, 68 mg. vitamin C, 0.8 mg. beta-carotene • **Serves 4**

Skillet Cassoulet

1 teaspoon olive oil

2 ounces reduced-fat turkey
kielbasa sausage, halved and
sliced ½-inch thick

1 medium onion, chopped

2 celery stalks, diced

2 medium carrots, diced

8 ounces skinless, boneless
chicken thighs, cut into 1-inch
chunks

2 garlic cloves, minced

1 bay leaf, preferably imported

½ teaspoon dried rosemary or
1 tablespoon fresh rosemary

½ teaspoon dried thyme or
1 tablespoon fresh thyme

¼ teaspoon freshly ground black
pepper

1 can (14½ ounces) stewed
tomatoes with juice

¼ cup white wine

2 cans (19 ounces each)
cannellini beans, rinsed and
drained

1 cup fresh breadcrumbs

¼ cup chopped Italian parsley

If you love the French country casserole called cassoulet—but don't have time to soak the dried beans, roast the duck, poach the sausage, blanch the salt pork, brown the lamb and bake the casserole (whew!)—this recipe will please you. And you'll love the big cuts in fat and calories, thanks to the use of turkey kielbasa and chicken.

1 In a large flameproof skillet, warm the oil over medium-high heat. Add the sausage, onions, celery and carrots; cover and cook, stirring occasionally, for 5 minutes, or until the vegetables are tender.

2 Add the chicken to the skillet and cook, turning occasionally, for 3 to 5 minutes, or until browned on all sides. Stir in the garlic, bay leaf, rosemary, thyme and black pepper, and cook for 30 seconds, or until fragrant. Add the tomatoes and their juice, then add the wine. Reduce the heat to medium-low and simmer, covered, for 10 minutes. Stir in the beans and simmer, covered, for 5 minutes longer. While the cassoulet is cooking, preheat the broiler.

3 In a small bowl, combine the breadcrumbs and parsley. Sprinkle the top of the cassoulet with the breadcrumb mixture. Broil for 2 minutes, or until the topping is golden.

Preparation time 25 minutes • **Total time** 40 minutes • **Per serving** 396 calories, 6.8 g. fat (16% of calories), 1.4 g. saturated fat, 57 mg. cholesterol, 861 mg. sodium, 15.7 g. dietary fiber, 7 mg. calcium, 6 mg. iron, 30 mg. vitamin C, 6.6 mg. beta-carotene • **Serves 4**

❧ ❧ ❧

To make your own breadcrumbs, trim the crusts from an unsliced loaf of bread.

Then grate the crustless bread on the large holes of a hand grater.

Or, place large chunks of the bread in a food processor and pulse to make crumbs.

HOISIN PORK AND VEGETABLES

- 2 tablespoons hoisin sauce
- 2 tablespoons dry sherry
- 2 tablespoons reduced-sodium soy sauce
- 1 tablespoon honey
- 1½ teaspoons cornstarch
- ½ teaspoon dark sesame oil
- ¼ teaspoon crushed red pepper flakes
- 8 ounces lean, boneless pork loin, cut into ¼-inch-wide strips
- 8 ounces whole-wheat spaghettini
- ⅔ cup water
- 6 cups broccoli florets or 8 cups trimmed, cut-up broccoli rabe (2-inch lengths)
- 2 medium carrots, sliced
- 3 teaspoons vegetable oil
- 2 cups thinly sliced red cabbage
- 1 medium yellow bell pepper, sliced
- ½ small red onion, sliced
- 2 garlic cloves, minced

Hoisin sauce, which gives this pork stir-fry savory richness, is a Chinese staple that's sold in most American supermarkets. If you like to create your own stir-fried dishes, there should be a bottle of hoisin sauce in your refrigerator. Made from soybeans, vinegar, garlic, chilies and spices, this sauce can season meat, poultry and shellfish (you can use it in cooking, or as a table condiment). If you buy hoisin sauce in a can, transfer it to a glass jar before you store it.

1 In a medium bowl, combine the hoisin sauce, sherry, soy sauce, honey, cornstarch, sesame oil and red pepper flakes. Stir in the pork and let marinate while you prepare the pasta and vegetables.

2 While the pork is marinating, bring a large covered pot of water to a boil over high heat. Add the spaghettini, return to a boil and cook for 10 to 12 minutes, or according to package directions until al dente. Drain in a colander.

3 While the spaghettini is cooking, in a large no-stick skillet, bring the ⅔ cup of water to a boil over high heat. Add the broccoli florets or broccoli rabe and the carrots, cover and cook for 2 minutes, or until the vegetables are just tender. Drain the vegetables in a colander and transfer to a medium bowl. Wipe the skillet dry.

4 In the dry skillet, warm 1 teaspoon of the oil over medium-high heat. Add the cabbage, bell peppers and onions, and stir-fry for 2 to 3 minutes, or until tender. Add the garlic and stir-fry for 30 seconds, or until fragrant. Transfer to the bowl with the other vegetables.

5 In the skillet, warm the remaining 2 teaspoons oil over medium-high heat. Add the pork and the marinade, and stir-fry for 2 to 3 minutes, or until the pork is cooked through. Add the vegetables and stir-fry for 1 to 2 minutes, or until heated through. Serve over the spaghettini.

Preparation time 25 minutes • **Total time** 35 minutes • **Per serving** 468 calories, 8.8 g. fat (16% of calories), 1.8 g. saturated fat, 33 mg. cholesterol, 557 mg. sodium, 15.8 g. dietary fiber, 155 mg. calcium, 5 mg. iron, 182 mg. vitamin C, 8 mg. beta-carotene • **Serves 4**

SEAFOOD JAMBALAYA

1 tablespoon olive oil

3 ounces baked ham, diced

1 medium green bell pepper, diced

1 medium onion, chopped

2 celery stalks, chopped

3 garlic cloves, minced

1 cup long-grain white rice

1 bay leaf, preferably imported

½ teaspoon dried oregano

½ teaspoon dried thyme

½ teaspoon freshly ground black pepper

¼ teaspoon salt

⅛ teaspoon ground red pepper

1½ cups defatted reduced-sodium chicken broth

1½ cups water

8 ounces sea scallops, tough muscle removed

8 ounces medium shrimp, peeled and deveined, with tails attached

1 cup diced ripe tomatoes

¼ cup chopped Italian parsley

Not many foods have found their way into the lyrics of American popular songs: Jambalaya (and its Cajun companions, crawfish pie and filé gumbo) has that rare distinction. One of the defining dishes of Louisiana cuisine, jambalaya is delightfully variable, subject to the whims of the person cooking it (although the rice, onions, celery and bell peppers are unvarying ingredients). The shrimp-scallop-and-ham jambalaya here is just one interpretation of a dish that is frequently made with sausage, crayfish or oysters.

1 In a large no-stick skillet, warm the oil over medium-high heat. Add the ham, bell peppers, onions, celery and garlic, and sauté for 4 to 5 minutes, or until the vegetables are softened.

2 Stir in the rice, bay leaf, oregano, thyme, black pepper, salt and ground red pepper, and sauté for 1 minute. Add the broth and water, and bring to a boil. Reduce the heat to medium-low, cover and simmer for 15 minutes, or until the rice is just tender.

3 Stir in the scallops, shrimp and tomatoes; cover and simmer for 5 minutes, or until the seafood turns opaque. Just before serving, sprinkle the jambalaya with the chopped parsley.

Preparation time 25 minutes • **Total time** 35 minutes • **Per serving** 383 calories, 7.2 g. fat (17% of calories), 1.5 g. saturated fat, 101 mg. cholesterol, 883 mg. sodium, 2.6 g. dietary fiber, 92 mg. calcium, 5 mg. iron, 38 mg. vitamin C, 0.4 mg. beta-carotene • **Serves 4**

To chop an onion, first cut off the tip and peel the onion. Make a series of parallel cuts toward (but not through) the root end.

Holding the partially sliced onion together, make a second, perpendicular series of cuts, without cutting all the way through.

Still holding the onion together, turn it on its side and cut crosswise: The onion will fall into tiny dice.

STIR-FRY CHICKEN CURRY WITH SPINACH

1¼ cups plus 2 tablespoons water

1 cup instant couscous

2 garlic cloves, minced

1 tablespoon curry powder

1 teaspoon grated fresh ginger

1 teaspoon tomato paste

1 teaspoon ground cumin

¼ teaspoon salt

¼ teaspoon freshly ground black pepper

Pinch of ground cloves

1½ teaspoons vegetable oil

1 medium onion, finely chopped

12 ounces skinless, boneless chicken thighs, cut into 1½-inch chunks

12 ounces sweet potatoes, peeled and cut into ½-inch dice

1 cup defatted reduced-sodium chicken broth

1 cup diced Golden Delicious apple

½ cup frozen peas

4 ounces spinach, trimmed and coarsely chopped

¼ cup chopped fresh cilantro

Curry is normally a slow-simmered production, as it takes at least an hour for cubes of lamb or beef to cook to the point of melting tenderness. An obvious shortcut for curry-lovers who are pressed for time is to use chicken instead of red meat. After the chicken chunks are stir-fried, they simmer—along with diced sweet potatoes—for just 15 minutes or so in a spicy sauce. In another noteworthy departure from tradition, the curry is served over couscous rather than rice.

1 In a small saucepan, bring 1¼ cups of the water to a boil over high heat. Add the couscous, cover and remove from the heat. Let stand while you prepare the chicken and vegetables.

2 In a small bowl, combine the remaining 2 tablespoons of water, the garlic, curry powder, ginger, tomato paste, cumin, salt, black pepper and cloves, and whisk until smooth; set aside.

3 In a large no-stick skillet, warm the oil over medium-high heat until very hot but not smoking. Add the onions and stir-fry for 2 to 3 minutes, or until golden. Add the chicken and stir-fry for 4 minutes, or until browned. Stir in the garlic and reserved spice mixture, and stir-fry for about 1 minute, or until fragrant.

4 Add the potatoes and broth. Reduce the heat to medium-low, cover and simmer, stirring occasionally, for 10 to 15 minutes, or until the chicken is cooked through and the potatoes are tender. Stir in the apples and peas, cover and simmer for 3 minutes. Stir in the spinach and cook, uncovered, for 1 minute, or until the spinach is wilted.

5 Fluff the couscous with a fork and divide among 4 plates. Top the couscous with the curry, then sprinkle with the cilantro.

Preparation time 35 minutes • **Total time** 45 minutes • **Per serving** 420 calories, 6.2 g. fat (13% of calories), 1.2 g. saturated fat, 71 mg. cholesterol, 433 mg. sodium, 6.5 g. dietary fiber, 86 mg. calcium, 4 mg. iron, 31 mg. vitamin C, 8.4 mg. beta-carotene • **Serves 4**

FIVE-SPICE CHICKEN WITH VEGETABLES

2 tablespoons reduced-sodium soy sauce

2 garlic cloves, minced

1½ teaspoons five-spice powder

1 teaspoon grated fresh ginger

1 teaspoon dark sesame oil

¼ teaspoon freshly ground black pepper

12 ounces thin-sliced chicken cutlets

⅓ cup defatted reduced-sodium chicken broth

1 tablespoon dry sherry

2 teaspoons cornstarch

⅛ teaspoon crushed red pepper flakes

3 teaspoons vegetable oil

6 ounces orzo pasta

½ pound green beans, trimmed

4 medium carrots, cut into julienne strips

3 cups small cauliflower florets

½ small red onion, thinly sliced

2 tablespoons water

Sliced scallion greens for garnish (optional)

Like pumpkin-pie spice or *fines herbes,* Chinese five-spice powder is a convenient ready-made seasoning blend. It's usually composed of ground anise or fennel seed, star anise, cloves, cinnamon and Szechuan peppercorns. You can find this unique spice blend at Asian markets, and many supermarkets stock it, too.

1 In a medium bowl, combine 2 teaspoons of the soy sauce, the garlic, five-spice powder, ginger, sesame oil and black pepper. Add the chicken and turn to coat. Refrigerate for 15 minutes.

2 Meanwhile, bring a large covered pot of water to a boil over high heat. In a small bowl, whisk together the broth, sherry, cornstarch, red pepper flakes and remaining 1 tablespoon plus 1 teaspoon soy sauce until smooth; set aside.

3 In a large no-stick skillet, warm 1½ teaspoons of the oil over medium-high heat until hot but not smoking. Add the chicken cutlets and cook, turning once, for 4 minutes, or until golden and cooked through. Transfer the chicken to a cutting board and cut into ¼-inch-wide strips.

4 Add the orzo to the boiling water, return to a boil and cook for 8 minutes, or according to package directions until al dente.

5 While the orzo is cooking, in the large skillet, warm the remaining 1½ teaspoons oil over medium-high heat until very hot but not smoking. Add the beans, carrots, cauliflower and onions, and cook, stirring, for 1 minute. Add the water, cover and cook for 2 minutes, or until the vegetables are just tender. Stir in the reserved chicken-broth mixture; reduce the heat to medium-low and simmer for 1 minute. Add the chicken and cook for 30 seconds longer.

6 Drain the orzo and divide it among 4 plates. Top with the chicken and vegetables, and garnish with sliced scallion greens, if desired.

Preparation time 25 minutes • **Total time** 35 minutes • **Per serving** 384 calories, 6.8 g. fat (16% of calories), 1 g. saturated fat, 49 mg. cholesterol, 454 mg. sodium, 6.5 g. dietary fiber, 86 mg. calcium, 4 mg. iron, 72 mg. vitamin C, 12.4 mg. beta-carotene • **Serves 4**

LONE STAR TURKEY TAMALE PIE

8 ounces skinless, boneless turkey cutlets, cut into chunks

1 teaspoon dried oregano

½ teaspoon fennel seeds

¼ teaspoon freshly ground black pepper

2 teaspoons olive oil

1 medium onion, chopped

3 garlic cloves, minced

2 medium zucchini, diced

2 tablespoons chili powder

1 teaspoon ground cumin

½ teaspoon ground coriander

¼ cup defatted reduced-sodium chicken broth

1 can (16 ounces) whole tomatoes in purée, coarsely chopped, with purée reserved

1 can (15 ounces) pinto beans, rinsed and drained

1 package (10 ounces) frozen corn kernels

1 can (4 ounces) chopped mild green chilies, rinsed and drained

3 cups water

¼ teaspoon salt

1 cup yellow cornmeal

2 ounces reduced-fat Cheddar cheese, shredded

Authentic Mexican tamales are not easy to prepare. They're made by enclosing a filling (such as chili-spiced chopped meat) in cornmeal dough and then in a cornhusk, securing the packets with a strip of cornhusk and then steaming the tamales. If you don't have this traditional technique down pat, try tamale pie, a favorite Southwestern casserole that captures the flavors without the work. You can see how much simpler it is to prepare the filling in a skillet, top it with a Cheddar-flavored cornmeal mixture and bake it in the oven.

1 Preheat the oven to 425°.

2 Process the turkey in a food processor until finely ground. Add the oregano, fennel seeds and black pepper, and pulse briefly.

3 In a large ovenproof skillet, warm the oil over medium-high heat. Add the onions and garlic, and sauté for 3 minutes, or until the onions are golden. Add the zucchini and sauté for 2 minutes. Stir in the turkey mixture, the chili powder, cumin and coriander, and cook, stirring constantly, for 1 minute. Add the broth and cook, stirring to break up any clumps of turkey, for 2 to 3 minutes, or until the turkey turns white.

4 Stir in the tomatoes and their purée, the beans, corn and chilies, and bring to a boil. Reduce the heat to medium-low and simmer for 5 minutes to blend the flavors; remove the pan from the heat.

5 Meanwhile, in a large saucepan, bring the water and salt to a boil over high heat. Gradually whisk in the cornmeal. Reduce the heat to low and cook, whisking frequently, for 5 minutes. Add the Cheddar and stir until melted.

6 Spoon the cornmeal mixture over the turkey mixture in the skillet. Bake for 15 minutes, or until the turkey mixture is bubbly and the cornmeal topping is lightly browned.

Preparation time 30 minutes • **Total time** 50 minutes • **Per serving** 453 calories, 7.7 g. fat (14% of calories), 2.4 g. saturated fat, 45 mg. cholesterol, 762 mg. sodium, 9 g. dietary fiber, 247 mg. calcium, 5 mg. iron, 37 mg. vitamin C, 1.8 mg. beta-carotene • **Serves 4**

❧ ❧ ❧

TUSCAN PORK WITH WHITE BEANS

1 pound well-trimmed, lean pork tenderloin

¼ teaspoon freshly ground black pepper

⅛ teaspoon salt

1 tablespoon plus 1 teaspoon olive oil

½ cup sliced shallots

¼ teaspoon dried thyme or 1 teaspoon fresh thyme

3 tablespoons balsamic vinegar

2 cans (19 ounces each) cannellini beans, rinsed and drained

1 can (14½ ounces) Italian-style stewed tomatoes with juice

¼ cup defatted reduced-sodium chicken broth

⅛ teaspoon crushed red pepper flakes

2 cups packed fresh spinach leaves or Swiss chard leaves, sliced

Beans have a long history in Tuscany, stretching back to the 16th century when they were first brought from the New World. White beans—cannellini—are eaten fresh when first picked in June; as the year progresses, the beans become increasingly drier, and cooking times must be adjusted accordingly. Canned beans eliminate any such guesswork from this recipe, in which the beans, bathed in a tart tomato sauce, serve as a foil for tasty pork medallions.

1 Cut the pork tenderloin crosswise into 8 pieces. Place each piece of tenderloin between 2 sheets of wax paper and pound to ½ inch thick. Sprinkle both sides of the pork with the black pepper and salt.

2 In a large no-stick skillet, warm 3 teaspoons of the oil over medium-high heat until very hot but not smoking. Add the pork and cook for 3 minutes per side, or until browned and cooked through. With a slotted spoon, transfer the pork to a plate; cover loosely to keep warm.

3 Add the remaining 1 teaspoon oil to the skillet. Add the shallots and thyme, and sauté for 1 minute. Stir in the vinegar and bring to a boil. Stir in the beans, tomatoes, broth and red pepper flakes, and return to a boil. Reduce the heat to medium-low and simmer for 5 minutes, or until slightly thickened. Stir in the spinach or Swiss chard and simmer for 1 minute, or until the spinach or chard is just wilted.

4 Divide the bean mixture among 4 plates. Top each portion with 2 pork medallions.

Preparation time 20 minutes • **Total time** 35 minutes • **Per serving** 428 calories, 10 g. fat (21% of calories), 2.1 g. saturated fat, 74 mg. cholesterol, 897 mg. sodium, 14.4 g. dietary fiber, 117 mg. calcium, 6 mg. iron, 29 mg. vitamin C, 2 mg. beta-carotene • **Serves 4**

Shallots look like miniature onions. When you remove the outer layer of skin, you'll see that they separate into cloves, like a head of garlic.

ON THE MENU
Make it a totally Tuscan meal: For starters, arrange individual salads of thinly sliced fennel and mushrooms, dressed with an olive-oil and balsamic vinaigrette. Serve whole-wheat Italian bread with the main course; and for a dessert that is quintessentially Tuscan, offer biscotti and ripe pears with a dessert wine or espresso.

KITCHEN TIP
Shallots, like garlic cloves, are easier to peel if you first blanch them in boiling water for 1 minute, then rinse them.

Poultry, Fish & Meat

❧ ❧ ❧

SERVE CHICKEN OR CHOPS,

SNAPPER OR SCALLOPS—AND

TAKE A HEALTHIER LOOK AT THE

HEARTIEST OF MEALS

ROSEMARY-ORANGE CHICKEN ON SPINACH

1 large navel orange

2–3 tablespoons orange juice

1 tablespoon olive oil

2 teaspoons balsamic vinegar

½ teaspoon dried rosemary, crumbled

¼ teaspoon light brown sugar

Pinch of crushed red pepper flakes

1 pound thin-sliced chicken cutlets

¼ teaspoon freshly ground black pepper

¼ teaspoon salt

1 pound washed spinach, tough stems removed

The novel interplay of seasonings in this dish will surprise and intrigue anyone who ever thought chicken was boring: There's the freshness of citrus, the mellow tang of balsamic vinegar, the pungency of rosemary and the bite of black and red pepper. If you can't find balsamic vinegar, which is carefully aged to produce its unique flavor, substitute a mild red wine vinegar.

1 Grate ½ teaspoon of zest from the orange; set the zest aside. Using a sharp paring knife, peel the orange, removing all of the white pith. Working over a bowl, cut between the membranes to divide the orange into sections. Squeeze the membranes between your fingers to release all the juice, then discard them. Pour all the juice from the bowl into a measuring cup, then add enough additional orange juice to measure ⅓ cup.

2 Add the orange zest, 1 teaspoon of the oil, the vinegar, ¼ teaspoon of the rosemary, the sugar and red pepper flakes to the orange juice, and whisk until blended; set aside.

3 Sprinkle the chicken with the remaining ¼ teaspoon rosemary, the black pepper and salt. In a large no-stick skillet, warm the remaining 2 teaspoons oil over high heat until hot but not smoking. Working in batches, if necessary, add the chicken and sauté for 2 to 3 minutes per side, or until lightly browned and cooked through. Transfer the chicken to a platter and cover loosely with a sheet of foil.

4 Add the spinach to the skillet and stir-fry over high heat for 1 to 2 minutes, or just until the spinach is wilted.

5 Arrange the spinach around the chicken on the platter and place the orange sections on the chicken.

6 Whisk the dressing briefly to reblend it, then pour the dressing over the chicken and spinach.

Preparation time 25 minutes • **Total time** 35 minutes • **Per serving** 199 calories, 5.1 g. fat (23% of calories), 1 g. saturated fat, 66 mg. cholesterol, 274 mg. sodium, 3.2 g. dietary fiber, 115 mg. calcium, 3 mg. iron, 54 mg. vitamin C, 3.4 mg. beta-carotene • **Serves 4**

❧ ❧ ❧

SWEET-AND-SOUR PORK CHOPS

¼ cup reduced-sodium ketchup

¼ cup frozen pineapple juice concentrate

3 tablespoons water

2 teaspoons cornstarch

2 teaspoons reduced-sodium soy sauce

¼ teaspoon crushed red pepper flakes

¼ teaspoon dry mustard

2 garlic cloves

1 slice (¼-inch-thick) peeled fresh ginger

1 large red bell pepper, cut into chunks

1 medium onion, cut into ¼-inch dice

1 can (8¼ ounces) juice-packed pineapple rings, drained and cut in half

1½ pounds well-trimmed thin-sliced pork chops (4 chops)

1 tablespoon chopped fresh cilantro (optional)

Pork goes particularly well with piquant sauces such as the sweet-and-sour basting mixture used here. Although the flavors are inspired by Chinese cuisine, the ingredients are all readily available in supermarkets. Reduced-sodium soy sauce contains about one-third less sodium than regular soy sauce—it isn't a low-sodium condiment, but is quite an improvement over the original.

1 Preheat the oven to 450°. Spray a roasting pan or the bottom of a broiler pan with no-stick spray.

2 Combine the ketchup, pineapple juice concentrate, water, cornstarch, soy sauce, crushed red pepper and mustard in a food processor. With the machine running, drop the garlic, then the ginger, through the feed tube and process until puréed.

3 Place the bell peppers, onions and pineapple in the prepared pan and toss with about 3 tablespoons of the ketchup mixture; spread into an even layer. Coat both sides of the chops with the remaining ketchup mixture and place the chops on top of the vegetables and pineapple.

4 Bake for 20 to 25 minutes, or until the vegetables are tender and the pork chops are cooked medium. Transfer the chops, vegetables and pineapple to a heated platter and sprinkle with the cilantro, if using.

Preparation time 20 minutes • **Total time** 45 minutes • **Per serving** 281 calories, 6.6 g. fat (21% of calories), 2 g. saturated fat, 77 mg. cholesterol, 294 mg. sodium, 1.5 g. dietary fiber, 62 mg. calcium, 2 mg. iron, 65 mg. vitamin C, 1 mg. beta-carotene • **Serves 4**

ON THE MENU
Serve this generous entrée with rice, cooked while the pork chops are in the oven. Underscore the Asian theme with almond cookies and tea for dessert.

NUTRITION NOTE
Improved methods of breeding and raising pigs have lowered the fat content of pork by more than 30 percent over the past ten years. Pork has always been an excellent source of B vitamins, especially thiamin. Like other types of meat, pork is a good source of iron.

MARKET AND PANTRY
Fresh ginger should be firm, its paper-thin tan skin tight and glossy. Avoid ginger roots that feel soft and flabby, or those with dull, wrinkled skin.

FISH FINGERS WITH SPICY SAUCE

Fish Fingers

- 1 pound lemon sole, scrod or tilefish fillets, about 1 inch thick
- 1 tablespoon fresh lime juice
- ⅛ teaspoon salt
- ⅛ teaspoon freshly ground black pepper
- ⅛ teaspoon ground red pepper (optional)
- ¾ cup unseasoned dry breadcrumbs
- 1 large egg white
- 2 teaspoons olive oil

Spicy Sauce

- ½ cup nonfat sour cream
- ¼ cup medium or mild salsa
- 1 tablespoon chopped fresh cilantro
- 1 teaspoon fresh lime juice
- Lime wedges, for garnish (optional)

Children love fish sticks—in fact, some turn up their noses at just about everything else. Unfortunately, a serving of fish sticks can have as much as 20 grams of fat, and some brands are also very high in sodium. The solution to this dietary dilemma is homemade fish fingers, put together quickly from fresh ingredients. The dipping sauce is a tangy blend of salsa and sour cream.

1 Preheat the oven to 400°. Spray a jelly-roll pan with no-stick spray.

2 To make the fish fingers: Cut the fish into 2-inch-long strips. Drizzle the fish with the lime juice and season with the salt and black pepper and the red pepper, if using.

3 Spread the breadcrumbs on a plate. In a medium bowl, lightly beat the egg white; add the fish and toss to coat. One piece at a time, roll the fish strips in the breadcrumbs to coat completely. Arrange the fish strips in a single layer in the prepared pan and drizzle them evenly with the oil.

4 Bake the fish fingers for 10 to 15 minutes, or until the crumb crust is lightly browned and the fish flakes when tested with a fork.

5 While the fish is cooking, make the sauce: In a small bowl, stir together the sour cream, salsa, cilantro and lime juice. Serve the fish with the sauce, garnished with lime wedges, if desired.

Preparation time 20 minutes • **Total time** 35 minutes • **Per serving** 220 calories, 4.8 g. fat (20% of calories), 1 g. saturated fat, 55 mg. cholesterol, 424 mg. sodium, 1 g. dietary fiber, 98 mg. calcium, 1 mg. iron, 12 mg. vitamin C, 0 mg. beta-carotene
Serves 4

FOR A CHANGE
For a less spicy dish, leave out the ground red pepper and choose a mild salsa.

KITCHEN TIPS
The fish fillets should be fairly thick to produce finger-size pieces. If you're using thin sole fillets, cut them into 2-inch-wide pieces; cut thicker scrod or tilefish fillets into 1-inch-wide pieces.

ON THE MENU
Accompany the fish fingers with carrot, celery and cucumber sticks (you can dip them in the sauce); try sherbet "floats" for a child-pleasing dessert.

COUNTRY CAPTAIN CHICKEN

2 garlic cloves, crushed

1 tablespoon curry powder or more to taste

2 teaspoons olive oil

1 teaspoon water

½ teaspoon dried thyme, crumbled

⅛ teaspoon freshly ground black pepper

2 pounds bone-in skinless chicken breast halves

1 large onion, sliced

1 large green bell pepper, cut into thin strips

2 large celery stalks with leaves, sliced

⅓ cup defatted chicken broth

1 can (14½ ounces) whole tomatoes, drained and coarsely chopped

3 tablespoons raisins

¼ cup chopped fresh cilantro (optional)

The route by which this dish came to America from India is uncertain, but tradition has it that the recipe was brought to Savannah by spice traders; indeed, Country Captain is still very popular in the South. The primary seasoning is curry powder, which may include turmeric, cardamom, coriander, cumin, ginger, mustard, pepper, cloves and fenugreek. Curry powders vary in strength, so let your taste be your guide as to how much you use. As befits a dish of Indian origin, Country Captain is usually served with rice.

1 Preheat the oven to 425°. Spray a 9 x 13-inch baking dish with no-stick spray.

2 In a cup, mix the garlic, 2 teaspoons of the curry powder, the oil, water, thyme and ground black pepper. Rub the mixture over both sides of the chicken breasts and place the chicken, bone side down, in the prepared baking dish. Bake for 15 minutes, or until the chicken is light golden brown.

3 Meanwhile, in a large, heavy saucepan, combine the onions, bell peppers, celery, broth and the remaining 1 teaspoon curry powder; cover and bring to a boil over high heat. Reduce the heat to medium, and simmer for 5 minutes, or until the vegetables are crisp-tender.

4 Uncover the pan, increase the heat to high and stir in the tomatoes and raisins; bring just to a boil. Taste the mixture and add more curry powder, if desired. Spoon the vegetable mixture evenly over the chicken, mixing it with any juices in the baking dish.

5 Cover the dish with a sheet of foil and bake for 10 minutes longer, or until the chicken is cooked through and the juices are bubbly. Divide the vegetables among 4 plates and top each portion with a chicken breast. Sprinkle with the cilantro, if desired.

Preparation time 15 minutes • **Total time** 50 minutes • **Per serving** 297 calories, 5.4 g. fat (16% of calories), 1 g. saturated fat, 101 mg. cholesterol, 388 mg. sodium, 3.4 g. dietary fiber, 88 mg. calcium, 3 mg. iron, 46 mg. vitamin C, 0.5 mg. beta-carotene • **Serves 4**

ROSEMARY-FENNEL LAMB CHOPS

1 teaspoon dried rosemary

1 teaspoon dried thyme

½ teaspoon garlic powder

¼ teaspoon fennel seeds

¼ teaspoon freshly ground black pepper

¼ teaspoon salt

1½ pounds rib lamb chops (4 chops)

Rubbing freshly ground herbs and spices into meat or poultry accomplishes the same purpose as marinating, but does it more quickly and produces a more intense flavor. You have a number of options for grinding the spices: A mortar and pestle is traditional for this job, and small but sturdy marble or porcelain sets are inexpensive. Handheld electric coffee mills (also sold as spice mills) are perfect for grinding spices. It's best, however, not to use the same mill for coffee and spices: Both have pervasive aromas and you may end up with coffee-flavored spices or spice-scented coffee.

1 In a clean coffee or spice mill, or in a mortar and pestle, grind the rosemary, thyme, garlic powder, fennel seeds, pepper and salt to a fine powder. Rub the spice mixture over both sides of the lamb chops and place them on a plate; cover and let stand at room temperature for 15 minutes.

2 Preheat the broiler. Place the chops on a broiler-pan rack and broil 4 to 5 inches from the heat source for 6 to 7 minutes, then turn the chops and cook for 5 to 6 minutes for medium-rare (the cooking time will depend on the thickness of the chops).

A small stone or ceramic mortar and pestle is an old-fashioned but highly efficient device for crushing herbs and spices.

Preparation time 10 minutes • **Total time** 40 minutes • **Per serving** 132 calories, 7.1 g. fat (49% of calories), 2.5 g. saturated fat, 50 mg. cholesterol, 182 mg. sodium, 0 g. dietary fiber, 22 mg. calcium, 2 mg. iron, 0 mg. vitamin C, 0 mg. beta-carotene
Serves 4

ON THE MENU
Complement the full-flavored lamb with a salad of tart-bitter greens such as chicory, arugula or mizuna (Japanese mustard greens). Rice pilaf, orzo (rice-shaped pasta) or couscous provides a fine foil for the meat's richness.

HEAD START
Grind the herbs and spices in advance and store them in a small jar with a tight-fitting lid or in a twist of plastic wrap.

MARKET AND PANTRY
Good-quality fresh lamb is pinkish (not dark red) and firm. Lamb chops will keep for two to four days in the refrigerator.

FOOD FACT
Fennel seeds come from common fennel, close kin to Florence fennel, of which we eat the root and stalks. (Both plants are related to the wildflower Queen Anne's lace.) Common fennel yields flat, greenish-tan seeds with a mild anise flavor.

SNAPPER WITH MUSTARD-DILL TOPPING

- **2 tablespoons plus 1 teaspoon reduced-calorie mayonnaise**

- **1 tablespoon snipped fresh dill**

- **1 tablespoon grated Parmesan cheese**

- **2 teaspoons fresh lemon juice**

- **1½ teaspoons coarse Dijon mustard**

- **¼ teaspoon freshly ground black pepper**

- **1 pound red snapper or striped bass fillets, cut into 4 pieces**

- **Lemon wedges and dill sprigs, for garnish (optional)**

Delectable red snapper is a warm-water fish that is caught in the Atlantic along the southeast coast of the United States and also in the Gulf of Mexico. Its skin is a shimmering pink or red, depending on the size of the fish. Other species of snapper, such as the gray, appear in American markets, but red snapper, even when sold as fillets, usually has its skin left on to identify it. Striped bass, which may be substituted for snapper, is a similarly lean, flavorful fish.

1 Preheat the broiler. Spray a broiler-pan rack with no-stick spray.

2 In a small bowl, mix the mayonnaise, snipped dill, Parmesan, lemon juice, mustard and pepper.

3 Place the fish fillets on the prepared broiler-pan rack and spread the mayonnaise mixture evenly over them.

4 Broil 4 to 6 inches from the heat for 6 to 8 minutes, or until the topping is well browned in spots and the fish just flakes when tested with a knife.

5 Serve the fish garnished with lemon wedges and dill sprigs, if desired.

Preparation time 5 minutes • **Total time** 15 minutes • **Per serving** 148 calories, 4.6 g. fat (28% of calories), 1.1 g. saturated fat, 46 mg. cholesterol, 200 mg. sodium, 0 g. dietary fiber, 58 mg. calcium, 0 mg. iron, 1 mg. vitamin C, 0.1 mg. beta-carotene
Serves 4

The "Canadian rule" can help you gauge cooking time for fish (see right).

Ⓞ Ⓞ Ⓞ

KITCHEN TIPS

Fish cooks very quickly and can overcook in a matter of minutes. When following a recipe, test the fish a little before the suggested cooking time has elapsed. If you're not using a recipe, the so-called Canadian rule (developed by the Canadian Department of Fisheries) can serve as a rough guide for baking or broiling: Measure the fish at its thickest point, then allow 10 minutes of cooking time for each inch of thickness. Even with this general guideline, it's important to test the fish for doneness. Using a sharp knife, make a small cut in the thickest part of the fish: The flesh should separate along its natural grain, but should still look very moist and just slightly translucent, as it will continue to cook from retained heat after you remove it from the oven. The description of fish "flaking" when tested does not mean that it should fall apart into flakes when you cut into it. If cooked to this point, the fish will be overdone and dry.

MOZZARELLA MEATBALLS

12 ounces lean, trimmed beef top round

1 large egg white

2 tablespoons unseasoned dry breadcrumbs

1 tablespoon grated Parmesan cheese

1 tablespoon chopped fresh Italian parsley

1 garlic clove, crushed

1½ teaspoons dried Italian herb seasoning

¼ teaspoon freshly ground black pepper

⅛ teaspoon salt

2 cans (8 ounces each) no-salt-added tomato sauce

1 medium zucchini, thinly sliced crosswise

2½ ounces part-skim mozzarella cheese, shredded

This knife-and-fork version of an Italian meatball hero demands delicious, crusty bread on the side; you could also serve the meatballs and vegetables atop a thick, toasted slice of Italian or French bread. One way to form the beef mixture into equal-size meatballs is to shape it into an 8-inch log, then cut it crosswise into 16 equal slices and roll them, with moistened hands, into balls.

1 Preheat the broiler. Spray a broiler-pan rack with no-stick spray.

2 Cut the beef into cubes and process it in a food processor until finely chopped. Add the egg white, breadcrumbs, Parmesan, parsley, garlic, 1 teaspoon of the Italian seasoning, the pepper and salt to the processor; process briefly to mix.

3 Shape the mixture into 16 meatballs, using a scant tablespoon for each. Arrange the meatballs on the prepared broiler-pan rack and broil 5 to 6 inches from the heat for 5 to 6 minutes, or until the meatballs are no longer pink in the center. Remove from the broiler.

4 Combine the tomato sauce, zucchini and remaining ½ teaspoon Italian seasoning in a deep medium skillet; bring to a boil over high heat, stirring frequently. Add the meatballs and return to a boil. Reduce the heat to medium-low, cover and simmer for 5 minutes to blend the flavors.

5 Sprinkle the meatballs with the mozzarella; cover and simmer for 1 to 2 minutes longer, or until the cheese is melted.

Preparation time 25 minutes • **Total time** 45 minutes • **Per serving** 229 calories, 7 g. fat (28% of calories), 3.1 g. saturated fat, 60 mg. cholesterol, 300 mg. sodium, 2.1 g. dietary fiber, 156 mg. calcium, 3 mg. iron, 23 mg. vitamin C, 1 mg. beta-carotene • **Serves 4**

Shape the meatballs lightly with your fingers; if the mixture is compacted too firmly, the meatballs will be tough.

KITCHEN TIP

The slicing slot on a grater—if it is sharp—can be used to slice the zucchini. Otherwise, try a food processor, or slice the zucchini with a good, heavy chef's knife—an indispensable kitchen tool.

MARKET AND PANTRY

Italian herb seasoning is an herb-and-spice blend that helps you achieve just the right flavor balance. It usually consists of oregano, basil, marjoram, thyme, summer savory, rosemary and sage.

BAKED CHICKEN OREGANATA

1 pound boneless, skinless chicken thighs, well trimmed

1 tablespoon lemon juice

2 garlic cloves, crushed

1 teaspoon dried oregano, crumbled

½ teaspoon freshly ground black pepper

¼ teaspoon dried mint, crumbled

⅛ teaspoon salt

¼ cup unseasoned dry breadcrumbs

2 tablespoons grated Parmesan cheese

2 large tomatoes (about 1 pound), each cut into 10 wedges

1 teaspoon olive oil

A thick, crunchy coat of Parmesan- and herb-flavored bread-crumbs keeps these skinless chicken thighs juicy, as do the tomatoes baked alongside. The dark meat of poultry is higher in fat than the white meat, but you can reduce the overall fat content of a dish made with chicken thighs by removing the skin and trimming all visible fat before cooking.

1 Preheat the oven to 450°. Coat a 9 x 13-inch baking dish with no-stick spray.

2 Place the chicken in a medium bowl with the lemon juice and garlic, and toss to combine.

3 In a cup, stir together the oregano, pepper, mint and salt. Place the breadcrumbs in a small bowl and stir in the Parmesan and half of the oregano mixture.

4 Scatter the breadcrumbs over the chicken; toss to coat the chicken with the crumbs. Place the chicken in the prepared baking dish and arrange the tomatoes around the chicken. Drizzle the oil over the chicken and sprinkle the remaining herb mixture over the tomatoes.

5 Bake for 25 to 30 minutes, or until chicken is cooked through and the tomatoes are soft and juicy. Serve the chicken and tomatoes topped with the pan juices.

Preparation time 15 minutes • **Total time** 45 minutes • **Per serving** 214 calories, 7.3 g. fat (31% of calories), 1.9 g. saturated fat, 96 mg. cholesterol, 282 mg. sodium, 1.8 g. dietary fiber, 77 mg. calcium, 2 mg. iron, 27 mg. vitamin C, 0.4 mg. beta-carotene • **Serves 4**

❧ ❧ ❧

ON THE MENU
Serve the chicken with spinach fettuccine or a rice pilaf, along with a salad of cucumbers and scallions.

KITCHEN TIPS
It's easy to make your own dry bread-crumbs. Lay bread slices on a baking sheet and bake at 300° until dry and very lightly browned. After the bread cools, tear it into pieces and process into crumbs in a food processor or blender: One slice of bread yields about ⅓ cup of crumbs. The dry crumbs, tightly sealed in a plastic bag, can be refrigerated for a week or frozen for about six months.

STEAK WITH MANY PEPPERS

12 ounces well-trimmed boneless sirloin steak

2 garlic cloves, minced

¾ teaspoon coarsely ground black pepper

¼ teaspoon salt

1 tablespoon balsamic vinegar

1 teaspoon extra-virgin olive oil

1 small red bell pepper, thinly sliced

1 small green bell pepper, thinly sliced

1 small yellow bell pepper, thinly sliced

1 medium onion, halved and cut into thin wedges

1 large ripe tomato, cut into thin wedges

1 tablespoon defatted chicken broth or water

1 tablespoon chopped fresh oregano or 2 tablespoons chopped fresh Italian parsley

You needn't give a moment's thought to garnishing this dish—the vivid colors of the bell peppers and tomatoes make it quite irresistible without any extra fuss or flourishes. To balance this entrée—in which most of the calories come from the meat—serve it with bread, rice or potatoes; the addition of carbohydrates will drop the percentage of calories from fat in the meal well below its current 32 percent.

1 Preheat the broiler. Spray a broiler pan rack with no-stick spray.

2 Rub both sides of the steak with the garlic, pepper and ⅛ teaspoon of the salt; place the steak on the prepared rack and drizzle it with 1 teaspoon of the vinegar. Broil 5 to 6 inches from the heat for about 5 minutes, then turn the steak and drizzle the second side with another teaspoon of vinegar. Broil for 4 to 5 minutes longer for medium-rare. Transfer the steak to a warmed platter, cover loosely with foil and let stand for 5 minutes.

3 While the steak is cooking, in a deep, medium no-stick skillet, warm the oil over high heat until hot. Add the bell peppers and onions, and toss to coat them with oil; cook, stirring, for 1 minute. Reduce the heat to medium-high, add the tomatoes and broth or water, and toss to combine. Cover and cook, stirring frequently, for 8 to 10 minutes, or until the vegetables are tender.

4 Uncover the skillet and add the remaining 1 teaspoon vinegar, ⅛ teaspoon salt and any juices that have collected on the steak platter; simmer for 1 minute. Remove from the heat and stir in the oregano or parsley.

5 Carve the steak into thin slices and arrange on the platter. Spoon the vegetables and pan juices around the steak.

Preparation time 10 minutes • **Total time** 35 minutes • **Per serving** 177 calories, 6.3 g. fat (32% of calories), 2 g. saturated fat, 57 mg. cholesterol, 199 mg. sodium, 1.9 g. dietary fiber, 31 mg. calcium, 3 mg. iron, 63 mg. vitamin C, 0.8 mg. beta-carotene • **Serves 4**

CHICKEN LEGS WITH CHILI BEANS

1¼ **pounds skinned chicken legs, drumsticks and thighs cut apart**

3 **garlic cloves, crushed**

2 **tablespoons chili powder**

1 **teaspoon olive oil**

1 **medium onion, chopped**

1 **medium green bell pepper, diced**

2 **tablespoons defatted chicken broth**

2 **teaspoons diced seeded, pickled jalapeño peppers**

1 **can (16 ounces) red kidney beans, rinsed and drained**

1 **can (14½ ounces) no-salt-added stewed tomatoes**

This hearty supper gets its tongue-tingling kick from chili powder and pickled jalapeños. Chili powder is a blend of ground dried chilies with other seasonings, which may include garlic, cumin, coriander, cloves, oregano, thyme and salt. Chili powder is sold in different "heats" and comes in salt-free versions, too. Not just for chili, the spice blend can also be added to soups and salad dressings.

1 Preheat the oven to 425°. Coat a jelly-roll pan with no-stick spray.

2 Place the chicken pieces in the pan and rub them with the garlic and 1 tablespoon of the chili powder. Drizzle with the oil. Bake for 20 to 25 minutes, or until the chicken is no longer pink near the bone.

3 Meanwhile, in a large no-stick skillet, combine the onions, bell peppers and broth, and sauté for 4 to 6 minutes, or until the vegetables are tender. Stir in the jalapeños and the remaining 1 tablespoon chili powder, and cook, stirring constantly, for 30 seconds.

4 Add the beans and stewed tomatoes, and bring to a simmer. Reduce the heat to low, cover and simmer, stirring occasionally, for 10 minutes. Serve the chili beans with the chicken.

Preparation time 15 minutes • **Total time** 45 minutes • **Per serving** 272 calories, 6.6 g. fat (22% of calories), 1.2 g. saturated fat, 77 mg. cholesterol, 333 mg. sodium, 9.1 g. dietary fiber, 95 mg. calcium, 4 mg. iron, 40 mg. vitamin C, 1.2 mg. beta-carotene • **Serves 4**

🌿 🌿 🌿

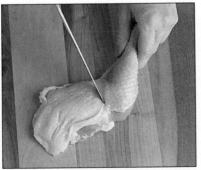

To cut apart the chicken thigh and leg, first cut through the joint from the top.

Then turn the thigh over, skin side down, and cut through the joint.

BEEF AND CORN SKILLET

½ **cup raw converted white rice**

1 **cup water**

8 **ounces lean, well-trimmed beef top round**

1 **tablespoon chili powder**

2 **teaspoons olive oil**

⅛ **teaspoon salt**

1 **large onion, thinly sliced**

1 **medium green bell pepper, thinly sliced**

1½ **cups crushed canned tomatoes**

1 **cup frozen corn kernels**

Two favorite ethnic cuisines come together in this stir-fry with a Tex-Mex twist. Although stir-frying is an Asian technique, this quick cooking method can be adapted to many other dishes. You can flavor stir-fried vegetables with Indian curry spices, toss stir-fried chicken strips with pasta and Italian seasoning or try this chili-sauced medley of beef, corn and bell peppers served over rice.

1 In a heavy, medium saucepan, combine the rice and water; bring to a boil over high heat. Reduce the heat to low, cover and simmer for 20 minutes, or until the rice is tender and the liquid has been absorbed.

2 While the rice is cooking, cut the beef into very thin strips and sprinkle with the chili powder; toss to coat.

3 In a large no-stick skillet, warm the oil over high heat until very hot. Add the beef and stir-fry for 2 to 3 minutes, or until the beef is no longer pink. Sprinkle the beef with the salt.

4 Add the onions and bell peppers; toss well to mix with the beef and the pan juices. Reduce the heat to medium-high and stir-fry for 4 to 5 minutes, or until the vegetables are tender and the beef is cooked through.

5 Stir in the tomatoes and corn; bring the mixture to a boil. Reduce the heat to medium and simmer for 3 to 4 minutes, or until the corn is hot. Serve the beef mixture over the hot rice.

Preparation time 10 minutes • **Total time** 40 minutes • **Per serving** 269 calories, 5.3 g. fat (18% of calories), 1.1 g. saturated fat, 32 mg. cholesterol, 269 mg. sodium, 4 g. dietary fiber, 54 mg. calcium, 3 mg. iron, 55 mg. vitamin C, 0.9 mg. beta-carotene
Serves 4

ON THE MENU
Tall, cold drinks are called for here, and cornsticks—cornbread shaped like little ears of corn—would be a fitting bread. For dessert, try an unusual combination: vanilla frozen yogurt topped with just a pinch of freshly ground black pepper.

FOOD FACT
Although beef is the source of much of the fat in the American diet, lean cuts still have a place in low-fat meals. Choose cuts from the round, or rump, such as eye of round, top round, bottom round roast, boneless rump roast and round steak.

TURKEY AND ZUCCHINI PARMIGIANA

1 large Spanish onion, cut into ¼-inch-thick slices

1 tablespoon olive oil

2 garlic cloves, crushed

1 tablespoon water

½ teaspoon dried basil

½ teaspoon dried oregano

¼ teaspoon freshly ground black pepper

¼ teaspoon crushed red pepper flakes

⅛ teaspoon salt

4 thin turkey breast cutlets (12 ounces)

2 medium zucchini, cut into ¼-inch-thick lengthwise slices

1 tablespoon unseasoned dry bread crumbs

1 can (14½ ounces) no-salt-added stewed tomatoes with juice

3 ounces part-skim mozzarella cheese, shredded

1 tablespoon grated Parmesan cheese

B roiling really brings out the flavor of vegetables, especially when they're cooked until lightly charred. The smoky savor of broiled onions and zucchini lends richness to this layering of turkey, vegetables and luscious melted cheese. Serve it with a side dish of your favorite pasta, or with thick slices of Italian peasant bread.

1 Preheat the broiler. Spray a jelly-roll pan with no-stick spray.

2 Arrange the onion slices in a single layer in the prepared pan and drizzle 1 teaspoon of the oil over them. Broil 5 to 6 inches from the heat, turning once, for 10 minutes, or until the onions are tender and lightly charred.

3 Meanwhile, in a cup, mix the remaining 2 teaspoons oil, the garlic, water, basil, oregano, black pepper, red pepper flakes and salt. Brush both sides of the turkey cutlets and zucchini slices with the oil mixture.

4 Using a metal spatula, push the onions toward the center of the pan, arranging them in four stacks. Place the turkey cutlets on top of the onions and arrange the zucchini slices around the edges. Broil for 7 to 9 minutes, or until the turkey is cooked through and the zucchini slices are tender.

5 Preheat the oven to 450°.

6 Sprinkle the bread crumbs in the bottom of a 9 x 9-inch baking dish. Transfer the turkey and onions to the baking dish, then place the zucchini on top.

7 Spoon the tomatoes and their juice over the turkey and vegetables. Sprinkle with the mozzarella and Parmesan, and bake for 10 minutes, or until the sauce is bubbly and the cheeses are melted.

Preparation time 15 minutes • **Total time** 55 minutes • **Per serving** 259 calories, 8.4 g. fat (29% of calories), 3.1 g. saturated fat, 66 mg. cholesterol, 280 mg. sodium, 3.8 g. dietary fiber, 244 mg. calcium, 3 mg. iron, 28 mg. vitamin C, 0.6 mg. beta-carotene • **Serves 4**

SCALLOP SAUTÉ WITH VEGETABLES

¾ **cup raw converted white rice**

1½ **cups water**

1 **pound sea scallops**

1 **tablespoon olive oil**

1 **medium zucchini, halved lengthwise and then cut crosswise into ¼-inch-thick slices**

½ **teaspoon dried basil, crumbled**

⅛ **teaspoon salt**

⅛ **teaspoon freshly ground black pepper**

⅛ **teaspoon crushed red pepper flakes (optional)**

½ **cup diced, drained roasted red peppers (from a jar)**

2 **tablespoons chopped fresh Italian parsley**

Scallops, unlike oysters and clams, really have no season: These succulent morsels, enclosed within fanlike shells, are harvested throughout the year on both the East and West coasts. Sweet, tender scallops are almost always sold shucked; the only preparation they sometimes require is the removal of a small piece of tough connective tissue that may remain after shucking.

1 In a heavy, medium saucepan, combine the rice and water; bring to a boil over high heat. Reduce the heat to low, cover and simmer for 20 minutes, or until the rice is tender and the liquid has been absorbed.

2 Meanwhile, rinse and pat dry the scallops. If any of the scallops are very large, cut them in half crosswise.

3 In a large no-stick skillet, warm the oil over high heat. Add the scallops, zucchini, basil, salt, black pepper and red pepper flakes, if using; sauté the scallops and zucchini for 4 to 5 minutes, or until the scallops are opaque at their thickest part and the zucchini slices are tender. Add the roasted red peppers and sauté for 30 seconds longer, or until the peppers are heated through.

4 Remove the skillet from the heat and stir in the parsley. Spoon the scallop mixture over the hot rice.

Preparation time 10 minutes • **Total time** 30 minutes • **Per serving** 271 calories, 4.6 g. fat (15% of calories), 0.6 g. saturated fat, 38 mg. cholesterol, 260 mg. sodium, 0.7 g. dietary fiber, 54 mg. calcium, 3 mg. iron, 27 mg. vitamin C, 0.6 mg. beta-carotene • **Serves 4**

If some of the scallops you buy have a rubbery piece of connective tissue on one side, just pull it off with your fingers.

FOR A CHANGE
Use yellow summer squash or pattypan squash instead of zucchini. Subtly flavor the rice with garlic by adding a peeled garlic clove to the cooking water. Remove the garlic before serving.

ON THE MENU
This meal is low enough in calories and fat to be a good choice when you want

to splurge on dessert at a family birthday party or other special occasion. Such an extra-light main dish lets you enjoy a slice of cake with a clear conscience.

FOOD FACT
Red pepper flakes are crushed, dried hot chilies; the seeds are included, making this is a very powerful spice—a pinch or two will usually suffice.

BASIL CHICKEN WITH POTATOES

1½ cups firmly packed basil leaves

¼ cup defatted chicken broth

2 garlic cloves, peeled

2 teaspoons extra-virgin olive oil

½ teaspoon dried thyme

½ teaspoon freshly ground black pepper

½ teaspoon salt

2 pounds skinless bone-in chicken breast halves (4)

1 pound small red potatoes, cut into wedges

6 ripe plum tomatoes, cut into wedges

8 pitted ripe olives, halved

Potatoes cooked in the same pan with a chicken or roast come out crisp, savory—and high in fat, having soaked up the greasy drippings from the meat. But when you're cooking skinless chicken breasts, that's not a problem. Here, the chicken, potatoes and tomatoes are kept moist with a basil-garlic baste that's made with just two teaspoons of oil. To speed preparation of this meal, the potatoes are parboiled for five minutes before they go into the oven.

1 Spray a 9 x 13-inch baking pan with no-stick spray.

2 In a food processor, combine the basil, broth, garlic, oil, thyme, pepper and salt, and process until puréed. Place the chicken in the baking pan and rub both sides of the breasts with ¼ cup of the basil mixture; set aside.

3 Preheat the oven to 425°.

4 Place the potatoes in a medium saucepan and cover with cold water. Cover the pan and bring to a boil over high heat, then reduce the heat to medium and simmer for 5 minutes. Drain the potatoes.

5 Arrange the potato and tomato wedges around the chicken breasts and spoon the remaining basil mixture over the vegetables. Sprinkle the olives over the chicken and vegetables.

6 Bake for 25 minutes, or until the chicken is cooked through and the potatoes are tender.

Preparation time 20 minutes • **Total time** 45 minutes • **Per serving** 355 calories, 6.4 g. fat (16% of calories), 1 g. saturated fat, 101 mg. cholesterol, 533 mg. sodium, 3 g. dietary fiber, 229 mg. calcium, 7 mg. iron, 37 mg. vitamin C, 0.8 mg. beta-carotene • **Serves 4**

MARKET AND PANTRY
Plum tomatoes, which are more solid and "meaty" than round tomatoes, are excellent for cooking; they hold their shape well and don't release much liquid.

ON THE MENU
Start with a salad of Bibb or Boston lettuce; use a little dark sesame oil in the vinaigrette and sprinkle the greens with toasted sesame seeds.

TURKEY TONKATSU WITH VEGETABLES

- 1 teaspoon vegetable oil
- 1 large egg white
- 3 tablespoons water
- ½ cup unseasoned dry bread crumbs
- 1 tablespoon plus ½ teaspoon grated fresh ginger
- 1 tablespoon reduced-sodium soy sauce
- 1 pound thin-sliced turkey breast cutlets (4)
- 3 cups cauliflower florets
- 2 cups thinly sliced carrots
- 3 tablespoons rice vinegar
- 1 tablespoon honey
- ¼ teaspoon salt
- ¼ teaspoon crushed red pepper flakes
- ¼ teaspoon freshly ground black pepper
- 2 scallions, thinly sliced on the diagonal
- 2 teaspoons dark sesame oil

Tonkatsu means "pork cutlet," but this turkey variation is lighter than the original. The crumbed cutlets are usually fried in oil; baking them in the oven cuts lots of fat from the dish. The pickled vegetables are *sunomono*—Japanese for "vinegared things."

1 Brush a jelly-roll pan with the vegetable oil.

2 In a shallow bowl, using a fork, beat the egg white and 1 tablespoon of the water until frothy. Place the bread crumbs on a plate.

3 On another plate, mix 1½ teaspoons of the ginger with the soy sauce. Dip both sides of each turkey cutlet into the soy-sauce mixture. Dip the cutlets into the egg white, let the excess drip off, then dredge in the bread crumbs, pressing the crumbs into the surface. Arrange the turkey in a single layer in the prepared pan. Cover with a sheet of wax paper and set aside.

4 Preheat the oven to 425°.

5 In a medium saucepan, bring 1 inch of water to a boil over high heat. Add the cauliflower and carrots, and return to a boil. Cook for 4 to 6 minutes, or until the vegetables are crisp-tender. Drain in a colander and transfer to a serving bowl.

6 In the same saucepan, combine the remaining 2 teaspoons ginger, the vinegar, honey, salt, red pepper flakes, black pepper and remaining 2 tablespoons water, and bring to a boil over high heat, stirring.

7 Add half the scallions to the bowl of vegetables, then pour on the hot dressing and toss to mix; place the bowl in the freezer to chill.

8 Drizzle the sesame oil over the turkey and bake for 5 minutes. Turn and bake for 5 minutes longer, or until browned, crisp and cooked through. Cut the turkey diagonally into strips. Garnish the pickled vegetables with the remaining scallions and serve with the turkey.

Preparation time 15 minutes • **Total time** 30 minutes • **Per serving** 280 calories, 5.1 g. fat (16% of calories), 0.9 g. saturated fat, 70 mg. cholesterol, 505 mg. sodium, 4.3 g. dietary fiber, 88 mg. calcium, 3 mg. iron, 60 mg. vitamin C, 0.9 mg. beta-carotene • **Serves 4**

CRISPY CHICKEN WITH NECTARINE SALSA

1 large egg white

2 tablespoons plus 1 teaspoon fresh lime juice

½ cup unseasoned dry bread crumbs

1½ teaspoons chili powder

1¼ teaspoons ground cumin

¼ teaspoon salt

1 pound skinless, boneless chicken breast halves (4)

12 ounces ripe nectarines, diced

½ cup finely diced red bell peppers

2 tablespoons chopped fresh cilantro

1 tablespoon minced red onion

1 tablespoon honey

½ teaspoon minced, seeded pickled jalapeño pepper

⅛ teaspoon freshly ground black pepper

2 teaspoons olive oil

Peruse the menus of the country's trendiest restaurants and you'll find salsas made with pineapples, mangoes, cranberries, bananas, and just about any other fruit you can think of. This sweet-hot nectarine-and-jalapeño salsa is the ideal companion for crisp-crusted chicken breasts.

1 Spray a jelly-roll pan with no-stick spray.

2 In a shallow bowl or pie plate, using a fork, lightly beat the egg white with 1 tablespoon of the lime juice until frothy. In another shallow bowl, mix the bread crumbs, chili powder, 1 teaspoon of the cumin and the salt. One at a time, dip the chicken breasts into the egg white, letting the excess drip off, then roll the chicken in the crumbs, pressing them into the surface. Place the chicken breasts, skinned-side up, on the prepared pan. Set the chicken aside, uncovered.

3 Preheat the oven to 450°.

4 In a medium bowl, combine the nectarines, bell peppers, cilantro, onions, honey, jalapeño, black pepper, the remaining 1 tablespoon plus 1 teaspoon lime juice and remaining ¼ teaspoon cumin. Cover and set aside.

5 Drizzle the chicken evenly with the oil and bake for 10 minutes. Turn the chicken and bake for 5 minutes longer, or until crisp, lightly browned, and cooked through.

6 Serve the chicken with the nectarine salsa.

Preparation time 20 minutes • **Total time** 35 minutes • **Per serving** 257 calories, 5.1 g. fat (18% of calories), 0.8 g. saturated fat, 66 mg. cholesterol, 283 mg. sodium, 2.3 g. dietary fiber, 51 mg. calcium, 2 mg. iron, 32 mg. vitamin C, 1 mg. beta-carotene
Serves 4

SUBSTITUTION
Use peaches if nectarines are not available. Or substitute unsweetened frozen peach slices when the fresh fruits are out of season.

FOOD FACT
Nectarines and peaches are closely related, and the two fruits have been cross-bred to produce sweetier, tastier peaches and bigger nectarines.

CHICKEN-VEGETABLE PACKETS

1 can (8 ounces) no-salt-added tomato sauce

2 tablespoons grated Parmesan cheese

1 tablespoon balsamic vinegar

½ teaspoon freshly ground black pepper

½ teaspoon dried basil

⅛ teaspoon salt

8 slices (¼ inch thick) Spanish onion

8 rings (¼ inch thick) green bell pepper

12 ounces thin-sliced chicken breast cutlets, divided into 4 equal portions

8 slices (¼ inch thick) peeled eggplant

8 slices (¼ inch thick) ripe tomato

8 diagonal slices (½ ounce each) crusty French or Italian bread

1½ teaspoons extra-virgin olive oil

1 garlic clove, peeled and halved

3 ounces shredded part-skim mozzarella cheese

It is usually rather delicate foods—herbed fish fillets for instance—that are cooked in packets because this method treats food gently, steaming it with no basting or turning required. Here, more robust ingredients go in the foil packets, where the flavors blend to perfection. Garlic toasts are served on the side.

1 Preheat the oven to 450°. Tear off four 12-inch pieces of heavy-duty aluminum foil.

2 In a medium bowl, mix the tomato sauce, Parmesan, vinegar, black pepper, basil and salt.

3 Dividing the ingredients evenly, in the center of each piece of foil make a bed of onions and bell peppers. Place a portion of chicken on the vegetables, then top with a heaping tablespoon of the tomato sauce, some eggplant and tomatoes. Spoon the remaining sauce on top. Fold the foil up and over the chicken and vegetables, and seal it well.

4 Place the packets in a jelly-roll pan and bake for 30 to 35 minutes, or until the vegetables are tender and the chicken is cooked through (check by opening one of the packets).

5 After the packets have baked for 20 minutes, place the bread on a baking sheet and bake for about 5 minutes, or until toasted. Remove the baking sheet from the oven, drizzle each piece of toast with some of the oil and rub with the cut sides of the garlic clove.

6 Place each packet on a plate, open it up and sprinkle with some of the mozzarella. Loosely reclose the foil and let stand for 1 to 2 minutes to melt the cheese.

7 Open up the packets; transfer the vegetables and chicken to plates. Pour the juices around the vegetables and chicken, and place two garlic toasts on each plate.

Preparation time 15 minutes • **Total time** 50 minutes • **Per serving** 302 calories, 8.2 g. fat (24% of calories), 3.3 g. saturated fat, 64 mg. cholesterol, 462 mg. sodium, 3 g. dietary fiber, 230 mg. calcium, 2 mg. iron, 28 mg. vitamin C, 0.6 mg. beta-carotene • **Serves 4**

LEMON-ROSEMARY CHICKEN BREASTS

2 large lemons

2 tablespoons packed light brown sugar

1½ teaspoons coarsely chopped fresh rosemary leaves or ½ teaspoon dried

¼ teaspoon salt

¼ teaspoon freshly ground black pepper

2 pounds skinless bone-in chicken breast halves (4)

1 teaspoon cornstarch dissolved in 1 tablespoon cold water

Fresh rosemary sprigs for garnish (optional)

Here's a quick dinner that you can put together even when there's no time to shop. You can keep all the ingredients on hand, including the rosemary, which will last in the refrigerator for up to ten days. Of course, you can use dried rosemary instead of fresh. If you're substituting the dried herb, crumble it between your fingers to release its fragrance.

1 Preheat the oven to 400°. Spray a 9 x 13-inch baking pan with no-stick spray.

2 Grate 2 teaspoons of zest from one lemon, then halve the lemon and squeeze 3 tablespoons of juice from it into a shallow medium bowl. Cut the other lemon into thin slices, discarding the ends.

3 Add the lemon zest, sugar, rosemary, salt and pepper to the bowl of lemon juice and whisk to blend. One at time, dip the chicken breasts into the lemon mixture, turning to coat both sides.

4 Arrange the chicken breasts, skinned side up, in the prepared pan and place some of the lemon slices on top of each. (If any of the lemon mixture remains in the bowl, spoon it over the chicken.) Bake, basting twice with the pan juices, for 25 to 30 minutes, or until the chicken is cooked through.

5 Transfer the chicken to plates. Pour the pan juices into a small saucepan, stir in the cornstarch mixture and bring to a boil over medium heat, stirring constantly until thickened. Spoon the pan juices over the chicken. Garnish with rosemary sprigs, if desired.

Preparation time 5 minutes • **Total time** 35 minutes • **Per serving** 232 calories, 2.5 g. fat (10% of calories), 1 g. saturated fat, 101 mg. cholesterol, 253 mg. sodium, 0 g. dietary fiber, 47 mg. calcium, 2 mg. iron, 30 mg. vitamin C, 0 mg. beta-carotene
Serves 4

KITCHEN TIPS
Wrap fresh rosemary in a small plastic bag and store it in the crisper drawer of the refrigerator.

ON THE MENU
Steamed green beans or yellow wax beans (or a mix of the two) and crisp rolls make this meal complete.

BAKED CHICKEN BARBECUE

1 **medium red bell pepper, cut into thin strips**

1 **medium green bell pepper, cut into thin strips**

1 **small onion, halved and sliced**

2 **garlic cloves, crushed through a press**

2 **tablespoons defatted chicken broth**

2 **tablespoons water**

2 **cans (8 ounces each) no-salt-added tomato sauce**

¼ **cup raisins**

3 **tablespoons molasses**

1 **tablespoon plus 1 teaspoon cider vinegar**

½–1 **teaspoon hot-pepper sauce**

1 **teaspoon dry mustard**

½ **teaspoon freshly ground black pepper**

¼ **teaspoon salt**

1 **pound 12 ounces skinned bone-in chicken legs, thighs and drumsticks separated (4 whole legs)**

Oven-baked barbecue is a Southern specialty quite distinct from either suburban backyard grilling or large-scale open-pit smoking. In this adaptation of the recipe, chicken legs take the place of the more usual short ribs; the chicken is baked in a tangy tomato sauce made with raisins, molasses and vinegar. Don't worry too much about overcooking the chicken: Most people prefer oven-barbecued meats "falling off the bone" tender.

1 Preheat the oven to 425°. Spray a roasting pan with no-stick spray.

2 In a heavy medium saucepan, combine the bell peppers, onions, garlic, broth and water; bring to a boil over high heat. Reduce the heat to medium; cover and simmer, stirring several times, for 5 minutes, or until the vegetables are crisp-tender.

3 Stir in the tomato sauce, raisins, molasses, vinegar, hot-pepper sauce, mustard, black pepper and salt; increase the heat to medium-high and bring to a boil.

4 Place the chicken pieces in the prepared pan. Spoon the sauce over the chicken and toss to coat the chicken.

5 Bake the chicken, turning the pieces and basting occasionally with the sauce, for 25 to 35 minutes, or until the chicken is cooked through and very tender.

Preparation time 10 minutes • **Total time** 45 minutes • **Per serving** 299 calories, 6.2 g. fat (19% of calories), 1.3 g. saturated fat, 108 mg. cholesterol, 340 mg. sodium, 3.3 g. dietary fiber, 66 mg. calcium, 4 mg. iron, 77 mg. vitamin C, 2 mg. beta-carotene
Serves 4

ON THE MENU
Cornbread and coleslaw are the classic accompaniments for barbecue. You could lighten up the coleslaw with a yogurt dressing, though, and add some shredded broccoli and red bell pepper to the standard cabbage and carrots. Iced tea and lemonade are the perfect drinks.

MAKE AHEAD
Cook the chicken a day ahead, cover with foil and refrigerate. Reheat covered, adding a little water if necessary.

FOR A CHANGE
Use quartered bone-in chicken breasts instead of the thighs.

JERK CHICKEN WITH MANGO

2 fresh jalapeño peppers, halved and partially seeded

½ small onion, halved

2 garlic cloves, peeled

1 slice (¼ inch thick) peeled fresh ginger

1 tablespoon paprika

1 tablespoon defatted chicken broth

2 teaspoons olive oil

2 teaspoons distilled white vinegar

1½ teaspoons dried thyme

1 teaspoon ground allspice

½ teaspoon freshly ground black pepper

¼ teaspoon salt

4 skinless bone-in chicken breast halves (2 pounds)

1 ripe mango, peeled and diced

1 tablespoon chopped fresh mint

Scallions and mint sprigs for garnish (optional)

A South American Indian word for strips of cured meat— *charqui*—may have given rise to the word "jerk," which is used in the Caribbean to describe meat that is rubbed with spices and then grilled, baked or smoked. For a lavish presentation, buy an extra mango to garnish the platter: Halve the unpeeled fruit, score the flesh into cubes and turn each half "inside out."

1 Preheat the oven to 450°. Spray a 9 x 13-inch baking pan with no-stick spray.

2 In a food processor, combine the jalapeños, onions, garlic, ginger, paprika, broth, oil, vinegar, thyme, allspice, black pepper and salt, and process until very finely chopped, stopping the machine a few times to scrape down the sides of the container.

3 Using a rubber spatula, spread the jalapeño mixture on both sides of the chicken breasts. Place them, skinned side up, in the prepared pan.

4 Bake the chicken for 30 to 35 minutes, or until lightly browned and cooked through. Place the chicken on plates and scatter the diced mango on top. Sprinkle the mango with the mint. Garnish with scallions and mint sprigs, if desired.

Preparation time 10 minutes • **Total time** 45 minutes • **Per serving** 268 calories, 5.1 g. fat (17% of calories), 1 g. saturated fat, 101 mg. cholesterol, 268 mg. sodium, 1 g. dietary fiber, 51 mg. calcium, 3 mg. iron, 38 mg. vitamin C, 2 mg. beta-carotene
Serves 4

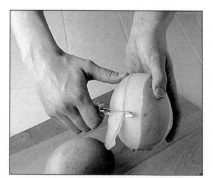

To prepare the mango used in the topping, first pare it with a vegetable peeler.

Slice off most of the flesh in two halves, cutting on either side of the flat pit.

Cut off the flesh that remains around the pit, then dice the mango.

TURKEY YAKITORI WITH VEGETABLES

1 **pound thin-sliced turkey breast cutlets**

3 **tablespoons no-sugar-added apricot spread**

2 **tablespoons low-sodium ketchup**

1 **tablespoon plus 2 teaspoons reduced-sodium soy sauce**

1 **tablespoon grated fresh ginger**

1 **large garlic clove, crushed**

2 **teaspoons dark sesame oil**

½ **teaspoon cider vinegar**

¼ **teaspoon hot-pepper sauce**

2 **medium red bell peppers, cut into 1½-inch squares**

12 **scallions, root ends trimmed, green tops left on**

Thread the strips of turkey ribbonwise onto the wooden skewers.

Whole restaurants in Japan are devoted to *yakitori*—skewered meats cooked over a charcoal fire—which are eaten either as snacks or, served with rice, as a main dish. Here, whole scallions and generous pieces of red pepper are grilled alongside skewered strips of turkey. You'll need eight 12-inch bamboo skewers for this recipe: Soak them in cold water for at least half an hour to prevent them from charring under the broiler.

1 Preheat the broiler. Spray the broiler-pan rack with no-stick spray.

2 Cut the turkey into eight 1-inch-wide strips.

3 In a medium bowl, combine the apricot spread, ketchup, soy sauce, ginger, garlic, oil, vinegar and hot-pepper sauce; stir well. Add the turkey strips and turn them until well coated with the sauce. Thread each strip on a 12-inch bamboo skewer and set aside.

4 Add the bell pepper squares to the sauce and toss until well coated. Arrange the peppers in a single layer on one side of the broiler pan. Place the scallions in the sauce (thin it with 1 teaspoon of water if necessary) and turn them to coat. Place the scallions on the other side of the broiler pan and broil the vegetables 5 to 6 inches from the heat for 5 to 6 minutes, or until the scallions are tender and very lightly charred.

5 Transfer the scallions to a warm platter and cover loosely with a sheet of foil to keep warm. Turn the peppers, spread them out a bit on the pan and broil for 5 to 6 minutes longer, or until tender and somewhat charred. Transfer the pepper squares to the platter.

6 Place the skewers of turkey on the broiler pan. Cover the exposed ends of the skewers with a strip of foil so they do not burn. Broil the turkey without turning for 4 to 5 minutes, or until cooked through. Serve the turkey with the bell peppers and scallions.

Preparation time 15 minutes • **Total time** 45 minutes • **Per serving** 213 calories, 3.2 g. fat (13% of calories), 0.6 g. saturated fat, 70 mg. cholesterol, 377 mg. sodium, 1.7 g. dietary fiber, 54 mg. calcium, 2 mg. iron, 79 mg. vitamin C, 1.4 mg. beta-carotene • **Serves 4**

❧ ❧ ❧

TANDOORI CHICKEN

1¼ cups nonfat yogurt

1 garlic clove, crushed through a press

1 teaspoon ground cumin

½ teaspoon ground coriander

¼ teaspoon freshly ground black pepper

¼ teaspoon salt

¼ teaspoon ground ginger

¼ teaspoon ground turmeric

Large pinch of ground red pepper

½ cup diced fresh tomatoes

½ cup diced peeled cucumbers

¼ cup minced fresh cilantro, plus cilantro sprigs for garnish (optional)

1 pound skinned boneless chicken thighs (8)

¾ cup uncooked converted white rice

¾ cup water

¾ cup defatted chicken broth

From the urn-shaped brick-and-clay oven known as a *tandoor* come some of India's best-loved foods. A fire is built in the tandoor, and when the coals are white-hot, skewered meats are lowered into the oven. The intense heat cooks kebabs or a halved chicken with remarkable speed. Some Indian breads, such as *naan* and *roti,* are made by slapping portions of dough against the searing-hot inner walls of the tandoor, where they cook in about one minute.

1 Preheat the oven to 425°. Spray a 7 x 11-inch baking pan with no-stick spray.

2 In a medium bowl, mix the yogurt with the garlic, cumin, coriander, black pepper, salt, ginger, turmeric and red pepper. Transfer ⅔ cup of the yogurt mixture to another medium bowl and stir in the tomatoes, cucumbers and minced cilantro; cover and refrigerate.

3 Add the chicken thighs to the remaining yogurt mixture and toss to coat well. Arrange the chicken in a single layer, skinned side up, in the prepared pan; spoon any remaining yogurt mixture over the chicken. Bake for 20 to 25 minutes, or until the chicken is cooked through.

4 Meanwhile, combine the rice, water and broth in a heavy medium saucepan; bring to a boil over high heat. Reduce the heat to low, cover and simmer for 20 minutes, or until the rice is tender and the liquid is absorbed.

5 Spread the rice on a platter and arrange the chicken thighs on top. Spoon the reserved yogurt-vegetable mixture over the chicken and rice; garnish with cilantro sprigs, if desired.

Preparation time 15 minutes • **Total time** 45 minutes • **Per serving** 322 calories, 5.4 g. fat (15% of calories), 1.3 g. saturated fat, 96 mg. cholesterol, 478 mg. sodium, 1 g. dietary fiber, 188 mg. calcium, 3 mg. iron, 11 mg. vitamin C, 0.1 mg. beta-carotene • **Serves 4**

FOODWAYS

In earlier times, chicken was rubbed with saffron and a natural coloring called cochineal to turn it a deep red in the tan-door. Today, artificial food coloring is sometimes added. In this version of tan-doori chicken, deep-yellow turmeric turns the chicken golden rather than red.

TURKEY CUTLETS MILANESE

1 large egg white

1 tablespoon water

½ cup unseasoned dry bread crumbs

½ teaspoon freshly ground black pepper

¼ teaspoon dried oregano, crumbled

1 pound thinly sliced turkey breast cutlets (4)

2 tablespoons defatted chicken broth

1 tablespoon plus 1 teaspoon extra-virgin olive oil

2 teaspoons red wine vinegar

1 small garlic clove, crushed through a press

1 teaspoon Dijon mustard

⅛ teaspoon salt

4 firmly packed cups (2 large bunches) arugula, watercress or spinach, washed and trimmed

1 large fresh tomato (about 10 ounces), cut into large dice

½ cup thinly sliced radishes

¼ cup thinly sliced sweet red or white onion

½ ounce Parmesan cheese, shaved with a vegetable peeler (about 2 tablespoons)

Egg-dipped, crumbed and gently sautéed in butter, thinly sliced veal *alla Milanese* turns out juicy and tender despite the delicacy of the meat. Thin turkey breast cutlets are a fine substitute for veal; baked with just a drizzling of olive oil, they emerge crisp-crusted and delicious. The somewhat sharp-flavored salad of greens, radishes, onions and Parmesan provides a refreshing contrast.

1 Preheat the oven to 450°. Spray a jelly-roll pan with no-stick spray.

2 In a shallow bowl or pie plate, using a fork, beat the egg white and water until frothy. In another shallow bowl, or on a sheet of wax paper, combine the bread crumbs, ¼ teaspoon of the pepper and the oregano.

3 One at time, dip the turkey cutlets into the egg mixture, letting the excess drip off, then coat with the crumbs, pressing them into the surface. Arrange the cutlets in a single layer in the prepared pan and let stand while you prepare the salad dressing.

4 In a medium bowl, whisk together the broth, 2 teaspoons of the oil, the vinegar, garlic, mustard, salt and the remaining ¼ teaspoon pepper; set aside.

5 Drizzle the turkey with the remaining 2 teaspoons oil and bake, turning once, for 6 to 8 minutes, or until lightly browned and cooked through.

6 Arrange the turkey cutlets on a heated platter. Add the arugula or other greens, the tomatoes, radishes and onions to the dressing, and toss to coat. Spoon the salad over the cutlets. Sprinkle with the Parmesan and serve.

Preparation time 20 minutes • **Total time** 30 minutes • **Per serving** 273 calories, 7.9 g. fat (26% of calories), 1.8 g. saturated fat, 73 mg. cholesterol, 421 mg. sodium, 3.2 g. dietary fiber, 166 mg. calcium, 3 mg. iron, 40 mg. vitamin C, 1.7 mg. beta-carotene • **Serves 4**

KITCHEN TIPS

If you're using arugula or spinach for the salad, tear any large leaves into pieces.

Use a vegetable peeler to pare shavings from a piece of Parmesan. This is easier to do if the cheese is at room temperature.

GRILLED GARLIC LIME GAME HENS

2 Cornish game hens (1½ pounds each), split

¼ cup plus 2 tablespoons fresh lime juice

1 tablespoon grated lime zest

3 garlic cloves, crushed through a press

1 teaspoon extra-virgin olive oil

¼ teaspoon salt

¼ teaspoon freshly ground black pepper

⅛ teaspoon crushed red pepper flakes

You'll discard the skin before eating these juicy game hens, but while the birds roast, the skin seals in the zesty marinade. Because the recipe is for the hens only, the ratio of calories from fat may seem high. You can restore the balance by serving the hens with a complex carbohydrate, such as rice, potatoes or couscous.

1 Place the hens in a shallow no-stick baking pan (or foil-lined pan) large enough to hold them in a single layer. In a small bowl, mix the lime juice, lime zest, garlic, oil, salt, black pepper and red pepper flakes.

2 Pour the mixture over the hens, rubbing it over both sides and especially under the skin. Cover and let stand for 10 minutes.

3 Meanwhile, preheat the broiler.

4 Broil the hens 5 to 6 inches from the heat for about 10 minutes per side, or until the hens are browned and the juices run clear, not pink, when the hens are pierced at the thigh with a sharp knife. Baste the hens with the pan juices while they are roasting.

5 Remove the skin from the hens before eating.

Preparation time 10 minutes • **Total time** 40 minutes • **Per serving** 253 calories, 10.2 g. fat (36% of calories), 2.6 g. saturated fat, 108 mg. cholesterol, 241 mg. sodium, 0 g. dietary fiber, 34 mg. calcium, 2 mg. iron, 9 mg. vitamin C, 0 mg. beta-carotene • **Serves 4**

❧ ❧ ❧

Use kitchen shears to split the Cornish hens down the backbone.

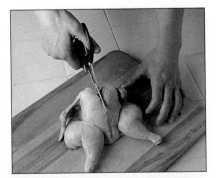
Then turn the birds over and split them along the breastbone.

CHICKEN BREASTS ARRABBIATA

1 tablespoon extra-virgin olive oil

1 cup chopped red bell peppers

1 cup chopped onions

¼ cup seeded, rinsed and chopped peperoncini

3 garlic cloves, crushed

½ teaspoon dried basil, crumbled

½ teaspoon sugar

½ teaspoon freshly ground black pepper

¼ teaspoon salt

⅛ teaspoon crushed red pepper flakes

3 cups coarsely chopped plum tomatoes

¼ cup defatted chicken broth

1 tablespoon no-salt-added tomato paste

1 pound skinless, boneless chicken breast halves (4 halves)

¼ cup chopped Italian parsley

Arrabbiata means "angry," and perhaps this dish got its name because it is somewhat "hot-tempered"—that is to say, spicy with peppers. There are four types of pepper in this recipe: sweet red bell peppers, pickled peperoncini, red pepper flakes and ground black pepper. Jars of peperoncini, slightly hot Italian pickled peppers, can be found in most supermarkets. Sometimes they're labeled "Tuscan peppers."

1 Preheat the broiler and broiler-pan rack.

2 In a large skillet, warm the oil over medium-high heat. Add the bell peppers, onions, peperoncini, garlic, basil, sugar, ¼ teaspoon of the black pepper, ⅛ teaspoon of the salt and the red pepper flakes, and stir to combine. Reduce the heat to medium and sauté for 3 to 4 minutes, or until the vegetables are tender.

3 Add the tomatoes, broth and tomato paste, increase the heat to medium-high and sauté for 2 to 3 minutes longer, or until the tomatoes start to release their juices.

4 Reduce the heat to medium, cover and simmer, stirring occasionally and mashing the tomatoes with a spoon, for 10 minutes, or until the tomatoes are reduced to a sauce.

5 Meanwhile, season the chicken on both sides with the remaining ¼ teaspoon black pepper and ⅛ teaspoon salt. Broil the chicken 4 to 5 inches from the heat for 5 minutes per side, or until browned and cooked through. Add the chicken to the tomato sauce, spoon the sauce over the chicken and bring to a simmer. Sprinkle with the parsley and remove from the heat.

6 To serve, place a piece of chicken on each of 4 plates and top with the sauce.

Preparation time 20 minutes • **Total time** 45 minutes • **Per serving** 220 calories, 5.6 g. fat (23% of calories), 0.9 g. saturated fat, 66 mg. cholesterol, 528 mg. sodium, 3.2 g. dietary fiber, 46 mg. calcium, 2 mg. iron, 83 mg. vitamin C, 1.6 mg. beta-carotene • **Serves 4**

STEAK OREGANATA WITH MUSHROOMS

2 teaspoons grated lemon zest

2 tablespoons fresh lemon juice

2 tablespoons defatted chicken broth

1 tablespoon coarsely chopped fresh oregano leaves or ½ teaspoon dried oregano

2 garlic cloves, crushed

1 teaspoon extra-virgin olive oil

¾ teaspoon cracked black pepper

¼ teaspoon salt

1 pound well-trimmed boneless sirloin steak

16 large cremini or white mushrooms, stems trimmed even with the caps

Oregano or parsley sprigs, for garnish (optional)

You don't need a 12-ounce steak for a satisfying meal if you serve meaty mushrooms alongside. Sharing the plate with the sirloin slices here are *cremini* (flavorful pale-brown Italian button mushrooms). Use white mushrooms if you can't get cremini.

1 Preheat the broiler and the broiler-pan rack.

2 In a medium bowl, combine the lemon zest, lemon juice, broth, oregano, garlic, oil, black pepper and salt.

3 Rub 1 tablespoon of the herb mixture into one side of the steak. Turn the steak and rub with another tablespoon of the herb mixture.

4 Add the mushrooms to the remaining herb mixture and toss to coat.

5 Place the steak in the center of the broiler-pan rack. Place the mushrooms, stem-side down, around the steak. Pour the herb mixture remaining in the bowl over the steak and mushrooms.

6 Broil the steak and mushrooms 4 to 6 inches from the heat for 5 minutes. Turn the steak and mushrooms, and broil for 5 to 7 minutes longer, or until the steak is medium-rare and the mushrooms are lightly browned and tender. Transfer the steak to a cutting board and the mushrooms to 4 warmed plates. Let the steak rest for 5 minutes.

7 Carve the steak into thin slices and arrange on the plates with the mushrooms. Garnish with oregano or parsley sprigs, if desired.

Cremini do not look quite so "tame" and tidy as white button mushrooms.

Preparation time 10 minutes • **Total time** 35 minutes • **Per serving** 214 calories, 7.9 g. fat (33% of calories), 2.6 g. saturated fat, 76 mg. cholesterol, 228 mg. sodium, 1.7 g. dietary fiber, 26 mg. calcium, 5 mg. iron, 10 mg. vitamin C, 0 mg. beta-carotene
Serves 4

FOOD FACT
In Italy, when people go hunting, it's not always game they're after—sometimes the "prey" is wild mushrooms. Cremini are among the more common wild mushrooms, and today they are cultivated by American growers—which of course makes them more plentiful and cheaper.

COD STEAKS SICILIAN-STYLE

1 tablespoon plus 1 teaspoon
extra-virgin olive oil

1 medium onion, halved and
thinly sliced

1 cup thinly sliced fennel

2 garlic cloves, minced

½ teaspoon dried thyme, crumbled

¼ teaspoon salt

¼ teaspoon freshly ground
black pepper

1 tablespoon honey

1¼ teaspoons grated orange zest

1 tablespoon balsamic vinegar

1 can (16 ounces) crushed
tomatoes

½ cup fresh orange juice

3 tablespoons golden raisins

1¼ pounds cod steaks (4 steaks)

Chopped fresh parsley, for
garnish (optional)

Sicilian food might be characterized as assertive: The flavors are bold, the seasonings wonderfully varied. Rather than a simple poached fish with lemon juice, you'll encounter seafood dishes like this deeply savory braise of sturdy cod cooked with onions, fennel, garlic, tomatoes and orange juice. Honey, orange zest and raisins are surprising—but typically Sicilian—additions. If cod steaks are not available, use thick cod fillets—or halibut or haddock steaks. If you use fillets, check for doneness earlier—the baking time will be shorter for the thinner cuts.

1 Preheat the oven to 425°.

2 In a large, heavy no-stick skillet, warm the oil over medium-high heat until hot but not smoking. Add the onions, fennel, garlic, thyme, salt and black pepper, and sauté, reducing the heat slightly if necessary to keep the vegetables from sticking, for 3 to 4 minutes, or until the vegetables are just tender and lightly browned.

3 Stir in the honey and orange zest, and cook, stirring, for 30 seconds. Add the vinegar and simmer for 30 seconds, or until the vinegar is nearly evaporated and the vegetables are glazed.

4 Stir in the tomatoes, orange juice and raisins, and bring to a boil. Reduce the heat to medium-low and simmer for 5 minutes, or until the sauce is slightly thickened.

5 Place the cod steaks in a 9 x 9-inch nonreactive baking dish. Spoon the sauce over the fish. Bake, uncovered, for 12 to 15 minutes, or until the fish flakes easily when tested with a fork.

6 Transfer the fish and sauce to 4 plates. Sprinkle with chopped parsley, if desired.

Preparation time 15 minutes • **Total time** 45 minutes • **Per serving** 240 calories, 5.9 g. fat (22% of calories), 0.9 g. saturated fat, 54 mg. cholesterol, 418 mg. sodium, 2.3 g. dietary fiber, 87 mg. calcium, 2 mg. iron, 41 mg. vitamin C, 0.5 mg. beta-carotene • **Serves 4**

Pork Tenderloin with Vegetables

1 pound small red potatoes, cut into 1-inch wedges

3 large carrots, cut into 1-inch chunks

1 tablespoon grated lemon zest

2 teaspoons dried rosemary, crumbled

1 teaspoon fennel seeds

¾ teaspoon cracked black pepper

½ teaspoon salt

1 pound well-trimmed pork tenderloin

1 tablespoon plus 1 teaspoon extra-virgin olive oil

1 large onion, cut into ½-inch-thick wedges

4 medium plum tomatoes, each cut into 4 wedges

⅓ cup defatted chicken broth

Fresh rosemary sprigs, for garnish (optional)

Pork is very popular in Italy. Like all meats, it is typically eaten in modest portions, combined with generous amounts of vegetables, beans or pasta. Here, pork tenderloin, the leanest cut, is roasted along with potatoes, carrots, onions and tomatoes. Fennel seeds and rosemary add an unmistakably Italian fragrance and flavor.

1 Preheat the oven to 450°. Spray a heavy no-stick roasting pan or a broiler pan with no-stick spray.

2 Place the potatoes and carrots in a medium saucepan with cold water to cover. Cover the pan and bring to a boil over high heat. Reduce the heat to medium and simmer for 5 minutes, or until the potatoes are just tender. Drain the vegetables in a colander.

3 Meanwhile, in a large bowl, combine the lemon zest, rosemary, fennel seeds, black pepper and salt. Rub the pork tenderloin with 2 teaspoons of the herb mixture. Place the tenderloin in the center of the roasting pan or broiler pan and drizzle with 1 teaspoon of the oil; set aside.

4 Add the drained potatoes and carrots, the onion wedges and tomato wedges to the herb mixture remaining in the bowl. Add the remaining 1 tablespoon oil and toss to coat. Arrange the vegetables around the roast. Drizzle the vegetables with the broth.

5 Roast the pork and vegetables for 25 to 30 minutes, or until the pork is cooked through but still juicy in the center and the vegetables are tender and lightly browned on the edges. Transfer the pork to a cutting board.

6 Slice the pork on the diagonal, transfer to a platter and serve surrounded by the vegetables. Drizzle with the pan juices, and garnish with rosemary sprigs, if desired.

Preparation time 10 minutes • **Total time** 55 minutes • **Per serving** 342 calories, 9.9 g. fat (26% of calories), 2 g. saturated fat, 74 mg. cholesterol, 454 mg. sodium, 5.8 g. dietary fiber, 58 mg. calcium, 3 mg. iron, 39 mg. vitamin C, 12.8 mg. beta-carotene • **Serves 4**

SOLE FLORENTINE

1 tablespoon extra-virgin olive oil

1 cup diced red bell peppers

2 garlic cloves, minced

4 cups loosely packed chopped fresh spinach

½ teaspoon dried thyme, crumbled

¼ teaspoon salt

¼ teaspoon freshly ground black pepper

1 pound sole fillets (4 fillets)

¼ cup unseasoned dry breadcrumbs

1 large egg white

2 tablespoons grated Parmesan cheese

2 tablespoons dry white wine

1 tablespoon defatted chicken broth

Fresh thyme sprigs, for garnish (optional)

Roll the fillets carefully, starting at the wide end and tucking in the filling as you go.

Florence is fabled for its food as well as for its art and architecture; and even humble spinach plays a role in the city's culinary glory. These spinach-stuffed sole fillets are baked in a small amount of wine, but you can substitute more broth if you wish.

1 Preheat the oven to 425°. Spray an 11 x 7-inch baking dish with no-stick spray.

2 In a large, heavy no-stick skillet, warm the oil over medium-high heat until hot but not smoking. Add the bell peppers and garlic, and sauté for 2 to 3 minutes, or until the peppers are tender. Transfer ¼ cup of the pepper mixture to a small bowl and set aside.

3 Increase the heat to medium-high heat and stir in the spinach, thyme, salt and black pepper. Cook, stirring, for about 1 minute, or until the spinach is wilted. Drain the spinach in a strainer, pressing down lightly to remove any excess moisture. Transfer the spinach to a medium bowl.

4 Cut the sole fillets in half lengthwise, removing any bones near the tops of the fillets.

5 Add the breadcrumbs, egg white and Parmesan to the spinach, and toss well. Spoon 2 rounded tablespoons of the spinach mixture onto the wide end of each piece of sole and roll up the fillet toward the narrow end. Place the rolls, seam-side down, in the prepared baking dish.

6 Sprinkle the rolls with the reserved bell pepper mixture, then drizzle with the wine and broth. Cover the baking dish with foil and bake for 10 to 12 minutes, or until the fish just flakes when tested with a fork and the filling is heated through.

7 Transfer 2 fish rolls with the bell pepper topping to each of 4 plates. Discard the pan juices. Garnish with fresh thyme sprigs, if desired.

Preparation time 15 minutes • **Total time** 45 minutes • **Per serving** 207 calories, 6.6 g. fat (28% of calories), 1.4 g. saturated fat, 56 mg. cholesterol, 418 mg. sodium, 2.9 g. dietary fiber, 164 mg. calcium, 3 mg. iron, 72 mg. vitamin C, 4.3 mg. beta-carotene • **Serves 4**

MINTED LAMB CHOPS WITH WHITE BEANS

3 anchovy fillets, rinsed and patted dry

1 teaspoon extra-virgin olive oil

1½ teaspoons dried mint

½ teaspoon freshly ground black pepper

1¼ pounds well-trimmed loin lamb chops (4 chops)

2 cups coarsely chopped plum tomatoes

1 garlic clove, crushed

3 cups canned cannellini beans, rinsed and drained

2 tablespoons defatted reduced-sodium beef broth

¼ teaspoon salt

2 tablespoons chopped fresh mint

Mint sprigs and additional chopped fresh mint, for garnish (optional)

The mountainous region of Abruzzi is home to flocks of fat sheep. And fresh, tender lamb—*agnello*—is welcomed as one of the pleasures of spring. It may be roasted with garlic and mint, braised in wine or simply grilled. These thick chops are anointed with a paste of anchovies and mint before broiling; they're served with *cannellini,* plump white beans that are also grown in Abruzzi.

1 On a cutting board, finely chop the anchovies. Sprinkle with the oil, dried mint and ¼ teaspoon of the black pepper, then mash to a paste with the flat side of a chef's knife or a fork. Rub the anchovy paste evenly over both sides of the lamb chops. Place the chops on a plate, cover loosely with plastic wrap and set aside at room temperature for 15 minutes.

2 Meanwhile, preheat the broiler and broiler-pan rack.

3 While the chops stand, in a medium no-stick skillet, combine the tomatoes and garlic, and sauté over medium-high heat for 2 minutes, or until the tomatoes begin to give up their juices. Reduce the heat to medium, cover and cook for 2 to 3 minutes longer, or until the tomatoes are softened.

4 Stir in the beans, broth, salt, 1 tablespoon of the chopped fresh mint and remaining ¼ teaspoon black pepper, and bring to a simmer. Reduce the heat to medium-low, cover and simmer, stirring occasionally, for 10 minutes to blend the flavors.

5 While the beans are simmering, broil the lamb chops 5 to 6 inches from the heat for 4 to 6 minutes per side for medium.

6 To serve, spoon the bean mixture onto 4 warmed dinner plates and top each portion with a lamb chop. Sprinkle with the remaining 1 tablespoon chopped mint, and garnish with mint sprigs, if desired.

Preparation time 10 minutes • **Total time** 40 minutes • **Per serving** 369 calories, 11.2 g. fat (27% of calories), 3.3 g. saturated fat, 82 mg. cholesterol, 637 mg. sodium, 9.6 g. dietary fiber, 78 mg. calcium, 4 mg. iron, 20 mg. vitamin C, 0.4 mg. beta-carotene • **Serves 4**

TURKEY-SAGE CUTLETS WITH MUSHROOMS

⅓ cup dried mushrooms, preferably porcini (¼ ounce)

1 cup boiling water

1 pound thin-sliced turkey cutlets (4 cutlets)

¼ teaspoon salt

¼ teaspoon freshly ground black pepper

1½ teaspoons grated lemon zest

4 large fresh sage leaves plus ½ teaspoon coarsely chopped fresh sage

1 tablespoon all-purpose flour

1 tablespoon grated Parmesan cheese

1 tablespoon plus 1 teaspoon olive oil

12 ounces white button mushrooms, sliced

3 tablespoons dry Marsala

Marsala, a fortified wine produced in western Sicily, gives this dish a light winy "bouquet." If you prefer, substitute 4 teaspoons of grape juice plus 4 teaspoons of beef broth.

1 Place the dried mushrooms in a large heatproof measuring cup and pour the boiling water over them; let stand for 10 to 15 minutes, or until softened. Meanwhile, line a small strainer with cheesecloth.

2 With a slotted spoon, transfer the mushrooms from the soaking liquid to a cutting board and chop. Place the strainer over a small bowl and pour the soaking liquid through it, leaving the sediment in the cup. Reserve about ¼ cup of the soaking liquid.

3 Season the cutlets with the salt and black pepper. Rub one side of each cutlet with the lemon zest. Place a sage leaf on the bottom half of the zested side of each cutlet, then fold the cutlets in half crosswise. In a small bowl, combine the flour and Parmesan; dust the cutlets with the mixture.

4 In a large no-stick skillet, warm 2 teaspoons of the oil over medium-high heat. Sauté the cutlets, turning once halfway through cooking, for 6 to 8 minutes, or until browned and cooked through. Transfer the cutlets to a platter and cover loosely to keep warm.

5 Add the remaining 2 teaspoons oil to the skillet and warm over medium-high heat. Add the fresh mushrooms and softened dried mushrooms, and sauté for 2 minutes. Drizzle with 2 tablespoons of the reserved soaking liquid and the Marsala. Sauté for 2 to 3 minutes, or until the mushrooms are tender and the liquid is absorbed. Add a little more soaking liquid if the pan gets too dry. Pour any juices from the platter over the mushrooms, sprinkle with the chopped sage and simmer for 30 seconds.

6 Serve the cutlets topped with the mushrooms.

Preparation time 10 minutes • **Total time** 30 minutes • **Per serving** 220 calories, 6 g. fat (24% of calories), 1.1 g. saturated fat, 71 mg. cholesterol, 219 mg. sodium, 1.2 g. dietary fiber, 40 mg. calcium, 3 mg. iron, 4 mg. vitamin C, 0 mg. beta-carotene
Serves 4

SHRIMP, POTATOES AND BROCCOLI RABE

12 ounces small red potatoes, quartered

1 large bunch broccoli rabe (about 1¼ pounds) or 4 cups broccoli florets

1 tablespoon plus 1 teaspoon extra-virgin olive oil

4 garlic cloves, minced

2 tablespoons chopped Italian parsley

¼ teaspoon crushed red pepper flakes

1 pound shrimp, peeled and deveined, with tails attached

2 tablespoons defatted chicken broth

½ teaspoon sugar

¼ teaspoon salt

Gather the broccoli rabe into a bunch so you can trim all the stems with one stroke of the knife.

The region known as Apulia forms the "heel" of the boot-shaped Italian peninsula. It juts out into the sea, with the Adriatic to the east and the Ionian Sea to the south and west. In Apulian cities such as Bari, fresh shellfish is sold at waterfront stands, to be eaten on the spot or taken home and cooked quickly and simply. This combination of shrimp, potatoes and robust greens captures the spirit of Apulian cuisine.

1 Place the potatoes in a medium saucepan with cold water to cover. Cover the pan and bring to a boil over high heat. Reduce the heat to medium and simmer for 8 to 10 minutes, or until the potatoes are fork-tender. Drain the potatoes in a colander, then return them to the saucepan. Cover to keep warm.

2 While the potatoes are cooking, trim the large, tough bottom stems from the broccoli rabe, if using. Cut the broccoli rabe into 2-inch pieces (you should have about 8 cups).

3 Fill a large, deep no-stick skillet with ½ inch of water. Cover and bring to a boil over high heat. Add the broccoli rabe or broccoli florets and return to a boil. Cook, uncovered, for 2 to 3 minutes, or until the broccoli is tender. Drain in a colander. Wipe the skillet dry.

4 In the same skillet, warm the oil over medium-high heat until hot but not smoking. Add the garlic, parsley and red pepper flakes, and sauté for 30 seconds, or until fragrant. Add the shrimp and sauté for 2 to 3 minutes, or until the shrimp are pink and opaque. With a slotted spoon, transfer the shrimp to a plate.

5 Add the drained potatoes and broccoli to the skillet. Add the broth, sugar and salt, and toss to mix well. Cook, tossing, for 1 to 2 minutes, or until heated through. Add the shrimp and toss to combine.

Preparation time 25 minutes • **Total time** 45 minutes • **Per serving** 254 calories, 6.8 g. fat (24% of calories), 1 g. saturated fat, 140 mg. cholesterol, 341 mg. sodium, 6 g. dietary fiber, 112 mg. calcium, 4 mg. iron, 109 mg. vitamin C, 1.3 mg. beta-carotene • **Serves 4**

PARMESAN PORK WITH ITALIAN SLAW

- 1 tablespoon extra-virgin olive oil
- 1 pound well-trimmed boneless pork cutlets, pounded to ¼ inch thick (4 cutlets)
- ¼ teaspoon freshly ground black pepper
- ¼ teaspoon salt
- 1 large egg white
- ½ cup unseasoned dry breadcrumbs
- 1 tablespoon grated Parmesan cheese
- 1 tablespoon chopped fresh oregano
- 2 teaspoons defatted chicken broth
- 2 teaspoons red wine vinegar
- ¼ teaspoon sugar
- 1 medium head radicchio, coarsely shredded (4 ounces)
- 2 heads Belgian endive, cut crosswise on the diagonal into thin slices
- 1 large tomato, quartered and sliced crosswise
- 2 tablespoons chopped red onion
- Fresh oregano leaves and oregano sprigs, for garnish (optional)

A surprising "slaw" of radicchio (an Italian chicory with thick, tight leaves that are a solid or variegated rosy red), Belgian endive, tomatoes and onions serves as a foil for these breaded, baked pork scallops. You can have the butcher pound the pork, or do it yourself with a wooden mallet or small, heavy skillet.

1 Preheat the oven to 450°. Coat a jelly-roll pan with 1 teaspoon of the oil.

2 Season the pork cutlets on both sides with the black pepper and ⅛ teaspoon of the salt.

3 In a glass pie plate or shallow bowl, lightly beat the egg white. On a plate, combine the breadcrumbs, Parmesan and 2 teaspoons of the chopped oregano.

4 One at a time, dip the cutlets into the egg white, letting the excess drip off, then dredge the cutlets in the breadcrumb mixture, pressing the mixture into both sides. Place the cutlets in a single layer in the prepared pan.

5 Drizzle the cutlets evenly with 1 teaspoon of the oil. Bake for 10 minutes, or until the undersides are lightly browned. Turn and bake for 5 minutes longer, or until browned and cooked through.

6 While the cutlets are cooking, make the dressing. In a medium bowl, whisk together the broth, vinegar, sugar, remaining 1 teaspoon each oil and oregano and the remaining ⅛ teaspoon salt.

7 Just before the cutlets are done, add the radicchio, endive, tomatoes and onions to the dressing, and toss to combine.

8 Transfer the cutlets to 4 plates and top with the salad. Garnish with oregano leaves and sprigs, if desired.

Preparation time 20 minutes • **Total time** 45 minutes • **Per serving** 262 calories, 10.9 g. fat (37% of calories), 3 g. saturated fat, 78 mg. cholesterol, 353 mg. sodium, 1.9 g. dietary fiber, 78 mg. calcium, 3 mg. iron, 16 mg. vitamin C, 0.5 mg. beta-carotene • **Serves 4**

PESTO SALMON

1¼ cups loosely packed fresh
   basil leaves

3 tablespoons defatted chicken
   broth

1 tablespoon blanched slivered
   almonds

1 tablespoon fresh lemon juice

2 teaspoons grated Parmesan
   cheese

2 teaspoons extra-virgin olive oil

¼ teaspoon salt

¼ teaspoon freshly ground
   black pepper

1 garlic clove, peeled

1 pound skinned salmon fillet, cut
   into 4 pieces

Lemon wedges and basil sprigs,
for garnish (optional)

Basil is one of the preeminent herbs in the Italian kitchen, and some of the finest basil is grown in Liguria, a coastal region of northern Italy. Pesto—a heady basil sauce—is the pride of Liguria and is used as a pasta sauce or as a last-minute addition to a bowl of minestrone. Here, a pesto made with almonds (rather than pine nuts) is slathered over salmon fillets before and after broiling.

1 To make the pesto, place the basil, broth, almonds, lemon juice, Parmesan, oil, salt and black pepper in a food processor. Turn the machine on, drop the garlic clove through the feed tube and process until puréed.

2 Place the pieces of salmon on a plate. Spoon 3 tablespoons of the pesto over the salmon and turn to coat both sides of each piece. Cover with plastic wrap and let stand at room temperature for 15 minutes. Reserve the remaining pesto at room temperature.

3 Meanwhile, preheat the broiler. Spray a jelly-roll pan with no-stick spray.

4 Place the salmon in the prepared pan. Spread any of the pesto remaining on the plate on top of each piece. Broil the salmon 4 to 5 inches from the heat for 6 to 8 minutes, or just until opaque in the center. (The cooking time will depend on the thickness of the fish.)

5 Transfer the salmon pieces to 4 dinner plates and top each piece with some of the reserved pesto. Garnish with lemon wedges and basil sprigs, if desired.

Preparation time 10 minutes • **Total time** 40 minutes • **Per serving** 222 calories, 11.6 g. fat (47% of calories), 1.7 g. saturated fat, 63 mg. cholesterol, 250 mg. sodium, 0.3 g. dietary fiber, 186 mg. calcium, 4 mg. iron, 7 mg. vitamin C, 0.4 mg. beta-carotene • **Serves 4**

FOR A CHANGE
The pesto would suit a number of other rich-fleshed fish, such as bluefish, snapper, tuna or swordfish. The fish could be broiled, grilled, steamed or poached.

ON THE MENU
Accompany the salmon with sautéed cherry tomatoes tossed with fresh herbs. If you pierce the tomatoes with a pin before heating them, they won't burst.

Drumsticks with Peppers and Onions

1½ **pounds small chicken drumsticks, skinned (8 drumsticks)**

1 **large green bell pepper, cut into 1-inch squares**

1 **large red bell pepper, cut into 1-inch squares**

1 **medium red onion, cut into ½-inch wedges**

8 **pimiento-stuffed green olives, halved crosswise**

4 **garlic cloves, cut into thin slivers**

3 **tablespoons balsamic vinegar**

½ **teaspoon dried thyme, crumbled**

¼ **teaspoon freshly ground black pepper**

¼ **teaspoon salt**

⅛ **teaspoon crushed red pepper flakes**

¾ **cup water**

¾ **cup defatted chicken broth**

¾ **cup converted white rice**

B raised chicken and vegetables is a simple enough recipe, but bright bell peppers, red onions and pimiento-stuffed green olives elevate this dish to company status. The flavors are as vivid as the colors, highlighted by lots of garlic and a splash of vinegar.

1 Preheat the oven to 425°.

2 Place the chicken, green and red bell peppers, onions, olives and garlic in a 13 x 9-inch baking dish. Drizzle with the vinegar, then sprinkle with the thyme, black pepper, salt and red pepper flakes. Toss to mix.

3 Bake the chicken and vegetables, uncovered, for 30 to 35 minutes, or until the chicken is cooked through and the vegetables are tender.

4 Meanwhile, in a medium saucepan, combine the water, broth and rice. Bring to a boil over high heat. Reduce the heat to low, cover and simmer for 20 minutes, or until the rice is tender and the liquid is absorbed.

5 Transfer the rice to a platter and top with the chicken, vegetables and pan juices.

Preparation time 15 minutes • **Total time** 50 minutes • **Per serving** 309 calories, 5.4 g. fat (16% of calories), 1 g. saturated fat, 83 mg. cholesterol, 613 mg. sodium, 2.4 g. dietary fiber, 64 mg. calcium, 3 mg. iron, 79 mg. vitamin C, 1 mg. beta-carotene
Serves 4

To slice the garlic without cutting yourself, stab the clove with a toothpick or skewer.

Hold the garlic in place on a cutting board as you slice it with a sharp paring knife.

VEGETABLES PARMESAN WITH MEAT SAUCE

1 medium eggplant

2 medium zucchini

2 teaspoons extra-virgin olive oil

½ teaspoon dried basil, crumbled

½ teaspoon dried oregano, crumbled

½ teaspoon freshly ground black pepper

¼ teaspoon salt

6 ounces lean beef top round, cut into chunks

3 garlic cloves, peeled

2 cans (8 ounces each) no-salt-added tomato sauce

1 large tomato, cut into ¼-inch-thick slices

1 ounce part-skim mozzarella cheese, shredded

1 ounce Parmesan cheese, coarsely grated

3 tablespoons unseasoned dry breadcrumbs

Classic eggplant parmigiana is loaded with fat—mainly because the eggplant is fried. Here, the vegetables bake, and even with a meat sauce and a cheese topping the dish is low in fat.

1 Preheat the oven to 475°. Spray 2 jelly-roll pans with no-stick spray.

2 Trim the eggplant and zucchini, and cut both into ¼-inch-thick slices. Place each vegetable in a separate medium bowl. In a small bowl, combine 1 teaspoon of the oil, ¼ teaspoon each of the basil, oregano and black pepper, and ⅛ teaspoon of the salt. Drizzle half the oil mixture over each vegetable and toss to coat well.

3 Place the eggplant in one of the prepared pans in a single layer and the zucchini in the other pan in a single layer. Place both pans in the oven and bake until the vegetables are tender and lightly browned (the zucchini should take about 10 minutes; the eggplant about 15 minutes). Remove from the oven; leave the oven on.

4 While the vegetables are cooking, in a food processor, combine the the beef, garlic, remaining ¼ teaspoon each basil, oregano and pepper, and the remaining ⅛ teaspoon salt, and pulse until finely ground.

5 In a medium, heavy no-stick skillet, warm the remaining 1 teaspoon oil over medium heat. Add the beef and cook, stirring, for 2 to 3 minutes, or until the beef loses its pink color. Stir in the tomato sauce and bring to a boil. Remove the skillet from the heat.

6 Spread ¾ cup of the meat sauce in the bottom of an 11 x 7-inch baking dish. Top with the eggplant and then the zucchini; cover with the tomato slices. Spoon the remaining meat sauce over the vegetables.

7 Sprinkle evenly with the mozzarella and Parmesan, then top with the breadcrumbs. Bake, uncovered, for 10 to 12 minutes, or until the cheeses are melted and the breadcrumbs are browned.

Preparation time 10 minutes • **Total time** 45 minutes • **Per serving** 246 calories, 8.6 g. fat (31% of calories), 3 g. saturated fat, 34 mg. cholesterol, 402 mg. sodium, 4.8 g. dietary fiber, 230 mg. calcium, 4 mg. iron, 36 mg. vitamin C, 1.3 mg. beta-carotene • **Serves 4**

CHICKEN BREASTS WITH PEARS

½ teaspoon dried thyme, crumbled

¼ teaspoon salt

¼ teaspoon freshly ground black pepper

1 pound skinless, boneless chicken breast halves (4)

2 teaspoons olive oil

½ cup pear nectar

¼ cup defatted chicken broth

2 teaspoons balsamic vinegar

2 teaspoons honey

2 large ripe pears (about 1 pound), cut into ½-inch dice

1 teaspoon cornstarch dissolved in 1 tablespoon defatted chicken broth or cold water

1 teaspoon unsalted butter or margarine

½ ounce toasted coarsely chopped walnuts

The technique used to create this dish is one you can use again and again for quick meals: The chicken breasts are sautéed in a skillet and removed, then a sauce is made in the same skillet, using a few simple ingredients. It's a one-pot meal that can be casual or celebratory, depending on the sauce and side dishes.

1 In a cup, mix the thyme, salt and pepper. Season the chicken on both sides with the herb mixture.

2 In a large, heavy no-stick skillet, warm the oil over medium-high heat. Add the chicken and sauté for 4 to 6 minutes per side, or until cooked through, reducing the heat slightly if necessary. Transfer to a large platter and cover loosely with foil to keep warm.

3 Add the pear nectar, broth, vinegar and honey to the skillet, and bring to a boil over medium-high heat, stirring frequently.

4 Add the pears to the skillet, bring to a boil and reduce the heat to medium-low. Cover and simmer, stirring occasionally, for 2 to 3 minutes, or until the pears are tender. Pour any juices that have collected on the chicken platter into the skillet. Stir in the cornstarch mixture, then the butter or margarine; return the sauce to a boil, stirring gently until slightly thickened. Remove the skillet from the heat.

5 Transfer the chicken to plates; spoon the pears and sauce over the chicken. Sprinkle with the walnuts.

Preparation time 10 minutes • **Total time** 30 minutes • **Per serving** 272 calories, 7.3 g. fat (24% of calories), 1.5 g. saturated fat, 68 mg. cholesterol, 273 mg. sodium, 3.1 g. dietary fiber, 35 mg. calcium, 2 mg. iron, 6 mg. vitamin C, 0 mg. beta-carotene
Serves 4

ON THE MENU
Accompany the chicken with sautéed kale and a mixture of brown and wild rice.

SUBSTITUTION
If pear nectar isn't available, you can substitute apple cider.

FOOD FACT
We owe the development of many modern pear varieties to the French nobility of the 17th, 18th and 19th centuries. Gentlemen cultivated pears as a hobby, and they perfected, among others, the Anjou, Comice and what we now call the Bartlett pear.

CHICKEN PICCATA WITH ESCAROLE

- 12 ounces skinless, boneless chicken breast halves (4)
- ½ teaspoon dried thyme, crumbled
- ¼ teaspoon freshly ground black pepper
- 1½ teaspoons olive oil
- 2 garlic cloves, minced
- 5 cups loosely packed cut-up escarole
- 1 cup halved cherry tomatoes
- ⅛ teaspoon salt
- 2 teaspoons cornstarch dissolved in ½ cup defatted chicken broth
- ½ teaspoon grated lemon zest
- 1 tablespoon fresh lemon juice
- 1 teaspoon unsalted butter or margarine

Although it is frequently served as a salad green, escarole is also delicious sautéed with garlic and served warm.

Classic sauces start out rich: Cream, butter and eggs are the basic of many of them. Beyond that, there's a technique called "enrichment," in which more of these luxurious ingredients are added after the sauce is made. Egg yolks and cream may be beaten in, or additional butter whisked into the sauce. Taking a tip from the great chefs, you can also enrich a light sauce like this one; one teaspoon of butter adds just a gram of fat per serving but makes a notable difference in the flavor.

1 Preheat the broiler and a broiler-pan rack.

2 Season both sides of the chicken breasts with the thyme and pepper. Place the chicken on the broiler-pan rack and broil 2 to 3 inches from the heat for about 5 minutes per side, or until it is browned and cooked through. Transfer the chicken to a warm platter and cover it loosely with foil.

3 Meanwhile, in a large, deep skillet, warm the oil over medium-high heat. Add the garlic and sauté, stirring constantly, for 30 seconds, or until fragrant. Add the escarole, increase the heat to high and sauté, tossing frequently, for 2 to 3 minutes, or until the greens begin to wilt. Add the cherry tomatoes and cook for 2 to 3 minutes, or until the tomatoes are warm and soft and the escarole is completely wilted. Add the salt, then transfer the vegetables to the warm platter.

4 In the same skillet, whisk together the cornstarch mixture, lemon zest and lemon juice, and bring to a boil over high heat, stirring constantly. Simmer, stirring, for 1 to 2 minutes, or until the sauce is slightly thickened and bubbly. Add the butter or margarine and any juices that have collected on the platter, and return to a boil, stirring. Cook just until the butter or margarine is melted and the sauce has thickened. Pour the sauce over the chicken and vegetables.

Preparation time 10 minutes • **Total time** 30 minutes • **Per serving** 148 calories, 4.1 g. fat (25% of calories), 1.1 g. saturated fat, 52 mg. cholesterol, 268 mg. sodium, 2.1 g. dietary fiber, 60 mg. calcium, 2 mg. iron, 13 mg. vitamin C, 1 mg. beta-carotene
Serves 4

GOLDEN CHICKEN CURRY

1 cup uncooked converted white rice

2 cups water

½ cup frozen peas

12 ounces skinless, boneless chicken breast halves, cut into ½-inch chunks

3 tablespoons all-purpose flour

1 tablespoon curry powder

¼ teaspoon salt

1 tablespoon olive oil

1 medium onion, chopped

1 large celery stalk, diced

2 garlic cloves, minced

1 cup defatted chicken broth

1 tart medium apple, such as a Macoun, diced

3 tablespoons golden raisins

¾ cup nonfat yogurt

¼ cup chopped fresh cilantro

Fruits go into many Indian dishes: Mangoes, papayas, tamarinds, lemons and limes are used in curries and chutneys. Here, apples and golden raisins give a chicken curry memorable flavor.

1 Combine the rice and water in a medium saucepan and bring to a boil over high heat. Reduce the heat to low, cover and simmer for 20 minutes, or until the rice is tender and the liquid is absorbed. Stir in the peas and remove the pan from the heat; cover and set aside.

2 While the rice is cooking, toss the chicken with 2 tablespoons of the flour, 1 teaspoon of the curry powder and the salt; reserve any excess flour mixture. In a large, heavy skillet, warm 2 teaspoons of the oil over high heat. Add the chicken and stir-fry for 2 to 3 minutes, or until the chicken turns golden (it will not be cooked through). With a slotted spoon, transfer the chicken to a clean plate.

3 Add the remaining 1 teaspoon oil to the skillet. Stir in the onions, celery, garlic, the reserved flour mixture and remaining 2 teaspoons curry powder; sauté, stirring, for 1 minute. Drizzle 2 tablespoons of the broth over the vegetables and reduce the heat to medium. Sauté, gradually adding 2 tablespoons more broth to the skillet, for 3 to 5 minutes, or until the onions are tender and the celery is crisp-tender.

4 Add the apples, raisins and the browned chicken to the skillet, and stir to mix with the vegetables. Add the remaining ¾ cup chicken broth, increase the heat to high and bring to a boil. Reduce the heat to medium-low, cover and simmer, stirring occasionally, for 10 minutes, or until the flavors are blended and the juices slightly thickened.

5 Place the yogurt in a medium bowl. Whisk in the remaining 1 tablespoon flour and the cilantro. Stir a spoonful of the curry sauce into the yogurt mixture; then, stirring constantly, add the yogurt mixture to the skillet. Cook, stirring and shaking the skillet, just until the sauce is heated through. Do not boil. As soon as the sauce is hot, remove the skillet from the heat. Serve the curried chicken mixture over the rice.

Preparation time 15 minutes • **Total time** 45 minutes • **Per serving** 423 calories, 5.6 g. fat (12% of calories), 0.9 g. saturated fat, 50 mg. cholesterol, 508 mg. sodium, 4.1 g. dietary fiber, 161 mg. calcium, 4 mg. iron, 11 mg. vitamin C, 0.1 mg. beta-carotene • **Serves 4**

CHICKEN MOZZARELLA

6 ounces ditalini pasta or other small macaroni

½ teaspoon dried thyme

½ teaspoon dried basil

⅛ teaspoon salt

⅛ teaspoon garlic powder

⅛ teaspoon crushed red pepper flakes

8 ounces thin-sliced chicken breast cutlets, cut into strips

1 teaspoon olive oil

2½ cups halved cherry tomatoes

1 medium zucchini (about 8 ounces), halved lengthwise and thinly sliced

1 cup coarsely diced red onion

¼ cup defatted chicken broth

¼ cup water

1 can (10 ounces) red kidney beans, rinsed and drained

3 ounces shredded part-skim mozzarella cheese

1 tablespoon chopped fresh Italian parsley (optional)

When the word "cheese"—or the name of a specific cheese—is in a recipe title, it's usually a good bet that the dish is loaded with fat. At a restaurant, you'd want to skip anything labeled "Parmigiana," "Mozzarella" or "Con Quattro Formaggi" (with four cheeses). This chicken-and-pasta combination breaks the rule, with less than seven grams of fat per serving.

1 Bring a covered medium pot of water to a boil over high heat. Add the pasta, return to a boil and cook for 5 to 8 minutes, or according to package directions until al dente. Drain in a colander and set aside.

2 While the pasta is cooking, in a cup, crumble together ¼ teaspoon of the thyme and ¼ teaspoon of the basil with the salt, garlic powder and red pepper flakes. Sprinkle the seasonings over both sides of the chicken strips.

3 Brush a large, heavy no-stick skillet with the oil and heat over medium-high heat. Add the chicken strips and sauté for about 2 minutes per side, or until lightly browned and cooked through. Transfer the cooked chicken to a clean plate.

4 Add the tomatoes, zucchini, onions, broth, water and the remaining ¼ teaspoon thyme and ¼ teaspoon basil to the skillet, and toss to blend well. Simmer, tossing frequently, for 4 to 5 minutes, or until the tomatoes have collapsed and the vegetables are tender. Add the beans and simmer for 2 to 3 minutes, or until heated through. Stir in the drained pasta.

5 Place the chicken on top of the pasta and vegetables; pour any chicken juices that have collected on the plate over the chicken and sprinkle with the cheese. Remove from the heat, cover and let stand for 3 to 4 minutes, or until the cheese is melted. Sprinkle with the parsley, if desired.

Preparation time 10 minutes • **Total time** 30 minutes • **Per serving** 375 calories, 6.7 g. fat (16% of calories), 2.6 g. saturated fat, 45 mg. cholesterol, 370 mg. sodium, 5.6 g. dietary fiber, 199 mg. calcium, 4 mg. iron, 23 mg. vitamin C, 0.4 mg. beta-carotene • **Serves 4**

Turkey Sauté with Apples

- 3 tablespoons all-purpose flour
- 1 teaspoon ground cumin
- ½ teaspoon freshly ground black pepper
- ¼ teaspoon salt
- ⅛ teaspoon ground cinnamon
- 1 pound thin-sliced turkey breast cutlets (4)
- 1 tablespoon olive oil
- 1 pound apples, cut into ½-inch-thick wedges
- ¾ cup defatted chicken broth
- 2 tablespoons honey
- ¾ cup water
- 1 teaspoon cider vinegar
- 2 tablespoons raisins
- 1 teaspoon unsalted butter or margarine

This handy kitchen tool simultaneously cores the apple and cuts it into wedges.

Welcome autumn—the glorious season of apples—with this tangy turkey sauté. You cook the apples with the skins on, so for extra color, use a selection of apples ranging from red to green to yellow. Try Empires, Granny Smiths and Golden Delicious, or Cortlands, Newtown Pippins and Gravensteins.

1 In a shallow bowl or pie plate, mix the flour, cumin, pepper, salt and cinnamon. Dredge the turkey in the flour mixture, patting it into the surface; reserve the excess flour mixture.

2 In a large, heavy no-stick skillet, warm the oil over medium-high heat. Add the turkey and sauté for 2 to 3 minutes per side, or until golden brown and cooked through. Transfer the turkey to a platter and cover loosely with foil to keep warm.

3 Add the apples, ½ cup of the broth and 1 tablespoon of the honey to the skillet. Cook over medium heat for 8 to 10 minutes, or until the apples are tender and nicely glazed, but not mushy; turn the apples frequently and scrape any brown bits from the bottom of the skillet. Remove the skillet from the heat. Spoon the apples over the turkey.

4 In a medium bowl, combine the reserved seasoned flour, remaining ¼ cup broth, remaining 1 tablespoon honey, the water and vinegar, and whisk until smooth. Pour this mixture into the skillet and bring to a boil over medium-heat, stirring constantly. Stir in the raisins. Simmer, stirring frequently, for 2 minutes, or until the sauce is thickened.

5 Stir in the butter or margarine, then remove the skillet from the heat. Pour the sauce over the turkey and apples.

Preparation time 15 minutes • **Total time** 40 minutes • **Per serving** 301 calories, 5.6 g. fat (18% of calories), 1.3 g. saturated fat, 73 mg. cholesterol, 378 mg. sodium, 2.7 g. dietary fiber, 32 mg. calcium, 2 mg. iron, 6 mg. vitamin C, 0 mg. beta-carotene
Serves 4

ON THE MENU
Serve the turkey and apples with broad noodles and broccoli.

KITCHEN TIPS
If honey becomes crystallized, set the jar in hot water for 10 to 15 minutes.

HOT-AND-SOUR TURKEY STIR-FRY

1 **cup uncooked converted white rice**

2½ **cups water**

8 **ounces turkey breast cutlets, cut into thin strips**

2 **tablespoons grated fresh ginger**

2 **tablespoons dry sherry or defatted chicken broth**

1 **tablespoon plus 1 teaspoon reduced-sodium soy sauce**

2 **garlic cloves, crushed through a press**

2 **teaspoons granulated sugar**

½ **teaspoon ground white pepper**

¼ **teaspoon crushed red pepper flakes**

⅛ **teaspoon salt**

1 **tablespoon plus 1 teaspoon olive oil**

4 **cups broccoli florets**

1 **large red bell pepper, cut into thin strips**

8 **ounces shiitake or white button mushrooms, cut into thick slices (if using shiitakes, stem them)**

½ **cup defatted chicken broth**

1 **tablespoon cornstarch dissolved in 2 tablespoons rice vinegar**

Sticklers for tradition will want to use a wok for this stir-fry, but a heavy skillet works perfectly well. The centuries-old design of the wok is perfect for stir-frying: Its sloping sides allow the food to be easily tossed and mixed, particularly if you use the traditional long-handled utensil that is a cross between a spoon and a spatula.

1 Combine the rice and 2 cups of the water in a heavy medium saucepan, and bring to a boil over high heat. Reduce the heat to low, cover and cook for 20 minutes, or until the rice is tender and the liquid is absorbed. Remove from the heat and set aside, covered.

2 While the rice is cooking, place the turkey strips in a shallow bowl. In a cup, combine the ginger, sherry or broth, soy sauce, garlic, sugar, white pepper, red pepper flakes and salt. Toss the turkey with 2 tablespoons of the ginger mixture.

3 In a large, deep no-stick skillet, warm 1½ teaspoons of the oil over high heat. Spread the turkey strips in the skillet and stir-fry for 2 to 3 minutes, or until the turkey is lightly browned and cooked through. Transfer the turkey to a plate.

4 Heat the remaining 2½ teaspoons oil in the skillet. Add the broccoli, bell peppers, mushrooms and the remaining ginger mixture, and stir-fry for 2 to 3 minutes, or until the peppers are crisp-tender and the broccoli is bright green.

5 Add the broth and the remaining ½ cup water to the skillet, and bring to a boil. Reduce the heat to medium-low, cover and simmer for 3 to 4 minutes, or until the broccoli is crisp-tender.

6 Increase the heat to high and stir in the turkey and any juices that have collected on the plate. Stir in the cornstarch mixture and bring to a boil, stirring constantly until the sauce is thickened. Serve the stir-fry over the rice.

Preparation time 20 minutes • **Total time** 40 minutes • **Per serving** 375 calories, 5.9 g. fat (14% of calories), 0.8 g. saturated fat, 35 mg. cholesterol, 459 mg. sodium, 6.5 g. dietary fiber, 102 mg. calcium, 4 mg. iron, 144 mg. vitamin C, 2 mg. beta-carotene • **Serves 4**

CHICKEN WITH GINGER-MUSTARD SAUCE

1 **pound thin-sliced chicken breast cutlets**

½ **teaspoon freshly ground black pepper**

¼ **teaspoon ground ginger**

⅛ **teaspoon salt**

2½ **teaspoons extra-virgin olive oil**

½ **cup defatted chicken broth**

1½ **teaspoons cornstarch, dissolved in ¼ cup cold water**

2 **teaspoons grated fresh ginger**

2 **teaspoons coarse Dijon mustard**

¼ **teaspoon dry mustard**

3 **tablespoons light sour cream**

There's more than one way to make a cream sauce, as every health- and flavor-conscious cook should know. One French recipe for mustard sauce calls for 1½ cups of heavy cream and a few tablespoons of butter, plus the pan juices from roasted pork that has been basted with butter and lard. In a simple but significant transformation, this ginger-mustard sauce is made in the skillet after you sauté skinless chicken in just 2½ teaspoons of oil; the cornstarch and the prepared and dry mustards thicken the sauce, with light sour cream as a last-minute enrichment.

1 Season the chicken on both sides with the pepper, ground ginger and salt.

2 In a large, heavy no-stick skillet, warm the oil over medium-high heat. Add the chicken and sauté for 2 to 3 minutes per side, or just until browned and cooked through. Transfer the chicken to a platter and cover loosely with foil to keep warm.

3 Whisk the broth, cornstarch mixture, fresh ginger, Dijon mustard and dry mustard into the skillet. Place over medium-high heat and bring to a boil, whisking constantly until the sauce thickens. Remove the skillet from the heat.

4 Pour any chicken juices that have collected on the platter into the sauce and whisk in the sour cream. Spoon the sauce over the chicken.

As you whisk the cornstarch mixture into the skillet, the sauce will thicken and become glossy.

Preparation time 10 minutes • **Total time** 25 minutes • **Per serving** 181 calories, 6.2 g. fat (31% of calories), 1.5 g. saturated fat, 70 mg. cholesterol, 342 mg. sodium, 0 g. dietary fiber, 16 mg. calcium, 1 mg. iron, 1 mg. vitamin C, 0 mg. beta-carotene
Serves 4

❧ ❧ ❧

KITCHEN TIPS

Cornstarch, a superfine flour made from the endosperm of the corn kernel, can thicken sauces without adding fat. Here are a few points to remember when cooking with cornstarch. If you stir the starch directly into hot liquid, it will almost certainly form lumps. To prevent this, combine the cornstarch with cold liquid (such as the water used here) and then add the mixture to the hot (not boiling) liquid. Whisk or stir constantly but gently as the cornstarch mixture is added and afterward: Too-vigorous beating—or too-high heat—will defeat the thickening power of the cornstarch.

CHICKEN CACCIATORE WITH RICE

¾ **cup uncooked converted white rice**

1½ **cups water**

1 **tablespoon olive oil**

1 **medium onion, diced**

2 **garlic cloves, minced**

8 **ounces small fresh mushrooms, quartered**

1 **medium red bell pepper, cut into large dice**

¾ **teaspoon freshly ground black pepper**

½ **teaspoon dried oregano, crumbled**

½ **teaspoon dried tarragon, crumbled**

⅛ **teaspoon salt**

¼ **cup dry white wine or defatted chicken broth**

1 **can (28 ounces) tomatoes in purée, drained, ½ cup of purée reserved**

2 **tablespoons no-salt-added tomato paste**

12 **ounces skinless, boneless chicken thighs, cut into ½-inch pieces**

Eating poultry without the skin eliminates much of its fat content; when you roast, broil or bake chicken, you can leave the skin on during cooking and remove it before you eat. However, when you stew or braise, the fat will end up in the sauce unless you remove the skin before cooking. Making chicken cacciatore with skinless thighs saves more than four grams of fat per serving.

1 Combine the rice and water in a heavy medium saucepan and bring to a boil over high heat. Reduce the heat to low, cover and simmer for 20 minutes, or until the rice is tender and the liquid is absorbed. Remove from the heat and set aside, covered (the rice will stay warm for a long time.)

2 Meanwhile, in a large, heavy no-stick skillet, warm the oil over medium-high heat. Add the onions and garlic, and stir to coat well with the oil. Stir in the mushrooms, bell peppers, black pepper, oregano, tarragon and salt; sauté, tossing the vegetables, for 3 minutes, or until they start to soften. Stir in the wine or broth and bring to a simmer. Reduce the heat to medium-low, cover and cook, stirring occasionally, for 4 to 5 minutes longer, or until the vegetables are tender.

3 Meanwhile, coarsely chop the tomatoes.

4 Add the chopped tomatoes with their reserved purée and the tomato paste to the skillet. Increase the heat to high and bring to a boil, stirring frequently. Reduce the heat to medium-low, cover and simmer, stirring occasionally, for 5 minutes. Uncover the pot and simmer for 5 minutes longer, or until the flavors are blended.

5 Stir in the chicken and simmer, uncovered, stirring occasionally, for 6 to 8 minutes longer, or until the chicken is cooked through. Serve the chicken cacciatore over the rice.

Preparation time 15 minutes • **Total time** 50 minutes • **Per serving** 368 calories, 7.3 g. fat (18% of calories), 1.4 g. saturated fat, 71 mg. cholesterol, 470 mg. sodium, 2.8 g. dietary fiber, 127 mg. calcium, 4 mg. iron, 78 mg. vitamin C, 2 mg. beta-carotene • **Serves 4**

SAUTÉED CHICKEN WITH PLUMS

1 teaspoon grated lemon zest

½ teaspoon dried thyme, crumbled

¼ teaspoon salt

¼ teaspoon freshly ground
black pepper

⅛ teaspoon ground nutmeg

1 pound skinless, boneless
chicken breast halves (4)

1 tablespoon olive oil

12 ounces ripe plums, cut into
½-inch wedges

⅓ cup apple juice

⅓ cup defatted chicken broth

3 tablespoons plum jam

1 teaspoon fresh lemon juice

2 teaspoons cornstarch, dissolved
in 1 tablespoon cold water

Fresh thyme sprigs for garnish
(optional)

Different varieties of plums will subtly alter the taste of this sauté: Santa Rosas and Casselmans are on the tart side, while Tragedy and Queen Ann plums are sweeter. Be careful not to overcook the plums; the time required will depend on their type and ripeness.

1 In a cup, mix the lemon zest, thyme, salt, pepper and nutmeg. Sprinkle the mixture over both sides of the chicken.

2 In a large, heavy no-stick skillet, warm the oil over medium-high heat. Add the chicken, skinned side down, and reduce the heat to medium. Sauté for 4 to 6 minutes per side, or until cooked through. Transfer the chicken to a clean plate and cover loosely with foil to keep warm.

3 Add the plums to the skillet and sauté for 1 minute, or until they start to soften. Add the apple juice, broth, jam and lemon juice, and bring to a boil. Reduce the heat to medium-low, cover the skillet and simmer, stirring occasionally, for 2 to 3 minutes, or until the plums have softened; be careful not to let them turn mushy.

4 Pour any chicken juices that have collected on the plate into the skillet and then stir in the cornstarch mixture. Increase the heat to medium and cook, stirring constantly but gently to keep the plums intact, until the mixture comes to a boil and thickens. Remove the skillet from the heat.

5 Place the chicken breasts on dinner plates. Spoon the plums and sauce over the chicken and garnish with thyme sprigs, if desired.

Preparation time 12 minutes • **Total time** 30 minutes • **Per serving** 254 calories, 5.5 g. fat (19% of calories), 0.9 g. saturated fat, 66 mg. cholesterol, 297 mg. sodium, 1.9 g. dietary fiber, 27 mg. calcium, 1.3 mg. iron, 20 mg. vitamin C, 0.2 mg. beta-carotene • **Serves 4**

❧ ❧ ❧

ON THE MENU
Serve the chicken with couscous or rice, topped with a little of the plum sauce.

Carrot sticks or sliced yellow summer squash or zucchini, simply steamed, make a colorful complement to the chicken.

PEPPER CHICKEN WITH PENNE

3 garlic cloves, crushed through a press

¾ teaspoon coarsely ground black pepper

¼ teaspoon crushed red pepper flakes

¼ teaspoon salt

12 ounces skinless, boneless chicken breast halves, cut crosswise into thin slices

1 tablespoon olive oil, preferably extra-virgin

8 ounces penne pasta

1 medium red bell pepper, cut into thin strips

1 medium green bell pepper, cut into thin strips

1 medium yellow bell pepper, cut into thin strips

1 can (16 ounces) tomatoes in juice, drained and coarsely chopped

½ cup defatted chicken broth

There are no less than five peppers in this recipe—black pepper, red pepper flakes and red, green and yellow bell peppers. Of course, the bell peppers are all the same vegetable, but they differ slightly in flavor; the yellow and red peppers are sweeter than the green. If all three colors are not available, feel free to prepare the recipe using whatever bell peppers are in your market.

1 Bring a large covered pot of water to a boil over high heat.

2 Meanwhile, on a plate, mix the garlic, black pepper, red pepper flakes and salt; add the chicken and toss until well coated.

3 In a large no-stick skillet, warm 1½ teaspoons of the oil over high heat. Add the chicken and stir-fry for 2 to 3 minutes, or until lightly browned and cooked through. Transfer the chicken to a clean plate.

4 Add the pasta to the boiling water and return to a boil. Cook for 10 to 12 minutes, or according to package directions until al dente. Drain the pasta in a colander and transfer to a warmed serving bowl.

5 Add the remaining 1½ teaspoons oil to the skillet and warm over medium-high heat. Add all the bell peppers to the skillet and stir-fry for 3 to 4 minutes, or until the peppers start to soften and brown. Add the tomatoes and broth, and bring to a boil. Reduce the heat to low, cover and simmer, stirring occasionally, for 3 to 4 minutes, or until the peppers are very tender.

6 Return the chicken to the skillet, adding any juices that have collected on the plate. Cover the skillet and simmer for 3 minutes, or until the chicken is heated through and the flavors are blended. Pour the chicken mixture over the pasta and toss to mix.

Preparation time 20 minutes • **Total time** 40 minutes • **Per serving** 380 calories, 6 g. fat (14% of calories), 1 g. saturated fat, 49 mg. cholesterol, 504 mg. sodium, 3.2 g. dietary fiber, 62 mg. calcium, 4 mg. iron, 87 mg. vitamin C, 1 mg. beta-carotene • **Serves 4**

CHICKEN PROVENÇALE

1 tablespoon extra-virgin olive oil

1 large red bell pepper, cut into thin strips

½ cup thinly sliced shallots

¾ teaspoon dried thyme, crumbled

½ teaspoon dried rosemary, crumbled

½ teaspoon freshly ground black pepper

⅛ teaspoon salt

¼ cup defatted chicken broth

12 ounces skinless, boneless chicken breasts, cut crosswise into ½-inch-wide strips

1 medium zucchini, halved lengthwise and cut crosswise into ¼-inch slices

½ cup coarsely chopped fresh basil

8 kalamata olives, sliced off pits

8 thin slices crusty French bread (about ½ ounce each)

1 garlic clove, peeled and halved

As a change from pasta, potatoes or rice, you can make bread the carbohydrate component of a meal. There are so many types of bread to choose from: French *baguettes* and *boules*, Italian loaves, round peasant breads, whole-grain, fruit and nut breads. Garlic-rubbed slices of toasted French bread complement this chicken and vegetable sauté, robust with herbs and olives.

1 In a large, heavy skillet, warm the oil over medium-high heat. Add the bell peppers, shallots, thyme, rosemary, black pepper and salt, and sauté for 2 to 3 minutes, or until the shallots begin to brown. Drizzle in 2 tablespoons of the broth; reduce the heat to medium-low, cover and simmer, stirring once or twice, for 2 to 3 minutes, or until the bell peppers are tender.

2 Add the chicken and zucchini to the skillet and drizzle in the remaining 2 tablespoons broth; increase the heat to high and stir-fry for 4 to 5 minutes, or until the chicken is cooked through and the zucchini is tender. Remove the skillet from the heat; add the basil and olives, and toss to mix. Cover and let stand while you prepare the garlic toasts.

3 Turn on the broiler (or a toaster oven). Place the bread on a baking sheet and broil 4 to 5 inches from the heat for 2 to 4 minutes, or until the top surface is lightly toasted.

4 Rub the tops of the toasts with the cut sides of the garlic clove. Serve the chicken sauté with the toasts.

Preparation time 20 minutes • **Total time** 40 minutes • **Per serving** 250 calories, 6.8 g. fat (24% of calories), 1.1 g. saturated fat, 49 mg. cholesterol, 451 mg. sodium, 1.9 g. dietary fiber, 113 mg. calcium, 3.6 mg. iron, 56 mg. vitamin C, 1 mg. beta-carotene • **Serves 4**

SUBSTITUTION
A half-cup of thinly sliced onions can stand in for the shallots. If necessary, use black olives instead of kalamatas.

ON THE MENU
For a Provençal-style dessert, serve orange or lemon sorbet in halved, hollowed-out orange or lemon shells.

TURKEY WITH CRANBERRY-ORANGE SAUCE

¾ teaspoon dried sage, crumbled

¾ teaspoon coarsely cracked black pepper

¼ teaspoon salt

1 pound thin-sliced turkey breast cutlets (4)

2 cups fresh or frozen cranberries

½ medium navel orange, scrubbed (but not peeled) and cut into small dice

¼ cup water

¼ cup no-sugar-added orange marmalade

2 tablespoons frozen orange juice concentrate

1 tablespoon granulated sugar

⅛ teaspoon ground cinnamon

1 tablespoon olive oil

With a wide variety of ready-to-cook turkey parts available at most supermarkets, this low-fat meat has become tremendously popular. You can choose from drumsticks, wings or thighs, boneless or bone-in breasts, breast cutlets (slices) and tenderloins (fillets). Thin-sliced cutlets are the quickest to cook.

1 In a cup, mix the sage, pepper and salt. Sprinkle both sides of the turkey cutlets with this mixture; cover and set aside.

2 In a heavy medium saucepan, stir together the cranberries, diced orange, water, marmalade, orange juice concentrate, sugar and cinnamon. Bring to a boil over high heat, stirring frequently. Reduce the heat to medium-low, cover and simmer for 4 minutes.

3 Uncover the pot and simmer, stirring occasionally, for 3 to 4 minutes longer, or until the cranberries have popped and softened and the sauce is thickened. Remove from the heat and cover to keep warm.

4 In a large no-stick skillet, warm the oil over high heat. Add the turkey, in batches, and sauté for 1½ to 3 minutes per side, or until browned and cooked through. Serve the turkey with the cranberry sauce.

Preparation time 10 minutes • **Total time** 30 minutes • **Per serving** 261 calories, 4.3 g. fat (15% of calories), 0.7 g. saturated fat, 70 mg. cholesterol, 192 mg. sodium, 0.6 g. dietary fiber, 31 mg. calcium, 2 mg. iron, 30 mg. vitamin C, 0 mg. beta-carotene
Serves 4

To crush peppercorns, spread them on a cutting board; lay the flat of a broad knife blade on them and rap it sharply with the heel of your hand.

MARKET AND PANTRY
Stock up on cranberries when they are most available—in the fall through the winter holidays. Cranberries keep for about a month in the refrigerator, and for up to a year in the freezer, in the unopened bag. Because the berries are dry packed, they pour readily from the bag when frozen; it's not necessary to thaw them before cooking. If you use a standard recipe for cranberry sauce (such as the one on the bag), you can reduce the sugar considerably and still have a tasty sauce. The sauce can also be sweetened with frozen fruit juice concentrates or with the addition of fruits such as pears or raisins.

HEAD START
Make the cranberry sauce ahead of time and serve it either warm or cold. If you like, make a double batch so you have some extra to serve at other meals.

SOUTHWESTERN CHICKEN SAUTÉ

- 1 tablespoon chili powder
- 1¼ teaspoons ground cumin
- ¼ teaspoon salt
- ⅛ teaspoon ground red pepper
- 1 pound skinless, boneless chicken breast halves (4)
- 2 teaspoons olive oil
- ½ cup defatted chicken broth
- 1 tablespoon cider vinegar
- 8 ounces ripe plum tomatoes, diced
- 1 cup frozen corn kernels
- 1 can (4 ounces) mild green chilies, rinsed and drained
- ¼ cup chopped fresh cilantro
- 1 lime, cut into wedges

Cilantro, or Chinese parsley, looks something like flat-leaf parsley. If you're not sure which is which, crush a leaf between your fingers—the aroma of cilantro is unmistakable.

The chicken is topped with a super-chunky warm "salsa" made with tomatoes, corn and chilies. A quick chili rub gets the chicken off to a flavorful start, and more of the chili mixture goes into the sauce. Chili powder is a spice blend, but ground red pepper is unadulterated "heat": Leave it out if you want a milder dish.

1 In a cup, mix the chili powder, cumin, salt and pepper. Rub both sides of the chicken breasts with 1 tablespoon of the spice mixture.

2 In a large, heavy no-stick skillet, warm the oil over medium-high heat. Add the chicken and sauté for 2 to 3 minutes per side, or until the spice coating is browned and the surface of the chicken is opaque. (The chicken will finish cooking later.) Transfer the chicken to a clean plate.

3 Add the broth, vinegar and the remaining spice mixture to the skillet; increase the heat to high and bring to a boil, stirring to get up the browned bits from the bottom of the skillet. Boil for 1 to 2 minutes, or until the liquid is slightly reduced.

4 Return the chicken to the skillet, adding any juices that have collected on the plate. Add the tomatoes, corn and chilies, and bring to a simmer. Spoon the corn and tomato mixture over the chicken; reduce the heat to medium, cover and simmer, stirring once or twice, for 5 minutes, or until the chicken is cooked through and the flavors are blended. Transfer the chicken and vegetables to a serving dish and sprinkle with the cilantro.

5 Serve the chicken and vegetables with the lime wedges.

Preparation time 10 minutes • **Total time** 30 minutes • **Per serving** 214 calories, 4.9 g. fat (20% of calories), 0.7 g. saturated fat, 66 mg. cholesterol, 410 mg. sodium, 2.6 g. dietary fiber, 37 mg. calcium, 2 mg. iron, 21 mg. vitamin C, 0.7 mg. beta-carotene • **Serves 4**

ON THE MENU
The perfect partner for the chicken and vegetables is a corn or flour tortilla or a slice of cornbread. And serve a salad of chilled blanched green beans and ripe tomato wedges with a vinaigrette dressing.

Pasta with Poultry

❧ ❧ ❧

QUICK-COOKING CHICKEN

AND TURKEY TURN PASTA

INTO HEARTY DINNERS, SATISFYING

SALADS AND MORE

PEPPER-SAUCED PENNE WITH SAUSAGE

3 medium red bell peppers, halved and cored

1 green bell pepper, halved and cored

1 yellow bell pepper, halved and cored

1 medium onion, sliced

6 ounces hot or sweet turkey sausage, cut into ½-inch slices

3 garlic cloves, sliced

1 teaspoon olive oil

⅓ cup defatted reduced-sodium chicken broth

8 ounces penne pasta

¼ teaspoon freshly ground black pepper

Readily available turkey sausage comes in both hot and sweet varieties, just as pork sausage does. For this recipe, use either one alone or a combination of the two.

1 Bring a large covered pot of water to a boil over high heat. Preheat the broiler. Spray the broiler-pan rack with no-stick spray.

2 While the water comes to a boil, arrange the bell peppers and onions on the prepared broiler rack and broil 4 to 5 inches from the heat, turning once, for 10 minutes, or until the peppers and onions are tender and lightly charred. Transfer the broiled vegetables to a plate.

3 Arrange the sausage in a single layer on the broiler-pan rack and broil, turning once, for 10 minutes, or until the sausage is lightly browned and cooked through. Remove from the heat.

4 While the sausage is cooking, in a small skillet combine the sliced garlic and the oil, and sauté, stirring constantly, for 1 to 2 minutes, or just until the garlic is lightly browned. Transfer the garlic to a plate.

5 Peel or scrape the charred skin from the peppers. Place the 3 red peppers, the onion, browned garlic and the broth in a food processor and process until puréed. Cut the green and yellow peppers into thin strips; set aside.

6 Add the pasta to the boiling water, return to a boil and cook for 10 to 12 minutes or according to package directions until al dente. Reserving ½ cup of the cooking liquid, drain the pasta in a colander.

7 Combine the red pepper purée, reserved cooking liquid, sausage and black pepper in the pasta cooking pot and bring to a boil over high heat; cook for 1 to 2 minutes to heat the sausage through. Add the pasta and roasted pepper strips, and toss until coated with sauce.

Preparation time 11 minutes • **Total time** 40 minutes • **Per serving** 337 calories, 6.9 g. fat (18% of calories), 2 g. saturated fat, 26 mg. cholesterol, 322 mg. sodium, 3.5 g. dietary fiber, 38 mg. calcium, 3 mg. iron, 142 mg. vitamin C, 2 mg. beta-carotene
Serves 4

SESAME NOODLES WITH LEMON CHICKEN

8 ounces thin-sliced chicken cutlets

1 tablespoon plus 1 teaspoon reduced-sodium soy sauce

1 tablespoon plus 1 teaspoon fresh lemon juice

1½ teaspoons grated fresh ginger

¼ teaspoon freshly ground black pepper

8 ounces spaghetti

2 tablespoons reduced-fat peanut butter

2 tablespoons defatted chicken broth

1 teaspoon dark sesame oil

¼ teaspoon crushed red pepper flakes

1 cup julienne-cut unpeeled kirby cucumbers

½ cup shredded carrots

¼ cup diagonally sliced scallions

To julienne the cucumbers, cut off the ends and then halve the cucumbers crosswise. Quarter each half lengthwise, then cut it into thin sticks.

Szechuan restaurants continue to flourish in the United States, with sesame noodles one of their most popular dishes. Chinese cooks use a rich golden sesame paste, but here, a mixture of peanut butter and fragrant dark sesame oil produces a remarkably similar flavor. The noodles can be served either warm or chilled.

1 Bring a large covered pot of water to a boil over high heat. Meanwhile, preheat the broiler and spray a jelly-roll pan with no-stick spray.

2 Arrange the chicken in a single layer in the prepared pan and drizzle with 2 teaspoons of the soy sauce, 1 teaspoon of the lemon juice, 1 teaspoon of the ginger and the black pepper. Rub the seasonings into the surface; cover and let stand while you cook the pasta.

3 Add the pasta to the boiling water, return to a boil and cook for 8 to 10 minutes or according to package directions until al dente. Reserving ¼ cup of the cooking liquid, drain the pasta in a colander.

4 Broil the chicken 4 to 5 inches from the heat for 6 to 7 minutes, or until the chicken is lightly browned and cooked through. Remove from the broiler.

5 In a small bowl, whisk together 3 tablespoons of the reserved pasta cooking liquid, the peanut butter, broth, sesame oil, red pepper flakes, the remaining 2 teaspoons soy sauce, remaining 1 tablespoon lemon juice and remaining ½ teaspoon ginger.

6 Place the pasta in a serving bowl. Cut the chicken into strips and add the chicken and any juices from the pan to the pasta. Pour the peanut sauce over the chicken, add the cucumber, carrots and scallions, and toss to mix. If the pasta seems a bit dry, add the remaining tablespoon of pasta cooking liquid or a little boiling water.

Preparation time 20 minutes • **Total time** 40 minutes • **Per serving** 350 calories, 6.1 g. fat (16% of calories), 1 g. saturated fat, 33 mg. cholesterol, 313 mg. sodium, 2.5 g. dietary fiber, 31 mg. calcium, 3 mg. iron, 7 mg. vitamin C, 2.4 mg. beta-carotene
Serves 4

CHICKEN CACCIATORE PASTA

1 tablespoon extra-virgin olive oil

1 large onion, sliced

3 garlic cloves, minced

½ teaspoon dried thyme, crumbled

½ teaspoon freshly ground black pepper

1 bay leaf, preferably imported

¼ teaspoon dried rosemary, crumbled

⅛ teaspoon salt

10 ounces small fresh mushrooms, quartered

2 tablespoons defatted chicken broth

1 can (16 ounces) crushed tomatoes in purée

2 tablespoons dry white wine (optional)

8 ounces cavatelli or other macaroni

8 ounces boneless, skinless chicken breast halves, cut into ½-inch chunks

The word *cacciatore* (hunter) suggests the sort of hearty dish that a hunter might put together after a day in the forests and fields. The main ingredient would be game (here updated with chicken), and the robust accompaniments traditionally include onions, tomatoes, mushrooms, garlic and wine.

1 Bring a large covered pot of water to a boil over high heat.

2 Meanwhile, heat the oil in a large, heavy skillet over high heat. Add the onions and garlic, and sauté for 3 to 4 minutes, or until the onions are tender and very lightly browned. Stir in the thyme, pepper, bay leaf, rosemary and salt, and cook, stirring constantly, for 30 seconds.

3 Stir in the mushrooms and broth and bring to a boil. Reduce the heat to medium-high and cook, stirring frequently, for 4 to 5 minutes, or until the mushrooms are tender. Stir in the tomatoes and the wine (if using), and return to a boil. Reduce the heat to low, cover and simmer for 10 minutes to blend the flavors.

4 Add the pasta to the boiling water, return to a boil and cook for 10 to 12 minutes or according to package directions until al dente. Drain in a colander.

5 Add the chicken to the sauce; increase the heat to medium, cover and simmer, stirring frequently, for 5 to 8 minutes longer, or until the chicken is cooked through. Remove and discard the bay leaf.

6 Transfer the pasta to a warmed serving bowl, spoon the sauce over the pasta and toss to mix.

Preparation time 15 minutes • **Total time** 45 minutes • **Per serving** 378 calories, 5.6 g. fat (13% of calories), 0.9 g. saturated fat, 33 mg. cholesterol, 326 mg. sodium, 3.2 g. dietary fiber, 84 mg. calcium, 4 mg. iron, 26 mg. vitamin C, 0.5 mg. beta-carotene • **Serves 4**

SMOKED TURKEY CARBONARA

8 ounces linguine

8 ounces asparagus, sliced diagonally into 1-inch pieces

2 large eggs

3 large egg whites

¼ cup skim milk

2 tablespoons grated Parmesan cheese

2 tablespoons chopped fresh Italian parsley

½ teaspoon freshly ground black pepper

⅛ teaspoon salt

Large pinch of ground nutmeg, preferably freshly grated

Large pinch of ground red pepper

3 ounces smoked turkey, cut into julienne

1 tablespoon olive oil

The term *carbonara* describes dishes cooked with bacon or ham; the best-known of these dishes is *pasta alla carbonara*, a luxuriously rich creation that calls for pancetta (an Italian cured bacon), Parmesan or Romano cheese, heavy cream—and one whole egg per serving. For this version, smoked turkey stands in for pancetta and skim milk substitutes for cream; two eggs (combined with two egg whites, which are virtually fat-free) serve four.

1 Bring a large covered pot of water to a boil over high heat. Add the pasta to the boiling water, return to a boil and cook, stirring frequently, for 9 to 11 minutes or according to package directions. Two minutes before the pasta is done, add the asparagus and cook until the asparagus is crisp-tender and the pasta is al dente. Drain the pasta and asparagus in a colander and rinse briefly under cold running water; drain again.

2 In a large bowl, whisk together the eggs, egg whites, milk, Parmesan, parsley, black pepper, salt, nutmeg and red pepper until well blended. Stir in the turkey. Add the pasta and asparagus, and toss, using 2 spoons, until the spaghetti is coated with the egg mixture.

3 In a large no-stick skillet, warm the oil over high heat. Add the pasta mixture and cook, tossing constantly with 2 wooden spoons, for 2 to 3 minutes, or until the eggs have set into small clumps and the pasta is hot.

Preparation time 10 minutes • **Total time** 20 minutes • **Per serving** 347 calories, 8.5 g. fat (22% of calories), 2.2 g. saturated fat, 120 mg. cholesterol, 428 mg. sodium, 2.1 g. dietary fiber, 103 mg. calcium, 3 mg. iron, 21 mg. vitamin C, 0.5 mg. beta-carotene • **Serves 4**

❧ ❧ ❧

Intensely fragrant freshly grated nutmeg makes a tremendous difference in both savory and sweet dishes. This miniature grater is specially made for nutmeg.

KITCHEN TIPS
Cooking the asparagus in the same pot with the pasta is a time-saver, but be sure to add the asparagus gradually so the water does not stop boiling.

MARKET AND PANTRY
Smoked turkey, cured over flavorful woods such as mesquite or apple, is widely available. Keep it well wrapped so its assertive aroma does not permeate other foods.

TURKEY TETRAZZINI

8 ounces wide egg noodles

1½ cups defatted reduced-sodium chicken broth

1 cup 1% low-fat milk

3 tablespoons cornstarch

½ teaspoon freshly ground black pepper

½ teaspoon dried thyme, crumbled

⅛ teaspoon salt

4 tablespoons grated Parmesan cheese

1½ teaspoons dry sherry (optional)

1 tablespoon unsalted butter or margarine

8 ounces fresh mushrooms, sliced

¾ cup thinly sliced scallions

4 ounces skinless roast turkey breast, cut into matchstick strips about the same length as the noodles

The name of Italian opera diva Luisa Tetrazzini lives on in the baked pasta dish created in her honor. An admiring chef devised a dinner of spaghetti, chicken and mushrooms in a sherried cream sauce, topped with Parmesan and baked until golden. Turkey is often substituted for chicken in the dish; to lighten this particular rendition, a mixture of low-fat milk and cornstarch takes the place of the cream sauce.

1 Preheat the oven to 450°. Spray a 9 x 9-inch or 11 x 7-inch baking dish with no-stick spray.

2 Bring a large covered pot of water to a boil over high heat. Add the noodles to the boiling water, return to a boil and cook for 5 to 6 minutes (the noodles should be slightly underdone). Drain in a colander and rinse briefly under gently running cold water to keep the noodles from sticking; drain again.

3 Meanwhile, in a medium saucepan, whisk together the broth, milk, cornstarch, pepper, thyme and salt. Bring to a boil over high heat, whisking constantly. Cook, stirring, until the sauce is thickened and smooth. Remove from the heat and stir in 3 tablespoons of the Parmesan and the sherry (if using).

4 In the pasta cooking pot, melt the butter or margarine over medium-high heat. Add the mushrooms and scallions, and sauté for 2 to 4 minutes, or until the mushrooms are tender (the pan will be dry at first; keep stirring and the mushrooms will release their liquid). Remove the pot from the heat and stir in the noodles, sauce and turkey. Toss until mixed, then transfer to the prepared pan.

5 Sprinkle the surface with the remaining 1 tablespoon Parmesan. Bake for 15 minutes, or until the sauce is bubbly and the top of the casserole is lightly browned.

Preparation time 10 minutes • **Total time** 45 minutes • **Per serving** 397 calories, 10 g. fat (23% of calories), 4.3 g. saturated fat, 91 mg. cholesterol, 493 mg. sodium, 2.8 g. dietary fiber, 206 mg. calcium, 4 mg. iron, 6 mg. vitamin C, 0.2 mg. beta-carotene • **Serves 4**

TURKISH-STYLE PASTA WITH CHICKEN

1 **cup plain nonfat yogurt**

¾ **cup defatted reduced-sodium chicken broth**

8 **ounces boneless, skinless chicken breast halves, cut crosswise into ½-inch strips**

6 **ounces wide egg noodles**

8 **ounces green beans, trimmed and cut into 1-inch lengths**

2 **medium kirby cucumbers, scrubbed, trimmed and thinly sliced**

⅓ **cup finely chopped red onions**

1½ **teaspoons ground cumin**

¼ **teaspoon ground coriander**

¼ **teaspoon turmeric**

¼ **teaspoon freshly ground black pepper**

¼ **teaspoon salt**

⅛ **teaspoon ground red pepper**

The refreshing combination of cucumbers and yogurt appears on tables all over the Near East and Asia Minor, often as chilled soups or creamy sauces. Here, yogurt (briefly drained to thicken it) is mixed with thinly sliced cucumbers, chopped onions, cumin, coriander and turmeric to serve as a sauce for egg noodles, poached chicken strips and green beans.

1 Bring a large covered pot of water to a boil over high heat.

2 Meanwhile, spoon the yogurt into a cheesecloth-lined strainer suspended over a bowl and let drain for 15 minutes.

3 While the yogurt drains, bring the broth to a boil in a covered, deep, medium skillet over high heat. Add the chicken breasts, reduce the heat to medium-low, cover and simmer, turning often, for 3 to 4 minutes, or until the chicken is cooked through. Using a slotted spoon, transfer the chicken to a plate; cover loosely to keep it moist. Boil the broth over high heat for 7 to 8 minutes, or until it is reduced to about 1 tablespoon of caramel-colored syrup.

4 Add the noodles and green beans to the boiling water; return to a boil and cook for 5 to 6 minutes or according to package directions until the noodles are al dente and the beans are tender. Drain the noodles and beans in a colander; transfer to a warmed serving bowl.

5 In a small bowl, mix the yogurt, cucumbers, onions, cumin, coriander, turmeric, black pepper, salt and red pepper. Pour the sauce over the noodles, add the chicken and reduced broth, and toss well.

Preparation time 15 minutes • **Total time** 35 minutes • **Per serving** 290 calories, 3 g. fat (10% of calories), 0.7 g. saturated fat, 74 mg. cholesterol, 351 mg. sodium, 2.7 g. dietary fiber, 169 mg. calcium, 4 mg. iron, 13 mg. vitamin C, 0.3 mg. beta-carotene • **Serves 4**

ON THE MENU
Precede this meal with a Near-Eastern appetizer, such as a dip made of roasted eggplant and garlic served with crisp baked pita triangles.

KITCHEN TIPS
The slicing slot on a metal grater—if it is sufficiently sharp—can be used to slice the cucumbers. Otherwise, cut them by hand or with a mechanical slicer.

FETTUCCINE WITH TURKEY "SAUSAGE"

- **8 ounces boneless, skinless turkey breast, cut into chunks**
- **½ teaspoon freshly ground black pepper**
- **½ teaspoon dried thyme**
- **¼ teaspoon dried sage or ¾ teaspoon minced fresh sage**
- **¼ teaspoon fennel seed**
- **¼ teaspoon crushed red pepper flakes**
- **2 teaspoons olive oil**
- **1 large onion, chopped**
- **2 garlic cloves, minced**
- **¾ cup defatted reduced-sodium chicken broth**
- **1 can (16 ounces) whole tomatoes in purée, finely chopped in a food processor or blender**
- **6 ounces fettuccine**

Fresh Italian sausage, an earthy blend of chopped pork, pepper, garlic, sage and fennel, comes in sweet and hot varieties, the latter spiked with red pepper. For a low-fat meal with all the flavor of Italian sausage, ground turkey is combined with the traditional seasonings, cooked with tomatoes and served over fettuccine.

1 Bring a large covered pot of water to a boil over high heat.

2 Meanwhile, process the turkey in a food processor until finely ground. Add the black pepper, thyme, sage, fennel seeds and red pepper flakes, and pulse until blended.

3 Heat the oil in a large, heavy skillet over medium-high heat. Add the onions and garlic, and stir to blend with the oil. Add 2 tablespoons of the broth and sauté for 4 to 5 minutes, or until the onions are tender. Stir in the turkey mixture and 2 tablespoons more broth, and cook, stirring to break up the clumps of turkey, for 2 to 3 minutes, or until the turkey turns white.

4 Stir in the tomatoes and the remaining ½ cup broth and bring to a boil. Reduce the heat to medium-low, cover and simmer, stirring occasionally, for 15 minutes, or until the flavors are blended.

5 Meanwhile, add the pasta to the boiling water, return to a boil and cook for 9 to 11 minutes or according to package directions until al dente. Drain in a colander and transfer to a warmed serving bowl. Pour the sauce over the pasta and toss to mix.

Preparation time 15 minutes • **Total time** 45 minutes • **Per serving** 305 calories, 4.7 g. fat (14% of calories), 0.8 g. saturated fat, 76 mg. cholesterol, 339 mg. sodium, 2.1 g. dietary fiber, 80 mg. calcium, 3 mg. iron, 22 mg. vitamin C, 0.5 mg. beta-carotene • **Serves 4**

As the turkey cooks, its color will change from translucent pink to opaque white.

MARKET AND PANTRY
It's best to grind turkey breast yourself rather than buying ground turkey, which may contain dark meat and skin. You can also have the butcher grind a piece of skinless turkey breast for you. Use ground turkey within a day of purchase, as it is more perishable than uncut poultry.

ON THE MENU
For dessert, offer sliced cantaloupe or honeydew with fresh figs.

FUSILLI, TURKEY AND ORANGE SALAD

8 ounces spinach fusilli

2 navel oranges

2 tablespoons frozen orange juice concentrate

2 tablespoons defatted chicken broth

1 tablespoon extra-virgin olive oil

2 teaspoons balsamic vinegar

¼ teaspoon salt

¼ teaspoon freshly ground black pepper

⅛ teaspoon crushed red pepper flakes

8 ounces thin turkey-breast slices, cut into ½-inch-wide strips

½ cup thinly shredded basil leaves

1½ cups thinly sliced celery or fennel

6 kalamata or ripe olives, sliced off pits

The combination of oranges and olives is distinctly Mediterranean, and orange-and-olive salads are popular in Italy, especially around Rome. Kalamata olives, used here, are available in many supermarkets. Rather than trying to halve and pit the olives, use a sharp paring knife to shave the flesh from the pits.

1 Bring a large covered pot of water to a boil over high heat. Preheat the broiler and spray a jelly-roll pan with no-stick spray.

2 Add the pasta to the boiling water, return to a boil and cook for 10 to 12 minutes or according to package directions until al dente. Drain in a colander and rinse briefly under cold running water; drain again.

3 Meanwhile, with a serrated knife, pare the peel and white pith from the oranges. Working over a medium bowl, cut out the orange sections between the membranes, letting the sections fall into the bowl. Squeeze the juice from the membranes over the oranges. Pour the juice into a salad bowl.

4 To the juice, add the orange juice concentrate, broth, oil, vinegar, ⅛ teaspoon salt, ⅛ teaspoon of the black pepper and the red pepper flakes, and whisk with a fork until blended; set aside.

5 Place the turkey strips in the prepared pan and toss with 2 tablespoons of the basil and the remaining ⅛ teaspoon salt and remaining ⅛ teaspoon black pepper. Arrange the turkey strips in a single layer and broil 3 to 4 inches from the heat for 4 to 5 minutes, turning the pieces once, until cooked through.

6 Add the pasta to the bowl of dressing and toss gently. Add the turkey (and any juices that have collected in the pan), the oranges, celery or fennel, olives and the remaining 6 tablespoons basil, and toss gently to coat.

Preparation time 25 minutes • **Total time** 40 minutes • **Per serving** 385 calories, 5.7 g. fat (13% of calories), 0.9 g. saturated fat, 47 mg. cholesterol, 307 mg. sodium, 8.7 g. dietary fiber, 143 mg. calcium, 4 mg. iron, 57 mg. vitamin C, 0.3 mg. beta-carotene • **Serves 4**

TEX-MEX PASTA BAKE

1 can (14½ ounces) no-salt-added stewed tomatoes

1 can (8 ounces) no-salt-added tomato sauce

½ cup hot or medium salsa

1 can (4 ounces) chopped green chilies, rinsed and drained

1 tablespoon fresh lime juice

1¼ teaspoons ground cumin

¼ teaspoon dried oregano, crumbled

8 ounces rigatoni pasta

1 can (10½ ounces) pinto or red kidney beans, rinsed and drained

½ cup frozen corn kernels

3 ounces skinless roast turkey, diced

2 ounces Monterey Jack cheese, shredded

Here's a dish for hearty appetites. It's a casserole of rigatoni with chunks of turkey, beans and corn kernels in a spicy tomato sauce, topped with velvety Monterey Jack cheese. For even more Tex-Mex flavor, make this pasta dish with pepper-jack cheese, which is Monterey Jack flecked with bits of jalapeño.

1 Preheat the oven to 450°. Spray a 9 x 13-inch baking dish with no-stick spray. Bring a large covered pot of water to a boil over high heat.

2 Meanwhile, in a medium saucepan combine the stewed tomatoes, tomato sauce, salsa, chilies, lime juice, cumin and oregano, and bring to a boil over high heat. Reduce the heat to medium, cover and simmer, stirring occasionally, for 5 minutes.

3 While the sauce simmers, add the pasta to the boiling water, return to a boil and cook for 11 to 13 minutes or according to package directions until al dente. Drain in a colander.

4 While the pasta cooks, add the beans, corn and turkey to the sauce, and bring to a boil; remove the pan from the heat.

5 Return the drained rigatoni to the pasta cooking pot; add the sauce and toss to mix. Transfer to the prepared baking dish and sprinkle with the cheese. Bake for 10 minutes, or until the cheese is melted and the sauce is bubbly.

Preparation time 12 minutes • **Total time** 45 minutes • **Per serving** 415 calories, 6.7 g. fat (14% of calories), 2.8 g. saturated fat, 33 mg. cholesterol, 474 mg. sodium, 7.4 g. dietary fiber, 176 mg. calcium, 5 mg. iron, 47 mg. vitamin C, 1 mg. beta-carotene • **Serves 4**

ON THE MENU
Serve a salad of grated carrots and jicama, a Mexican tuber that looks something like a turnip and tastes like a cross between water chestnuts and apples. Pare jicama with a swivel-bladed vegetable peeler before grating it; dress the salad with lime juice and sprinkle it with chopped cilantro.

HEADSTART
Make the tomato sauce through step 2 in advance. Bring it to a simmer before adding the beans, corn kernels and turkey.

NUTRITION NOTE
Beans and other legumes are excellent sources of both soluble and insoluble fiber.

THAI CHICKEN AND NOODLES

1¼ cups loosely packed cilantro sprigs

¼ cup defatted chicken broth

2 tablespoons fresh lime juice

1 tablespoon plus 1 teaspoon reduced-sodium soy sauce

1 tablespoon grated fresh ginger

2 teaspoons granulated sugar

1 teaspoon dark sesame oil

½ teaspoon crushed red pepper flakes

1 garlic clove, peeled

8 ounces thin-sliced chicken cutlets, cut into strips

8 ounces thin egg noodles or vermicelli

1 large red bell pepper, cut into thin strips

½ cup grated radishes

Use the fine side of a grater for shredding pungent fresh ginger. You need not peel the ginger before grating it.

T hai restaurants are still a relative novelty in the United States, and some Thai ingredients, such as spicy galanga root and citrus-scented lemongrass, are available only in specialty stores. However, these exotic flavors can be approximated, as they are here, with ginger and lime juice.

1 Bring a large covered pot of water to a boil over high heat.

2 Meanwhile, combine the cilantro, broth, lime juice, soy sauce, ginger, sugar, oil and red pepper flakes in a food processor. With the machine running, drop the garlic clove through the feed tube and process until puréed. Put the chicken in a medium bowl, add ¼ cup of the cilantro sauce and toss to mix well. Cover and let stand at room temperature for 10 minutes.

3 Transfer the chicken mixture to a medium no-stick skillet. Cook over medium-high heat, tossing frequently, for 3 to 4 minutes, or until the chicken is cooked through. Remove the pan from the heat.

4 Add the pasta to the boiling water, return to a boil and cook for 2 to 4 minutes or according to package directions until al dente. One minute before the pasta is done, stir in the bell pepper strips. Drain the pasta and peppers in a colander; transfer to a serving bowl.

5 Add the remaining cilantro sauce and the chicken mixture to the noodles, and toss to coat. Scatter the radishes on top.

Preparation time 20 minutes • **Total time** 40 minutes • **Per serving** 317 calories, 4.5 g. fat (13% of calories), 0.8 g. saturated fat, 87 mg. cholesterol, 316 mg. sodium, 2.2 g. dietary fiber, 39 mg. calcium, 3 mg. iron, 55 mg. vitamin C, 1 mg. beta-carotene
Serves 4

MARKET AND PANTRY
Fragrant dark sesame oil, made from toasted sesame seeds, is essential in many Asian cuisines; it is most often used as a seasoning rather than as a cooking oil. it can be found in Asian food stores, gourmet shops and some supermarkets. Do not substitute light sesame oil.

ON THE MENU
For a light first course, serve bowls of broth flavored with ginger and scallions.

RIGATONI WITH HERBED CHICKEN

- 8 ounces boneless, skinless chicken breast halves, cut into ½-inch chunks

- 3 garlic cloves, crushed

- ½ teaspoon dried basil, crumbled

- ¼ teaspoon dried thyme, crumbled

- ¼ teaspoon fennel seeds

- ⅛ teaspoon freshly ground black pepper

- ⅛ teaspoon crushed red pepper flakes

- 2 teaspoons extra-virgin olive oil

- 2 cans (14½ ounces each) no-salt-added tomatoes in juice, coarsely chopped, 1 cup of juice reserved

- 1 tablespoon no-salt-added tomato paste

- 8 ounces rigatoni pasta

- 3 tablespoons chopped fresh basil or 2 tablespoons chopped fresh Italian parsley

- ½ cup part-skim ricotta cheese

Ricotta cheese often goes into the filling for stuffed pastas such as manicotti and ravioli, but it can also be used with quick sauce-topped pastas. Here, part-skim ricotta—which is lower in fat but richer in calcium than whole-milk ricotta—tops a plate of sturdy rigatoni with a chunky chicken and tomato sauce.

1 Bring a large covered pot of water to a boil over high heat.

2 Put the chicken in a medium bowl; add the garlic, basil, thyme, fennel seeds, black pepper and red pepper flakes, and mix well.

3 In a large no-stick skillet, warm the oil over high heat until very hot. Add the chicken chunks, and sauté for 2 to 3 minutes, or until the chicken turns light golden. Stir in the tomatoes and the reserved juice, and the tomato paste, and bring to a boil, stirring to get up any browned bits that have adhered to the bottom of the skillet. Reduce the heat to medium-low and simmer, stirring frequently, for 10 minutes, or until the sauce has thickened slightly.

4 Meanwhile, add the pasta to the boiling water, return to a boil and cook for 12 to 14 minutes or according to package directions until al dente. Reserving ¼ cup of the pasta cooking liquid, drain the rigatoni in a colander.

5 Stir the basil or parsley into the tomato and chicken mixture. Combine the rigatoni and the reserved cooking liquid in a warmed serving bowl. Pour the sauce over the pasta, then top with the ricotta.

Preparation time 15 minutes • **Total time** 35 minutes • **Per serving** 387 calories, 6.9 g. fat (16% of calories), 2.2 g. saturated fat, 42 mg. cholesterol, 110 mg. sodium, 3.2 g. dietary fiber, 184 mg. calcium, 5 mg. iron, 35 mg. vitamin C, 1 mg. beta-carotene • **Serves 4**

FOOD FACTS

Black and red pepper, despite their common name, come from different plants. Black pepper is the dried, unripe berries ("peppercorns") of the *Piper nigrum* vine, while red pepper flakes are dried, crushed chili peppers, which, like bell peppers, belong to the *Capsicum* family.

ON THE MENU

Serve a tricolor salad made with Belgian endive, arugula and radicchio.

SPICY CHICKEN AND PASTA SALAD

½ cup defatted reduced-sodium chicken broth

6 ounces boneless, skinless chicken breast halves, cut crosswise into ½-inch-thick strips

8 ounces gemelli or fusilli pasta

2 cups small broccoli florets

1 cup carrot sticks

1 cup snow peas

¼ cup loosely packed Italian parsley sprigs

2 scallions, cut up

1 fresh jalapeño pepper, halved, seeded and cut into chunks

3 tablespoons reduced-fat mayonnaise

2 tablespoons nonfat sour cream

1 tablespoon fresh lemon juice

The pasta called *gemelli* is made up of two short strands twisted together at one end—hence the name, which means "twins." You may not find gemelli in your supermarket, but fusilli or rotini would provide an equally good foil for the creamy, chili-laced dressing, strips of chicken and crisp-tender vegetables.

1 Bring a large covered pot of water to a boil over high heat.

2 Meanwhile, bring the broth to a boil in a covered medium skillet over high heat. Stir in the chicken strips, return to a boil and reduce the heat to low; cover and simmer, turning occasionally, for 3 to 4 minutes, or until the chicken is cooked through. With a slotted spoon, transfer the chicken to a plate; cover chicken loosely with foil. Increase the heat to high and boil the broth for 3 to 5 minutes, or until reduced to a syrupy consistency. Remove the pan from the heat.

3 While the broth is cooking down, add the pasta to the boiling water and return to a boil; cook for 8 to 10 minutes or according to package directions until al dente. About 4 minutes before the pasta is done, add the broccoli and carrots. One minute before the pasta is done, add the snow peas. Cook until the vegetables are crisp-tender and the pasta is done. Drain in a colander and cool under cold running water; drain again. Transfer the pasta and vegetables to a salad bowl.

4 Combine the parsley, scallions, jalapeño, mayonnaise, sour cream, lemon juice and the reduced broth in a food processor, and process until puréed.

5 Pour the dressing over the salad, add the chicken and toss to mix.

To string a snow-pea pod, pinch the stem end with your fingers, then pull downward on the string.

Preparation time 20 minutes • **Total time** 35 minutes • **Per serving** 348 calories, 4.9 g. fat (13% of calories), 1 g. saturated fat, 28 mg. cholesterol, 207 mg. sodium, 5.8 g. dietary fiber, 87 mg. calcium, 4 mg. iron, 88 mg. vitamin C, 5.5 mg. beta-carotene • **Serves 4**

TURKEY-MACARONI CASSEROLE

8 ounces macaroni, such as elbows

4 ounces fresh mushrooms, sliced

3 tablespoons defatted chicken broth

8 ounces part-skim ricotta cheese

2 ounces shredded part-skim mozzarella cheese

2 large egg whites

2 tablespoons grated Parmesan cheese

2 tablespoons skim milk

1/4 teaspoon freshly ground black pepper

4 ounces skinless roast turkey breast, diced

1/2 cup coarsely chopped fresh basil leaves

1 can (8 ounces) no-salt-added tomato sauce

Macaroni-with-meat casseroles have a long history in America, and these days they are often made with a packaged mix. But for flavor and nutrition, nothing beats a homemade noodle bake put together from fresh ingredients.

1 Preheat the oven to 375°. Spray an 11 x 7-inch baking dish with no-stick spray.

2 Bring a large covered pot of water to a boil over high heat. Add the pasta to the boiling water, return to a boil and cook for 6 to 7 minutes or according to package directions until al dente. Drain in a colander, rinse briefly under cold running water and drain again.

3 While the pasta is cooking, combine the mushrooms and broth in a large no-stick skillet. Bring the broth to a boil over high heat and sauté for 4 to 6 minutes, or until the mushrooms are tender. Remove the skillet from the heat.

4 In a large bowl combine the ricotta, mozzarella, egg whites, Parmesan, milk and pepper; beat together with a wooden spoon until well blended. Stir in the mushrooms and their broth, the turkey and basil, then add the drained pasta. Spoon the mixture into the prepared baking dish.

5 Pour the tomato sauce over the pasta mixture and bake for 20 to 25 minutes, or until hot and bubbly.

Preparation time 15 minutes • **Total time** 55 minutes • **Per serving** 421 calories, 9.3 g. fat (20% of calories), 4.9 g. saturated fat, 51 mg. cholesterol, 294 mg. sodium, 2.6 g. dietary fiber, 354 mg. calcium, 5 mg. iron, 11 mg. vitamin C, 0.6 mg. beta-carotene • **Serves 4**

Using skinless turkey breast instead of beef in this casserole keeps the fat content healthfully low.

FOOD FACT

Ricotta cheese was originally made by cooking the whey drained off during the production of other types of cheese. Today, this versatile cheese is made by combining whey with whole or skim milk.

KITCHEN TIPS

Many foods, like the mushrooms in this recipe, can be sautéed without fat, using broth, wine, juice or even water instead of oil or butter. A no-stick pan is an asset when you use this fat-cutting technique.

PASTA CAESAR SALAD WITH CHICKEN

3 tablespoons nonfat mayonnaise

1 ounce Parmesan cheese, coarsely grated

2 tablespoons Italian parsley sprigs

1 tablespoon plus 1 teaspoon fresh lemon juice

1 tablespoon defatted reduced-sodium chicken broth

2 garlic cloves, crushed

1 teaspoon anchovy paste

½ teaspoon freshly ground black pepper

6 ounces cavatappi pasta

8 ounces thin-sliced chicken cutlets, cut into 1-inch pieces

⅛ teaspoon salt

1 bunch arugula or watercress, washed, tough stems removed

Caesar salad is said to have been created in the 1920s by chef Caesar Cardini, owner of a restaurant in Tijuana, Mexico. The greens, garlicky dressing and a lightly cooked egg are often tossed together with a flourish at tableside. For this variation, Caesar dressing, flavored with anchovy paste and Parmesan, is tossed with pasta, tart greens and morsels of broiled chicken.

1 Bring a large covered pot of water to a boil over high heat. Preheat the broiler. Spray a jelly-roll pan with no-stick spray.

2 Meanwhile, combine the mayonnaise, 1 tablespoon of the Parmesan, the parsley sprigs, 1 tablespoon of the lemon juice, the broth, half of the garlic, the anchovy paste and ¼ teaspoon of the pepper in a food processor or blender, and process until smooth.

3 Add the pasta to the boiling water, return to a boil and cook for 8 to 10 minutes or according to package directions until al dente. Drain in a colander and cool briefly under cold running water; drain again.

4 Place the chicken in the prepared pan. Drizzle the remaining 1 teaspoon lemon juice over the chicken. Sprinkle with the remaining crushed garlic, the remaining ¼ teaspoon pepper and the salt, and toss to mix. Broil 3 to 4 inches from the heat for 3 to 5 minutes, or until the chicken is cooked through and lightly browned. Remove from the heat.

5 Transfer the pasta to a salad bowl. Add the arugula or watercress, the dressing, the chicken and any juices that have collected in the pan, and the remaining Parmesan. Toss to coat well.

Preparation time 15 minutes • **Total time** 30 minutes • **Per serving** 274 calories, 3.9 g. fat (13% of calories), 1.7 g. saturated fat, 39 mg. cholesterol, 394 mg. sodium, 2.1 g. dietary fiber, 172 mg. calcium, 2 mg. iron, 23 mg. vitamin C, 1.3 mg. beta-carotene • **Serves 4**

GARLICKY SPAGHETTI WITH TURKEY

8 ounces perciatelli or spaghetti

8 ounces green beans, trimmed and cut in half

1 tablespoon plus 1 teaspoon extra-virgin olive oil

½ teaspoon crushed red pepper flakes

3 garlic cloves, crushed

6 ounces julienne-cut skinless roast turkey breast

¾ cup julienne-cut roasted red peppers (freshly roasted or from a jar)

1 tablespoon cider vinegar

¼ teaspoon salt

Store-bought roasted peppers are a convenience, but nothing rivals the flavor of freshly roasted bell peppers. The method shown below is simple and quick, using quartered, stemmed and seeded peppers rather than whole ones.

1 Bring a large covered pot of water to a boil over high heat.

2 Add the pasta to the boiling water, return to a boil and cook for 10 to 12 minutes or according to package directions until al dente. About 5 minutes before the pasta is cooked, add the beans and cook until the pasta is al dente and the beans are crisp-tender. Drain in a colander and transfer to a large serving bowl.

3 In a small skillet, stir together the oil and pepper flakes. Place over medium heat and cook, stirring constantly, for 2 minutes. Stir in the garlic and cook, stirring constantly, for 30 seconds, or until fragrant. Immediately pour the hot oil mixture over the pasta and beans.

4 Add the turkey, red peppers, vinegar and salt to the pasta mixture, and toss to combine.

Preparation time 10 minutes • **Total time** 30 minutes • **Per serving** 350 calories, 7.7 g. fat (20% of calories), 1.5 g. saturated fat, 33 mg. cholesterol, 179 mg. sodium, 2.3 g. dietary fiber, 47 mg. calcium, 4 mg. iron, 40 mg. vitamin C, 0.8 mg. beta-carotene • **Serves 4**

❧ ❧ ❧

Arrange quartered, stemmed, seeded peppers, skin-side up, on a foil-lined baking pan. Broil until well charred.

Place the roasted peppers in a bowl and cover it. Let the peppers steam for a few minutes to loosen their skins.

Scrape off the charred skin with a table knife. If neccessary, rub off stubborn patches of char under cold running water.

Pasta with Meat

❧ ❧ ❧

OLD AND NEW FAVORITES—FROM

CHUNKY SAUCE TO SATISFYING SALAD—

MADE WITH THE LEANEST CUTS OF

BEEF, VEAL, PORK AND LAMB

PASTA WITH SWEET PEPPERS AND HAM

1½ teaspoons extra-virgin olive oil

2 large red bell peppers, coarsely diced

1 large onion, coarsely diced

4 garlic cloves, minced

½ teaspoon dried oregano, crumbled

¼ teaspoon crushed red pepper flakes

3 ounces boiled ham, diced

½ cup defatted low-sodium chicken broth

8 ounces penne rigate (ribbed penne) or regular penne pasta

1 ounce Parmesan cheese, coarsely grated

¼ cup chopped fresh Italian parsley

⅛ teaspoon freshly ground black pepper

A shaker of domestic grated Parmesan is handy for hurry-up meals, but its flavor cannot rival that of freshly grated Italian cheese. Domestic Parmesan, aged for as little as 10 months, is a firm, mild cheese, while the best imported Parmesan, designated "Parmigiano Reggiano," is aged for at least two years to develop a well-rounded, sharp-sweet flavor and a granular texture. With a good Parmesan cheese, you can use less and still enjoy a full flavor.

1 Bring a large covered pot of water to a boil over high heat.

2 Meanwhile, in a medium saucepan over high heat, warm the oil until very hot but not smoking. Add the bell peppers, onions, garlic, oregano and red pepper flakes. Sauté, stirring, for 2 to 3 minutes, or until the vegetables begin to soften and release their juices. Stir in the ham, then add 3 tablespoons of the broth and bring to a simmer. Reduce the heat to medium, cover and simmer, stirring occasionally, for 8 to 9 minutes, or until the vegetables are very tender. (If the pan gets too dry, add an additional tablespoon of broth.)

3 Meanwhile, add the pasta to the boiling water, return to a boil and cook for 10 to 12 minutes or according to package directions until al dente. Reserving ½ cup of the pasta cooking liquid, drain the pasta in a colander and transfer to a warmed serving bowl.

4 Add the remaining broth and the reserved pasta cooking liquid to the vegetable mixture. Increase the heat to high, bring to a boil and simmer for 3 minutes to reduce the liquid slightly.

5 Pour the sauce over the pasta. Add the Parmesan, parsley and black pepper, and toss to coat well.

A French rotary grater with interchangeable drums can produce fine or coarse shreds or chips of cheese, nuts or chocolate.

Preparation time 15 minutes • **Total time** 45 minutes • **Per serving** 348 calories, 7.1 g. fat (18% of calories), 2.5 g. saturated fat, 18 mg. cholesterol, 467 mg. sodium, 3.6 g. dietary fiber, 141 mg. calcium, 4 mg. iron, 155 mg. vitamin C, 2.7 mg. beta-carotene • **Serves 4**

BOW-TIES WITH CURRIED BEEF

1 cup plain nonfat yogurt

8 ounces lean, trimmed boneless beef sirloin or top round steak

2 garlic cloves, crushed

1½ teaspoons curry powder

1½ teaspoons ground cumin

6 ounces bow-tie pasta

⅓ cup defatted chicken broth

¼ cup water

1½ cups small cauliflower florets

1½ cups snow peas

¼ cup chopped fresh cilantro

¼ teaspoon salt

Pinch of ground red pepper

Yogurt-cheese funnels are made of fine plastic mesh. Stand the funnel over a bowl or cup and spoon in the yogurt; place in the refrigerator until the yogurt is as thick as you like.

Yogurt, when briefly drained, gets as thick as sour cream, providing a low-fat base for creamy sauces. If you use drained yogurt often (it can substitute for heavy cream or cream cheese, too), buy an inexpensive yogurt funnel like the one shown.

1 Line a coffee-filter cone with a paper filter (or line a small strainer with a white paper towel) and place over a small bowl. Spoon the yogurt into the filter or strainer and let drain for 15 minutes.

2 While the yogurt drains, bring a large covered pot of water to a boil over high heat. Meanwhile, preheat the broiler and the broiler pan and rack. Rub the steak with the garlic, ½ teaspoon of the curry powder and ½ teaspoon of the cumin. Let stand for 5 minutes.

3 Place the steak on the broiler-pan rack and broil 4 to 6 inches from the heat source for 5 minutes per side, or until medium-rare. Transfer to a plate and let stand for 5 minutes.

4 While the steak broils, add the pasta to the boiling water, return to a boil and cook for 10 to 12 minutes or according to package directions until al dente. Drain in a colander and transfer to a serving bowl.

5 In a medium skillet, bring the broth and water to a boil over high heat. Add the cauliflower, reduce the heat to medium-high, cover and cook for 3 to 4 minutes, or until crisp-tender. Uncover the pan, stir in the snow peas and cook for 1 to 2 minutes longer, or until crisp-tender. Pour the vegetable mixture over the pasta.

6 Mix the drained yogurt with the cilantro, the remaining 1 teaspoon curry powder, remaining 1 teaspoon cumin and the salt and red pepper. Add the yogurt mixture to the pasta and toss to coat.

7 Transfer the steak to a cutting board; pour any juices from the plate over the pasta. Thinly slice the steak, add it to the pasta and toss.

Preparation time 10 minutes • **Total time** 35 minutes • **Per serving** 314 calories, 4.4 g. fat (12% of calories), 1.4 g. saturated fat, 39 mg. cholesterol, 301 mg. sodium, 3.6 g. dietary fiber, 175 mg. calcium, 5 mg. iron, 60 mg. vitamin C, 0.1 mg. beta-carotene • **Serves 4**

Pasta with Meat • 243

PASTA WITH VEAL AND LEMON

1 tablespoon plus 1 teaspoon
extra-virgin olive oil

1 ½ cups thinly sliced shallots

1 teaspoon granulated sugar

2 teaspoons grated lemon zest

1 ½ cups defatted chicken broth

1 cup julienne-cut carrots

8 ounces tricolor fusilli

8 ounces veal scaloppine, cut into
½-inch-wide strips

¼ teaspoon freshly ground black
pepper

1 tablespoon all-purpose flour

1 tablespoon fresh lemon juice

1 tablespoon cornstarch dissolved
in 1 tablespoon cold water

1 ripe medium tomato, diced

Here is a light dish based on veal piccata. Shallots, rather than the traditional garlic, are used in this recipe; to save peeling time, choose large-cloved shallots.

1 Bring a large covered pot of water to a boil over high heat.

2 Meanwhile, in a heavy, medium skillet, warm 1 teaspoon of the oil over medium-high heat. Add the shallots, sprinkle with the sugar and 1 teaspoon of the lemon zest, and stir well; reduce the heat to medium-low. Drizzle in 1 tablespoon of the broth and cook, stirring frequently, for about 12 minutes, or until the shallots are lightly browned and very tender. (Add up to ⅓ cup more broth as necessary.)

3 Stir in the carrots and add ¼ cup more broth; increase the heat to medium-high and bring to a boil. Cover and simmer, stirring once or twice, for 3 to 4 minutes, or until the carrots are just tender. Remove the skillet from the heat and set aside.

4 Add the pasta to the boiling water and return to a boil. Cook for 9 to 11 minutes or according to package directions until al dente. Drain the pasta in a colander, then transfer it to a serving bowl.

5 Toss the veal with the remaining 1 teaspoon lemon zest and the pepper, then with the flour. In a large no-stick skillet heat the remaining 1 tablespoon oil over high heat. Add the veal and sauté for 2 to 3 minutes, or until just cooked through. Transfer the veal to a plate.

6 Add the remaining broth and the lemon juice to the no-stick skillet; cook over high heat for 3 minutes, stirring to get up any browned bits from the bottom of the pan. Stir in the cornstarch mixture and bring to a boil, stirring constantly. Stir in the tomatoes and cook, stirring frequently, for 2 minutes, or until the tomatoes just start to soften. Add the shallot mixture, the veal and any juices that have collected on the plate, and heat through. Pour over the pasta and toss to mix.

Preparation time 20 minutes • **Total time** 45 minutes • **Per serving** 404 calories, 7 g. fat (16% of calories), 1.1 g. saturated fat, 44 mg. cholesterol, 452 mg. sodium, 4.5 g. dietary fiber, 60 mg. calcium, 4 mg. iron, 19 mg. vitamin C, 4.9 mg. beta-carotene
Serves 4

GREEK-STYLE PASTA WITH MEAT

6 ounces lean, trimmed boneless
leg of lamb or beef top round,
cut into chunks

2 teaspoons olive oil

1 large onion, chopped

3 garlic cloves, minced

¼ teaspoon dried oregano

¼ teaspoon dried thyme

¼ teaspoon dried mint

¼ teaspoon freshly ground black
pepper

Large pinch of ground
cinnamon

1 can (16 ounces) crushed
tomatoes in purée

1 can (8 ounces) no-salt-added
tomato sauce

10 ounces orzo pasta

1 ounce feta cheese, crumbled

The pasta most associated with Greece is one shaped like grains of rice. In the United States, it is usually sold as *orzo*, which is the Italian word for barley. Most small pasta shapes—orzo, ring-shaped *anellini*, thimble-shaped *ditalini* and the tiny "butter-flies" called *farfalline*, for example—are used in soup, but *orzo* is often served like rice. Here, it is the base for a meat sauce seasoned with the distinctively Greek combination of oregano and cinnamon.

1 Bring a large covered pot of water to a boil over high heat.

2 Process the lamb or beef in a food processor just until ground.

3 Warm the oil in a large, heavy skillet over medium-high heat. Add the onions and garlic, and sauté for 3 to 5 minutes, or until the onions are tender and lightly browned. Crumble in the ground meat and cook, stirring, for 2 to 3 minutes, or until it is no longer pink; add a tablespoon of water if the pan gets too dry. Stir in the oregano, thyme, mint, pepper and cinnamon; cook, stirring constantly, for 30 seconds.

4 Stir in the crushed tomatoes and tomato sauce and bring to a boil. Reduce the heat to low and simmer, stirring occasionally, for 10 minutes, or until the flavors are blended.

5 While the sauce simmers, add the pasta to the boiling water, return to a boil and cook for 6 to 8 minutes or according to package directions until al dente. Drain in a colander and transfer to a warmed serving bowl.

6 Spoon the meat sauce over the pasta and sprinkle with the feta.

Feta cheese is packed in brine. Rinse the cheese in cold water before using if you find it too salty or if you're trying to cut down on your intake of sodium.

Preparation time 15 minutes • **Total time** 40 minutes • **Per serving** 432 calories, 7.1 g. fat (15% of calories), 2.2 g. saturated fat, 34 mg. cholesterol, 305 mg. sodium, 3.5 g. dietary fiber, 110 mg. calcium, 5 mg. iron, 31 mg. vitamin C, 0.9 mg. beta-carotene • **Serves 4**

RADIATORE WITH MEXICAN PORK STEW

6 ounces lean, boneless loin pork chops, cut into ½-inch cubes

3 teaspoons chili powder

2 teaspoons olive oil

1 large green bell pepper, finely diced

1 large onion, minced

1 can (4 ounces) chopped green chilies, rinsed and drained

3 garlic cloves, minced

1 teaspoon ground cumin

½ teaspoon dried oregano, crumbled

⅛ teaspoon salt

1 can (10½ ounces) red kidney beans, rinsed and drained

1 cup defatted reduced-sodium chicken broth

6 ounces radiatore pasta

1 cup frozen corn kernels

¼ cup chopped fresh cilantro or 2 tablespoons chopped fresh Italian parsley

This dish was inspired by Mexican *posole*, which is made with hominy (hulled corn). Here, corn kernels stand in for hominy, but the other ingredients—bell pepper, onion, chilies, garlic, cumin and oregano—are traditional. To tenderize the pork, pound the chops lightly, using a rolling pin or meat mallet.

1 Bring a large covered pot of water to a boil over high heat.

2 Meanwhile, place the pork cubes on a sheet of wax paper; sprinkle with 1 teaspoon of the chili powder and toss to coat. Let stand for 5 minutes.

3 In a large, heavy saucepan, warm the oil over high heat until hot but not smoking. Add the pork and sauté for 1 to 2 minutes, or until lightly browned. Using a slotted spoon, transfer the pork to a plate.

4 Add the bell peppers, onions, chilies, garlic, cumin, oregano, salt and the remaining 2 teaspoons chili powder to the pan. Sauté for 2 to 3 minutes, or until the vegetables start to soften. Add the beans and broth, and bring to a boil. Reduce the heat to low, cover and simmer, stirring occasionally, for 10 minutes, or until the vegetables are tender.

5 While the stew is cooking, add the pasta to the boiling water, return to a boil and cook for 10 to 12 minutes or according to package directions until al dente. Drain the pasta in a colander and transfer to a warmed serving bowl.

6 Remove 1 cup of the stew and purée in a food processor or blender. Stir the purée back into the pan, then add the corn and pork, along with any juices that have accumulated on the plate. Increase the heat to medium and simmer the stew, uncovered, for 5 minutes.

7 Remove the pan from the heat and stir in the cilantro or parsley. Pour the stew over the pasta and toss to mix.

Preparation time 17 minutes • **Total time** 45 minutes • **Per serving** 379 calories, 6.7 g. fat (16% of calories), 1.2 g. saturated fat, 27 mg. cholesterol, 550 mg. sodium, 7.1 g. dietary fiber, 69 mg. calcium, 4 mg. iron, 51 mg. vitamin C, 0.7 mg. beta-carotene • **Serves 4**

TORTELLONI WITH VEGETABLE SAUCE

2 cans (14½ ounces each) no-salt-added stewed tomatoes with their juice

2 tablespoons no-salt-added tomato paste

1 medium zucchini, thinly sliced

1 medium yellow squash, thinly sliced

2 garlic cloves, crushed

2 teaspoons dried Italian herb seasoning

12 ounces fresh or frozen meat tortelloni

2 teaspoons cornstarch

2 tablespoons grated Parmesan cheese

¼ cup chopped fresh basil, or 2 tablespoons chopped Italian parsley

Filled pastas such as tortelloni and the smaller tortellini are sold both fresh and frozen in many supermarkets. They are almost a meal in themselves, requiring just a simple sauce and a salad to make a well-balanced dinner. This sauce, made with tomatoes and summer squash, can also be served over unfilled pasta such as rotelle.

1 Bring a large covered pot of water to a boil over high heat.

2 Meanwhile, in a cup, set aside 1 tablespoon of the juice from the stewed tomatoes. In a large, heavy saucepan, stir together the stewed tomatoes with their remaining juice and the tomato paste. Stir in the zucchini, yellow squash, garlic and Italian seasoning; cover and bring to a boil over medium-high heat. Reduce the heat to low; simmer, stirring occasionally, for 5 minutes, or until the vegetables are tender.

3 Add the pasta to the boiling water, return to a boil and cook for 8 to 10 minutes or according to package directions until al dente. Drain the pasta in a colander and transfer to a warmed serving bowl.

4 Stir the cornstarch into the reserved tomato juice. Stir the cornstarch mixture and the Parmesan into the vegetable sauce and bring to a boil, stirring constantly; the sauce will thicken slightly. Remove the pan from the heat and stir in the basil or parsley.

5 Pour the vegetable sauce over the pasta and serve.

Preparation time 11 minutes • **Total time** 25 minutes • **Per serving** 355 calories, 5.4 g. fat (14% of calories), 0.7 g. saturated fat, 52 mg. cholesterol, 496 mg. sodium, 5.8 g. dietary fiber, 224 mg. calcium, 5 mg. iron, 40 mg. vitamin C, 1.1 mg. beta-carotene • **Serves 4**

ON THE MENU
Try an Italian salad of thinly sliced fennel, sliced mushrooms (either nut-brown crem-ini or white button mushrooms) and shav-ings of Parmesan, lightly dressed with a lemon vinaigrette.

FOR A CHANGE
There are lots of stuffed pastas, with a variety of fillings, to sample: *cappelletti* (little hats), the filled pasta crescents called *agnolotti* and triangular *pansotti* as well as the more familiar tortellini and ravioli.

PENNE AND STEAK SALAD

- ½ cup (1 ounce) sun-dried tomatoes (not packed in oil)
- 1 cup water
- 6 ounces penne pasta
- 8 ounces lean, trimmed boneless beef sirloin or top round steak
- 2 garlic cloves, crushed
- ½ teaspoon coarsely cracked black pepper
- 2 tablespoons defatted beef broth
- 1 tablespoon fresh lemon juice
- 2 teaspoons reduced-sodium soy sauce
- 1½ teaspoons grated fresh ginger
- 1 teaspoon Dijon mustard
- 1 teaspoon extra-virgin olive oil
- 1 bunch watercress, washed, tough stems removed
- 1 cup thinly sliced kirby or English cucumbers

Soak the sun-dried tomatoes in boiling water for a few minutes to soften them, then rinse and drain the tomatoes before cutting them up.

Hearty and light at the same time, warm salads are welcome in any weather. This one has a lovely balance of crisp and tender textures, spicy and fresh flavors, and a vibrant red-white-and-green color scheme: Slices of juicy garlic-rubbed steak are combined with penne, sun-dried tomatoes, watercress and cucumbers, and tossed with a soy-ginger-mustard dressing.

1 Bring a large covered pot of water to a boil over high heat. Preheat the broiler and a broiler pan and rack.

2 Put the dried tomatoes and water in a small saucepan and bring to a boil over high heat. Remove the pan from the heat, cover and let stand for 5 minutes, or until the tomatoes have softened. Drain the tomatoes in a small strainer, then rinse under cold running water until cool. Cut the tomatoes into small pieces.

3 Add the pasta to the boiling water, return to a boil and cook for 10 to 12 minutes or according to package directions until al dente. Drain in a colander and rinse briefly under cold running water; drain again.

4 Rub the steak with half of the garlic and all of the pepper. Place the steak on the broiler-pan rack and broil 4 to 6 inches from the heat for 5 minutes per side, or until medium-rare. Transfer the steak to a plate and let stand for 5 minutes while you make the dressing.

5 In a salad bowl, whisk together the broth, lemon juice, soy sauce, ginger, mustard, oil and the remaining garlic.

6 Transfer the steak to a cutting board. Add any juices that have collected on the plate to the salad dressing. Carve the steak into thin slices.

7 Add the pasta, dried tomatoes, watercress, cucumbers and steak to the salad bowl, and toss to mix.

Preparation time 15 minutes • **Total time** 35 minutes • **Per serving** 290 calories, 5.3 g. fat (17% of calories), 1.5 g. saturated fat, 38 mg. cholesterol, 223 mg. sodium, 3.9 g. dietary fiber, 80 mg. calcium, 4 mg. iron, 43 mg. vitamin C, 2 mg. beta-carotene
Serves 4

WARM PASTA ANTIPASTO SALAD

6 ounces bow-tie pasta

2 teaspoons extra-virgin olive oil

1 large red bell pepper, quartered, then cut crosswise into thin slices

1 medium red onion, thinly sliced

2 garlic cloves, minced

½ teaspoon freshly ground black pepper

¼ teaspoon dried Italian herb seasoning, crumbled (see page 13)

⅛ teaspoon salt

1 small zucchini, thinly sliced

2 tablespoons defatted reduced-sodium chicken broth

2 tablespoons water

2 cups halved cherry tomatoes

1 can (10½ ounces) cannellini beans, rinsed and drained

2 ounces sliced provolone cheese, cut into strips

2 ounces thinly sliced ham, cut into strips

1 tablespoon red wine vinegar

6 kalamata or ripe olives, sliced off pits

As you enter a fine Italian restaurant, you'll pass a table laden with a mouth-watering array of *antipasti*—roasted peppers, olives, marinated vegetables and beans, cheeses, smoked meats and chilled seafood—that serve to sharpen the appetite for the meal to come. This bountiful salad combines the *antipasti* with the pasta course. As a time-saver, the sauce is started before the pasta is done.

1 Bring a large covered pot of water to a boil over high heat.

2 Add the pasta to the boiling water, return to a boil and cook, stirring frequently, for 10 to 12 minutes or according to package directions until al dente. Drain in a colander and cool under cold running water until the pasta is just warm.

3 While the pasta is cooking, in a large, deep skillet, warm the oil over high heat. Add the bell peppers, onions, garlic, black pepper, Italian seasoning and salt, and sauté for 3 to 4 minutes, or until the bell peppers are crisp-tender. Stir in the zucchini, broth and water, and bring to a boil. Reduce the heat to medium, cover and cook, stirring occasionally, for 3 to 4 minutes, or until the zucchini is tender. Add the tomatoes and toss gently to mix; cover and cook for 1 minute longer, or until the tomatoes are just heated but not cooked. Transfer the vegetable mixture to a serving bowl.

4 Add the drained pasta, beans, cheese, ham, vinegar and olives to the bowl, and toss to mix.

Preparation time 20 minutes • **Total time** 40 minutes • **Per serving** 358 calories, 9.6 g. fat (24% of calories), 3.5 g. saturated fat, 18 mg. cholesterol, 558 mg. sodium, 6.2 g. dietary fiber, 166 mg. calcium, 4 mg. iron, 71 mg. vitamin C, 1.2 mg. beta-carotene • **Serves 4**

MAKE-AHEAD
You can make the salad in advance and serve it chilled or at room temperature.

FOOD FACT
Firm, golden, smoky-flavored provolone cheese is a specialty of southern Italy.

Provolone melts beautifully and is excellent for sandwiches and casseroles.

ON THE MENU
End the meal with oranges—peeled, sliced crosswise, sprinkled with cinnamon and a pinch of sugar, and thoroughly chilled.

PASTA WITH LAMB AND ROSEMARY PESTO

1 large lemon

6 ounces spinach, washed, tough stems removed

3 tablespoons defatted beef broth

½ teaspoon dried rosemary leaves

¼ teaspoon freshly ground black pepper

¼ teaspoon salt

⅛ teaspoon crushed red pepper flakes

1 garlic clove, peeled

8 ounces lean, trimmed, boneless lamb steak

8 ounces long fusilli or fettuccine

3 large carrots, halved lengthwise and cut into long diagonal slices

1 tablespoon grated Parmesan cheese

P esto *alla Genovese*, known to every lover of Italian food, is made from basil, garlic, olive oil, Parmesan and pine nuts. Here is a very different pesto, composed of spinach, rosemary, garlic and lemon juice. The fragrant herb mixture is rubbed on lamb steak before it's broiled and is also tossed with the pasta.

1 Bring a large covered pot of water to a boil over high heat.

2 Meanwhile, with a swivel-bladed vegetable peeler, remove a 2-inch strip of zest from the lemon. Squeeze 2 tablespoons of juice from the lemon. Combine the lemon juice, spinach, broth, rosemary, black pepper, salt and crushed red pepper in a food processor. With the machine running, drop the lemon zest and the garlic through the feed tube and process until puréed.

3 Preheat the broiler, broiler pan and broiler rack. Place the lamb steak on a plate and spread 2 tablespoons of the rosemary pesto over it, coating both sides. Let stand for 5 minutes.

4 Place the lamb on the broiler-pan rack and broil 4 to 5 inches from the heat source for 4 to 5 minutes per side for medium-rare. Transfer to a clean plate and let stand for 5 minutes.

5 While the lamb broils, add the pasta to the boiling water, return to a boil and cook for 8 to 10 minutes or according to package directions until al dente. Three minutes before the pasta is done, add the carrots and cook until tender. Drain the pasta and carrots in a colander and transfer to a heated serving bowl. Toss the pasta and carrots with the remaining pesto.

6 Transfer the lamb to a cutting board. Pour any juices that have collected on the plate into the pasta. Carve the lamb into thin slices, place on top of the pasta and toss gently, then sprinkle with the Parmesan.

Use a small rubber spatula—or your hands—to spread the rosemary pesto over the lamb steak.

Preparation time 10 minutes • **Total time** 35 minutes • **Per serving** 351 calories, 6.1 g. fat (16% of calories), 2.1 g. saturated fat, 41 mg. cholesterol, 292 mg. sodium, 4.6 g. dietary fiber, 97 mg. calcium, 4 mg. iron, 20 mg. vitamin C, 14 mg. beta-carotene • **Serves 4**

THAI NOODLES WITH BEEF AND BASIL

8 ounces lean beef top round, cut into chunks

3 garlic cloves, crushed

1 tablespoon reduced-sodium soy sauce

1 teaspoon anchovy paste

1 teaspoon dried mint

½ teaspoon granulated sugar

¼ teaspoon crushed red pepper flakes

2½ teaspoons olive oil

1 large red bell pepper, halved and thinly sliced crosswise

1 medium red onion, thinly sliced

¼ cup defatted reduced-sodium beef broth

2 large tomatoes, coarsely chopped in a food processor or by hand

1 tablespoon plus 2 teaspoons fresh lime juice

8 ounces medium-thin egg noodles

½ cup coarsely chopped fresh basil

Rather than using the saltshaker, Thai cooks season most of their savory dishes with a few drops of *nam pla*, an intensely aromatic sauce made by fermenting a mixture of fresh anchovies and salt for a year or longer. Although Thai food is becoming more popular each year, *nam pla* is not yet widely available; here, a combination of soy sauce and anchovy paste takes its place.

1 Bring a large covered pot of water to a boil over high heat.

2 Meanwhile, place the beef chunks in a food processor and process until finely ground. Add the garlic, soy sauce, anchovy paste, mint, sugar and red pepper flakes, and pulse just until blended.

3 In a large, deep no-stick skillet, warm 2 teaspoons of the oil over high heat until hot but not smoking. Add the bell peppers and onions, and sauté for 5 minutes, or until the vegetables are crisp-tender. (If the pan gets too dry, add a little of the broth.)

4 Crumble in the beef mixture; drizzle with 2 tablespoons of the broth and sauté for 2 to 3 minutes, or until the meat is no longer pink. Add the remaining 2 tablespoons broth, the tomatoes and lime juice, and toss to blend well. Bring to a boil, reduce the heat to low, cover and simmer, stirring occasionally, for 5 minutes, or until the flavors are blended.

5 Meanwhile, add the noodles to the boiling water, return to a boil and cook for 6 to 8 minutes or according to package directions until al dente. Drain in a colander and transfer to a large warmed serving bowl. Toss the noodles with the remaining ½ teaspoon olive oil to prevent sticking.

6 Pour the beef mixture over the noodles, then add the basil and toss gently to mix.

Preparation time 25 minutes • **Total time** 45 minutes • **Per serving** 372 calories, 7.6 g. fat (18% of calories), 1.6 g. saturated fat, 87 mg. cholesterol, 290 mg. sodium, 3.6 g. dietary fiber, 94 mg. calcium, 6 mg. iron, 71 mg. vitamin C, 1.3 mg. beta-carotene • **Serves 4**

Pasta with Vegetables

❧ ❧ ❧

THE BEST OF THE GARDEN'S

SEASONAL BOUNTY, PARTNERED

WITH PASTA, MAKES QUICK,

COLORFUL MEALS

CHILI BEAN PASTA

1 tablespoon plus 1 teaspoon olive oil

1 large onion, chopped

1 large red bell pepper, diced

1 can (4 ounces) chopped green chilies, rinsed and drained

3 garlic cloves, minced

1 large fresh jalapeño pepper, partially seeded and diced

1¼ teaspoons ground cumin

¼ teaspoon freshly ground pepper

1 can (16 ounces) crushed tomatoes in purée

1 can (10½ ounces) black beans, rinsed and drained

1 can (8 ounces) no-salt-added tomato sauce

2 tablespoons water

8 ounces fusilli pasta

¼ cup chopped fresh cilantro or 2 tablespoons chopped fresh Italian parsley

Much of the heat in chili peppers lies in their seeds and ribs, so you can fine-tune the hotness of a dish by including more or less of these potent parts of the jalapeño. Wear thin rubber or plastic gloves when preparing hot chilies, and don't touch your mouth, nose and especially your eyes when working with them. If you choose not to wear gloves, wash your hands thoroughly with soap and water, and even after you do so, avoid touching your eyes.

1 Bring a large covered pot of water to a boil over high heat.

2 Meanwhile, warm the oil in a large, deep skillet over high heat. Add the onions, bell peppers, green chilies, garlic and jalapeños, and stir to coat with the oil. Reduce the heat to medium-high and cook, stirring frequently, for 3 to 5 minutes, or until the vegetables are tender. Add the cumin and ground pepper; cook, stirring, for 30 seconds.

3 Add the crushed tomatoes, beans, tomato sauce and water to the vegetables, and bring to a boil. Reduce the heat to low, cover and simmer, stirring occasionally, for 15 minutes, or until the flavors are blended. Uncover, increase the heat to medium and simmer for 5 minutes longer.

4 While the sauce simmers, add the pasta to the boiling water. Return to a boil and cook for 10 to 12 minutes or according to package directions until al dente. Drain in a colander and transfer to a warmed serving bowl.

5 Pour the sauce over the pasta, sprinkle with the cilantro or parsley and toss to mix well.

Preparation time 12 minutes • **Total time** 45 minutes • **Per serving** 389 calories, 6.3 g. fat (14% of calories), 0.8 g. saturated fat, 0 mg. cholesterol, 494 mg. sodium, 6.2 g. dietary fiber, 95 mg. calcium, 5 mg. iron, 135 mg. vitamin C, 2.3 mg. beta-carotene • **Serves 4**

LEMONY ASPARAGUS AND PASTA SALAD

8 ounces penne pasta

1 pound asparagus, trimmed and cut diagonally into 2-inch pieces

2 tablespoons reduced-calorie mayonnaise

2 tablespoons defatted chicken broth or vegetable broth

1 tablespoon fresh lemon juice

2 teaspoons Dijon mustard

1 garlic clove, crushed

¼ teaspoon freshly ground black pepper

2 ounces shredded sharp Cheddar cheese

¼ cup diagonally sliced scallions

Finding pasta shapes that echo other ingredients in a recipe is part of the fun of creative pasta cookery. Asparagus spears, cut into 2-inch lengths, are much the same shape as penne, or pasta "quills." Similarly, carrot slices would work well with rotelli, or wagon-wheel pasta, and ribbons of zucchini or yellow squash with fettuccine. Here, the asparagus and pasta are cooked together: Be sure to add the asparagus before the penne is done so that the pasta does not overcook.

1 Bring a large covered pot of water to a boil over high heat. Add the pasta, return to a boil and cook for 10 to 12 minutes or according to package directions until al dente. About three minutes before the pasta is done, add the asparagus and cook until crisp-tender. Drain the pasta and asparagus in a colander, cool under cold running water and drain again.

2 In a salad bowl, whisk together the mayonnaise, broth, lemon juice, mustard, garlic and pepper. Add the pasta and asparagus, and toss to coat well. Sprinkle with the Cheddar and scallions, and serve.

Preparation time 10 minutes • **Total time** 25 minutes • **Per serving** 309 calories, 7.9 g. fat (23% of calories), 3.6 g. saturated fat, 17 mg. cholesterol, 241 mg. sodium, 2.1 g. dietary fiber, 133 mg. calcium, 3 mg. iron, 23 mg. vitamin C, 0.4 mg. beta-carotene • **Serves 4**

Cut the asparagus into pieces about the same size and shape as the penne.

SUBSTITUTION

Frozen asparagus can be used when fresh is not available. It's not necessary to cook the asparagus along with the pasta; just thaw it in the refrigerator, then place it in a colander and pour the boiling cooking liquid over it when you drain the pasta.

MARKET AND PANTRY

Asparagus can be expensive, so you want to be sure to get the best spears with the least waste. Look for plump stalks that are fresh and green all the way down: If the bottom of the stalk is hard, dry and white, it will be unusable. The tips of the spears should consist of tightly closed, moist-looking buds. The best way to store this delicate vegetable is to treat it as if it were a bouquet of flowers: Trim the bottoms of the stalks, then stand them in a tall container and add 1 inch of cold water. Cover with a plastic bag to hold in the moisture. Fresh asparagus will keep for about 3 days in the refrigerator.

PASTA WITH CAULIFLOWER AND CHEDDAR

8 ounces whole-wheat linguine

3 cups small cauliflower florets

1½ cups 1% low-fat milk

2 tablespoons cornstarch

½ teaspoon dry mustard

½ teaspoon freshly ground black pepper

¼ teaspoon dried thyme, crumbled

¼ teaspoon hot pepper sauce

⅛ teaspoon salt

4 ounces extra-sharp Cheddar cheese, shredded

2 tablespoons grated Parmesan cheese

¼ cup thinly sliced scallion greens

Ivory white cauliflower could almost pass for pasta, especially when blanketed with a creamy sauce, and it makes a most interesting meal when paired with sturdy whole-wheat linguine. Some "secret ingredients" help cut the fat content of the two-cheese sauce: It's based on a blend of low-fat milk and cornstarch (rather than whole milk), and the sharp Cheddar flavor is underscored with dry mustard and hot pepper sauce so that you use less cheese than usual.

1 Bring a large covered pot of water to a boil over high heat. Add the pasta, return to a boil and cook for 9 to 11 minutes, or according to package directions. Four minutes before the pasta is done, stir in the cauliflower and cook until the cauliflower is tender and the pasta is al dente. Reserving ½ cup of the cooking liquid, drain the pasta and cauliflower in a colander.

2 While the pasta is cooking, in a heavy medium saucepan, whisk together the milk, cornstarch, mustard, pepper, thyme, hot pepper sauce and salt until smooth. Place the pan over medium-high heat and bring to a boil, stirring constantly. Cook, stirring, for 1 minute, or until the sauce is quite thick; remove the pan from the heat.

3 Transfer the pasta and cauliflower to a warmed serving bowl; add the reserved pasta cooking liquid and toss to mix well.

4 Add the Cheddar and Parmesan to the sauce and whisk until smooth. Pour the sauce over the pasta and cauliflower, and toss to mix. Sprinkle with the scallions.

Preparation time 10 minutes • **Total time** 30 minutes • **Per serving** 401 calories, 12 g. fat (27% of calories), 7.3 g. saturated fat, 36 mg. cholesterol, 373 mg. sodium, 8.7 g. dietary fiber, 412 mg. calcium, 3 mg. iron, 56 mg. vitamin C, 0.3 mg. beta-carotene • **Serves 4**

KITCHEN TIPS
You'll need a head of cauliflower that weighs about 2 pounds to yield the 3 cups of florets required for this recipe. Take off any leaves and wash the head of cauliflower. Halve it, using a large, heavy knife, then remove the dense core. Break the head into large florets or cut them apart with a small knife. Then, if necessary, divide the florets into smaller sections.

PENNE WITH BROCCOLI AND CHICK-PEAS

1 tablespoon extra-virgin olive oil

2 large red onions, sliced

3 garlic cloves, minced

4 cups small broccoli florets

1 cup defatted reduced-sodium chicken broth or vegetable broth

8 ounces penne pasta

1 can (10½ ounces) chick-peas, rinsed and drained or 1¼ cups drained cooked chick-peas (see below)

½ teaspoon freshly ground black pepper

3 tablespoons freshly grated Parmesan cheese

If using dried chick-peas (see directions at right), drain the soaking water and then add fresh water for cooking. This helps make the chick-peas easier to digest.

C hick-peas are a favorite legume around the Mediterranean. They are the main ingredient in the Middle Eastern fritters called *falafel* as well as *hummus*, a rich, creamy paste used as a sandwich spread or dip. The French prepare many soups, stews and salads with these nutty-tasting legumes, and a savory oversized pancake called *socca*, beloved in Nice, is made from chick-pea flour.

1 Bring a large covered pot of water to a boil over high heat.

2 Meanwhile, heat the oil in a large, deep skillet over high heat. Add the onions and garlic, and stir well to coat with the oil. Reduce the heat to medium and cook, stirring frequently, for 7 to 8 minutes, or until the onions are very tender and light golden brown. (Add a tablespoon of the broth if the pan gets too dry.)

3 Stir in the broccoli and broth; increase the heat to high and bring to a boil. Reduce the heat to medium-high, cover and simmer, stirring occasionally, for 6 to 7 minutes, or until the broccoli is tender.

4 Meanwhile, add the pasta to the boiling water, return to a boil and cook for 10 to 12 minutes or according to package directions until al dente. Reserving ¼ cup of the cooking liquid, drain the pasta in a colander.

5 Add the chick-peas and pepper to the broccoli and cook for 2 to 3 minutes, or until heated through. Add the penne and the reserved cooking liquid to the vegetables, and toss to coat the pasta. Transfer the mixture to a heated serving bowl and sprinkle with the Parmesan.

Preparation time 10 minutes • **Total time** 35 minutes • **Per serving** 404 calories, 7.7 g. fat (17% of calories), 1.6 g. saturated fat, 4 mg. cholesterol, 366 mg. sodium, 9.7 g. dietary fiber, 172 mg. calcium, 4 mg. iron, 102 mg. vitamin C, 1.3 mg. beta-carotene • **Serves 4**

KITCHEN TIP

Here's how to presoak and cook dried chick-peas: Place them in a large saucepan and add cold water to cover. Bring to a boil and cook for 2 minutes; cover and let stand for 1 hour. Drain, add fresh water (2 cups for each ½ cup of chick-peas) and bring to a boil. Simmer, partially covered, for about 90 minutes, or until the chick-peas are tender but firm.

FETTUCCINE WITH TOMATO-BASIL SAUCE

- 1 tablespoon extra-virgin olive oil
- 1 large onion, chopped
- 3-4 garlic cloves, minced
- ¼ teaspoon salt
- ¼ teaspoon freshly ground black pepper
- ¼ teaspoon crushed red pepper flakes (optional)
- 2 pounds ripe tomatoes, coarsely chopped in a food processor or by hand
- 3 tablespoons no-salt-added tomato paste
- 8 ounces spinach fettuccine
- ¾ cup coarsely chopped fresh basil, plus basil sprigs for garnish
- 2 tablespoons coarsely grated Parmesan cheese

There are several different varieties of basil. This "basil bouquet" is composed of common basil, also called sweet basil, and cinnamon basil, which has a uniquely spicy scent and flavor.

Tomatoes and basil, which share the same season, make one of the most delicious combinations imaginable. To preserve their summer-fresh flavors in this dish, the tomatoes are cooked only briefly, and the basil is added at the last possible moment. The Parmesan that tops the pasta should be grated just before serving. Instead of using a grater, you can shave slivers of Parmesan with a swivel-bladed vegetable peeler, a cheese plane or a sharp paring knife.

1 Bring a large covered pot of water to a boil over high heat.

2 Meanwhile, warm the oil in a large, heavy saucepan over high heat. Add the onions and garlic, and sauté for 3 to 4 minutes, or until tender. Add the salt, black pepper and red pepper flakes (if using). Stir in the tomatoes and tomato paste, and bring to a boil. Reduce the heat to low, cover and simmer, stirring occasionally, for 15 minutes, or until the tomatoes begin to cook down into a sauce.

3 While the sauce simmers, add the pasta to the boiling water, return to a boil and cook for 9 to 11 minutes or according to package directions until al dente. Reserving ¼ cup of the cooking liquid, drain the pasta in a colander. Transfer the pasta to a warmed serving bowl and toss with the reserved cooking liquid.

4 Stir the chopped basil into the sauce and spoon the sauce over the pasta. Top with the Parmesan and garnish with the basil sprigs.

Preparation time 20 minutes • **Total time** 45 minutes • **Per serving** 353 calories, 8.1 g. fat (21% of calories), 1.8 g. saturated fat, 56 mg. cholesterol, 265 mg. sodium, 8.3 g. dietary fiber, 179 mg. calcium, 5 mg. iron, 55 mg. vitamin C, 1.4 mg. beta-carotene • **Serves 4**

ON THE MENU
Although the spinach in the fettuccine contributes a vivid green color, it doesn't really "count" as a vegetable. So serve the pasta with steamed broccoli dressed with lemon juice and garlic; or chilled cooked zucchini and carrots tossed with a red-wine vinaigrette; or a big mixed salad.

MARKET AND PANTRY
The time to make this dish is when red-ripe tomatoes are at markets and farm-stands. When you buy beautiful tomatoes, handle them with care. Store them at room temperature for no more than 2 to 3 days and never refrigerate them: The cold will destroy their flavor and texture.

BAKED PASTA PRIMAVERA

6 ounces ziti

2 cups small broccoli florets

1¼ cups diagonally sliced carrots

8 ounces asparagus, cut diagonally into 1-inch pieces

1 small zucchini, halved lengthwise and sliced ¼ inch thick

3 cans (8 ounces each) no-salt-added tomato sauce

¾ teaspoon dried Italian herb seasoning (see page 13)

¼ teaspoon freshly ground black pepper

¾ cup part-skim ricotta cheese

3 ounces shredded part-skim mozzarella cheese

2 tablespoons grated Parmesan cheese

The original recipe for pasta primavera was prepared with a light cream sauce, but this popular dish of pasta and vegetables is open to many variations. The basic idea is to use spring vegetables—such as asparagus or peas—or at least young, tender specimens of summer vegetables, such as the small broccoli florets and zucchini called for here.

1 Preheat the oven to 425°. Bring a large covered pot of water to a boil over high heat.

2 Add the ziti to the boiling water, return to a boil and cook for 9 minutes or according to package directions until al dente. Four minutes before the ziti is done, stir in the broccoli florets and carrots. Two minutes before the ziti is done, stir in the asparagus and zucchini. Cook until the pasta is al dente and the vegetables are crisp-tender. Drain in a colander.

3 In the pasta cooking pot, combine the tomato sauce, Italian seasoning and pepper; bring to a boil over high heat. Remove from the heat, stir in the pasta and vegetables, and toss until mixed. Pour the mixture into a 9 x 13-inch baking dish.

4 Spoon dollops of ricotta onto the pasta mixture, then sprinkle on the mozzarella and Parmesan. Bake for 12 to 15 minutes, or until the mozzarella is melted and the sauce is bubbly.

Preparation time 16 minutes • **Total time** 45 minutes • **Per serving** 393 calories, 9.5 g. fat (22% of calories), 5 g. saturated fat, 29 mg. cholesterol, 275 mg. sodium, 7.4 g. dietary fiber, 354 mg. calcium, 4 mg. iron, 89 mg. vitamin C, 8.2 mg. beta-carotene
Serves 4

KITCHEN TIPS
This recipe will save you time because it calls for adding the raw vegetables to the already-cooking pasta. However, adding cold ingredients could stop the boiling, so be sure to have the vegetables at room temperature.

HEADSTART
You can cut up the vegetables in advance and refrigerate them in plastic bags until needed. Combine the carrots and broccoli in one bag, the asparagus and zucchini in another. If time is really tight, buy cut-up vegetables at a salad bar.

MACARONI AND CHEESE SALAD

6 ounces elbow macaroni

⅓ cup chopped fresh cilantro

¼ cup hot or medium salsa

3 tablespoons reduced-fat sour cream

Grated zest of 1 lime

2 tablespoons fresh lime juice

1 teaspoon ground cumin

½ teaspoon freshly ground black pepper

1 medium green bell pepper, diced

1 medium yellow or red bell pepper, diced

2 ounces shredded sharp Cheddar cheese

½ cup sliced scallions

Instead of a mayonnaise-dressed pasta salad, enliven your next buffet or barbecue with this colorful macaroni-and-vegetable mixture. Like the best party dishes, it can be made a day in advance, and the flavor will intensify if you prepare the salad ahead of time and refrigerate it overnight.

1 Bring a large covered pot of water to a boil over high heat. Add the pasta to the boiling water, return to a boil and cook for 7 to 9 minutes or according to package directions until al dente. Drain in a colander and rinse under cold running water; drain again.

2 While the pasta is cooking, in a salad bowl, whisk together the cilantro, salsa, sour cream, lime zest and juice, cumin and black pepper.

3 Add the macaroni, bell peppers, Cheddar and scallions to the dressing, and toss to combine.

Preparation time 12 minutes • **Total time** 25 minutes • **Per serving** 257 calories, 7 g. fat (25% of calories), 3.8 g. saturated fat, 19 mg. cholesterol, 185 mg. sodium, 2 g. dietary fiber, 131 mg. calcium, 3 mg. iron, 68 mg. vitamin C, 0.9 mg. beta-carotene
Serves 4

❧ ❧ ❧

This citrus zester shaves fine shreds of zest that are easy to measure in a spoon. Press the tool firmly against the fruit and pull it toward you.

This utensil, called a channel knife, cuts a thicker strip of zest, which can be chopped into smaller pieces for recipes or left whole for garnishing.

WATERCRESS AND TOMATO SPAGHETTI

1 cup water

1 ounce (½ cup) sun-dried tomatoes (not packed in oil)

2 teaspoons extra-virgin olive oil

6 scallions, thinly sliced

3 garlic cloves, minced

3 large ripe tomatoes (1½ pounds), coarsely chopped in a food processor or by hand

¼ teaspoon salt

⅛–¼ teaspoon crushed red pepper flakes

6 kalamata or ripe olives, sliced off pits

8 ounces spaghetti

1 bunch watercress, washed, tough stems removed

1 tablespoon grated Parmesan cheese

When tomatoes are dried—either in the sun or in special ovens—their flavor is concentrated, just as drying turns grapes into sugar-sweet raisins. The dried tomatoes, if not packed in oil, are usually softened by soaking them in boiling water before cooking. On their own, sun-dried tomatoes are a potent seasoning; in this recipe, they reinforce the flavor of fresh tomatoes.

1 Place the water and dried tomatoes in a small saucepan and bring to a boil over high heat. Remove from the heat and let stand for 5 minutes, or until softened. Drain the tomatoes, cool briefly under cold running water and cut into small pieces.

2 Bring a large covered pot of water to a boil over high heat.

3 Meanwhile, heat the oil in a large no-stick skillet over high heat. Add the scallions and garlic, and sauté for 1 to 2 minutes, or until the scallions have wilted. Stir in the fresh and dried tomatoes, the salt and red pepper, and cook until the tomatoes start to release their juices and the juices come to a boil. Reduce the heat to medium; cover and simmer, stirring occasionally, for 10 minutes, or until the flavors are blended. Stir in the olives.

4 While the sauce simmers, add the pasta to the boiling water, return to a boil and cook for 8 to 10 minutes or according to package directions until al dente. Drain in a colander.

5 Place the watercress in a warmed serving bowl. Add the pasta, then pour the sauce over the pasta. Toss to mix the ingredients and to wilt the watercress. Sprinkle the pasta with the Parmesan.

Preparation time 20 minutes • **Total time** 45 minutes • **Per serving** 318 calories, 5.2 g. fat (15% of calories), 1 g. saturated fat, 1.2 mg. cholesterol, 264 mg. sodium, 6.8 g. dietary fiber, 125 mg. calcium, 4 mg. iron, 77 mg. vitamin C, 2.7 mg. beta-carotene • **Serves 4**

FOR A CHANGE
Instead of watercress, toss the pasta with trimmed arugula, a long-leaved green with a similar mildly bitter flavor.

ON THE MENU
For a refreshing Italian-style dessert, finish the meal with lemon sorbet dusted with finely ground espresso powder.

GREEK-STYLE PASTA AND TOMATO SALAD

8 ounces corkscrew pasta

2½ ounces crumbled feta cheese

⅓ cup plain nonfat yogurt

1 tablespoon fresh lemon juice

¾ teaspoon dried mint

¼ teaspoon ground cumin

¼ teaspoon freshly ground black pepper

⅛ teaspoon salt

1 garlic clove, peeled

1 bunch watercress, washed, tough stems removed

2 cups halved cherry tomatoes

½ cup sliced radishes

Most people have sampled Greek salad, a flavorful toss of greens, cucumbers, tomatoes, ripe olives and tangy feta cheese with a dressing made of Greek olive oil, lemon juice and oregano. For this hearty pasta salad, feta cheese is used in a creamy yogurt-based dressing that is served over pasta, watercress, tomatoes and radishes.

1 Bring a large covered pot of water to a boil over high heat. Add the pasta to the boiling water, return to a boil and cook for 11 to 13 minutes or according to package directions until al dente. Drain in a colander and rinse under cold running water; drain again. Transfer to a salad bowl.

2 While the pasta cooks, combine the feta, yogurt, lemon juice, mint, cumin, pepper and salt in a food processor or blender. With the machine running, drop the garlic clove through the feed tube and process until the dressing is smooth.

3 Pour the dressing over the pasta. Add the watercress, cherry tomatoes and radishes, and toss to coat well.

Preparation time 15 minutes • **Total time** 30 minutes • **Per serving** 288 calories, 5 g. fat (16% of calories), 2.8 g. saturated fat, 16 mg. cholesterol, 311 mg. sodium, 3.3 g. dietary fiber, 195 mg. calcium, 3 mg. iron, 33 mg. vitamin C, 1.4 mg. beta-carotene
Serves 4

Cut the thick stems from the watercress at the point where the bunch is tied.

Holding the cress by the remaining stems, rinse the leaves in a basin of water.

RAVIOLI WITH PEAS AND RED PEPPERS

½ cup defatted reduced-sodium chicken broth

1 package (10 ounces) frozen peas

¼ cup loosely packed Italian parsley sprigs

1 garlic clove, peeled

¼ teaspoon freshly ground black pepper

9 ounces fresh or frozen cheese ravioli

1 medium red bell pepper, diced

2 teaspoons grated Parmesan cheese

You don't need to make your own pasta in order to serve it fresh: Small pasta shops are springing up everywhere, offering such specialties as pumpkin ravioli, wild-mushroom tortellini and broccoli-rabe agnolotti. Cooking times vary for filled pastas; you need to know the approximate time in advance so you can cook the bell peppers and peas in the same pot as the ravioli without overcooking either the vegetables or the pasta. If directions don't come with fresh ravioli, be sure to ask about the recommended cooking time.

1 Bring a large covered pot of water to a boil over high heat.

2 Meanwhile, in a small saucepan, combine the broth, 1 cup of the peas, the parsley sprigs and garlic. Cover and bring to a boil over high heat. Cook for 1 minute; remove from the heat.

3 Purée the pea mixture in a food processor or blender until very smooth; stir in the black pepper and set aside.

4 Add the ravioli to the boiling water and return to a boil, stirring frequently. Cook for 4 to 5 minutes, or according to package directions. Two minutes before the ravioli are done, add the bell peppers and the remaining 1 cup peas to the pot. Return to a boil and cook for 2 minutes longer, or until the peppers are crisp-tender, the peas are heated through, and the ravioli are tender. Drain in a colander and transfer to a warmed serving bowl.

5 Add the pea purée to the ravioli and toss gently to combine. Sprinkle with the Parmesan.

Preparation time 12 minutes • **Total time** 30 minutes • **Per serving** 272 calories, 9 g. fat (30% of calories), 4.7 g. saturated fat, 57 mg. cholesterol, 450 mg. sodium, 3.2 g. dietary fiber, 188 mg. calcium, 3 mg. iron, 52 mg. vitamin C, 1.1 mg. beta-carotene
Serves 4

KITCHEN TIPS
It's not necessary to thaw frozen peas, and they will probably turn mushy if you do. The peas take only minutes to cook, and if you're using them in a salad, you don't even need to cook them—just place them in a strainer and rinse them under cold tap water. Frozen peas straight from the freezer are a great snack—one even vegetable-spurning kids may like.

PIZZA PASTA

2 large green bell peppers, cut into quarters

8 ounces spaghetti

4 ounces fresh mushrooms, sliced

3 tablespoons defatted chicken broth

3 cans (8 ounces each) no-salt-added tomato sauce

1 teaspoon dried Italian herb seasoning

¼ teaspoon garlic powder

⅛ teaspoon salt

⅛ teaspoon crushed red pepper flakes

4 ounces shredded part-skim mozzarella cheese

2 tablespoons grated Parmesan cheese

The flavors of pizza are instantly identifiable, but it's a treat to taste them in a new context. Here, spaghetti is baked with classic pizza ingredients: tomato sauce, garlic, mozzarella, peppers, mushrooms and Parmesan.

1 Bring a large covered pot of water to a boil over high heat. Preheat the broiler and a broiler pan and rack.

2 Arrange the peppers in a single layer on the broiler-pan rack and broil 2 to 3 inches from the heat, turning once, for 8 to 10 minutes, or until the peppers are tender and very lightly charred. Transfer the peppers to a cutting board and set aside to cool slightly, then cut each quarter into 4 pieces.

3 While the peppers are broiling, add the pasta to the boiling water, return to a boil and cook for 9 to 11 minutes or according to package directions until al dente. Drain the pasta in a colander.

4 In the pasta cooking pot, combine the mushrooms and broth, and bring to a boil over high heat. Sauté for 4 to 6 minutes, or until the mushrooms are tender.

5 Stir in the tomato sauce, roasted peppers, Italian seasoning, garlic powder, salt and crushed red pepper. Reduce the heat to medium-high and bring to a simmer, then reduce the heat to medium-low, cover and simmer for 5 minutes to blend the flavors.

6 Add the spaghetti to the sauce and toss to coat well. Transfer the mixture to a 9 x 13-inch flameproof baking pan or a 2-quart flameproof oval baking dish; sprinkle with the mozzarella and Parmesan, and broil, watching closely, for 1 to 3 minutes, or until the cheeses are melted and the sauce is bubbly.

Preparation time 10 minutes • **Total time** 40 minutes • **Per serving** 378 calories, 7.2 g. fat (17% of calories), 3.5 g. saturated fat, 18 mg. cholesterol, 341 mg. sodium, 5 g. dietary fiber, 235 mg. calcium, 4 mg. iron, 73 mg. vitamin C, 1.5 mg. beta-carotene • **Serves 4**

❧ ❧ ❧

SHELLS WITH DOUBLE-MUSHROOM SAUCE

½ ounce (¼ cup) dried mushrooms

1 cup boiling water

1 tablespoon olive oil

¾ cup diced shallots or chopped scallions (white parts only)

3 garlic cloves, minced

½ teaspoon freshly ground black pepper

½ teaspoon dried thyme

12 ounces white button mushrooms, coarsely chopped in a food processor or by hand

1 cup defatted reduced-sodium chicken broth

1 tablespoon plus 2 teaspoons cornstarch dissolved in 2 tablespoons dry white wine or water

6 ounces medium pasta shells or penne pasta

¼ cup chopped fresh Italian parsley

2 tablespoons grated Parmesan cheese

Even the cheapest dried mushrooms, sold in supermarkets, have a deeply savory, woodsy taste. Cook them with white button mushrooms and you might think you're eating fresh wild mushrooms, which are indeed a luxury item. If the dried mushrooms are in large pieces, chop them after soaking; if small, use them as is.

1 Put the dried mushrooms in a large glass measuring cup. Pour the boiling water over them and let stand for 5 minutes, or until softened. Meanwhile, line a small strainer with cheesecloth.

2 Using a slotted spoon, lift the mushrooms out of the soaking liquid and transfer them to small bowl. Place the strainer over the bowl and pour the soaking liquid through it, leaving the sediment in the cup.

3 Bring a large covered pot of water to a boil over high heat.

4 Meanwhile, in a large, heavy saucepan, warm the oil over medium-high heat. Add the shallots or scallions and garlic, and sauté for 3 to 4 minutes, or until the shallots are tender. Stir in the pepper and thyme, then the fresh mushrooms, and sauté for 5 minutes, or until the mushrooms release their juices.

5 Add the dried mushrooms and mushroom soaking liquid, the broth and the cornstarch mixture to the pan, and bring to a boil; cook, stirring constantly, for 1 to 3 minutes, or until thickened. Reduce heat to low, cover and simmer, stirring occasionally, for 15 minutes, or until the flavors are blended.

6 Meanwhile, add the pasta to the boiling water, return to a boil and cook for 8 to 10 minutes or according to package directions until al dente. Drain the pasta in a colander and transfer to a warmed serving bowl. Pour the sauce over the pasta, sprinkle with the parsley and Parmesan, and serve.

Preparation time 11 minutes • **Total time** 45 minutes • **Per serving** 278 calories, 5.7 g. fat (19% of calories), 1.2 g. saturated fat, 2.4 mg. cholesterol, 231 mg. sodium, 2.6 g. dietary fiber, 82 mg. calcium, 4 mg. iron, 10 mg. vitamin C, 0.1 mg. beta-carotene • **Serves 4**

PASTA SALAD WITH CHICK-PEAS

1 pound ripe tomatoes

1 medium cucumber, peeled and diced

¼ cup chopped red onions

2 tablespoons chopped fresh dill

2 tablespoons chopped fresh mint

1 tablespoon extra-virgin olive oil

1 tablespoon red wine vinegar

1 small garlic clove, crushed

½ teaspoon freshly ground black pepper

¼ teaspoon salt

1 can (19 ounces) chick-peas, rinsed and drained

8 ounces fresh spinach linguine, cut in half

Y ou'll find fresh pasta in many supermarkets, in the dairy section or in a special display with ready-made sauces. If you don't use fresh pasta right away, wrap it airtight and store it in the refrigerator for up to one week or in the freezer for up to a month.

1 Bring a medium saucepan of water to a boil over high heat. One at a time, add the tomatoes and blanch for 20 seconds, or until the skins begin to wrinkle. Cool the tomatoes in a bowl of cold water and slip off the skins. Coarsely chop the tomatoes and place in a salad bowl.

2 Add the cucumber, onions, dill, mint, oil, vinegar, garlic, pepper and salt to the tomatoes, and mix well; stir in the chick-peas. Cover and let stand at room temperature for 10 minutes.

3 Return the water in the pot to a boil, add the pasta and bring to a boil again. Cook, stirring frequently, for 3 to 5 minutes, or until the pasta floats to the surface and is al dente. Drain in a colander and rinse briefly under cold running water.

4 Add the pasta to the chick-pea mixture and toss thoroughly.

Preparation time 15 minutes • **Total time** 35 minutes • **Per serving** 323 calories, 8.2 g. fat (23% of calories), 0.7 g. saturated fat, 64 mg. cholesterol, 345 mg. sodium, 5.4 g. dietary fiber, 87 mg. calcium, 4 mg. iron, 28 mg. vitamin C, 0.5 mg. beta-carotene • **Serves 4**

ᵇᵉ   ᵇᵉ   ᵇᵉ

Drop a tomato into the pot of boiling water; remove it when the skin wrinkles.

After the tomato has cooled slightly, you can easily peel off the skin.

Pasta with Escarole and Cannellini

1 tablespoon extra-virgin olive oil

1 medium onion, chopped

1 large carrot, diced

2 large celery stalks with leaves, diced

3–4 garlic cloves, crushed

½–¾ teaspoon freshly ground black pepper

½ teaspoon dried basil, crumbled

¼ teaspoon salt

6 cups loosely packed cut escarole (1-inch pieces), well washed

½ cup defatted chicken or vegetable broth

1 can (19 ounces) cannellini beans, rinsed and drained

8 ounces pasta twists

Escarole's ruffled pale-green leaves have a slight bitterness reminiscent of the taste of chicory, a close relative. The inner leaves have a milder flavor than the outer leaves. Although escarole is often used in salads, it is delicious when braised in broth and served as a side dish or, as it is here, partnered with pasta and white beans.

1 Bring a large covered pot of water to a boil over high heat.

2 Meanwhile, warm the oil in a large, heavy saucepan over medium-high heat. Stir in the onions, carrots, celery and garlic, and sauté for 1 minute. Add the pepper, basil and salt, and reduce the heat to medium-low; cover and cook, stirring frequently, for 5 to 7 minutes, or until the vegetables are tender.

3 Add the escarole and broth to the vegetables, and raise the heat to high. Cook, tossing frequently, for 2 to 3 minutes, or until the escarole is wilted. Stir in the beans and reduce the heat to medium; cover and simmer for 3 to 5 minutes, or until the beans are heated through.

4 Meanwhile, add the pasta to the boiling water, return to a boil and cook for 10 to 12 minutes or according to package directions until al dente. Reserving 2 tablespoons of the cooking liquid, drain the pasta in a colander.

5 Combine the pasta, the reserved cooking liquid and the escarole mixture in a heated serving bowl, and toss to combine well.

Preparation time 15 minutes • **Total time** 35 minutes • **Per serving** 390 calories, 5.6 g. fat (13% of calories), 0.7 g. saturated fat, 0 mg. cholesterol, 483 mg. sodium, 11 g. dietary fiber, 126 mg. calcium, 5 mg. iron, 15 mg. vitamin C, 5.4 mg. beta-carotene • **Serves 4**

FOR A CHANGE
Fennel, which is very similar to celery in texture, has a mild licorice-like flavor that would add a new dimension to this dish. Use 1 cup of diced fennel to replace the celery.

NUTRITION NOTE
When choosing greens, the general rule is: The darker the leaves, the more nutritious. Escarole, for instance, is a richer source of beta-carotene, vitamin C and calcium than iceberg lettuce.

NOODLES WITH KALE AND POTATOES

2 teaspoons olive oil

1 teaspoon unsalted butter or margarine

6 packed cups torn kale, tough stems removed

1 large onion, sliced

8 ounces small new potatoes, cut into wedges

1 cup defatted reduced-sodium chicken broth or vegetable broth

1 teaspoon caraway seeds

½ teaspoon freshly ground black pepper

¼ teaspoon salt

6 ounces wide egg noodles

2 scallions, thinly sliced

To stem kale, fold the leaves forward and hold them near the stem; pull the stem from bottom to top so it peels off the top portion of the midrib along with the stem. Young kale does not require stemming if the leaves and stems are tender.

In the days when "starches" were considered fattening, a dish made with both noodles and potatoes would have been out of the question. Now, however, we recognize starches as energy-giving complex carbohydrates and know that they should make up the greatest proportion of our daily diets.

1 Bring a large covered pot of water to a boil over high heat.

2 Meanwhile, heat the oil and butter in a large, heavy saucepan over medium-high heat until the butter melts. Stir in the kale and onions, and sauté for 2 to 3 minutes, or until the kale is wilted.

3 Stir in the potatoes, broth, caraway seeds, pepper and salt; increase the heat to high and bring to a boil. Reduce the heat to medium-low, cover and simmer, stirring occasionally, for 20 to 22 minutes, or until the potatoes are tender.

4 When the potatoes are nearly done, add the noodles to the boiling water and return to a boil. Cook for 4 to 6 minutes or according to package directions until al dente. Drain in a colander and transfer to a warmed serving bowl.

5 Spoon the vegetable mixture over the noodles and sprinkle with the scallions.

Preparation time 12 minutes • **Total time** 45 minutes • **Per serving** 332 calories, 6.4 g. fat (17% of calories), 1.4 g. saturated fat, 43 mg. cholesterol, 366 mg. sodium, 11.6 g. dietary fiber, 208 mg. calcium, 5 mg. iron, 167 mg. vitamin C, 6.9 mg. beta-carotene • **Serves 4**

FOOD FACT
New potatoes are any variety of potatoes—red or white, baking or boiling—that have been recently dug and not stored. They have a thin "feathering" skin.

SUBSTITUTION
If kale is not available, use green cabbage, cut into narrow strips.

NUTRITION NOTE
Kale, a nutritional superstar, is an excellent source of vitamin C, calcium, beta-carotene and iron.

MARKET AND PANTRY
Look for deep green kale with no yellowed or withered leaves. Wrap the kale in damp paper towels, then in a plastic bag.

Pasta with Seafood

❧ ❧ ❧

A TEMPTING VARIETY, FROM

A COMFORTING SALMON-NOODLE

CASSEROLE TO AN ELEGANT

SCALLOP SAUTÉ

ANGEL HAIR WITH GRILLED SALMON

1½ teaspoons ground cumin

¼ teaspoon freshly ground black pepper

⅛ teaspoon salt

8 ounces salmon fillet, halved lengthwise, then cut crosswise into ½-inch-thick pieces

2 garlic cloves, minced

1½ teaspoons extra-virgin olive oil

1 small bay leaf, preferably Turkish

⅛ teaspoon fennel seeds

1 can (16 ounces) crushed tomatoes in purée

2 tablespoons frozen orange juice concentrate

2 teaspoons fresh lemon juice

8 ounces angel-hair (capelli d'angelo) pasta

1 package (10 ounces) frozen French-cut green beans, thawed

Salmon fillets may have tiny "feather bones" remaining in the flesh; these should be removed. Find them by running your fingers along the center portion of the top surface of the fish.

1 Bring a large covered pot of water to a boil over high heat. Preheat the broiler and spray a jelly-roll pan with no-stick spray.

2 In a cup, mix ¾ teaspoon of the cumin, ⅛ teaspoon of the pepper and the salt. Sprinkle the spice mixture over both sides of the salmon; arrange the salmon in a single layer in the prepared pan. Cover and let stand at room temperature for about 10 minutes.

3 Meanwhile, in a heavy, medium saucepan, combine the garlic, 1 teaspoon of the oil, the bay leaf, fennel seeds and the remaining ¾ teaspoon cumin and ⅛ teaspoon pepper. Cook, stirring, over high heat for 1 to 2 minutes, or until the garlic is fragrant and the mixture sizzles.

4 Stir in the tomatoes and orange juice concentrate, and bring to a boil; reduce the heat to low, cover and simmer, stirring occasionally, for 10 minutes, or until the flavors are blended. Remove the pan from the heat; remove and discard the bay leaf.

5 Drizzle the salmon with the lemon juice and broil 3 to 4 inches from the heat for 2 to 3 minutes, without turning, until the fish flakes easily with a fork. Remove from the broiler.

6 Add the pasta to the boiling water, return to a boil and cook for 2 minutes; add the green beans and cook, stirring frequently, for 2 to 3 minutes longer, or until the pasta is al dente and the beans are heated through. Drain the pasta and beans in a colander; transfer to a heated serving bowl and toss with the remaining ½ teaspoon oil. Add the sauce to the pasta and beans, and toss to coat. Add the salmon and any juices that have collected in the pan and toss gently.

Preparation time 15 minutes • **Total time** 40 minutes • **Per serving** 380 calories, 6.6 g. fat (16% of calories), 1 g. saturated fat, 31 mg. cholesterol, 282 mg. sodium, 2.7 g. dietary fiber, 102 mg. calcium, 4 mg. iron, 41 mg. vitamin C, 0.7 mg. beta-carotene
Serves 4

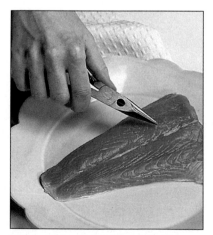

Use needle-nose pliers or tweezers to remove feather bones, which run from the center outward on the top of the fillet.

PASTA WITH SHRIMP AND BROCCOLI RABE

1 tablespoon olive oil

1 large onion, thinly sliced

3 garlic cloves, minced

6 ounces fusilli bucati or regular fusilli pasta

6 cups trimmed, cut-up broccoli rabe (2-inch lengths) or 4 cups broccoli florets

½ cup defatted chicken broth

12 ounces medium shrimp, peeled and deveined, tails left on

1 cup sliced roasted red peppers (from a jar)

½ teaspoon freshly ground black pepper

⅛ teaspoon salt

Fusilli—springy pasta "spindles"—come in several versions, long and short, solid and hollow, plain or colored with tomato or spinach; any of these would be fine for this dish. Hollow fusilli are called *fusilli bucati* or *fusilli col buco,* implying that their centers have been pierced or drilled out.

1 Bring a large covered pot of water to a boil over high heat.

2 Meanwhile, in a large, heavy saucepan, warm the oil over high heat. Add the onions and garlic, and toss to coat well with the oil. Reduce the heat to medium-low, cover and simmer, stirring occasionally, for 10 minutes, or until the onions are very tender.

3 Add the pasta to the boiling water, return to a boil and cook for 10 to 12 minutes or according to package directions until al dente. Drain the pasta in a colander and transfer to a warmed serving bowl.

4 While the pasta is cooking, add the broccoli rabe and broth to the onions; increase the heat to medium-high and bring to a boil. Cook, tossing frequently, for 3 to 4 minutes, or until the broccoli rabe is tender.

5 Add the shrimp, roasted peppers, black pepper and salt to the broccoli rabe and cook, tossing frequently, for 3 to 4 minutes, or until the shrimp are pink and just cooked through.

6 Pour the sauce over the pasta, toss to coat well and serve.

Broccoli rabe, also called *rapini,* is wonderful with pasta. It is usually blanched or sautéed to tone down its assertive, slightly bitter flavor.

Preparation time 22 minutes • **Total time** 40 minutes • **Per serving** 328 calories, 6 g. fat (16% of calories), 0.8 g. saturated fat, 105 mg. cholesterol, 357 mg. sodium, 4.9 g. dietary fiber, 138 mg. calcium, 6 mg. iron, 118 mg. vitamin C, 3.1 mg. beta-carotene • **Serves 4**

❧ ❧ ❧

ZITI WITH HERBED SWORDFISH

8 ounces swordfish, cut into
1-inch cubes

3 garlic cloves, crushed

1 teaspoon grated lemon zest

¾ teaspoon dried rosemary,
crumbled

¼ teaspoon freshly ground black
pepper

Large pinch of crushed red
pepper flakes (optional)

2 teaspoons extra-virgin olive oil

1 medium onion, chopped

1 can (14½ ounces) no-salt-added
stewed tomatoes

1 medium yellow summer squash,
halved lengthwise and cut into
¼-inch slices

½ cup defatted chicken broth

2 tablespoons fresh lemon juice

6 ounces ziti pasta

People who adore beef usually love swordfish, too, for this big saltwater fish, caught on both coasts, has dark, "meaty" flesh. Because swordfish is dense and firm, it can be cut into chunks that hold their shape whether they're simmered, stir-fried or skewered.

1 Bring a large covered pot of water to a boil over high heat.

2 Place the swordfish on a large plate and mix with 1 crushed garlic clove, the lemon zest, ¼ teaspoon of the rosemary, ⅛ teaspoon of the black pepper and the pepper flakes (if using). Cover and let stand at room temperature for 10 minutes.

3 Meanwhile, in a large, heavy saucepan, warm the oil over high heat until hot but not smoking. Stir in the onions and the remaining 2 garlic cloves, and sauté for 4 to 5 minutes, or until the onions are tender.

4 Add the stewed tomatoes, summer squash, broth, lemon juice, the remaining ½ teaspoon rosemary and remaining ⅛ teaspoon pepper, and bring to a boil. Reduce the heat to medium, cover and simmer, stirring occasionally, for 5 minutes, or until the squash is tender and the flavors are blended.

5 Meanwhile, add the pasta to the boiling water, return to a boil and cook for 10 to 12 minutes or according to package directions until al dente. Reserving ½ cup of the cooking liquid, drain the pasta in a colander. Transfer the pasta to a large heated serving bowl and toss with the reserved cooking liquid.

6 Add the swordfish cubes to the sauce, cover and simmer gently for 3 to 4 minutes, or until the fish is opaque in the center. Spoon the sauce and fish over the pasta.

Preparation time 10 minutes • **Total time** 45 minutes • **Per serving** 307 calories, 5.8 g. fat (17% of calories), 1.1 g. saturated fat, 22 mg. cholesterol, 198 mg. sodium, 4.6 g. dietary fiber, 71 mg. calcium, 3 mg. iron, 26 mg. vitamin C, 0.5 mg. beta-carotene • **Serves 4**

PICNIC MACARONI-TUNA SALAD

6 ounces elbow macaroni

¼ cup plain nonfat yogurt

2 tablespoons reduced-calorie mayonnaise

2 tablespoons snipped fresh dill

2 tablespoons red wine vinegar

1 teaspoon Dijon mustard

½ teaspoon freshly ground black pepper

1 can (6⅛ ounces) water-packed tuna, drained

1 can (15 ounces) black beans, rinsed and drained

1 medium red bell pepper, diced

2 large celery stalks, sliced

¼ cup sliced radishes

¼ cup chopped red onion

Just about any mayonnaise-based salad dressing can be lightened by substituting low-fat or nonfat yogurt for all or some of the mayo. In this case, nonfat yogurt is combined with reduced-calorie mayonnaise; the addition of fresh dill, vinegar and mustard ensures that not a bit of flavor is lost even though the fat content is considerably reduced. Crunchy celery, bell peppers, radishes and red onion add up to an unusually appetizing macaroni salad, and black beans make this dish a nutritional superstar.

1 Bring a large covered pot of water to a boil over high heat. Add the pasta, return to a boil and cook for 8 to 9 minutes or according to package directions until al dente. Drain in a colander and cool briefly under gently running cold water; drain again.

2 In a salad bowl, whisk together the yogurt, mayonnaise, dill, vinegar, mustard and black pepper.

3 Break the tuna into flakes and put it in a small strainer. Rinse under cold running water and drain well.

4 Add the macaroni, tuna, beans, bell peppers, celery, radishes and onions to the salad bowl, and toss to coat with the dressing.

Preparation time 23 minutes • **Total time** 35 minutes • **Per serving** 314 calories, 3.6 g. fat (10% of calories), 0.7 g. saturated fat, 19 mg. cholesterol, 427 mg. sodium, 5 g. dietary fiber, 86 mg. calcium, 5 mg. iron, 41 mg. vitamin C, 0.7 mg. beta-carotene
Serves 4

Kitchen shears or regular scissors make quick work of mincing herbs such as dill. Pat the herbs thoroughly dry after rinsing them so that the leaves do not stick to the scissor blades.

ON THE MENU
Serve the salad on a bed of curly greens and accompany it with wedges of juicy ripe tomato.

NUTRITION NOTE
The majority of Americans don't need to worry about consuming too much protein; in fact, most get more protein than necessary, with an unfortunate bonus of saturated fat and cholesterol if red meat is the main source of protein. This macaroni salad is a fine example of a more healthful way to eat protein: One serving supplies 22 grams of protein, or about half the daily requirement for the average woman, but has less than 4 grams of fat. Most of the protein in the salad comes from the tuna, macaroni and beans. These ingredients also provide good amounts of iron, a mineral that many people think they can get only by eating red meat.

Noodle Bake with Salmon and Peas

1 tablespoon unsalted butter or margarine

2 large celery stalks, diced

6 scallions, thinly sliced

¼ cup plus 1 tablespoon all-purpose flour

½ teaspoon dried tarragon, crumbled

½ teaspoon freshly ground black pepper

1½ cups skim milk

½ cup defatted reduced-sodium chicken broth

6 ounces wide egg noodles

1 can (7½ ounces) red salmon

1 cup frozen peas

3 tablespoons diced roasted red pepper

1 tablespoon unseasoned dry bread crumbs

1 tablespoon grated Parmesan cheese

Anyone with fond memories of tuna-noodle casserole will delight in this flavorful lower-fat update. Be sure to undercook the noodles slightly so that they don't turn mushy when baked.

1 Preheat the oven to 425°. Spray a 2-quart casserole with no-stick spray. Bring a large covered pot of water to a boil over high heat.

2 In a heavy, medium saucepan, melt the butter or margarine over medium heat. Stir in the celery and scallions, and sauté for 3 minutes, or until the vegetables are tender. Sprinkle in the flour, tarragon and pepper, and cook, stirring constantly, for 1 minute. Pour in the milk and broth, and whisk to blend well. Remove the pan from the heat, cover and set aside for 1 minute. (This helps make the sauce smooth.)

3 Place the uncovered pan of sauce over high heat and bring to a boil, whisking frequently. Cook, stirring constantly, for 2 to 3 minutes, or until thickened. Remove from the heat, cover and keep warm.

4 Add the noodles to the boiling water and return to a boil. Cook for just 3 to 4 minutes. Reserving ¼ cup of the cooking liquid, drain the noodles in a colander. Cool briefly under cold running water, separating the noodles with your fingers.

5 While the noodles are cooking, rinse and drain the salmon. Remove any skin and large bones, then break the salmon into large flakes.

6 Pour the sauce into the noodle cooking pot. Add the noodles and the reserved ¼ cup cooking liquid, and toss gently. Add the salmon, peas and roasted red peppers, and toss gently to mix. Transfer the mixture to the prepared casserole.

7 Mix together the bread crumbs and Parmesan, and sprinkle over the noodles. Bake for 15 to 20 minutes, or until the sauce is bubbly and the top is lightly browned.

Preparation time 5 minutes • **Total time** 45 minutes • **Per serving** 380 calories, 9.1 g. fat (21% of calories), 3.3 g. saturated fat, 70 mg. cholesterol, 473 mg. sodium, 3.9 g. dietary fiber, 291 mg. calcium, 4 mg. iron, 24 mg. vitamin C, 0.6 mg. beta-carotene • **Serves 4**

Noodles with Shrimp and Bok Choy

1 cup defatted reduced-sodium
  chicken broth

½ cup water

1 tablespoon dry sherry
  (optional)

2 garlic cloves, crushed

1 tablespoon grated fresh ginger

2 teaspoons reduced-sodium soy
  sauce

1 teaspoon dark sesame oil

1 medium fresh jalapeño pepper,
  cut in half

12 ounces small or medium shrimp
  (thawed if frozen), peeled and
  deveined

6 ounces fresh or dried
  capellini pasta

6 cups cut-up bok choy or napa
  cabbage (1-inch pieces)

½ cup drained canned sliced water
  chestnuts

¼ cup thinly sliced scallion greens

Capellini stands in for thin Chinese noodles in this pasta-in-broth meal. Fresh capellini is the quickest-cooking pasta of all: Test it after three minutes by biting a strand; if the pasta is properly al dente, drain and rinse it immediately to keep it from over-cooking. To freshen the flavor of the water chestnuts, drain them and place them in a small strainer, then pour some of the cooking liquid over them when you drain the pasta. Or simply drain the water chestnuts and rinse them under cool running water.

1 Bring a large covered pot of water to a boil over high heat.

2 In a large, heavy saucepan, combine the broth, water, sherry (if using), garlic, ginger, soy sauce, sesame oil and the jalapeño; cover and bring to a boil over high heat. Reduce the heat to medium-low and simmer for 5 minutes to blend the flavors. Remove and discard the jalapeño.

3 While the broth is simmering, remove the tails from the shrimp, if necessary. Cut the shrimp into 1-inch pieces.

4 Add the pasta to the boiling water, return to a boil and cook for 3 to 5 minutes or according to package directions until al dente. Drain in a colander and rinse briefly under cold running water; drain again.

5 Stir the shrimp, bok choy or napa cabbage and water chestnuts into the broth. Increase the heat to high and bring to a simmer, stirring frequently. Reduce the heat to low and cook, stirring frequently, for 3 to 5 minutes, or until the shrimp are pink and the bok choy is just crisp-tender.

6 Divide the pasta among 4 large, warmed soup bowls. Divide the broth, shrimp and vegetables among the 4 bowls and sprinkle each portion with scallions.

Preparation time 20 minutes • **Total time** 40 minutes • **Per serving** 240 calories, 3.8 g. fat (14% of calories), 0.6 g. saturated fat, 136 mg. cholesterol, 444 mg. sodium, 1 g. dietary fiber, 159 mg. calcium, 4 mg. iron, 55 mg. vitamin C, 2 mg. beta-carotene
Serves 4

MEDITERRANEAN SEASHELL SALAD

2 tablespoons frozen apple juice concentrate

2 tablespoons chopped fresh Italian parsley

1 tablespoon coarse Dijon mustard

1 tablespoon extra-virgin olive oil

1 tablespoon red wine vinegar

½ teaspoon ground cumin

¼ teaspoon freshly ground black pepper

1 medium yellow or red bell pepper, thinly sliced

1 cup thinly sliced fennel or celery

¼ cup thinly sliced red onions

6 ounces medium pasta shells

3 tablespoons golden raisins

1 can (3¾ ounces) water-pack sardines, drained and gently rinsed

Fresh sardines, quickly grilled, broiled or fried, are a great delicacy, and the tiny iridescent fish are a highlight of summer meals around the Mediterranean basin. In Sicily, filleted sardines are combined with macaroni, sweet fennel, onions, pine nuts and golden raisins—a typically Sicilian juxtaposition of sweet and savory flavors—in a casserole called *pasta con le sarde*. This unbaked version of the dish is made with canned sardines and a sprightly apple-juice dressing. A timesaving trick: The raisins are plumped by adding them to the pasta during the last few moments of cooking time.

1 Bring a large covered pot of water to a boil over high heat.

2 Meanwhile, in a salad bowl, whisk together the apple juice concentrate, parsley, mustard, oil, vinegar, cumin and black pepper.

3 Add the bell peppers, fennel or celery and onions to the dressing, and stir to blend. Cover and let stand at room temperature for 10 minutes.

4 While the vegetables marinate, add the pasta to the boiling water, return to a boil and cook for 9 to 11 minutes or according to package directions until al dente. One minute before the pasta is done, add the raisins. Drain the pasta and raisins in a colander, rinse briefly under cold running water and drain again.

5 Add the pasta and raisins to the salad bowl, and toss to mix. Add the sardines and toss gently.

Preparation time 10 minutes • **Total time** 25 minutes • **Per serving** 303 calories, 9.1 g. fat (27% of calories), 0.6 g. saturated fat, 0 mg. cholesterol, 178 mg. sodium, 2.2 g. dietary fiber, 111 mg. calcium, 3 mg. iron, 49 mg. vitamin C, 0.7 mg. beta-carotene • **Serves 4**

A fennel bulb, like a bunch of celery, is made up of many layers, so when you slice it crosswise it will fall into thin strips.

NUTRITION NOTE
Sardines have a lot to offer nutritionally. Although they are higher in fat than tuna, the fat is rich in omega-3s, polyunsaturated fatty acids that may be protective against heart disease. In addition, sardines are rich in iron, and the bone-in types are an excellent source of calcium.

LINGUINE WITH SCALLOPS PROVENÇALE

8 ounces fresh linguine

⅓ cup defatted reduced-sodium chicken broth plus ⅓ cup water

1 tablespoon plus ½ teaspoon extra-virgin olive oil

1 large onion, thinly sliced

1 medium red bell pepper, thinly sliced

1 medium green bell pepper, thinly sliced

3 garlic cloves, minced

12 ounces sea scallops, tough muscle removed

2 cups halved cherry tomatoes

1 medium zucchini, cut into ¼-inch-thick slices

1 tablespoon fresh lemon juice

½ teaspoon freshly ground black pepper

¼ teaspoon salt

½ cup coarsely chopped fresh basil

From Provence, in southwestern France, come dishes that speak of the sun. Olives and olive oil are hallmarks of robustly flavored Provençal dishes, as are tomatoes, garlic and fresh herbs. For this colorful dish, sautéed scallops, cherry tomatoes and zucchini are tossed with linguine, lemony broth and fresh basil.

1 Bring a large covered pot of water to a boil over high heat. Add the pasta, return to a boil and cook for 3 to 4 minutes or according to package directions until the pasta floats to the surface and is al dente. Drain in a colander and transfer to a heated serving bowl. Toss the pasta with 2 tablespoons of the broth-water mixture and ½ teaspoon of the oil.

2 In a large, deep skillet, warm the remaining 1 tablespoon oil over high heat. Stir in the onions, bell peppers and garlic, and sauté, stirring often, for 5 minutes, or until the vegetables begin to soften.

3 Stir in the scallops, cherry tomatoes and zucchini, and sauté, tossing frequently, for 4 to 6 minutes, or until the vegetables are crisp-tender and the scallops are just cooked through. Add the remaining broth mixture, the lemon juice, black pepper and salt, and bring just to a boil, stirring. Remove the pan from the heat.

4 Pour the scallop mixture over the pasta; sprinkle with the basil and toss to mix.

Preparation time 15 minutes • **Total time** 40 minutes • **Per serving** 335 calories, 7.5 g. fat (20% of calories), 0.7 g. saturated fat, 93 mg. cholesterol, 381 mg. sodium, 2.4 g. dietary fiber, 130 mg. calcium, 4 mg. iron, 73 mg. vitamin C, 1.2 mg. beta-carotene • **Serves 4**

To ensure even cooking, halve or quarter any particularly large scallops.

FOR A CHANGE
For an even more colorful dish, use spinach or tomato pasta.

ON THE MENU
A suitably sunny dessert is perfectly ripe fruit. Choose peaches or nectarines, strawberries, raspberries or cherries.

MARKET AND PANTRY
Scallops are almost always sold shucked, so there's no guesswork involved in selecting the best: Perfectly fresh scallops smell sweet and ocean-fresh; they look plump and moist. Scallops are very perishable and should be used within a day or two of purchase.

GREEN NOODLES WITH GARLICKY SHRIMP

- **12 ounces medium shrimp, thawed if frozen**
- **4 garlic cloves (1 crushed, 3 thinly sliced)**
- **1 tablespoon extra-virgin olive oil**
- **½ teaspoon dried oregano, crushed**
- **¼ teaspoon freshly ground black pepper**
- **¼ teaspoon salt**
- **⅛–¼ teaspoon crushed red pepper flakes**
- **8 ounces fresh spinach fettuccine or regular fettuccine**
- **½ cup defatted chicken broth**
- **12 ounces fresh spinach, tough stems removed, well washed**

Because most seafood has rather delicate flesh, it can benefit from even very brief marinating. Allowing the shrimp to marinate in olive oil, garlic, herbs and spices for just five minutes suffuses them with an impressive jolt of flavor.

1 Bring a large covered pot of water to a boil over high heat.

2 Meanwhile, peel and devein the shrimp; leave the tails on. Place the shrimp in a medium bowl and add the crushed clove of garlic, ½ teaspoon of the olive oil, the oregano, ⅛ teaspoon of the black pepper, ⅛ teaspoon of the salt and the red pepper; toss to combine. Cover and let stand for 5 minutes.

3 While the shrimp marinates, add the pasta to the boiling water; return to a boil and cook, stirring frequently, for 3 to 4 minutes or according to package directions until the pasta floats to the surface and is tender. Drain the pasta in a colander and transfer to a serving bowl. Mix in ¼ cup of the broth to keep the pasta from sticking together.

4 Sauté the shrimp in a heavy, medium no-stick skillet over high heat for 4 to 6 minutes, or until the shrimp are pink and cooked through. Remove from the heat and set aside.

5 In the pasta cooking pot, combine the remaining 2½ teaspoons olive oil, the sliced garlic, the remaining ⅛ teaspoon salt and remaining ⅛ teaspoon black pepper; sauté, stirring constantly, for 2 to 3 minutes, or until the garlic turns light brown and is very fragrant. Slowly pour in the remaining ¼ cup broth (the broth will boil up).

6 Add the spinach, in batches, and cook for 1 to 2 minutes, or until the spinach is just wilted.

7 Spoon the spinach mixture and the shrimp over the pasta, and toss to mix.

Preparation time 25 minutes • **Total time** 45 minutes • **Per serving** 314 calories, 7.7 g. fat (22% of calories), 0.8 g. saturated fat, 204 mg. cholesterol, 490 mg. sodium, 1.6 g. dietary fiber, 152 mg. calcium, 6 mg. iron, 19 mg. vitamin C, 2.6 mg. beta-carotene • **Serves 4**

LINGUINE WITH SMOKED SALMON

8 ounces spinach linguine or regular linguine

¼ cup reduced-fat sour cream

3 tablespoons snipped fresh dill

2 teaspoons distilled white vinegar

1½ teaspoons bottled white horseradish

¼ teaspoon freshly ground black pepper

⅛ teaspoon salt

1½ cups halved yellow or red pear tomatoes, plum tomatoes or cherry tomatoes

1 cup thinly sliced kirby or hot-house cucumber

3 ounces sliced smoked salmon, cut into thin strips

⅓ cup thinly sliced scallions

Gourmet shops and even supermarket deli counters and mail-order gourmet catalogues offer a number of choices in smoked salmon. You can go the economy route and buy what's called lox—salty brine-cured salmon—or be a bit more extravagant, since the recipe calls for only three ounces of fish. Some of the pricier choices are cold-smoked "Nova," a domestic product; imported Scottish smoked salmon (or "Scottish-style" salmon prepared on this side of the Atlantic) and alder-smoked salmon from the Pacific Northwest.

1 Bring a large covered pot of water to a boil over high heat. Add the pasta, return to a boil and cook for 9 to 11 minutes or according to package directions until al dente. Drain in a colander, cool briefly under cold running water and drain again.

2 In a salad bowl, combine the sour cream, dill, vinegar, horseradish, pepper and salt, and whisk with a fork until blended. Add the drained pasta, the tomatoes, cucumbers, salmon and scallions, and toss gently but thoroughly.

Preparation time 15 minutes • **Total time** 25 minutes • **Per serving** 284 calories, 4.1 g. fat (13% of calories), 1.4 g. saturated fat, 10 mg. cholesterol, 267 mg. sodium, 7.4 g. dietary fiber, 61 mg. calcium, 2 mg. iron, 16 mg. vitamin C, 0.3 mg. beta-carotene • **Serves 4**

❧ ❧ ❧

FOR A CHANGE
Smoked trout could stand in for the smoked salmon, but be particularly gentle when tossing the pasta, as the trout will break apart more readily than salmon.

ON THE MENU
A crisp *ficelle*—a long, thin loaf of French bread—would be welcome with this pasta. For dessert, fill a glass bowl with well-chilled melon balls tossed with fresh mint.

Joining the ever-popular cherry tomatoes as appealing garnishes and ingredients are diminutive yellow pear tomatoes, which you may find in farmers' markets in midsummer.

Side Dishes

❧ ❧ ❧

THE GREENS, GRAINS AND

OTHER ACCOMPANIMENTS

THAT MAKE ANY MEAL

COMPLETE

RICE WITH CONFETTI VEGETABLES

1 ½ cups water

¾ cup converted white rice

¼ teaspoon salt

⅛ teaspoon freshly ground black pepper

⅓ cup defatted chicken broth

1 cup shredded zucchini

1 cup shredded carrots

½ cup finely diced red bell pepper

¼ cup frozen green peas

¼ cup thinly sliced scallions

2 tablespoons chopped Italian parsley

½ teaspoon grated lemon zest

Citizens of Venice herald the arrival of spring with a bowl of *risi e bisi*—a slightly soupy mélange of rice and the tiniest of garden-fresh peas, flavored with ham, onions, parsley and Parmesan. Here, fluffy cooked rice is combined with peas (if your market stocks them, use the small frozen peas sold as petits pois) as well as shredded carrots, zucchini and bits of bell pepper and scallion. You can shred the carrots and zucchini by hand or with the shredding blade of a food processor.

1 In a medium saucepan, combine the water, rice, salt and black pepper, and bring to a boil over high heat. Reduce the heat to low, cover and simmer for 20 minutes, or until the rice is tender and the liquid is absorbed. Remove from the heat and set aside, covered.

2 In a large no-stick skillet, bring the broth to a boil over high heat. Add the zucchini, carrots, bell peppers, peas and scallions, and return to a boil. Reduce the heat to medium-low and simmer the vegetables, stirring frequently, for 3 to 4 minutes, or until tender.

3 Using a slotted spoon, transfer the vegetables to the pan with the rice. Add the parsley and lemon zest, and stir to combine.

Preparation time 15 minutes • **Total time** 40 minutes • **Per serving** 161 calories, 0.5 g. fat (3% of calories), 0.1 g. saturated fat, 0 mg. cholesterol, 242 mg. sodium, 2.4 g. dietary fiber, 45 mg. calcium, 2 mg. iron, 34 mg. vitamin C, 5.2 mg. beta-carotene • **Serves 4**

ON THE MENU
This side dish really brightens up a plate, so serve it with simple foods such as baked chicken or grilled fish. Because it's a combination of grain and vegetables, no other accompaniment is needed.

FOR A CHANGE
To transform the confetti rice into a main dish, add diced smoked turkey, ham or roast chicken breast; chunks of canned tuna or salmon; or rinsed and drained canned black beans or kidney beans.

Spicy Green Beans with Anchovies

1 cup water

½ cup sun-dried tomatoes (not oil-packed)

1 garlic clove, peeled

1 pound green beans, trimmed and halved crosswise

2 tablespoons chopped Italian parsley

4 anchovy fillets, rinsed, patted dry and chopped

1 tablespoon balsamic vinegar

1 teaspoon extra-virgin olive oil

⅛ teaspoon salt

⅛ teaspoon freshly ground black pepper

⅛ teaspoon crushed red pepper flakes, or more to taste

This unusual vegetable combination could fit into several different places in a traditional Italian menu: Offer it as an appetizer, as a side dish, or, atop a bed of greens, as a salad course, served after the main dish. And the beans are equally good hot or cold. If anchovies are not to your liking, simply leave them out.

1 In a small saucepan, bring the water to a boil over high heat. Remove the pan from the heat, stir in the sun-dried tomatoes, cover and let stand for 8 to 10 minutes, or until the tomatoes are softened. Reserving 2 tablespoons of the soaking liquid, drain the tomatoes, and cut into small pieces with kitchen shears, or chop with a knife.

2 Pour ½ inch of water into a large, deep skillet; cover and bring to a boil over high heat. Add the garlic and cook for 1 minute; remove with a slotted spoon and set aside. Add the green beans to the skillet, return to a boil and cook, uncovered, for 5 to 6 minutes, or until the beans are tender. Drain the beans in a colander.

3 While the beans are cooking, in a serving bowl, combine the parsley, anchovies, vinegar, oil, salt, black pepper, red pepper flakes and the reserved 2 tablespoons soaking liquid. Using a garlic press, crush the garlic clove into the bowl and stir well to combine.

4 Add the beans and sun-dried tomatoes to the bowl, and toss to coat.

Preparation time 10 minutes • **Total time** 20 minutes • **Per serving** 73 calories, 1.6 g. fat (20% of calories), 0.3 g. saturated fat, 2 mg. cholesterol, 230 mg. sodium, 3.3 g. dietary fiber, 51 mg. calcium, 1 mg. iron, 18 mg. vitamin C, 0.5 mg. beta-carotene • **Serves 4**

FOOD FACT
Although you can now buy balsamic vinegar in supermarkets, its price will never be comparable with that of more common vinegars. (The finest balsamic vinegars inhabit the same price range as superb vintage wines.) Why spend dollars on a bottle of balsamic when you can get a pint of cider vinegar for pennies? Because no other vinegar has its sweet, complex flavor, and none is so carefully made. Only sweet trebbiano grapes go into balsamic vinegar, which is aged for at least 12 years in wooden casks. To get an authentic balsamic, bottled in Italy, look for a code on the label: Vinegars labeled API MO are from Modena, while those marked API RE are from Reggio.

PARMESAN-BAKED PLUM TOMATOES

8 medium plum tomatoes (about 1¼ pounds)

¼ teaspoon salt

⅛ teaspoon freshly ground black pepper

¾ teaspoon olive oil

16 small fresh basil leaves

2 tablespoons unseasoned dry breadcrumbs

1 tablespoon grated Parmesan cheese

As with so many other everyday kitchen tasks, your finger is the best tool for spreading the oil over the tomatoes.

Baked tomato halves are eaten all over Italy; plum tomatoes, which are less watery than spherical tomatoes, are especially good when cooked by this method. Some traditional recipes call for the tomatoes to bake in a deep pool of olive oil, but here the tops are rubbed with just a little oil. The baking time will depend to some extent on the ripeness of the tomatoes: If they are very ripe, check them for doneness a little sooner in the second phase of baking.

1 Preheat the the oven to 425°. Spray a jelly-roll pan with no-stick spray.

2 Cut the tomatoes in half lengthwise, trimming the stem ends, if desired. Arrange the tomatoes, cut-side-up, in a single layer in the prepared pan. Sprinkle the tomatoes with the salt and black pepper, then drizzle with the oil. With your finger, spread the oil and seasonings evenly over the surface of the tomatoes. Place a basil leaf on top of each tomato half.

3 In a cup, mix the breadcrumbs and Parmesan. Sprinkle the breadcrumb mixture evenly over the tomatoes. Bake for 10 minutes, or until the breadcrumbs are browned. Lay a sheet of foil over the tomatoes and bake for 10 minutes longer, or until the tomatoes are softened and heated through.

Preparation time 5 minutes • **Total time** 30 minutes • **Per serving** 57 calories, 2 g. fat (33% of calories), 0.4 g. saturated fat, 1 mg. cholesterol, 199 mg. sodium, 1.8 g. dietary fiber, 40 mg. calcium, 1 mg. iron, 25 mg. vitamin C, 0.5 mg. beta-carotene • **Serves 4**

FOODWAYS

It's hard to imagine Italian food without tomatoes. However, as strongly as tomatoes are identified with Italian cuisine, they are New World natives and were not introduced to Italy until the 16th century. These first tomatoes were small and yellow, hence the Italian word for tomatoes—

pomodori, or golden apples. By the 18th century larger red tomatoes had been bred and were beginning to be popular as a salad ingredient; only later did people begin to cook them. Today, tomatoes are grown all over Italy, but the best plum tomatoes—most of which go into cans—come from San Marzano.

POTATO CAKE WITH SAGE AND GARLIC

1 pound thin-skinned potatoes, preferably yellow-fleshed

2 teaspoons olive oil

¼ teaspoon salt

¼ teaspoon cracked black pepper

4 garlic cloves, cut into thin slivers

1½ teaspoons slivered fresh sage or ½ teaspoon dried sage

Arrange the potato slices in concentric rings in the skillet.

Allover Europe you'll find irresistible variations on potatoes layered in a pan: This simple Italian dish is much like a French potato *galette* and a close cousin of Swiss *rösti*. However, when you taste the garlic and sage you'll immediately recognize it as an Italian creation. Yellow-fleshed potatoes, such as the Yukon Gold variety, make an especially pretty potato cake.

1 Preheat the oven to 450°. Generously coat an ovenproof 8- or 9-inch skillet or a 9-inch pie plate with no-stick spray.

2 By hand, or using the slicing blade of a food processor, cut the potatoes into very thin slices. Arrange the potato slices in overlapping concentric circles in the prepared pan.

3 Drizzle the oil evenly over the potatoes, sprinkle with the salt and black pepper then scatter the garlic on top. Sprinkle with the sage.

4 Bake for 30 minutes, or until the potatoes are crisp at the edges and tender in the center. Serve directly from the skillet or pie plate.

Preparation time 5 minutes • **Total time** 45 minutes • **Per serving** 124 calories, 3.5 g. fat (25% of calories), 0.3 g. saturated fat, 0 mg. cholesterol, 144 mg. sodium, 2 g. dietary fiber, 8 mg. calcium, 1 mg. iron, 18 mg. vitamin C, 0 mg. beta-carotene
Serves 4

KITCHEN TIP

If you buy small, uniformly sized potatoes, you can slice them in a food processor: Fit the processor with the slicing blade and drop the potatoes, one at a time, through the feed tube.

BRAISED GREENS WITH BEANS

3 garlic cloves, crushed

1 teaspoon extra-virgin olive oil

3 cups torn escarole, rinsed

4 cups trimmed, loosely packed fresh spinach

1 bunch watercress, tough stems removed

1 can (19 ounces) red kidney beans, rinsed and drained

1 teaspoon balsamic vinegar

¼ teaspoon sugar

¼ teaspoon salt

⅛ teaspoon freshly ground black pepper

This hearty accompaniment for a light meal brings together three types of greens with meaty red kidney beans in garlicky olive oil; balsamic vinegar and a touch of sugar are added later to make a mild sweet-and-sour sauce. In Italy, many vegetables are cooked in olive oil with garlic. While sturdy vegetables like broccoli are usually blanched first, greens such as escarole, spinach and watercress, used here, can go right into the skillet, where they'll wilt in a matter of minutes.

1 In a large, heavy saucepan, combine the garlic and oil. Cook over medium-high heat, stirring constantly, for 1 to 2 minutes, or until the garlic is fragrant.

2 Add the escarole, increase the heat to high and cook, stirring frequently, for 1 to 2 minutes, or until wilted. Add the spinach and watercress, and cook, stirring frequently, for 1 to 2 minutes, or until all the greens are wilted and tender.

3 Add the beans, vinegar, sugar, salt and black pepper. Reduce the heat to medium-low and stir to combine. Cover and cook for 5 minutes, or until the beans are heated through and the flavors are blended.

Preparation time 15 minutes • **Total time** 30 minutes • **Per serving** 139 calories, 2.3 g. fat (15% of calories), 0.3 g. saturated fat, 0 mg. cholesterol, 395 mg. sodium, 9.4 g. dietary fiber, 189 mg. calcium, 4 mg. iron, 46 mg. vitamin C, 5 mg. beta-carotene • **Serves 4**

MARKET AND PANTRY
Watercress is sold in fat little bunches, which are sometimes set in a tub of water to keep them fresh. Choose a bunch with crisp, dark green leaves and stems. For cooking, you need only cut off the tough bottom part of the stems; for salads, you just pinch off individual sprigs or leaves.

SOFT POLENTA WITH GORGONZOLA

3½ cups cold water

½ teaspoon salt

1 cup yellow cornmeal

¼ cup 1% low-fat milk

1 ounce Gorgonzola cheese
without rind, crumbled

1 tablespoon plus 1 teaspoon
Neufchâtel cream cheese

½ teaspoon chopped fresh thyme
or 1 tablespoon chopped
parsley

¼ teaspoon freshly ground black
pepper

Polenta, a sort of mush or porridge made from meal, can be prepared with oats, spelt, barley, millet, chestnut flour or buckwheat, but today it is most commonly made from coarse-ground yellow cornmeal. Corn was a gift from the New World to Europe, and cornmeal polenta did not become popular in Italy until the 17th century. Creamy and bland, polenta needs a jolt of flavor that is often supplied by a sharp cheese, such as pungent Gorgonzola.

1 In a large, heavy no-stick saucepan, combine the water and salt, and bring to a boil over high heat. Whisking constantly, add the cornmeal in a slow, steady stream.

2 Reduce the heat to medium-low and cook the cornmeal mixture, stirring frequently and vigorously with a wooden spoon, for 15 minutes, or until the cornmeal is thickened, glossy and very smooth. Stir in the milk and remove the pan from the heat.

3 Stir in the Gorgonzola and Neufchâtel, the thyme or parsley and the black pepper. Stir until the cheeses are melted. Serve immediately.

Preparation time 10 minutes • **Total time** 35 minutes • **Per serving** 171 calories, 4.1 g. fat (21% of calories), 2.3 g. saturated fat, 10 mg. cholesterol, 399 mg. sodium, 1.9 g. dietary fiber, 65 mg. calcium, 2 mg. iron, 1 mg. vitamin C, 0.2 mg. beta-carotene • **Serves 4**

Gorgonzola, which originated near Milan, has a powerful flavor. One ounce is sufficient to flavor a big pot of polenta.

American Neufchâtel is a reduced-fat cream cheese. It gives the polenta a rich texture without adding a lot of fat.

BAKED FENNEL WITH TOMATO SAUCE

1 large or 2 medium fennel bulbs (about 1½ pounds)

1 can (14½ ounces) no-salt-added stewed tomatoes

1 tablespoon no-salt-added tomato paste

2 garlic cloves, crushed

1 tablespoon chopped fresh thyme leaves or ¼ teaspoon dried thyme

¼ teaspoon fennel seeds

¼ teaspoon dried tarragon, crumbled

⅛ teaspoon salt

⅛ teaspoon freshly ground black pepper

⅛ teaspoon crushed red pepper flakes

1 tablespoon grated Parmesan cheese

Fennel (*finocchio* in Italian) was once considered an appropriate food to be eaten at the end of a meal, perhaps to refresh the palate after a succession of heavy dishes. Crisp and sweet, with an aniselike fragrance, it would certainly succeed in that purpose. Fennel's sweet spiciness, however, is today more often tempered with savory ingredients, making it a tempting side dish for simple grilled poultry or fish. Here, fennel is slow-baked in an herbed tomato sauce and topped with Parmesan.

1 Preheat the oven to 425°.

2 Cut off and discard the stalks from the fennel. Halve the fennel bulb and cut into ¾-inch-thick wedges.

3 Put the fennel in a large saucepan and add cold water to cover. Cover the pan and bring to a boil over high heat. Reduce the heat to medium and simmer for 8 to 10 minutes, or until the fennel is fork-tender. Drain in a colander and arrange the fennel in a single layer in a 9 x 9-inch nonreactive baking dish.

4 While the fennel is cooking, in a small saucepan, combine the stewed tomatoes, tomato paste, garlic, thyme, fennel seeds, tarragon, salt, black pepper and red pepper flakes. Bring to a boil over medium-high heat, then immediately remove the pan from the heat.

5 Pour the tomato sauce over the fennel, sprinkle with the Parmesan and bake for about 15 minutes, or until the cheese is melted and the sauce is bubbly.

Preparation time 5 minutes • **Total time** 45 minutes • **Per serving** 62 calories, 0.7 g. fat (10% of calories), 0.2 g. saturated fat, 1 mg. cholesterol, 250 mg. sodium, 3.9 g. dietary fiber, 127 mg. calcium, 2 mg. iron, 30 mg. vitamin C, 0.5 mg. beta-carotene • **Serves 4**

SUBSTITUTION
If fennel is not available, you can cook celery in the same fashion: The fennel seeds in the sauce will give the celery a mild fennel flavor.

NUTRITION NOTE
Fennel is a good source of calcium, roughly comparable to such better-known sources for that mineral as spinach, beet greens and collards.

ROASTED ASPARAGUS WITH GREEN SAUCE

1 **pound fresh asparagus spears, trimmed**

1 **teaspoon grated lemon zest**

1 **teaspoon extra-virgin olive oil**

¼ **teaspoon salt**

¼ **teaspoon freshly ground black pepper**

⅓ **cup packed Italian parsley sprigs**

⅓ **cup sliced scallions**

2 **tablespoons defatted chicken broth**

2 **garlic cloves, sliced**

½ **teaspoon dried tarragon, crumbled**

⅔ **cup plain nonfat yogurt**

1 **tablespoon fresh lemon juice**

1 **tablespoon low-fat mayonnaise**

Lemon wedges (optional)

Asparagus has been grown in Italy since Roman times; the asparagus grown in Ravenna, in the Emilia-Romagna region, was praised by the ancients, including famed historian Pliny the Elder. Here is a pleasing way to present the succulent spears (which may be served hot, warm or chilled): with a creamy lemon-herb sauce. Roasting, an unusual method for green vegetables, cooks the asparagus slowly and evenly. Note that the cooking time will depend on the thickness (or thinness) of the asparagus stalks.

1 Preheat the oven to 425°. Spray an 11 x 7-inch baking dish with no-stick spray.

2 Arrange the asparagus in the prepared pan. Sprinkle with the lemon zest, then drizzle with the oil. Sprinkle with ⅛ teaspoon each of the salt and black pepper. Turn the asparagus to coat it with the seasonings. Bake, turning the asparagus a few times, for 20 to 25 minutes, or until the spears are tender.

3 Meanwhile, in a small skillet, combine the parsley, scallions, broth, garlic and tarragon. Bring to a boil over high heat, then cover and simmer, stirring occasionally, for 3 to 4 minutes, or until the scallions are tender.

4 Transfer the mixture to a food processor. Add the yogurt, lemon juice, mayonnaise and the remaining ⅛ teaspoon each salt and black pepper, and purée until smooth. Transfer to a small bowl.

5 Serve the asparagus with the green sauce on the side. Offer lemon wedges, if desired.

Preparation time 15 minutes • **Total time** 30 minutes • **Per serving** 71 calories, 2 g. fat (26% of calories), 0.2 g. saturated fat, 1 mg. cholesterol, 238 mg. sodium, 1.6 g. dietary fiber, 122 mg. calcium, 1 mg. iron, 44 mg. vitamin C, 0.8 mg. beta-carotene • **Serves 4**

Vegetables & Salads

❧ ❧ ❧

MAIN DISHES AND

ACCOMPANIMENTS FROM A ZESTY

COLE SLAW TO A WARM SHRIMP

AND POTATO SALAD

THREE-BEAN SALAD WITH TURKEY

2 tablespoons unsweetened apple juice

1 tablespoon plus 2 teaspoons extra-virgin olive oil

2 tablespoons cider vinegar

1 tablespoon chopped fresh Italian parsley

1 teaspoon coarse Dijon mustard

½ teaspoon freshly ground black pepper

¼ teaspoon dried tarragon, crumbled

1 can (10½ ounces) black beans, rinsed and drained

1 can (10½ ounces) chick-peas, rinsed and drained

½ cup chopped red onion

½ cup very thinly sliced celery

12 ounces green beans, trimmed and cut into ½-inch lengths

6 ounces sliced skinless roast turkey breast, cut into julienne strips

Although it's called a vinaigrette, oil—not vinegar—is traditionally the main ingredient in this classic dressing. But you can tip the proportions in a healthier direction by replacing some of the oil with broth or, in this case, apple juice. Vary the taste of your vinaigrette with a selection of vinegars, such as cider, rice-wine and balsamic. The amount of vinegar you use in this recipe depends upon your personal taste and the sharpness of the vinegar you choose.

1 In a salad bowl, whisk together the apple juice, oil, vinegar, parsley, mustard, black pepper and tarragon.

2 Add the black beans, chick-peas, onions and celery to the dressing, and toss to coat well. Cover and let stand at room temperature for 10 minutes while you prepare the green beans.

3 In a medium saucepan, bring ½ inch of water to a boil over high heat. Add the green beans and return to a boil. Reduce the heat to medium and simmer for 4 to 6 minutes, or until the beans are tender. Drain in a colander and cool under cold running water.

4 Add the green beans and turkey to the salad bowl, and toss to coat with the dressing. Taste the salad and add more vinegar if the dressing seems bland.

Preparation time 15 minutes • **Total time** 40 minutes • **Per serving** 255 calories, 10.2 g. fat (36% of calories), 1.5 g. saturated fat, 36 mg. cholesterol, 290 mg. sodium, 5.6 g. dietary fiber, 71 mg. calcium, 3 mg. iron, 16 mg. vitamin C, 0 mg. beta-carotene
Serves 4

ON THE MENU
Unlike the standard three-bean salad, this one is a main dish and needs only thick slices of hearty rye bread or sourdough peasant bread to make it a meal.

FOR A CHANGE
Use cannellini, kidney or pinto beans instead of chick-peas. Try yellow wax beans instead of the green beans, or substitute lean ham for the roast turkey.

MAPLE CARROTS

8 large carrots, cut into thin
  diagonal slices

1 tablespoon pure maple syrup

2 teaspoons unsalted butter or
  margarine

  Large pinch of ground
  cinnamon

  Pinch of ground ginger

1 tablespoon chopped fresh
  cilantro (optional)

Carrots are among the most popular vegetables in America, and it's fortunate that they are so well-liked: A super source of beta-carotene, carrots also provide good amounts of potassium and both soluble and insoluble fiber. Keep carrot sticks on hand for snacks, add grated carrots to salads and sandwiches and, for a change, serve steamed carrot slices, glazed with maple syrup and butter, as an appetizing addition to a simple dinner. Instead of slicing the carrots, you might like to try roll-cutting them (see below).

1 In a deep, medium skillet, bring ½ inch of water to a boil over high heat. Add the carrots and return to a boil. Reduce the heat to medium and simmer for 5 to 6 minutes, or until the carrots are tender. Drain the carrots in a colander; dry the skillet.

2 Add the maple syrup, butter or margarine, cinnamon and ginger to the skillet, and return to medium heat. Cook, stirring constantly, until the butter melts and bubbles. Add the carrots and the cilantro, if using, and toss until the carrots are glazed and heated through.

Preparation time 10 minutes • **Total time** 10 minutes • **Per serving** 66 calories, 2.1 g. fat (28% of calories), 1.2 g. saturated fat, 5 mg. cholesterol, 30 mg. sodium, 2.6 g. dietary fiber, 27 mg. calcium, 1 mg. iron, 8 mg. vitamin C, 14 mg. beta-carotene
Serves 4

To roll-cut carrots, first cut off the end of a carrot on a sharp diagonal.

Keeping the knife at the same angle, roll the carrot 180° and make a second cut.

Calico Slaw with Poppyseed Dressing

⅓ cup nonfat mayonnaise

1 tablespoon frozen orange juice concentrate

2 teaspoons fresh lemon juice

1 teaspoon poppy seeds

½ teaspoon honey

¼ teaspoon freshly ground black pepper

1½ cups finely shredded green cabbage

1½ cups finely shredded red cabbage

½ cup thinly sliced red bell peppers

½ cup stringed and julienne-cut snow peas

¼ cup coarsely grated carrot

Poppyseed dressing is usually associated with fruit salads, but this citrusy-sweet version is also tasty on a colorful toss of cabbage, peppers, snow peas and carrots. To bring out the flavor of the poppy seeds, cook them in a dry skillet over medium heat just until they smell toasty. Immediately transfer the seeds to a plate and let them cool a bit before adding them to the dressing.

1 In a salad bowl, combine the mayonnaise, orange juice concentrate, lemon juice, poppy seeds, honey and black pepper; whisk together until well blended.

2 Add the green and red cabbages, bell peppers, snow peas and carrots; toss until the vegetables are well coated with the dressing.

Preparation time 25 minutes • **Total time** 25 minutes • **Per serving** 55 calories, 0.5 g. fat (8% of calories), 0 g. saturated fat, 0 mg. cholesterol, 150 mg. sodium, 2.1 g. dietary fiber, 49 mg. calcium, 1 mg. iron, 70 mg. vitamin C, 1.6 mg. beta-carotene • **Serves 4**

❧ ❧ ❧

Cut the head of cabbage in half lengthwise, through its core.

Remove the wedge-shaped core section from each cabbage half.

Halve each half again, then lay each quarter flat on a board and shred it crosswise.

SHRIMP AND POTATO SALAD

3 cups water

2 tablespoons plus 2 teaspoons cider vinegar

2 garlic cloves, peeled

1 bay leaf, preferably imported (Turkish)

¼ teaspoon crushed red pepper flakes

⅛ teaspoon salt

12 ounces medium shrimp (thawed if frozen), rinsed

12 ounces small new red potatoes, cut into ½-inch-thick wedges

3 tablespoons reduced-calorie mayonnaise

2 tablespoons plain nonfat yogurt

1 teaspoon Dijon mustard

½ teaspoon celery seed

¼ teaspoon freshly ground black pepper

1 kirby cucumber, thinly sliced

4 radishes, sliced

2 scallions, sliced

The bay leaf may seem an insignificant part of this recipe: After all, it's discarded after cooking, as bay leaves usually are. However, every ingredient counts, and for a more subtle flavor you might try the small Turkish bay leaves rather than the long, narrow domestic ones. Both are available in supermarkets. Like all dried herbs, bay leaves lose their fragrance after a while. If the ones in your spice collection look dusty or browned, it's time to replace them.

1 In a large saucepan, combine the water, 1 tablespoon of the cider vinegar, the garlic, bay leaf, crushed red pepper and salt. Cover and bring to a boil over high heat. Reduce the heat to medium and simmer for 5 minutes to blend the flavors.

2 Add the shrimp to the pot, stir well and simmer for 4 to 5 minutes, or until the shrimp turn pink and firm. Using a slotted spoon (reserve the cooking liquid), transfer the shrimp to a bowl. Rinse briefly with cold water until cool enough to handle and set aside.

3 Add the potatoes to the pot of cooking liquid; increase the heat to high, cover and bring to a boil. Meanwhile, peel and devein the shrimp.

4 Reduce the heat to medium-low and simmer the potatoes for 10 to 15 minutes, or until fork-tender. Reserving 1 tablespoon of the cooking liquid for the dressing, drain the potatoes in a colander; remove and discard the garlic cloves and bay leaf. Transfer the potatoes to a salad bowl and set aside.

5 In a cup, mix the reserved cooking liquid with the remaining 1 tablespoon plus 2 teaspoons cider vinegar, the mayonnaise, yogurt, mustard, celery seeds and black pepper.

6 Add the shrimp, cucumbers, radishes and scallions to the potatoes, then pour on the dressing and toss to coat well.

Preparation time 15 minutes • **Total time** 45 minutes • **Per serving** 187 calories, 4.6 g. fat (22% of calories), 1 g. saturated fat, 109 mg. cholesterol, 248 mg. sodium, 1.9 g. dietary fiber, 67 mg. calcium, 3 mg. iron, 17 mg. vitamin C, 0 mg. beta-carotene
Serves 4

WARM CHICKEN AND ORZO SALAD

6 ounces orzo or other small pasta

1¾ cups defatted reduced-sodium chicken broth

½ cup water

12 ounces boneless, skinless chicken breasts, trimmed and cut into 1-inch chunks

4 cups broccoli florets

¼ cup packed Italian parsley sprigs

2 tablespoons extra-virgin olive oil

2 tablespoons red wine vinegar

1 tablespoon Dijon mustard

¼ teaspoon salt

½ teaspoon freshly ground black pepper

1 garlic clove, peeled

¼ cup diced, drained roasted red peppers (from a jar)

Pasta salads, often party fare, also make delightful family dinners. This one starts with the tried-and-true pairing of chicken and rice, but the "rice" is really orzo, a grain-shaped pasta. The dish tastes best when served warm, but if necessary, you can prepare it ahead of time and refrigerate it. Just be sure to take the salad out of the refrigerator a little while before serving time so that it can return to room temperature.

1 Bring a covered medium saucepan of water to a boil over high heat. Add the pasta to the boiling water, return to a boil and cook for 8 to 10 minutes or according to package directions until al dente. Drain in a colander, rinse briefly under cold running water and drain again. Transfer the pasta to a large salad bowl.

2 While the pasta is cooking, bring 1½ cups of the broth and the water to a boil in a medium skillet. Add the chicken and return to a boil. Reduce the heat to medium-low, cover and simmer, stirring occasionally, for 6 to 8 minutes, or until the chicken is cooked through. Using a slotted spoon, transfer the chicken to the bowl of orzo; reserve the broth in the skillet.

3 Return the broth to a boil over high heat. Add the broccoli and return to a boil. Cook for 3 to 5 minutes, or until the broccoli is crisp-tender. Drain the broccoli in a colander, cool briefly under cold running water and drain again. Add the broccoli to the bowl of orzo.

4 Combine the parsley, oil, vinegar, mustard, salt, black pepper and the remaining ¼ cup broth in a food processor. With the processor running, drop the garlic clove through the feed tube; process the mixture until puréed.

5 Pour the dressing over the pasta mixture. Add the roasted peppers and toss the salad to mix well. Serve warm.

Preparation time 10 minutes • **Total time** 20 minutes • **Per serving** 365 calories, 9.4 g. fat (23% of calories), 1.4 g. saturated fat, 49 mg. cholesterol, 400 mg. sodium, 5.8 g. dietary fiber, 83 mg. calcium, 4 mg. iron, 109 mg. vitamin C, 2 mg. beta-carotene • **Serves 4**

❧ ❧ ❧

BUTTERMILK MASHED POTATOES

1 **pound baking potatoes, such as russets, peeled and cut into 1-inch chunks**

1 **cup water**

½ **cup defatted chicken broth**

2 **garlic cloves, unpeeled**

¼ **cup low-fat buttermilk**

2 **tablespoons thinly sliced scallions**

⅛ **teaspoon freshly ground pepper, preferably white**

Large pinch of salt

Mashed potatoes give meals the comforting taste of home. Traditionally, the potatoes would be finished with butter and cream, but there are other ways to add richness: For this recipe, the potatoes are cooked in broth with garlic cloves, then mashed with buttermilk and sliced scallions. Mash the potatoes smooth, or leave them truly "homestyle"—a bit lumpy.

1 In a medium saucepan, combine the potatoes, water, broth and garlic cloves. Cover and bring to a boil over high heat. Reduce the heat to medium-low and simmer for 12 to 15 minutes, or until the potatoes are fork-tender.

2 Just before the potatoes are done, place the buttermilk in a small, heavy saucepan and warm it over low heat.

3 Drain the potatoes well; discard the garlic cloves. Return the potatoes to the pan and mash them with a potato masher.

4 Stir the warmed buttermilk, scallions, ground pepper and salt into the potatoes and serve.

Preparation time 10 minutes • **Total time** 30 minutes • **Per serving** 96 calories, 0.5 g. fat (5% of calories), 0.1 g. saturated fat, 1 mg. cholesterol, 191 mg. sodium, 1.8 g. dietary fiber, 24 mg. calcium, 1 mg. iron, 17 mg. vitamin C, 0 mg. beta-carotene **Serves 4**

❧ ❧ ❧

This type of potato masher requires a fair amount of pressure.

The more open wire masher is a little easier to use because there's less resistance.

An electric mixer on low speed is the easiest way to mash potatoes.

BROCCOLI WITH CORN AND CRISP GARLIC

1 **lemon**

3 **cups small broccoli florets**

¾ **cup frozen corn kernels**

1 **teaspoon extra-virgin olive oil**

3 **garlic cloves, thinly sliced**

¼ **teaspoon freshly ground black pepper**

⅛ **teaspoon salt**

As readily available as broccoli is today, it wasn't until the mid-20th century that this vegetable gained popularity in the United States. In Italy, where broccoli has been a mainstay for centuries, it is often dressed, as it is here, with garlicky oil.

1 Using a swivel-bladed vegetable peeler, remove 2 or 3 wide bands of zest from the lemon; cut enough zest into thin strips to measure a scant tablespoon. Squeeze 1 tablespoon of juice from the lemon.

2 In a covered, deep medium skillet, bring ½ inch of water to a boil over high heat. Add the broccoli and return to a boil. Cook, turning the pieces occasionally, for 3 to 4 minutes, or until the broccoli is crisp-tender. Add the corn during the last minute or so of cooking time. Drain the broccoli and corn in a colander, and transfer to a heated platter; cover and keep warm.

3 In a small skillet, warm the oil over medium heat. Add the garlic, black pepper and salt, and sauté, stirring constantly, for about 1 minute, or until the garlic just begins to brown. Add the lemon zest and lemon juice, and stir to combine; immediately pour the garlic mixture over the broccoli and corn.

Preparation time 10 minutes • **Total time** 25 minutes • **Per serving** 72 calories, 1.7 g. fat (21% of calories), 0.2 g. saturated fat, 0 mg. cholesterol, 94 mg. sodium, 4 g. dietary fiber, 49 mg. calcium, 1 mg. iron, 0 mg. vitamin C, 1 mg. beta-carotene
Serves 4

❧ ❧ ❧

First, shave wide strips of peel from the lemon, removing only the colored zest.

Then, with a sharp paring knife, cut each piece of lemon zest into thin strips.

Mashed Sweet Potatoes with Honey

1 **pound sweet potatoes, peeled and cut into 1-inch chunks**

¼ **cup apricot nectar**

1 **tablespoon honey**

⅛ **teaspoon ground cinnamon**

Large pinch of freshly ground black pepper

It seems a pity to serve sweet potatoes only during the holidays—and it's practically a crime to bury their velvety texture and wonderful natural sweetness under a layer of marshmallows and brown sugar. This notably nutritious vegetable, available all year round in most supermarkets, can be boiled, steamed, baked, roasted or even grilled. Bring out the sweet potato's savory side with the same toppings you'd use for white potatoes—such as yogurt and chives—or enhance its sweetness with a touch of honey and some apricot nectar.

1 Place the sweet potatoes in a medium saucepan and add enough cold water to cover them. Cover the pan and bring to a boil over high heat. Reduce the heat to medium-low and simmer for 12 to 15 minutes, or until the potatoes are fork-tender.

2 Meanwhile, in a small saucepan, warm the apricot nectar over medium-low heat.

3 Drain the potatoes in a colander and return them to the saucepan in which they were cooked. Add the apricot nectar, honey, cinnamon and black pepper, and mash until smooth.

Preparation time 10 minutes • **Total time** 35 minutes • **Per serving** 111 calories, 0.3 g. fat (2% of calories), 0 g. saturated fat, 0 mg. cholesterol, 11 mg. sodium, 0.5 g. dietary fiber, 20 mg. calcium, 1 mg. iron, 27 mg. vitamin C, 10 mg. beta-carotene • **Serves 4**

MARKET AND PANTRY

Although sweet potatoes look quite sturdy, they are highly susceptible to decay. Buy potatoes that are smooth, firm and free of shriveled or dark areas. Store them in a cool, dry place (about 55° is best), not in the refrigerator, where their natural sugars will turn to starch, robbing the potatoes of their unique flavor.

FOR A CHANGE

Season the mashed sweet potatoes with nutmeg, allspice, ginger or cloves.

ON THE MENU

These lightly sweet and spicy potatoes are delicious with pork or poultry. For a holiday meal, offer both mashed sweet and white potatoes.

ROMAINE SALAD WITH PEPPER DRESSING

3 **tablespoons nonfat sour cream**

2 **tablespoons low-fat buttermilk**

2 **teaspoons red wine vinegar**

½ **teaspoon coarsely ground black pepper**

⅛ **teaspoon celery seeds**

⅛ **teaspoon salt**

3 **cups cut-up romaine lettuce (1-inch pieces)**

¾ **cup sliced radishes**

Although green salads are virtually fat-free, commercial salad dressings can turn a plate of lettuce into the fattiest part of the meal. Two tablespoons of blue-cheese dressing, for instance—the amount a salad-bar ladle might hold—can add 14 grams of fat. The packet of dressing that accompanies a fast-food salad may contain as much as 30 grams of fat. Of course, this doesn't mean you have to settle for a "naked" salad: Just base your dressing on low-fat ingredients, such as the buttermilk and nonfat sour cream used here. For a change, make the salad with red-leaf lettuce or radicchio and use white radishes (see below).

1 In a salad bowl, combine the sour cream, buttermilk, vinegar, black pepper, celery seeds and salt; whisk with a fork until blended.

2 Add the romaine and the radishes, and toss to coat well with the dressing.

Preparation time 15 minutes • **Total time** 15 minutes • **Per serving** 22 calories, 0.3 g. fat (10% of calories), 0 g. saturated fat, 0 mg. cholesterol, 94 mg. sodium, 1.2 g. dietary fiber, 46 mg. calcium, 1 mg. iron, 15 mg. vitamin C, 0.7 mg. beta-carotene • **Serves 4**

Red "button" radishes, the most familiar type, are available everywhere.

Mild-tasting white icicle radishes, like button radishes, do not require peeling.

Sharp-flavored daikon, a giant Japanese radish, should be peeled before using.

TOMATO AND CORN SUCCOTASH

1 cup trimmed, halved green beans

1 teaspoon olive oil

1 medium onion, chopped

1 garlic clove, minced

¼ teaspoon dried thyme, crumbled

⅛ teaspoon freshly ground black pepper

⅛ teaspoon salt

Large pinch of sugar

2 tablespoons defatted chicken broth or water

2 small ripe tomatoes, coarsely chopped

1 cup fresh or frozen corn kernels

As prepared in colonial America, succotash was a simple stew of corn and lima beans, enriched with salt pork and milk. The dish evolved in time, with the addition of other seasonal ingredients—such as bell peppers and tomatoes—and creative seasonings. For this colorful rendition, fresh corn is combined with green beans and tomatoes; the flavor is accentuated with onions, garlic and thyme.

1 In a deep medium skillet, bring ½ inch of water to a boil over high heat. Add the green beans and return to a boil. Cook for 3 to 5 minutes, stirring occasionally, until the beans are crisp-tender. Drain the beans in a colander; dry the skillet.

2 Add the oil to the same skillet, then stir in the onions, garlic, thyme, black pepper, salt and sugar. Sauté over medium-high heat for 1 minute, then stir in 1 tablespoon of the broth or water and sauté for 4 to 5 minutes, or until the onions are tender.

3 Stir in the blanched green beans, the tomatoes, corn and the remaining 1 tablespoon broth or water, and bring to a simmer. Reduce the heat to medium-low, cover and simmer, stirring occasionally, for 5 minutes, or until the tomatoes release their juices and all the vegetables are tender.

Preparation time 10 minutes • **Total time** 35 minutes • **Per serving** 81 calories, 1.9 g. fat (21% of calories), 0.2 g. saturated fat, 0 mg. cholesterol, 114 mg. sodium, 3.1 g. dietary fiber, 26 mg. calcium, 1 mg. iron, 20 mg. vitamin C, 0.4 mg. beta-carotene • **Serves 4**

MARKET AND PANTRY
Corn loses its natural sweetness very quickly after it's picked. Short of growing your own corn, the best guarantee of freshness is to buy corn at the farm where it is harvested, or at a farmer's market.

KITCHEN TIP
You can buy a special cutter to remove the kernels from fresh corn: This metal trough, about the size of an ear of corn, has a center opening fitted with blades. When you slide an ear of corn across the blades, they cut off the kernels, which drop through the opening. It's easy to cut the kernels from corn with a knife, too. Trim one end of an ear of corn so that you can stand it upright on a cutting board. Slide the blade of a sharp knife down the ear to cut off the kernels. Press gently so that you don't cut off any of the fibrous cob along with the tender kernels.

SPINACH WITH MUSHROOMS

2 large shallots or 1 small onion, chopped

¼ cup defatted chicken broth or water

¾ teaspoon olive oil

4 ounces small fresh mushrooms, quartered

1 pound washed spinach, tough stems removed

⅛ teaspoon salt

⅛ teaspoon freshly ground black pepper

We've come a long way since the time when cookbooks directed that spinach and other tender greens be "stewed" for half an hour, turning them into a gray mush with little nutritional value. When spinach is cooked just long enough to wilt it, the leaves stay a vibrant green and little of the vitamin C is lost.

1 In a large no-stick skillet, combine the shallots or onions, 2 tablespoons of the broth or water and the oil. Place the skillet over medium-high heat and cook, stirring constantly, for 3 to 4 minutes, or until the shallots or onions are tender.

2 Add the mushrooms and the remaining 2 tablespoons broth or water, and cook, stirring frequently, for 4 to 6 minutes, or until the mushrooms are tender.

3 Increase the heat to high. Add the spinach by handfuls and stir constantly until the spinach wilts; cook for 1 minute longer, season with the salt and pepper, and serve.

Preparation time 15 minutes • **Total time** 25 minutes • **Per serving** 39 calories, 1.3 g. fat (30% of calories), 0.2 g. saturated fat, 0 mg. cholesterol, 197 mg. sodium, 2.5 g. dietary fiber, 86 mg. calcium, 3 mg. iron, 24 mg. vitamin C, 3 mg. beta-carotene
Serves 4

Wash the spinach and gently pat it dry with a kitchen towel.

Hold the leaves between your fingers and pull off the stem from each leaf.

MEXICAN TACO SALAD

4 **corn tortillas**

8 **ounces lean, trimmed beef top round**

1 **tablespoon chili powder**

½ **teaspoon olive oil**

2 **tablespoons defatted beef broth**

1 **large tomato, diced**

1 **can (10½ ounces) pinto beans or red kidney beans, rinsed and drained**

1 **tablespoon chopped, seeded canned jalapeño chilies (optional)**

2 **cups shredded iceberg lettuce**

1 **small red onion, sliced**

1 **tablespoon fresh lime juice**

1½ **ounces Cheddar cheese, shredded**

¼ **cup chopped fresh cilantro**

Y ou're far better off making a taco salad at home than ordering one at a fast-food restaurant. Served with a deep-fried flour tortilla, cheese, sour cream and dressing, one popular fast-food taco salad packs about 900 calories and 60 grams of fat—a terrific incentive to shop for some lean, flavorful ingredients and assemble this beefy salad in your own kitchen.

1 Preheat the oven to 400°.

2 Stack the tortillas and cut them into 8 wedges each. Arrange the tortilla wedges in a single layer on a baking sheet and bake for 8 to 10 minutes, or until crisp and lightly browned. Remove the baking sheet from the oven and let the tortilla chips cool on the baking sheet.

3 While the tortilla chips are baking, cut the beef into cubes and process in a food processor until finely ground. Add the chili powder and pulse just until mixed.

4 In a medium no-stick skillet, warm the oil over high heat until hot but not smoking. Crumble in the beef, add the broth and sauté for 2 to 3 minutes, or until the meat is no longer pink. Add the tomatoes, beans and jalapeños, if using, and sauté for 3 to 4 minutes, or until the tomatoes are softened and the mixture is just heated through.

5 Arrange the shredded lettuce and onions in a shallow serving bowl; drizzle with the lime juice. Spoon the beef mixture on top and sprinkle the Cheddar over it. Scatter the tortilla chips around the beef and sprinkle with the cilantro.

Preparation time 15 minutes • **Total time** 35 minutes • **Per serving** 249 calories, 7.5 g. fat (27% of calories), 3.1 g. saturated fat, 44 mg. cholesterol, 310 mg. sodium, 5.2 g. dietary fiber, 172 mg. calcium, 3 mg. iron, 18 mg. vitamin C, 1 mg. beta-carotene • **Serves 4**

Stack the tortillas and cut them in half, then stack the two halves and cut them into wedges.

ON THE MENU
Accompany the taco salad with your favorite bottled salsa. Offer a refreshing pitcher of pink lemonade, made by mixing a small amount of cranberry juice into fresh lemonade. For a dessert with Mexican flair, dust scoops of chocolate frozen yogurt with ground cinnamon.

LAMB AND LENTIL SALAD WITH PEPPERS

1½ cups lentils, picked over and rinsed

1½ cups defatted reduced-sodium chicken broth

1½ cups water

2 garlic cloves (1 whole and 1 minced)

2 teaspoons ground cumin

½ teaspoon ground turmeric

¼ teaspoon salt

Pinch of ground cloves

¼ cup fresh orange juice

2 tablespoons fresh lemon juice

1 tablespoon plus 1 teaspoon olive oil

1 teaspoon grated lemon zest

1 teaspoon grated orange zest

½ teaspoon freshly ground black pepper

8 ounces lean, well-trimmed, boneless lamb steak, cut into 1-inch cubes

½ teaspoon dried oregano

1 jar (7 ounces) roasted red peppers, cut into julienne strips

4 scallions, thinly sliced

2 carrots, thinly sliced

2 celery stalks, thinly sliced

8 cups colorful mixed greens, torn into bite-size pieces

Thin strips of lemon zest, for garnish (optional)

There's a subtle taste of India in this rib-sticking salad: Lentils are a staple in Indian kitchens, and lamb is very popular with those who eat meat. In addition, two spices commonly found in Indian cuisine—turmeric and cumin—are used to flavor the lentils. Adding a whole garlic clove to the lentils while they cook (and then discarding it) imparts a delicate, garlicky flavor; you can use this trick any time you're cooking legumes, grains or pasta.

1 In a medium saucepan, combine the lentils, chicken broth, water, whole garlic clove, cumin, turmeric, ⅛ teaspoon of the salt and the cloves; bring to a boil over high heat. Reduce the heat to medium-low and simmer, uncovered, for 20 to 25 minutes, or until the lentils are just tender. Drain the lentils in a colander; remove the garlic clove. Return the lentils to the pan and keep warm.

2 Preheat the broiler.

3 To make the dressing, in a large bowl, whisk together the orange juice, lemon juice, oil, lemon zest, orange zest, black pepper, minced garlic and remaining ⅛ teaspoon of salt.

4 Place the lamb on the broiler-pan rack and drizzle with 1 table-spoon of the dressing. Sprinkle the lamb with the oregano. Broil the lamb 4 to 5 inches from the heat for 5 minutes, turning once, for medium-rare.

5 Meanwhile, add the peppers, scallions, carrots, celery and the reserved lentils to the bowl with the dressing and toss to mix.

6 Arrange the greens on a platter and mound the lentil mixture in the center. Spoon the broiled lamb cubes on top. Garnish with lemon zest, if desired.

Preparation time 25 minutes • **Total time** 55 minutes • **Per serving** 458 calories, 10.7 g. fat (20% of calories), 2.5 g. saturated fat, 39 mg. cholesterol, 573 mg. sodium, 11.9 g. dietary fiber, 156 mg. calcium, 11 mg. iron, 82 mg. vitamin C, 10 mg. beta-carotene • **Serves 4**

Two-Potato Salad with Chicken

- 1 pound sweet potatoes, peeled and cut into 1-inch chunks
- 1 pound all-purpose potatoes, peeled and cut into 1-inch chunks
- 3 medium carrots, cut into 1-inch chunks
- ¼ teaspoon salt
- 12 ounces skinless, boneless chicken breast halves
- ½ teaspoon freshly ground black pepper
- ¼ teaspoon paprika
- ¼ cup reduced-calorie mayonnaise
- ¼ cup plain nonfat yogurt
- 3 tablespoons sweet pickle relish
- 1 tablespoon Dijon mustard
- 1 garlic clove, minced
- 1 medium green bell pepper, diced
- 2 celery stalks, diced
- 2 scallions, chopped

For an indoor-outdoor meal, grill the chicken on the backyard barbecue while the vegetables chill. You could also bring the cooked vegetables in a picnic cooler to a grilling site farther afield (at a park or beach) and prepare the dish on the spot. When time is short, you can even make the salad with grilled or barbecued chicken breast from the supermarket, or with leftover roast chicken.

1 Preheat the broiler. Spray a broiler-pan rack with no-stick spray.

2 Place the sweet potatoes, all-purpose potatoes, carrots and salt in a large saucepan with cold water to cover and bring to a boil over high heat. Reduce the heat to medium-low and simmer, covered, for 10 to 15 minutes, or until the potatoes are just tender. Drain in a colander. Spread the vegetables in a shallow baking dish and place in the freezer for 10 minutes to chill.

3 While the vegetables are chilling, sprinkle the chicken with ¼ teaspoon of the black pepper and the paprika. Place the chicken on the prepared rack and broil 4 to 5 inches from the heat, turning the pieces several times, for 6 to 8 minutes, or until cooked through. Remove from the broiler, cool briefly and cut into 1-inch pieces.

4 To make the dressing, in a large bowl, whisk together the mayonnaise, yogurt, pickle relish, mustard, garlic and the remaining ¼ teaspoon black pepper.

5 Add the chilled vegetables, bell peppers, celery and scallions to the dressing, and toss to mix. Add the chicken and toss gently.

Preparation time 35 minutes • **Total time** 45 minutes • **Per serving** 375 calories, 7.2 g. fat (17% of calories), 1.7 g. saturated fat, 57 mg. cholesterol, 468 mg. sodium, 6.7 g. dietary fiber, 91 mg. calcium, 3 mg. iron, 60 mg. vitamin C, 19.1 mg. beta-carotene • **Serves 4**

ON THE MENU
You don't need to add much to this very appealing summer supper: Start with ice-cold cucumbers and onions tossed with rice vinegar, and put out bowls of chilled berries for dessert.

Mexican Tuna Cobb Salad

¼ **cup chopped fresh cilantro**

¼ **cup fat-free mayonnaise**

¼ **cup plain nonfat yogurt**

3 **tablespoons drained canned chopped green chilies**

2 **tablespoons minced red onion**

2 **tablespoons fresh lime juice**

1 **teaspoon grated lime zest**

¼ **teaspoon salt**

⅛ **teaspoon freshly ground black pepper**

8 **cups Romaine lettuce, thinly sliced**

1 **can (19 ounces) pinto or red kidney beans, rinsed and drained**

1 **can (6⅛ ounces) water-packed tuna, drained and flaked**

4 **plum tomatoes, diced**

1 **small cucumber, peeled, seeded and diced**

1 **medium yellow or red bell pepper, diced**

½ **medium avocado, peeled and diced**

½ **cup diced radishes**

2 **tablespoons chopped fresh cilantro, for garnish (optional)**

Baked tortilla chips (optional)

Robert Cobb, manager of the original Brown Derby restaurant, might not recognize this as the salad he invented and brought to fame back in the 1920s, but it's fun to improvise on his idea of a "chopped" salad. Here, the components are tuna, beans, tomatoes, cucumbers, bell peppers, avocado and radishes, arranged on a bed of Romaine and accented with a creamy cilantro dressing. Accompany the salad with low-fat oven-baked tortilla chips or warm corn tortillas—and be sure everyone gets a good look at this impressive salad before you dish it out.

1 To make the dressing, in a small bowl, combine the cilantro, mayonnaise, yogurt, chilies, onions, lime juice, lime zest, salt and black pepper, and whisk until blended.

2 In a large bowl, toss the lettuce with ¼ cup of the dressing.

3 Arrange the lettuce on a platter. Spoon the beans, tuna, tomatoes, cucumbers, bell peppers, avocados, radishes and some of the dressing in parallel rows on top of the lettuce. Place the remaining dressing in a small bowl to serve on the side. If desired, sprinkle the salad with chopped cilantro and serve with baked tortilla chips.

Preparation time 35 minutes • **Total time** 45 minutes • **Per serving** 231 calories, 5.2 g. fat (20% of calories), 0.8 g. saturated fat, 17 mg. cholesterol, 668 mg. sodium, 7.7 g. dietary fiber, 122 mg. calcium, 5 mg. iron, 90 mg. vitamin C, 2.7 mg. beta-carotene • **Serves 4**

❧ ❧ ❧

To seed the cucumber, first peel it, then slice it in half lengthwise.

Using the tip of a teaspoon or a melon baller, scrape out the seeds.

SESAME NOODLES WITH GRILLED SALMON

8 ounces spaghetti

6 ounces snow peas, trimmed and halved

1 tablespoon plus 2 teaspoons reduced-sodium soy sauce

1 teaspoon light brown sugar

1 teaspoon fresh lemon juice

¼ teaspoon grated fresh ginger

12 ounces skinned salmon fillet, cut into 4 equal pieces

½ cup plain nonfat yogurt

2 tablespoons reduced-fat peanut butter

2 garlic cloves, minced

½ teaspoon dark sesame oil

¼ teaspoon hot-pepper sauce

2 medium carrots, shredded

1 medium red bell pepper, cut into julienne strips

2 scallions, cut into julienne strips

½ cup loosely packed fresh cilantro leaves, chopped

Reduced-sodium soy sauce, for dipping (optional)

Cold sesame noodles—a key to the reputation of any Szechuan restaurant—make a terrific foundation for a main-dish salad. Marinated broiled salmon fillets are an unexpected and highly satisfying addition to the sauced noodles; snow peas, peppers, carrots and scallions add lots of color and crunch.

1 Preheat the broiler. Spray a broiler-pan rack with no-stick spray.

2 Bring a large covered pot of water to a boil over high heat. Add the pasta, return to a boil and cook for 8 to 9 minutes, or according to package directions until al dente. Thirty seconds before the pasta is done, stir in the snow peas. Drain the pasta and snow peas in a colander and cool briefly under gently running cold water; drain again.

3 While the pasta is cooking, combine 2 teaspoons of the soy sauce, the brown sugar, lemon juice and ginger in a shallow baking dish; add the salmon, turning to coat.

4 Arrange the salmon on the prepared broiler rack and spoon the soy mixture on top. Broil the salmon 4 to 5 inches from the heat for 8 to 10 minutes, or until lightly browned and cooked through. Remove from the broiler.

5 Meanwhile, make the dressing. In a large bowl, whisk together the yogurt, peanut butter, garlic, sesame oil, hot-pepper sauce and the remaining 1 tablespoon soy sauce until blended.

6 Add the drained pasta and snow peas, the carrots, bell peppers, scallions and cilantro to the dressing, and toss to mix. Divide the sesame noodles among 4 plates and top each portion with a piece of grilled salmon. Serve with additional soy sauce, if desired.

Preparation time 35 minutes • **Total time** 45 minutes • **Per serving** 452 calories, 10.1 g. fat (20% of calories), 1.6 g. saturated fat, 47 mg. cholesterol, 374 mg. sodium, 4.4 g. dietary fiber, 119 mg. calcium, 5 mg. iron, 67 mg. vitamin C, 6.8 mg. beta-carotene • **Serves 4**

LEMON-DILL SHRIMP CAESAR

12 slices (3½ ounces) Italian or French bread, cut ½-inch thick

3 garlic cloves (1 halved and 2 minced)

¼ cup buttermilk

3 tablespoons chopped fresh dill

1 ounce Romano cheese, coarsely grated

½ teaspoon anchovy paste

¼ teaspoon freshly ground black pepper

1 pound medium shrimp, peeled and deveined, with tails attached

2 teaspoons extra-virgin olive oil

½ teaspoon grated lemon zest

6 cups Romaine lettuce, torn into bite-size pieces

2 cups stemmed and halved cherry tomatoes

1 bunch watercress or arugula, tough stems removed

8 ounces small fresh mushrooms, sliced

Lemon slices, for garnish (optional)

Caesar salad has made a major comeback in the past few years after having been out of fashion for a decade or two: This classic salad is now turning up on restaurant menus nationwide. For an update, still-warm broiled shrimp, savory with a garlic-lemon marinade, are tossed with Romaine, watercress, cherry tomatoes and mushrooms. The dressing is a creamy dilled Caesar, minus the egg.

1 Preheat the broiler. Rub the bread slices with the halved garlic. Place the bread in a jelly-roll pan and broil 4 to 5 inches from the heat for 2 minutes per side, or until toasted. Transfer the bread from the pan to a plate, leaving the broiler on.

2 To make the dressing, in a large bowl, whisk together the buttermilk, dill, Romano, anchovy paste and black pepper; set aside.

3 Place the shrimp in the jelly-roll pan and sprinkle with the olive oil, minced garlic and lemon zest. Toss the shrimp to coat evenly and arrange in a single layer in the pan. Broil the shrimp 4 to 5 inches from the heat, turning once, for 3 to 4 minutes, or until opaque.

4 Meanwhile, add the Romaine, tomatoes, watercress or arugula and mushrooms to the bowl with the dressing and toss to mix. Add the broiled shrimp and toss gently. Divide the salad among 4 plates and serve with 3 bread slices each. Garnish with lemon slices, if desired.

Preparation time 25 minutes • **Total time** 35 minutes • **Per serving** 267 calories, 7.5 g. fat (25% of calories), 1 g. saturated fat, 148 mg. cholesterol, 441 mg. sodium, 4.6 g. dietary fiber, 257 mg. calcium, 5 mg. iron, 51 mg. vitamin C, 2.7 mg. beta-carotene • **Serves 4**

FOR A CHANGE
Romaine is the usual lettuce for Cobb salad, but you could use Bibb, Boston or mesclun (a mix of colorful baby lettuce leaves) instead of the watercress or arugula called for here.

HEAD START
You can wash and dry the greens ahead of time; refrigerate them in loosely closed plastic bags. Make the dressing in advance, too, and refrigerate it in a tightly closed jar.

SMOKED CHICKEN SALAD WITH FRUIT

¼ **cup fresh lime juice**

1 **tablespoon vegetable oil**

1 **teaspoon honey**

⅛ **teaspoon crushed red pepper flakes**

¼ **teaspoon grated lime zest**

½ **large ripe papaya, peeled and sliced (12 ounces)**

2 **medium plums, sliced very thin**

2 **plum tomatoes, sliced**

2 **scallions, chopped**

½ **teaspoon grated fresh ginger**

8 **cups Boston lettuce, torn into bite-size pieces**

1 **large bunch watercress, tough stems removed**

6 **ounces skinless smoked chicken breast, cut into julienne strips**

2 **tablespoons sliced natural almonds, toasted**

The inventive partnering of plums and papaya with plum tomatoes and scallions makes this salad a standout. Savory smoked chicken and tart watercress provide a pleasing counterpoint to the sweetness of the fruit. To reduce the percentage of calories from fat, eat the salad with crusty bread. For the topping, buy almonds labeled "natural" (this means they're not blanched) and toast them in a skillet (see below).

1 To make the dressing, in a medium bowl, whisk together 3 tablespoons of the lime juice, the oil, honey, red pepper flakes and lime zest.

2 In a large bowl, combine the papaya, plums, plum tomatoes, scallions, ginger and remaining 1 tablespoon lime juice.

3 Add the lettuce and watercress to the fruit mixture, along with 3 tablespoons of the dressing, and toss to coat.

4 Add the smoked chicken to the remaining dressing and toss to coat. Divide the greens and fruit mixture among 4 plates. Top with the smoked chicken and sprinkle with the almonds.

Preparation time 20 minutes • **Total time** 20 minutes • **Per serving** 219 calories, 9.4 g. fat (36% of calories), 1.6 g. saturated fat, 38 mg. cholesterol, 451 mg. sodium, 4.6 g. dietary fiber, 184 mg. calcium, 3 mg. iron, 93 mg. vitamin C, 3.8 mg. beta-carotene • **Serves 4**

To toast the almonds, place them in a small dry skillet and toast over medium heat, shaking the pan frequently.

After 5 to 10 minutes of cooking, the almonds should be golden brown and very fragrant.

Tip the almonds onto a plate so that they stop cooking, then let them cool slightly before adding them to the salad.

THAI BEEF SALAD

12 ounces lean, trimmed boneless beef sirloin or top round steak

2 garlic cloves (1 halved and 1 minced)

¼ teaspoon freshly ground black pepper

¼ cup rice wine vinegar

2 teaspoons vegetable oil

1 teaspoon dark sesame oil

1 teaspoon sugar

½ teaspoon grated fresh ginger

¼ teaspoon salt

¼ teaspoon crushed red pepper flakes

2 scallions, thinly sliced

12 cups green-leaf lettuce, torn into bite-size pieces

1 cup thinly sliced kirby or English cucumbers

1 cup loosely packed fresh cilantro leaves, chopped

1 cup loosely packed fresh mint leaves, chopped

1 small ripe mango or papaya, peeled and diced

1 cup bean sprouts

2 medium carrots, cut into julienne strips

1 tablespoon chopped unsalted dry-roasted peanuts

Lime wedges, for garnish (optional)

There is a category of delicious Thai salads called, appropriately enough, *yum:* These salads consist of greens topped with meat or poultry, fish or shellfish. *Yum gong,* for instance, comes with curry-flavored shrimp, while *yum pla muok* is made with spiced squid and pickled garlic. This dish is based on *yum nuer,* a salad topped with slices of spicy grilled beef. A sprinkling of fresh herbs is characteristic of *yums;* here, fresh cilantro and mint are added to the dressing instead.

1 Preheat the broiler. Spray the broiler-pan rack with no-stick spray.

2 Rub the steak on both sides with the halved garlic clove, then sprinkle with the black pepper. Place the steak on the prepared broiler-pan rack and broil 4 to 6 inches from the heat, turning once, for 5 minutes per side, or until medium rare. Transfer the steak to a plate and let stand for 5 minutes.

3 Meanwhile, make the dressing. In a large bowl, whisk together the vinegar, vegetable oil, sesame oil, sugar, ginger, salt, red pepper flakes and minced garlic.

4 Transfer the steak to a cutting board and pour any juices remaining on the steak plate into a medium bowl. Add 1 tablespoon of the dressing and the scallions to the juices, and stir to combine.

5 Carve the steak into ¼-inch-thick slices. Add the steak to the bowl with the scallions and toss to coat.

6 Add the lettuce, cucumbers, cilantro and mint to the dressing in the large bowl and toss to coat. Arrange the lettuce mixture on 4 plates. Mound the steak mixture on top, then top with the mangoes or papayas, bean sprouts and carrots. Sprinkle the salads with the chopped peanuts. Garnish with lime wedges, if desired.

Preparation time 25 minutes • **Total time** 30 minutes • **Per serving** 266 calories, 10 g. fat (34% of calories), 2.5 g. saturated fat, 57 mg. cholesterol, 211 mg. sodium, 4.2 g. dietary fiber, 166 mg. calcium, 6 mg. iron, 56 mg. vitamin C, 9.4 mg. beta-carotene • **Serves 4**

❧ ❧ ❧

MIXED-GRAIN AND CHICK-PEA TABBOULEH

5¾ cups water

½ cup barley

½ teaspoon salt

½ cup instant couscous

½ cup bulgur

⅓ cup fresh orange juice

3 tablespoons red wine vinegar

1 tablespoon plus 1 teaspoon
extra-virgin olive oil

2 garlic cloves, minced

1 teaspoon honey

½ teaspoon freshly ground black
pepper

½ cup slivered dried apricots

½ cup chick-peas, rinsed and
drained

1 medium yellow bell pepper,
diced

1 cup diced kirby or English
cucumber

1 cup stemmed and halved cherry
tomatoes

4 scallions, thinly sliced

½ cup chopped Italian parsley

¼ cup chopped fresh mint

8 Boston lettuce leaves

3 ounces feta cheese, crumbled

Chopped fresh mint and mint
sprigs, for garnish (optional)

Middle Eastern *tabbouleh* is traditionally a one-grain dish, made solely from bulgur (a specially prepared form of cracked wheat), along with chopped herbs, tomatoes, lemon juice and olive oil. This "tabbouleh extraordinaire" includes other favorite Middle Eastern ingredients—couscous, barley, chick-peas and apricots, as well as a sprinkling of feta cheese. Serve the salad with wedges of pita bread or strips of seed-topped crackerbread.

1 In a medium saucepan, combine 4 cups of the water, the barley and ⅛ teaspoon of the salt, and bring to a boil over high heat. Reduce the heat to medium-low, cover and simmer for 35 minutes, or until the barley is tender. Transfer the barley to a colander, rinse under cold running water and drain.

2 While the barley is cooking, in another medium saucepan, bring the remaining 1¾ cups of water and ⅛ teaspoon of the salt to a boil over high heat. Stir in the couscous and bulgur, and remove from the heat. Cover and let stand for 10 minutes, or until the grains have absorbed the liquid. Fluff the couscous and bulgur with a fork, transfer to a jelly-roll pan and place in the freezer for 10 minutes to chill.

3 While the grains are chilling, make the dressing. In a large bowl, whisk together the orange juice, vinegar, oil, garlic, honey, black pepper and remaining ¼ teaspoon salt. Stir in the apricots.

4 Add the barley, chilled couscous and bulgur, chick-peas, bell peppers, cucumbers, tomatoes, scallions, parsley and mint to the dressing and toss well.

5 Divide the lettuce among 4 plates. Spoon the grain mixture into the center and sprinkle with the feta cheese. Sprinkle with chopped mint and garnish with mint sprigs, if desired.

Preparation time 30 minutes • **Total time** 45 minutes • **Per serving** 457 calories, 11.6 g. fat (22% of calories), 4.1 g. saturated fat, 19 mg. cholesterol, 614 mg. sodium, 13.1 g. dietary fiber, 197 mg. calcium, 5 mg. iron, 49 mg. vitamin C, 1.5 mg. beta-carotene • **Serves 4**

❧ ❧ ❧

SCALLOP AND ORANGE TOSS

3 medium navel oranges

1 tablespoon plus 1 teaspoon extra-virgin olive oil

1 tablespoon plus 1 teaspoon red wine vinegar

½ teaspoon grated lemon zest

¼ teaspoon freshly ground black pepper

⅛ teaspoon salt

12 cups fresh spinach leaves, tough stems removed

4 ounces radicchio, thinly sliced

1 medium red bell pepper, diced

2 ounces trimmed Canadian bacon, finely diced

⅓ cup thinly sliced shallots

1 pound sea scallops, tough muscle removed

Eye-catching radicchio is expensive, but the firm leaves of each small head are tightly packed, so there's little waste.

Because the ingredients for this salad are few and their preparation simple, it's important that everything be of the very best quality. Take an extra moment at the market to select the plumpest scallops, the heaviest, juiciest oranges and the freshest, crispest spinach; splurge a bit on the radicchio and extra-virgin olive oil. Buy some pretty dinner rolls, too, and heat them while you make the salad. When you sit down to the meal, you'll agree it was worth every minute and the few extra pennies.

1 Using a serrated knife, pare the peel and white pith from the oranges. Working over a medium bowl, cut out the sections from between the membranes and set the sections aside. Squeeze 3 tablespoons of orange juice from the membranes into the bowl.

2 To the orange juice, add 3 teaspoons of the oil, the vinegar, lemon zest, ⅛ teaspoon of the black pepper and the salt; whisk to combine.

3 In a large bowl, combine the reserved orange sections, spinach, radicchio and bell peppers.

4 In a medium no-stick skillet, warm the remaining 1 teaspoon oil over medium-high heat. Stir in the bacon and shallots, and cook for 2 minutes, or until golden. Stir in the scallops and the remaining ⅛ teaspoon black pepper, and sauté for 2 minutes, or until the scallops are opaque. With a slotted spoon, transfer the scallop mixture to a plate.

5 Add the orange dressing to the skillet and cook, stirring, for 30 seconds to warm.

6 Add the warm dressing to the bowl with the orange sections and spinach mixture, and toss to mix. Divide the spinach mixture among 4 plates and top with the scallop mixture.

Preparation time 30 minutes • **Total time** 35 minutes • **Per serving** 268 calories, 7.3 g. fat (23% of calories), 1.2 g. saturated fat, 45 mg. cholesterol, 590 mg. sodium, 7.6 g. dietary fiber, 264 mg. calcium, 6 mg. iron, 152 mg. vitamin C, 7.8 mg. beta-carotene • **Serves 4**

PASTA, CANNELLINI AND ESCAROLE SALAD

10 ounces fusilli pasta

3 large carrots, thinly sliced

1 tablespoon plus 1 teaspoon extra-virgin olive oil

2 ounces sliced Canadian bacon, cut into thin strips

⅓ cup thinly sliced shallots

2 garlic cloves, minced

½ teaspoon dried thyme or 1 tablespoon fresh thyme

8 cups loosely packed cut escarole (1-inch pieces), well washed

¼ cup defatted reduced-sodium chicken broth

½ teaspoon freshly ground black pepper

⅛ teaspoon salt

2 cups stemmed and halved cherry tomatoes

1 can (19 ounces) cannellini beans, rinsed and drained

2 tablespoons balsamic vinegar

Fresh thyme sprigs, for garnish (optional)

Italians prize the pairing of greens and beans, as welcome in salads as it is in soups (such as minestrone) and pasta dishes. In this Italian-inspired pasta salad, robust escarole, sautéed with Canadian bacon and garlic, shares the spotlight with the large white beans called cannellini.

1 Bring a large covered pot of water to a boil over high heat. Add the pasta to the boiling water, return to a boil and cook, stirring frequently, for 9 to 11 minutes, or according to package directions until al dente. Three minutes before the pasta is done, stir in the carrots and cook until the carrots are tender. Reserving 2 tablespoons of the cooking liquid, drain the pasta and the carrots in a colander; rinse under cold running water and drain again.

2 While the pasta is cooking, in a large skillet, warm the oil over medium-high heat. Add the bacon, shallots, garlic and thyme, and sauté for 2 minutes, or until the bacon is golden. Stir in the escarole, broth, black pepper, salt and reserved pasta liquid, and bring to a boil. Reduce the heat to medium and cook, stirring, for about 1 minute, or until the escarole is tender. Transfer the escarole mixture to a salad bowl.

3 Add the drained pasta and carrots, the cherry tomatoes, beans and vinegar to the salad bowl, and toss to mix. Garnish with thyme sprigs, if desired.

Preparation time 20 minutes • **Total time** 30 minutes • **Per serving** 499 calories, 8.1 g. fat (14% of calories), 1.3 g. saturated fat, 7 mg. cholesterol, 542 mg. sodium, 13.1 g. dietary fiber, 144 mg. calcium, 6 mg. iron, 31 mg. vitamin C, 14.4 mg. beta-carotene • **Serves 4**

MARKET AND PANTRY

You'll find two kinds of fusilli in the market—long and cut. Long fusilli is like curly strands of spaghetti, while cut fusilli is similar to rotelle, rotini or twists. The cut fusilli is an ideal choice for a salad such as this one.

SUBSTITUTION

You might like to use fresh spinach instead of escarole in this salad, but keep in mind that the more tender spinach leaves may cook in less than a minute. If you can't find cannellini, Great Northern beans will do.

TURKEY AND TWO-RICE SLAW

2 cups water

1 cup defatted reduced-sodium chicken broth

½ cup wild rice

1 garlic clove, crushed

1 bay leaf, preferably imported

1 cup long-grain white rice

2 tablespoons cider vinegar

1 tablespoon plus 1 teaspoon vegetable oil

1 tablespoon honey

¼ teaspoon freshly ground black pepper

⅛ teaspoon salt

2 cups shredded red cabbage

2 cups shredded green cabbage

1 cup thinly sliced fennel or celery

5 ounces skinless smoked turkey breast, diced

2 Red Delicious apples, diced

⅓ cup dried cranberries or raisins

2 scallions, thinly sliced

2 tablespoons chopped pecans

Coleslaw, that perennial picnic favorite, takes its name from the Dutch words *kool sla*, meaning cabbage salad. While both red and green cabbages are in this slaw, there's much more going on: In fact, the cabbage takes a back seat to such "exotic" ingredients as wild rice, smoked turkey, fennel and dried cranberries.

1 In a large saucepan, bring the water and broth to a boil over high heat. Stir in the wild rice, garlic and bay leaf; reduce the heat, cover and simmer for 20 minutes. After 20 minutes, stir in the white rice; cover and cook for 18 to 20 minutes longer, or until both the white and wild rice are tender.

2 While the rice is cooking, make the dressing. In a large bowl, whisk together the vinegar, oil, honey, black pepper and salt.

3 Drain the rice; remove the bay leaf and garlic. Add the rice to the bowl with the dressing and toss to mix. Stir in the red and green cabbages and the fennel or celery. Add the turkey, apples, cranberries or raisins and scallions, and toss gently. Divide the salad among 4 plates and sprinkle with the pecans.

Preparation time 25 minutes • **Total time** 40 minutes • **Per serving** 465 calories, 9.6 g. fat (19% of calories), 1.4 g. saturated fat, 18 mg. cholesterol, 720 mg. sodium, 5.8 g. dietary fiber, 83 mg. calcium, 4 mg. iron, 45 mg. vitamin C, 0.2 mg. beta-carotene • **Serves 4**

❦ ❦ ❦

The rather heart-shaped fennel bulb is topped with stalks and feathery leaves that are usually removed before sale.

This cross-section of a fennel bulb shows its layered structure. Cut out the solid core before slicing the fennel.

ITALIAN BREAD SALAD WITH SWORDFISH

4 **cups cubed sourdough or Italian bread**

2 **garlic cloves, minced**

2 **tablespoons balsamic vinegar**

1 **tablespoon plus 1 teaspoon extra-virgin olive oil**

½ **teaspoon dried thyme**

¼ **teaspoon salt**

¼ **teaspoon crushed red pepper flakes**

12 **ounces swordfish steaks**

5 **ounces fresh spinach, tough stems removed**

1 **large bunch arugula or watercress, tough stems removed**

2 **plum tomatoes, diced**

1 **yellow or red bell pepper, sliced**

½ **medium red onion, sliced**

½ **cucumber, peeled, seeded and thinly sliced**

¼ **cup coarsely chopped fresh basil**

Bread and salad are a natural combination, but what's bread salad? It's a Tuscan dish called *panzanella,* devised as a way of using up a stale loaf. In Tuscany, dense whole-wheat bread is typically soaked in water, squeezed dry and then combined with tomatoes, herbs and dressing for a salad that's soft and soothing. This version is crisper: The fresh bread cubes are toasted like croutons.

1 Preheat the oven to 375°.

2 In a jelly-roll pan, toss the bread cubes with half the minced garlic. Bake for 10 minutes, or until golden. Remove from the oven and set aside to cool.

3 Preheat the broiler. Spray a broiler pan-rack with no-stick spray.

4 To make the dressing, in a large bowl, whisk together the vinegar, oil, thyme, salt, red pepper flakes and the remaining garlic.

5 Place the swordfish on the prepared broiler-pan rack and baste one side with 2 teaspoons of the dressing. Broil 4 to 6 inches from the heat, turning once without basting the second side, for 4 minutes per side, or until the swordfish just flakes when tested with a fork.

6 Transfer the swordfish to a cutting board and cut into 1-inch cubes.

7 Add the bread cubes, spinach, arugula or watercress, tomatoes, bell peppers, onions, cucumbers and basil to the bowl with the remaining dressing, and toss to combine. Divide the spinach mixture among 4 plates and top with the swordfish.

Preparation time 30 minutes • **Total time** 45 minutes • **Per serving** 281 calories, 9.9 g. fat (31% of calories), 1.9 g. saturated fat, 33 mg. cholesterol, 467 mg. sodium, 4.2 g. dietary fiber, 169 mg. calcium, 4 mg. iron, 79 mg. vitamin C, 3.5 mg. beta-carotene • **Serves 4**

FOOD FACT
Swordfish, caught off the U.S. coasts and also in Canadian, South American and Caribbean waters, is always in good supply. Its flesh ranges from pale pink to red, but always turns ivory white when cooked.

TROPICAL CHICKEN SALAD

2 tablespoons sliced natural almonds

2 teaspoons ground cumin

1 cup defatted chicken broth

12 ounces skinless, boneless chicken breast halves, cut into 1-inch chunks

1 tablespoon cornstarch dissolved in 1 tablespoon cold water

¼ cup apricot nectar

1 tablespoon fresh lime juice

1 tablespoon honey

¼ teaspoon freshly ground black pepper

⅛ teaspoon crushed red pepper flakes

2 tablespoons chopped fresh cilantro

2 cups fresh pineapple chunks (or juice-packed canned pineapple, drained)

Half of a ripe papaya, peeled, seeded and cut into chunks (1 cup)

1 ripe mango, peeled and cut into chunks (1 cup)

4 cups (1 large bunch) watercress or spinach, washed and trimmed

Pineapples, with their natural "armor," have been shipped to this country since the eighteenth century, but thinner-skinned mangoes and papayas are not such good travelers. Fortunately, they're now grown in Hawaii, Florida and California, and are available in most supermarkets. When ripe, mangoes and papayas will yield to gentle pressure; if necessary, ripen them in paper bags for a few days.

1 In a heavy, medium no-stick skillet, toast the almonds over medium-high heat, tossing frequently, for about 4 minutes, or until lightly browned. Tip the almonds onto a plate to stop the cooking.

2 Add the cumin to the skillet and cook over medium heat, stirring frequently, for about 4 minutes, or until the cumin is toasted and fragrant. Immediately transfer half of the cumin to a salad bowl; pour the broth into the skillet and bring to a boil over high heat.

3 Add the chicken to the skillet and reduce the heat to medium; cover and cook, stirring frequently, for 3 to 4 minutes, or until the chicken is cooked through. With a slotted spoon, transfer the chicken to a plate; cover it with wax paper to keep it moist.

4 Increase the heat to high and bring the cooking liquid to a boil. Boil for about 3 minutes, or until the liquid is reduced to about ¼ cup. Stir in the cornstarch mixture and return to a boil, whisking constantly (the mixture will be extremely thick). Remove from the heat.

5 Scrape the thickened liquid into the salad bowl and whisk in the apricot nectar, lime juice, honey, black pepper and red pepper; continue whisking until smooth. Stir in the cilantro.

6 Add to the bowl the chicken and any juices that have collected on the plate, the pineapple, papaya and mango, and toss gently to mix.

7 Spread the watercress or spinach on a large platter. Top with the chicken salad and sprinkle with the toasted almonds.

Preparation time 25 minutes • **Total time** 35 minutes • **Per serving** 238 calories, 3.7 g. fat (14% of calories), 0.5 g. saturated fat, 49 mg. cholesterol, 322 mg. sodium, 2.7 g. dietary fiber, 90 mg. calcium, 2 mg. iron, 71 mg. vitamin C, 3 mg. beta-carotene
Serves 4

CHICKEN SALAD NIÇOISE

1 pound small red potatoes, cut into 1-inch wedges

1 cup defatted chicken broth

½ cup water

2 garlic cloves, peeled

½ teaspoon freshly ground black pepper

¼ teaspoon dried thyme

12 ounces skinless, boneless chicken breast halves, cut crosswise into 1-inch strips

8 ounces green beans

1 tablespoon plus 1 teaspoon extra-virgin olive oil

1 tablespoon plus 2 teaspoons white wine vinegar

1 teaspoon Dijon mustard

⅛ teaspoon salt

4 ripe plum tomatoes, cut into wedges

1 medium kirby cucumber, halved crosswise and cut into wedges

8 kalamata olives

⅓ cup julienne-cut basil leaves

You've probably eaten a bountiful *salade Niçoise* made with canned tuna, and perhaps you've also enjoyed a modern version with fresh tuna. The same vegetables and dressing that set off the fish so beautifully work equally well with poached chicken.

1 Place the potatoes in a medium saucepan and add cold water to cover; cover the pan and bring to a boil over high heat. Reduce the heat to medium and simmer for 10 to 12 minutes, or until the potatoes are fork-tender. Drain in a colander and set aside to cool slightly.

2 While the potatoes are cooking, in another medium saucepan, combine the broth, water, garlic cloves, ¼ teaspoon of the pepper and the thyme; bring to a boil over high heat. Reduce the heat to medium, stir in the chicken strips and simmer, stirring frequently, for 3 to 4 minutes, or until the chicken is cooked through. Using a slotted spoon, transfer the chicken to a plate; cover loosely with wax paper and set aside. Remove and discard the garlic cloves.

3 Add the green beans to the poaching liquid, increase the heat to high and bring to a boil. Simmer, stirring occasionally, for 5 to 6 minutes, or until the beans are crisp-tender. Using a slotted spoon, transfer the beans to a small strainer and rinse briefly under cold running water to stop the cooking.

4 Measure out and discard ½ cup of the poaching liquid. Increase the heat under the saucepan to high and bring to a boil. Boil for about 3 minutes, or until the liquid is reduced to about 2 tablespoons. Transfer the reduced liquid to a large bowl. Whisk in the oil, vinegar, mustard, salt and the remaining ¼ teaspoon pepper. Add the cooked potatoes, chicken and green beans, and toss to coat well.

5 Transfer the chicken, potatoes and green beans to a shallow serving bowl. Add the tomato and cucumber wedges and the olives, and sprinkle the salad with the basil.

Preparation time 20 minutes • **Total time** 45 minutes • **Per serving** 289 calories, 7.5 g. fat (23% of calories), 1.1 g. saturated fat, 49 mg. cholesterol, 379 mg. sodium, 4.9 g. dietary fiber, 78 mg. calcium, 4 mg. iron, 52 mg. vitamin C, 0.8 mg. beta-carotene • **Serves 4**

CHICKEN AND RADIATORE SALAD

8 ounces radiatore pasta

12 ounces fresh asparagus spears, trimmed and cut diagonally into 1-inch lengths

3 medium carrots, thinly sliced

½ cup defatted chicken broth

½ cup water

3 tablespoons fresh lemon juice

2 garlic cloves, halved

¾ teaspoon dried tarragon

12 ounces skinless, boneless chicken breast halves, cut into ¾-inch chunks

2 cups loosely packed spinach leaves, well washed

¾ cup cut-up scallions

½ cup packed Italian parsley sprigs

¼ cup reduced-calorie mayonnaise

1 teaspoon Dijon mustard

¾ teaspoon freshly ground black pepper

¼ teaspoon salt

1 medium kirby cucumber, thinly sliced

Many of America's favorite salads and dressings originated in California, including a blend of mayonnaise, tarragon vinegar, garlic and fresh herbs created in San Francisco in the 1920s and dubbed "Green Goddess dressing." That's the inspiration for the herb dressing here; it's tossed with mouth-filling radiatore pasta, crisp-tender asparagus and chunks of poached chicken.

1 Bring a large covered pot of water to a boil over high heat. Add the radiatore and return to a boil. Cook for 7 minutes, then stir in the asparagus and carrots and cook for 1 to 2 minutes longer, or until the vegetables are crisp-tender and the pasta is al dente. Drain in a colander, rinse briefly under cold running water and drain again.

2 Meanwhile, combine the broth, water, 1 teaspoon of the lemon juice, the garlic cloves and tarragon in a medium skillet; cover and bring to a boil over high heat. Add the chicken and reduce the heat to medium; cover and simmer, stirring frequently, for 4 to 5 minutes, or until the chicken is just cooked through. Using a slotted spoon, transfer the chicken to a bowl; cover loosely with a sheet of wax paper to keep moist.

3 Stir the spinach, scallions and parsley into the broth mixture and place over high heat. Cook, stirring frequently, for 1 to 2 minutes, or until the greens are just wilted. Drain the greens and garlic cloves through a large strainer set over a bowl; reserve 3 tablespoons of the cooking liquid and discard the remainder.

4 Combine the greens, garlic and reserved cooking liquid in a food processor, and process until puréed. Add the mayonnaise, mustard, pepper, salt and the remaining 2 tablespoons plus 2 teaspoons lemon juice, and process just until blended.

5 Combine the pasta mixture, chicken and cucumbers in a salad bowl. Add the dressing and toss to mix.

Preparation time 20 minutes • **Total time** 40 minutes • **Per serving** 406 calories, 6.6 g. fat (15% of calories), 1.5 g. saturated fat, 54 mg. cholesterol, 430 mg. sodium, 5.7 g. dietary fiber, 116 mg. calcium, 6 mg. iron, 50 mg. vitamin C, 11 mg. beta-carotene • **Serves 4**

❧ ❧ ❧

CHINESE CHICKEN AND NOODLE SALAD

1 cup defatted chicken broth

3 tablespoons rice vinegar

1 slice (¼ inch thick) fresh ginger plus 1 tablespoon grated ginger

12 ounces skinless, boneless chicken breast halves

8 ounces vermicelli pasta

2 tablespoons reduced-sodium soy sauce

1 garlic clove, crushed through a press

2 teaspoons dark sesame oil

1 teaspoon granulated sugar

¼ teaspoon crushed red pepper flakes

3 cups shredded napa cabbage

1 cup julienne-cut snow peas

½ cup shredded carrots

½ cup minced fresh cilantro

There are macaroni salads made with mayonnaise and pasta salads made with pesto, but the Chinese pairing of noodles and sesame sauce is in a class by itself. This version is lower in fat than the traditional Szechuan noodles dish.

1 Bring a large covered pot of water to a boil over high heat.

2 In a medium skillet, combine the broth, 1 tablespoon of the vinegar and the ginger slice; cover and bring to a boil over high heat.

3 Add the chicken breasts to the skillet; reduce the heat to medium-low (the liquid should be barely simmering). Cover and simmer, turning the chicken two or three times, for 8 to 10 minutes, or until cooked through. Transfer the chicken to a plate; cover loosely with a sheet of wax paper and let stand until cool enough to handle. Remove the ginger from the poaching liquid and reserve ½ cup of the liquid.

4 While the chicken cools, add the pasta to the boiling water; return to a boil and cook for 6 to 8 minutes, or according to package directions until al dente. Drain in a colander, rinse briefly under cold running water and drain again. Transfer the pasta to a salad bowl and toss with ¼ cup of the reserved poaching liquid.

5 In a small bowl, whisk the remaining ¼ cup poaching liquid with the remaining 2 tablespoons vinegar, the grated ginger, soy sauce, garlic, sesame oil, sugar and red pepper flakes.

6 Cut the chicken into fine shreds. Add the chicken to the pasta, then add the cabbage, snow peas, carrots and cilantro. Pour the dressing over the salad and toss to coat.

When crinkly napa cabbage is cut crosswise, it falls naturally into strips that separate easily.

Preparation time 15 minutes • **Total time** 40 minutes • **Per serving** 371 calories, 4.6 g. fat (11% of calories), 0.8 g. saturated fat, 49 mg. cholesterol, 496 mg. sodium, 3.3 g. dietary fiber, 89 mg. calcium, 4 mg. iron, 40 mg. vitamin C, 3 mg. beta-carotene
Serves 4

ON THE MENU
Cups of hot tea or glasses of iced tea are just the thing to serve with this Chinese-style salad. For dessert, offer a platter of navel oranges and thin almond cookies or vanilla wafers.

TURKEY AND SWEET POTATO SALAD

¾ cup nonfat yogurt

1 pound sweet potatoes, peeled and cut into 1-inch chunks

½ cup defatted chicken broth

¼ cup water

3 tablespoons frozen orange juice concentrate, thawed

2 teaspoons curry powder

12 ounces skinless, boneless turkey breast, cut into ½-inch cubes

2 celery stalks, diagonally sliced

3 scallions, diagonally sliced

3 tablespoons raisins

¼ cup mango chutney

⅛ teaspoon hot-pepper sauce

⅛ teaspoon salt

3 tablespoons coarsely chopped toasted pecans

When Thanksgiving is a distant memory, cook some fresh turkey and sweet potatoes for this delectable warm salad, tossed with an orange-curry-chutney dressing that's like nothing you've ever eaten on "Turkey Day."

1 Line a small strainer with cheesecloth or paper towels and suspend it over a small bowl. Spoon the yogurt into the strainer and let drain for 15 minutes. Discard the whey and dry the bowl; turn the drained yogurt into the bowl.

2 While the yogurt is draining, place the sweet potatoes in a medium saucepan and add cold water to cover. Cover and bring to a boil over high heat. Reduce the heat to medium and simmer for 9 to 11 minutes, or until the sweet potatoes are fork-tender but not mushy. Drain in a colander and cool briefly under gently running cold water.

3 In a medium skillet, combine the broth, water, 1 tablespoon of the orange juice concentrate and 1 teaspoon of the curry powder; cover and bring to a boil over high heat.

4 Stir the turkey cubes into the broth mixture, reduce the heat to medium, cover and cook, stirring frequently, for 4 to 5 minutes, or until the turkey is cooked through. Reserving 3 tablespoons of the cooking liquid, drain the turkey in a colander.

5 Place the sweet potatoes in a large salad bowl and add the turkey, celery, scallions and raisins.

6 To the yogurt, add the reserved turkey cooking liquid, the remaining 2 tablespoons orange juice concentrate, remaining 1 teaspoon curry powder, the chutney, hot-pepper sauce and salt, and stir to blend.

7 Pour the dressing over the salad and toss gently to coat. Sprinkle with the pecans and serve.

Preparation time 20 minutes • **Total time** 40 minutes • **Per serving** 342 calories, 4.7 g. fat (12% of calories), 0.6 g. saturated fat, 54 mg. cholesterol, 479 mg. sodium, 4.2 g. dietary fiber, 143 mg. calcium, 2 mg. iron, 41 mg. vitamin C, 9.9 mg. beta-carotene • **Serves 4**

COBB SALAD WITH PARMESAN DRESSING

½ cup low-fat buttermilk

3 tablespoons grated Parmesan cheese

2 tablespoons light sour cream

1 tablespoon distilled white vinegar

¾ teaspoon coarsely cracked black pepper

⅛ teaspoon salt

3 cups loosely packed torn red-leaf lettuce

1 medium head Boston lettuce, torn into bite-size pieces (about 3 cups)

1 can (16 ounces) chick-peas, rinsed and drained

4 ounces julienne-cut skinless roast turkey breast

Whites of 4 hard-cooked eggs, coarsely chopped

Half of a ripe medium avocado, cut into chunks

1½ cups halved cherry tomatoes

½ cup thinly sliced radishes

A California classic, the Cobb salad was a signature dish of the Brown Derby restaurant in Hollywood. It's a sort of salad-bar-in-a-dish, with finely chopped greens, herbs, chicken, eggs, bacon, tomatoes and blue cheese arrayed in broad bands in a big bowl. The salad is first displayed in all its multicolored glory, then tossed with a vinaigrette. Here, the components are cut into more substantial pieces and arranged on a platter; toss the salad gently before serving, or simply pour on the dressing and pass the platter around.

1 To make the dressing, in a small bowl, whisk together the buttermilk, Parmesan, sour cream, vinegar, pepper and salt.

2 Spread the red-leaf and Boston lettuces in a large, shallow bowl or on a platter. Arrange the chick-peas, turkey, egg whites, avocados, cherry tomatoes and radishes in even bands over the lettuce.

3 Drizzle the dressing over the salad, toss if desired and serve.

Preparation time 30 minutes • **Total time** 30 minutes • **Per serving** 243 calories, 8.7 g. fat (32% of calories), 2.2 g. saturated fat, 30 mg. cholesterol, 384 mg. sodium, 5.3 g. dietary fiber, 188 mg. calcium, 4 mg. iron, 30 mg. vitamin C, 1 mg. beta-carotene • **Serves 4**

Halve the avocado, then tap the blade of a heavy knife against the pit; use the knife like a screwdriver to twist out the pit.

Grasp the skin at the blossom end and pull. The skin should come off smoothly, leaving the flesh unmarked.

DILLED CHICKEN AND POTATO SALAD

1 cup defatted chicken broth

½ cup water

3 tablespoons cider vinegar

¾ teaspoon freshly ground black pepper

¼ teaspoon dill seeds

1¼ pounds small red potatoes, cut into 1-inch chunks

⅓ cup nonfat yogurt

8 ounces skinless, boneless chicken breast halves, cut into ¾-inch cubes

3 tablespoons reduced-calorie mayonnaise

2 tablespoons snipped fresh dill

1 large red bell pepper, coarsely diced

1 large ripe tomato, diced

⅓ cup sliced scallions

Cooking the potatoes in well-seasoned broth gives you a head start on a full-flavored potato salad. After the potatoes are done, the chicken is poached in the same broth. The warm potatoes and chicken are combined, while still warm, in a tart yogurt dressing, and the salad is best if served immediately. Instead of fresh dill, you might try parsley, thyme, tarragon or another favorite herb.

1 In a medium saucepan, combine the broth, water, 2 tablespoons of the vinegar, ½ teaspoon of the black pepper and the dill seeds. Cover and bring to a boil over high heat.

2 Add the potatoes to the broth mixture and return to a boil. Reduce the heat to medium, cover and simmer for 10 to 15 minutes, or until the potatoes are fork-tender. Using a slotted spoon, transfer the potatoes to a salad bowl.

3 While the potatoes are cooking, line a small strainer with cheesecloth or paper towels and suspend it over a small bowl. Spoon the yogurt into the strainer and let drain for 15 minutes. Discard the whey and dry the bowl. Turn the yogurt into the bowl.

4 Add the chicken cubes to the broth mixture, cover and simmer, stirring frequently, for 2 to 4 minutes, or until the chicken is cooked through. Drain the chicken in a colander, then add it to the potatoes. Set aside the chicken and potatoes to cool slightly.

5 To the yogurt, add the mayonnaise, fresh dill, remaining 1 tablespoon vinegar and remaining ¼ teaspoon black pepper, and whisk until blended. Pour the dressing over the chicken and potatoes. Add the bell peppers, tomatoes and scallions, and toss to mix.

Preparation time 30 minutes • **Total time** 30 minutes • **Per serving** 246 calories, 4.6 g. fat (17% of calories), 1 g. saturated fat, 37 mg. cholesterol, 376 mg. sodium, 3.5 g. dietary fiber, 67 mg. calcium, 2 mg. iron, 79 mg. vitamin C, 1 mg. beta-carotene
Serves 4

FOODWAYS

Potato salad is popular in many parts of the world. The Germans make theirs with bacon; the French toss hot potatoes with white wine. Scandinavians mix diced potatoes with chopped apples and beets.

FRUITED CHICKEN AND COUSCOUS SALAD

½ cup defatted chicken broth

⅔ cup water

¾ cup instant couscous

¼ cup slivered dried apricots

2 tablespoons golden raisins

2 medium navel oranges

2 tablespoons fresh lemon juice

2 tablespoons chopped red onion

1 tablespoon extra-virgin olive oil

1 tablespoon honey

½ teaspoon freshly ground black pepper

¼ teaspoon salt

⅛ teaspoon ground red pepper

12 ounces skinless, boneless chicken breast halves, cut crosswise into ½-inch-wide strips

½ teaspoon ground coriander

1 large red bell pepper, cut into thin strips

½ cup thinly sliced fennel or celery

4 cups colorful mixed greens, torn into bite-size pieces

Couscous is a granular pasta made from semolina flour and water. Delicately flavored, it readily absorbs savory or sweet sauces, gravies and dressings. In Morocco, couscous is steamed slowly over a pot of spicy stew, but the instant couscous you'll find in your supermarket just needs to steep briefly in boiling liquid.

1 In a medium saucepan, bring the broth and water to a boil over high heat. Stir in the couscous, apricots and raisins, and remove the pan from the heat. Cover and let stand for 5 minutes, or until the couscous has absorbed the liquid. Spread the couscous in a shallow baking dish and place in the freezer for 10 minutes to chill.

2 Preheat the broiler. Spray a jelly-roll pan with no-stick spray.

3 Using a serrated knife, pare the peel and pith from the oranges. Working over a medium bowl, cut out the sections from between the membranes; set the sections aside. Squeeze the juice from the membranes into a large bowl: You should have about 3 tablespoons of juice.

4 To the orange juice, add 1 tablespoon of the lemon juice, the red onions, oil, honey, ¼ teaspoon of the black pepper, ⅛ teaspoon of the salt and half of the ground red pepper.

5 Place the chicken strips in the prepared pan and sprinkle with the coriander, the remaining 1 tablespoon lemon juice, remaining ¼ teaspoon black pepper, remaining ⅛ teaspoon salt and remaining ground red pepper. Toss the chicken to season evenly.

6 Broil the chicken 4 to 5 inches from the heat, turning the pieces several times, for 4 to 6 minutes, or until cooked through.

7 Add the chilled couscous, the chicken, bell peppers and fennel or celery to the dressing, and toss to mix. Add the orange sections and toss gently. Spread the greens on a platter and mound the couscous mixture in the center.

Preparation time 20 minutes • **Total time** 30 minutes • **Per serving** 363 calories, 5.5 g. fat (14% of calories), 0.3 g. saturated fat, 49 mg. cholesterol, 339 mg. sodium, 4 g. dietary fiber, 95 mg. calcium, 3 mg. iron, 106 mg. vitamin C, 2 mg. beta-carotene
Serves 4

❧ ❧ ❧

THAI RICE AND TURKEY SALAD

1 cup uncooked converted white rice

2½ cups water

½ cup defatted chicken broth

1 tablespoon grated fresh ginger

2 garlic cloves, crushed through a press

12 ounces skinless, boneless turkey breast, cut crosswise into strips

3 tablespoons no-salt-added peanut butter

3 tablespoons fresh lime juice

1 teaspoon honey

½ teaspoon anchovy paste

¼ teaspoon salt

¼ teaspoon crushed red pepper flakes

2 cups shredded napa cabbage

1 large red bell pepper, diced

½ cup diced red onion

3 tablespoons coarsely chopped fresh mint

3 cups small tender kale leaves or spinach, well washed

2 tablespoons coarsely chopped roasted unsalted peanuts

Balance is the keynote of Thai meals, and menus are carefully planned to touch on five flavors: sweet, hot, sour, salty and even a touch of bitter. A root called *galanga*, citrusy lemongrass and *nam pla*, a pungent fish sauce, are Thai staples. Here, ginger, lime juice and anchovy paste stand in for these exotic ingredients.

1 In a heavy medium saucepan, combine the rice and 2 cups of the water, and bring to a boil over high heat. Reduce the heat to low, cover and simmer for 20 minutes, or until the rice is tender and the liquid is absorbed. Spread the rice in a shallow baking pan and place it in the freezer for about 10 minutes to chill slightly.

2 Meanwhile, in a medium skillet, combine the remaining ½ cup water with the broth, ginger and garlic; cover and bring to a boil over high heat. Reduce the heat to medium and simmer for 5 minutes to blend the flavors. Stir in the turkey strips, cover and cook, stirring frequently, for 3 to 4 minutes, or until the turkey is cooked through.

3 Using a slotted spoon, transfer the turkey to a plate; cover loosely with a sheet of wax paper to keep it moist.

4 Increase the heat under the skillet to high and return the broth to a boil. Boil rapidly for 5 to 6 minutes, or until the broth is thickened and reduced to about ¼ cup.

5 In a salad bowl, whisk together the peanut butter, lime juice, honey, anchovy paste, salt and red pepper flakes. Whisk in the reduced broth and continue whisking until smooth (whisk in a few drops of hot water if the mixture becomes too thick). Add the cooled rice, the turkey strips and any juices that have collected on the plate, and stir gently; then add the cabbage, bell peppers, onions and mint, and toss to mix.

6 Arrange the kale or spinach leaves on a platter. Mound the salad in the center and sprinkle with the peanuts.

Preparation time 20 minutes • **Total time** 45 minutes • **Per serving** 432 calories, 10.2 g. fat (21% of calories), 1 g. saturated fat, 53 mg. cholesterol, 359 mg. sodium, 5.7 g. dietary fiber, 154 mg. calcium, 4 mg. iron, 126 mg. vitamin C, 3.9 mg. beta-carotene • **Serves 4**

Cool Delights

❧ ❧ ❧

SPARKLING SORBETS,

CHILLED PUDDINGS, SHIMMERING

GELATIN DESSERTS AND COLD

COMPOTES TO REFRESH THE PALATE

GINGERED CANTALOUPE SORBET

1 large ripe cantaloupe, peeled,
seeded and cut into chunks
(about 4 cups)

½ cup sugar

2 tablespoons light corn syrup

1 tablespoon fresh lemon juice

1 tablespoon peeled grated fresh
ginger

2 tablespoons minced crystallized
ginger

Mint sprigs, for garnish
(optional)

Fine-quality crystallized ginger comes in good-size chunks and slices.

You don't need an ice-cream machine to make sorbet—just a food processor—and you can produce flavors you'll never find at the supermarket, like this sublime gingered melon ice. It contains both pungent fresh ginger and sweet-hot crystallized ginger—lively accents to the fragrant sweetness of the melon.

1 Place the cantaloupe, sugar, corn syrup, lemon juice and fresh ginger in a food processor, and process until smooth. Add the crystallized ginger and pulse just until mixed. Pour into a 9 x 9-inch metal baking pan, cover with foil and freeze for at least 6 hours, or overnight, or until frozen hard.

2 Remove the sorbet from the freezer and let stand for a few minutes until softened. Break the sorbet into chunks. In batches, place the sorbet in a food processor and pulse until creamy and smooth.

3 Transfer the sorbet to a freezer container, cover and freeze for at least 1 hour, or until you are ready to serve.

4 To serve, soften at room temperature for a few minutes. Spoon the sorbet into 4 dessert dishes or goblets. Garnish with mint sprigs, if desired.

Preparation time 10 minutes • **Total time** 20 minutes plus chilling time • **Per serving** 211 calories, 0.5 g. fat (2% of calories), 0 g. saturated fat, 0 mg. cholesterol, 32 mg. sodium, 1.3 g. dietary fiber, 37 mg. calcium, 2 mg. iron, 73 mg. vitamin C, 3.1 mg. beta-carotene • **Serves 4**

MARKET AND PANTRY
Crystallized ginger is made by cooking slices of fresh ginger in a sugar syrup, then coating it with granulated sugar. This turns the ginger into a tasty confection with a consistency like that of firm dried fruit. The crystallized ginger sold in small jars in supermarket spice racks can be very expensive. Better bets are gourmet or candy shops, or Asian markets, where the ginger is sold by the pound. It's usually much cheaper and also of better quality.

FRESH FRUIT TERRINE

1 **envelope plus 1 teaspoon unflavored gelatin**

½ **cup cold water**

2 **cups cranberry juice cocktail**

3 **tablespoons sugar**

3 **medium nectarines, cut into thin wedges (about 3 cups)**

1¾ **cups sliced fresh strawberries**

Nectarine slices and halved strawberries, for garnish (optional)

For smooth slices, use a thin serrated knife and dip the blade into hot water before making each cut.

There's just no comparison, in terms of flavor, between this "stained-glass" dessert and one made from a boxed dessert mix. However, the method and preparation time are pretty much the same, so why not start from scratch? The slices of nectarine and berries are so pretty that you don't need to use a fancy mold—a simple loaf pan will do. This gives the dessert the shape of a classic French *terrine,* and makes turning it out of the mold easier, too.

1 Spray an 8 x 4-inch loaf pan with no-stick spray.

2 In a medium metal bowl, sprinkle the gelatin over the cold water and let stand for 2 minutes to soften.

3 In a small saucepan, combine the cranberry juice cocktail and sugar, and bring to a boil over high heat, stirring to dissolve the sugar. Pour the boiling juice mixture over the softened gelatin and stir until the gelatin is completely dissolved.

4 Place the bowl with the cranberry-gelatin mixture over a larger bowl of ice water and let sit, stirring occasionally, for 8 to 10 minutes, or until the mixture is cold and just starts to jell. Stir in the fruits and turn the mixture into the prepared loaf pan. Cover with plastic wrap and chill for at least 6 hours, or overnight, until set.

5 To unmold, dip the pan briefly into a basin of hot water and invert over a platter. Shake to loosen the terrine, then remove the pan.

6 If desired, surround the terrine with nectarine slices and halved strawberries, or cut the terrine into 8 slices, place a slice on each of 8 dessert plates and garnish each serving with the fresh fruits.

Preparation time 10 minutes • **Total time** 30 minutes plus chilling time • **Per serving** 94 calories, 0.5 g. fat (5% of calories), 0 g. saturated fat, 0 mg. cholesterol, 4 mg. sodium, 1.7 g. dietary fiber, 10 mg. calcium, 0 mg. iron, 44 mg. vitamin C, 0.2 mg. beta-carotene • **Serves 8**

CREAMY BANANA PUDDING

¾ cup sweetened condensed milk

1 tablespoon plus 1 teaspoon fresh lemon juice

2 cups vanilla nonfat yogurt

½ cup reduced-fat sour cream

1 teaspoon vanilla extract

⅓ cup cold water

1 envelope unflavored gelatin

4 large bananas

20 reduced-fat vanilla wafers

One of the South's most beloved desserts, this family-pleaser depends for its flavor on sweet, ripe bananas. Some of the other ingredients in this version, however, are not traditional. Instead of whole milk, butter, eggs and heavy cream, the pudding is made with vanilla nonfat yogurt and reduced-fat sour cream. Gelatin, rather than cornstarch, serves as a thickener.

1 In a medium bowl, whisk the condensed milk with 1 tablespoon of the lemon juice until slightly thickened. Whisk in the yogurt, sour cream and vanilla until smooth.

2 Pour the cold water into a small saucepan. Sprinkle the gelatin over the water and let soften for 2 minutes. Cook the gelatin mixture over medium heat, stirring constantly, for 1 to 2 minutes, or until the gelatin is completely dissolved and the mixture is heated through. Stir the dissolved gelatin into the yogurt mixture.

3 Slice 3 of the bananas into ¼-inch-thick rounds. Drizzle with the remaining 1 teaspoon lemon juice. Fold the bananas into the pudding. Pour the pudding into 8 dessert glasses or a serving bowl, cover and chill for at least 2 hours, or until the pudding is set but still has a soft texture.

4 Just before serving, slice the remaining banana into ¼-inch-thick slices. Arrange the banana slices and the vanilla wafers on top of the pudding. To soften the cookies, let the pudding stand for a few minutes before serving.

Preparation time 5 minutes • **Total time** 25 minutes plus chilling time • **Per serving** 273 calories, 5.9 g. fat (19% of calories), 2.8 g. saturated fat, 16 mg. cholesterol, 131 mg. sodium, 1.2 g. dietary fiber, 169 mg. calcium, 1 mg. iron, 8 mg. vitamin C, 0.1 mg. beta-carotene • **Serves 8**

SUBSTITUTION

If you can't get reduced-fat vanilla wafers, you can use the regular kind and still end up with a healthful dessert: Even the regular wafers are relatively low in fat. Eight of them have 5.1 grams of fat, while the same quantity of reduced-fat wafers have 3.5 grams of fat.

SPICED PLUMS WITH CHANTILLY SAUCE

¾ **cup plain nonfat yogurt**

1 **pound ripe prune plums or black plums**

⅓ **cup purple grape juice**

3 **tablespoons Damson plum preserves**

1 **tablespoon sugar**

⅛ **teaspoon ground allspice**

Two 2-inch-long strips lemon zest

Half a cinnamon stick or a large pinch of ground cinnamon

2 **tablespoons reduced-fat sour cream**

2 **tablespoons confectioners' sugar**

1 **vanilla bean or ½ teaspoon vanilla extract**

Halve the vanilla bean lengthwise, then scrape out the seeds. Save the vanilla bean halves and bury them in sugar to make vanilla sugar.

The gracefully named *crème Chantilly,* a classic French dessert topping, consists of sweetened whipped heavy cream flavored with a touch of vanilla or a liqueur, such as chocolate *crème de cacao* or cherry-flavored *kirsch.* Here, yogurt cream, made by draining the whey from yogurt, takes the place of the whipped cream. Using a vanilla bean rather than extract gives the sauce a richer flavor.

1 Line a strainer with cheesecloth or a double layer of paper towels and place the strainer over a medium bowl. Spoon the yogurt into the strainer and let drain for 30 minutes. Discard the whey, wipe out the bowl and spoon the yogurt into the bowl; set aside.

2 While the yogurt is draining, halve and pit the plums. If using black plums, cut them into quarters.

3 In a medium, heavy nonreactive saucepan, combine the grape juice, preserves, sugar and allspice, and stir well. Add the plums, lemon zest and cinnamon stick or ground cinnamon, and stir to combine.

4 Bring the plum mixture to a boil over medium-high heat. Reduce the heat to medium-low, cover and simmer, stirring occasionally, for 5 to 10 minutes, or until the plums are tender but not mushy. Pour the plums and syrup into a medium bowl, cover with vented plastic wrap and refrigerate for about 1 hour, or until chilled.

5 Meanwhile, make the Chantilly sauce. Whisk the sour cream and confectioners' sugar into the drained yogurt. If using the vanilla bean, cut the bean in half lengthwise and scrape the seeds into the yogurt; whisk to blend. Or, if using the vanilla extract, add to the yogurt and whisk to blend.

6 Discard the cinnamon stick, if using, then spoon the plums and syrup into 4 dessert dishes. Top each serving with 2 heaping tablespoons of the Chantilly sauce.

Preparation time 10 minutes • **Total time** 35 minutes plus chilling time • **Per serving** 163 calories, 1.7 g. fat (9% of calories), 0.6 g. saturated fat, 3 mg. cholesterol, 26 mg. sodium, 2.4 g. dietary fiber, 64 mg. calcium, 0 mg. iron, 17 mg. vitamin C, 0.2 mg. beta-carotene • **Serves 4**

❧ ❧ ❧

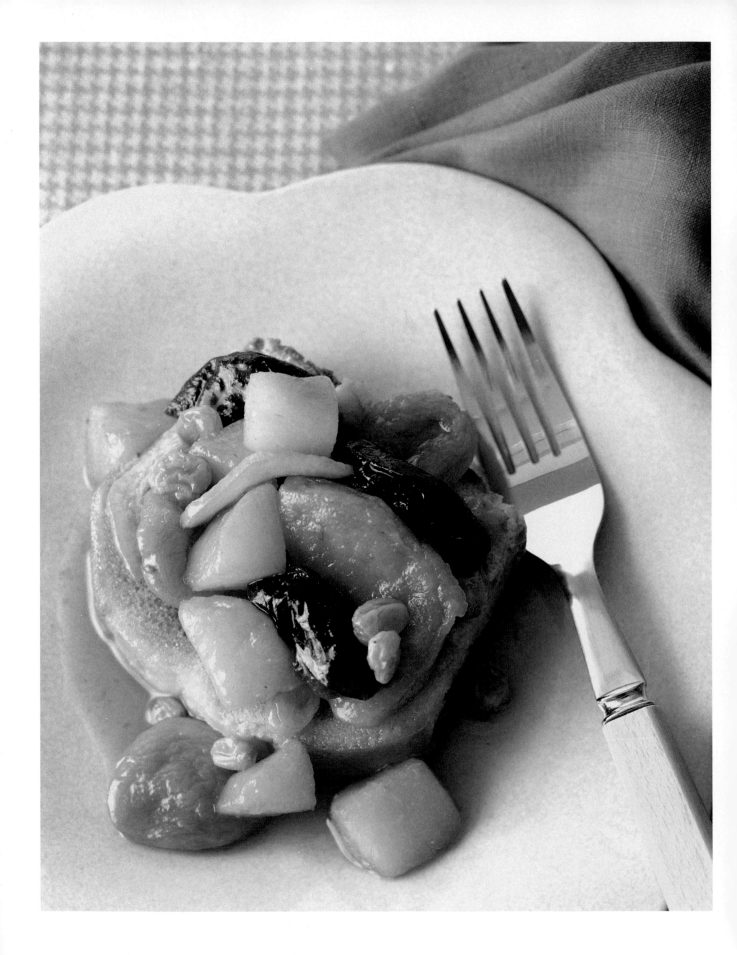

FRUIT COMPOTE WITH POUND CAKE

1 cup water

½ cup apple juice

1 medium Golden Delicious apple, peeled, quartered and cut into ½-inch wedges

1 medium pear, peeled, cored and cut into ¾-inch chunks

⅓ cup dried apricot halves

⅓ cup halved pitted prunes

3 tablespoons packed dark brown sugar

2 tablespoons golden raisins

1 large lemon

¼ teaspoon ground nutmeg

1 bay leaf, preferably imported

One (13.6-ounce) fat-free pound cake

A combination of fresh and dried fruits, this nutmeg-spiced compote captures the essence of autumn. Served over fat-free pound cake, it makes a remarkably nutritious dessert. For a change, spoon the compote over fat-free frozen yogurt or a slice of warm homemade gingerbread; or present the mixture in goblets with crisp gingersnaps on the side.

1 In a large, heavy saucepan, combine the water, apple juice, apples, pears, apricots, prunes, sugar and raisins.

2 Cut the lemon in half, then cut one half into thin slices. Cut the slices in half crosswise. Squeeze enough juice from the other lemon half into a small bowl to measure 2 tablespoons.

3 Add the lemon slices, lemon juice, nutmeg and bay leaf to the fruit mixture, and stir to combine. Bring to a simmer over medium-high heat. Reduce the heat to medium-low, cover and continue to simmer for 15 to 20 minutes, or until the fruits are very tender.

4 Pour the mixture into a medium bowl, cover and chill until ready to serve. Remove the bay leaf.

5 Just before serving, cut the pound cake into eight ¾-inch-thick slices. Place a slice of cake on each of 8 dessert plates. Spoon about ⅓ cup of the compote over each slice.

Preparation time 10 minutes • **Total time** 40 minutes plus chilling time • **Per serving** 218 calories, 0.3 g. fat (1% of calories), 0 g. saturated fat, 0 mg. cholesterol, 167 mg. sodium, 2.6 g. dietary fiber, 27 mg. calcium, 1 mg. iron, 21 mg. vitamin C, 0.4 mg. beta-carotene • **Serves 8**

NUTRITION NOTE
A box or bag of dried fruits is a "prize package," nutritionally speaking. Prunes are one of the best sources of fiber and supply lots of beta-carotene, iron, potassium and B vitamins as well. Dried apricots are an outstanding source of beta-carotene and a good source of iron. Although grapes are not tremendously nutritious, drying them concentrates their nutrients; in fact, raisins supply good amounts of iron, potassium and fiber.

Summer Fruits with Spiced Yogurt

1½ cups plain nonfat yogurt

½ medium cantaloupe

2 large nectarines

3 large plums

½ cup halved red seedless grapes

2 tablespoons honey

⅛ teaspoon ground cardamom

8 drops rosewater or almond extract

After spooning the yogurt into the cheese-cloth-lined strainer, stir the yogurt to break it up a bit and start the whey separating.

The delicate fragrance of the yogurt sauce may be familiar to lovers of Indian cuisine. The thickened yogurt is blended with cardamom and rosewater, two ingredients featured in many Indian sweets: Whole cardamom pods or ground cardamom seeds flavor coconut pudding and coconut fudge as well as hot tea, and rosewater lends a delicate perfume to rice pudding, cashew fudge and *lassi*—a yogurt "milkshake."

1 Line a strainer with cheesecloth or a double layer of paper towels and place the strainer over a medium bowl. Spoon the yogurt into the strainer and let drain for 20 minutes. Discard the whey, wipe out the bowl and spoon the yogurt into the bowl.

2 While the yogurt is draining, peel and seed the cantaloupe, and cut it into bite-size chunks. Place the cantaloupe in a medium serving bowl. Slice the nectarines and plums, and add to the cantaloupe. Add the grapes and stir to combine.

3 Add the honey, cardamom and rosewater or almond extract to the drained yogurt, and whisk to blend.

4 Drizzle the fruits with some of the spiced yogurt and serve the rest of the yogurt on the side.

Preparation time 5 minutes • **Total time** 30 minutes • **Per serving** 116 calories, 0.7 g. fat (5% of calories), 0 g. saturated fat, 0 mg. cholesterol, 24 mg. sodium, 2.3 g. dietary fiber, 81 mg. calcium, 0 mg. iron, 25 mg. vitamin C, 1.1 mg. beta-carotene • **Serves 6**

MARKET AND PANTRY
Rosewater is made from roses specially grown for their fragrance. It is sold in gourmet shops, Middle Eastern stores and many pharmacies.

SUBSTITUTION
If you're unable to get rosewater, or don't care for it, use almond extract instead. Be sure to buy pure almond extract—the imitation type has a distinctly inferior flavor.

RHUBARB-STRAWBERRY COMPOTE

⅓ cup strawberry all-fruit
   preserves

¼ cup sugar

2 tablespoons water

3 cups sliced rhubarb, cut into
   2-inch pieces (about 12 ounces)

3 cups thinly sliced strawberries

Mint sprigs, for garnish
   (optional)

Stewed rhubarb and strawberries make up the ever-popular filling for an early-summer pie (rhubarb is sometimes called "pie plant"); the combination offers a pleasing balance of sweet and tart. However, some standard recipes call for 2 to 3 cups of sugar—with almost sickeningly sweet results. Here, strawberry all-fruit preserves are used in the compote, so only ¼ cup of granulated sugar is needed. And if you save this recipe until local strawberries are in season, you'll find that they add plenty of their own sweetness.

1 In a medium, heavy nonreactive saucepan, combine the preserves, sugar and water, and whisk until smooth. Add the rhubarb and stir to coat. Bring to a simmer over medium heat. Reduce the heat to medium-low, cover and continue to simmer gently, turning the rhubarb occasionally with a rubber spatula so it stays intact, for 10 to 12 minutes, or until the rhubarb is very tender.

2 Remove the mixture from the heat and pour into a serving bowl or 4 dessert glasses. With a rubber spatula, gently fold in the strawberries. Cover with vented plastic wrap and chill for 1 hour, or until ready to serve. Garnish with mint sprigs, if desired.

Preparation time 5 minutes • **Total time** 50 minutes plus chilling time • **Per serving** 156 calories, 0.6 g. fat (3% of calories), 0 g. saturated fat, 0 mg. cholesterol, 5 mg. sodium, 3 g. dietary fiber, 89 mg. calcium, 1 mg. iron, 71 mg. vitamin C, 0.1 mg. beta-carotene • **Serves 4**

MARKET AND PANTRY
Rhubarb resembles Swiss chard, with its thick, fleshy stalks and fanlike leaves. But while chard is served as a vegetable, rhubarb has come to be unofficially considered a fruit: Though undeniably tart, it is used in desserts, jams and wines. Both hothouse and field-grown rhubarb are available; the color of the field-grown plant—both stems and leaves—is brighter, and the flavor is more intense. Field-grown rhubarb is sold only in the spring, while hothouse rhubarb is available practically all year round. Always remove and discard the leaves: They contain high levels of oxalic acid, which is toxic. You can freeze uncooked rhubarb (cut it into 2-inch pieces first) for six months to a year.

AMARETTI PUDDING

2 cups 1% low-fat milk

⅓ cup packed light brown sugar

¼ cup cornstarch

¼ teaspoon salt

½ cup skim milk

1 teaspoon vanilla extract

5 large amaretti cookies
(1¼ ounces), crumbled

Velvety desserts like this vanilla pudding need something crunchy for contrast. Here, crumbled *amaretti*—crisp almond-flavored macaroons from Italy—top the pudding. You can find amaretti, in brightly colored tins or bags, at gourmet shops, Italian grocery stores and many supermarkets. If you can't buy them, however, try another crisp topping, such as crumbled chocolate or vanilla wafers, your favorite breakfast cereal or a few spoonfuls of toasted coconut.

1 In a medium, heavy saucepan, warm the low-fat milk over medium heat just until small bubbles form around the edge and the milk is steaming. Remove the pan from the heat and set aside.

2 Meanwhile, in a medium bowl, whisk together the sugar, cornstarch and salt until blended. (You may need to break up the lumps of sugar with your fingers.) Gradually whisk in the skim milk until the mixture is smooth.

3 Pour the reserved low-fat milk into the sugar mixture and whisk until blended. Return the mixture to the saucepan and bring to a boil over medium heat, stirring constantly. Continue to boil, stirring, for 1 minute. Remove from the heat and stir in the vanilla.

4 Ladle the pudding into 4 dessert dishes or glasses, cover and refrigerate for about 1½ hours, or until chilled.

5 Just before serving, sprinkle each pudding with some amaretti crumbs.

Preparation time 10 minutes • **Total time** 30 minutes plus chilling time • **Per serving** 203 calories, 2.3 g. fat (10% of calories), 0.8 g. saturated fat, 6 mg. cholesterol, 224 mg. sodium, 0.1 g. dietary fiber, 204 mg. calcium, 0 mg. iron, 2 mg. vitamin C, 0.2 mg. beta-carotene • **Serves 4**

KITCHEN TIP
As anyone who's ever made gravy knows, cornstarch sometimes forms lumps when stirred into liquid. Combining the cornstarch with the sugar, and then whisking in the milk, helps keep this from happening.

Margarita Fruits

3 cups whole strawberries, hulled and quartered

2 tablespoons granulated sugar

2 tablespoons frozen orange juice concentrate

½ teaspoon grated lime zest

2 tablespoons fresh lime juice

1 tablespoon tequila (optional)

3 cups honeydew balls

Lime wedges, raw sugar and grated lime zest, for garnish (optional)

The Mexican cocktail called a *margarita* is made from tequila, orange liqueur and lime juice—a potent mixture that belies its innocent name (*margarita* is Spanish for "daisy"). To provide a sharp foil for its fruitiness, the drink is often served in a glass edged with coarse salt. Here, the dessert goblets are edged with raw sugar, available in most supermarkets.

1 In a medium bowl, combine the strawberries and granulated sugar. Let stand for 25 minutes, or until the juices begin to flow.

2 In a small bowl, combine the orange juice concentrate, lime zest, lime juice, and tequila, if using. Add the strawberries and their juice and the honeydew balls, and mix gently with a rubber spatula.

3 If desired, for a traditional margarita presentation, moisten the rims of 4 goblets with lime wedges. Place the raw sugar on a plate and dip the rim of each goblet into the sugar to coat it.

4 Carefully spoon the fruits and juice into the goblets and garnish each serving with lime zest, if desired.

Preparation time 10 minutes • **Total time** 25 minutes • **Per serving** 119 calories, 0.6 g. fat (4% of calories), 0 g. saturated fat, 0 mg. cholesterol, 14 mg. sodium, 4.2 g. dietary fiber, 28 mg. calcium, 1 mg. iron, 111 mg. vitamin C, 0.1 mg. beta-carotene • **Serves 4**

❧ ❧ ❧

Scoop out the seeds and fibers from the honeydew with a tablespoon.

Then insert a melon baller deep into the flesh to make balls that are nearly round.

LIME-MANGO MOLDS WITH FRUIT SAUCE

1 large ripe mango (about 1¼ pounds)

½ cup cold water

¼ cup sugar

3 tablespoons fresh lime juice

2 tablespoons honey

1 envelope unflavored gelatin

1 tablespoon chopped fresh cilantro

1 cup hulled whole strawberries

½ cup fresh raspberries or ½ cup frozen raspberries, thawed

4 strawberries, cut into fans, for garnish (optional)

These individual gelatin desserts glow with the colors of an island sunset. And the mango and lime evoke the flavors of the tropics. A touch of fresh cilantro provides an unexpected accent to the fruits.

1 Spray four 5- to 6-ounce decorative molds, custard cups or small soufflé dishes with no-stick spray.

2 Cut the fruit off the mango (see pages 14–15 for instructions), then place the pieces of mango in a food processor. Add ¼ cup of the cold water, 2 tablespoons of the sugar, the lime juice and honey, and process until puréed. Pour the purée into a medium bowl.

3 In a small saucepan, sprinkle the gelatin over the remaining ¼ cup water and let stand for 2 minutes. Cook the gelatin mixture over low heat, stirring, until the mixture is hot and the gelatin is dissolved.

4 Pour the dissolved gelatin into the mango purée and stir to combine. Stir in the cilantro. Divide the mango purée evenly among the prepared molds. Cover each with plastic wrap and chill for about 2 hours, or until the gelatin is set.

5 Meanwhile, place the whole strawberries, the raspberries and remaining 2 tablespoons sugar in a blender or food processor, and blend or process until puréed. Press the mixture through a fine strainer set over a medium bowl to remove the seeds. Cover and chill until ready to serve.

6 To unmold, briefly rub the outsides of the molds, cups or dishes with a kitchen towel or sponge dipped in hot water and invert over 4 dessert plates. Shake a few times to loosen the gelatin.

7 Spoon the fruit sauce around each gelatin dessert. Place a strawberry fan on top of each, if desired.

Preparation time 5 minutes • **Total time** 30 minutes plus chilling time • **Per serving** 179 calories, 1.5 g. fat (8% of calories), 0.1 g. saturated fat, 0 mg. cholesterol, 7 mg. sodium, 2.8 g. dietary fiber, 21 mg. calcium, 0 mg. iron, 56 mg. vitamin C, 2.3 mg. beta-carotene • **Serves 4**

LEMON-MINT WATERMELON GRANITA

3 pounds watermelon, seeded and
cut into chunks (about 4 cups)

⅓ cup sugar

⅓ cup fresh lemon juice

2 tablespoons light corn syrup

2 tablespoons slivered mint leaves

¾ teaspoon grated lemon zest

Even colder than a well-chilled watermelon, this refreshing dessert takes the form of a *granita*, a super-crunchy Italian ice. To produce the pleasantly granular texture, periodically stir and scrape the partially frozen mixture with a fork. This technique brings the iciest portions into the less-frozen center and maintains the crystalline quality of the ice.

1 Place the watermelon chunks, sugar, lemon juice and corn syrup in a blender or food processor, in batches if necessary, and process to a smooth purée. Add the slivered mint and lemon zest, and pulse just to mix.

2 Pour the watermelon mixture into a 9-inch square metal baking pan and place in the freezer. Freeze, scraping the frozen edges toward the middle every 30 minutes or so, for 2 to 3 hours, or until the granita is slushy and granular.

3 Cover and freeze for at least 2 to 3 hours longer, or until frozen hard.

4 To serve, scrape the surface of the ice with a metal spoon to create a granular texture, then spoon into 4 goblets or dessert dishes.

Preparation time 15 minutes • **Total time** 25 minutes plus chilling time • **Per serving** 150 calories, 0.7 g. fat (4% of calories), 0 g. saturated fat, 0 mg. cholesterol, 16 mg. sodium, 0.6 g. dietary fiber, 16 mg. calcium, 0 mg. iron, 26 mg. vitamin C, 0.4 mg. beta-carotene • **Serves 4**

MARKET AND PANTRY
You'll find two types of watermelon in the market, at least during the summer: picnic and icebox. Picnic watermelons weigh up to 50 pounds—they're the massive blimp-shaped fruits you'd serve at a barbecue. Icebox melons are bred to fit into the refrigerator: They're round or oval and weigh from 5 to 10 pounds. Some icebox watermelons are seedless. With its deep-colored, crunchy flesh, a seedless melon would be ideal for this recipe.

POACHED PEACHES WITH RASPBERRIES

2 cups white grape juice

2 cups water

½ cup honey

1 cinnamon stick, broken in half

1 teaspoon allspice berries or ¼ teaspoon ground allspice

4 whole cloves or ⅛ teaspoon ground cloves

4 large ripe peaches

1 cup fresh raspberries

Use whole allspice berries (left) and cloves (right) to flavor syrups, sauces and beverages; it's easy to strain the spices out after cooking, if necessary.

Dame Nellie Melba, a turn-of-the-century opera singer, inspired the most famous pairing of peaches and raspberries, a dish known to this day as *pêche Melba*. The great French chef Georges Escoffier created the recipe for poached peaches and raspberry sauce served over vanilla ice cream. For this elegant adaptation, the peaches are simmered in a warmly spiced mixture of grape juice, cinnamon, allspice and cloves. You can save the syrup (refrigerate it in a covered jar) and use it to cook other fruits.

1 In a large nonreactive saucepan, combine the grape juice, water, honey, cinnamon stick, allspice and cloves. Cover and bring to a boil over high heat. Reduce the heat to medium and simmer for 5 minutes to blend the flavors.

2 Add the whole peaches, increase the heat to medium-high and bring just to a boil. Reduce the heat to medium, cover and simmer for 20 minutes, or until the peaches are fork-tender. Remove the pan from the heat and let the peaches cool in the pan, uncovered, for 10 minutes.

3 Remove the peaches from the syrup, reserving the syrup. Slip off the skins, halve the peaches and remove the stones.

4 Spoon 1 cup of the syrup into a medium bowl and place the peach halves in the syrup. (Save the remaining syrup for another use.) Cover with vented plastic wrap and chill for about 1 hour, or until ready to serve.

5 To serve, place 2 peach halves in each of 4 dessert dishes. Pour ¼ cup of syrup over each portion and top each with ¼ cup of raspberries.

Preparation time 5 minutes • **Total time** 50 minutes plus chilling time • **Per serving** 152 calories, 0.3 g. fat (2% of calories), 0 g. saturated fat, 0 mg. cholesterol, 2 mg. sodium, 4.1 g. dietary fiber, 21 mg. calcium, 1 mg. iron, 29 mg. vitamin C, 0.6 mg. beta-carotene • **Serves 4**

Warm Pleasures

❧ ❧ ❧

FRUIT PASTRIES, WARM SOUFFLÉS,

CRISPS, CRUMBLES AND

OLD-FASHIONED PUDDINGS—

THE SWEET COMFORTS OF HOME

CHERRY CLAFOUTI

1 teaspoon unsalted butter or
margarine, at room temperature

⅓ cup granulated sugar

1 cup 1% low-fat milk

⅔ cup all-purpose flour

2 large eggs

2 large egg whites

1 teaspoon vanilla extract

⅛ teaspoon almond extract

2 cups pitted sweet cherries

1½ teaspoons confectioners' sugar

A *clafouti* is a thick, sweet pancake, studded with fruit and baked. This summer treat is traditionally made with fresh black cherries; you can substitute frozen unsweetened Bing cherries in other seasons. If you don't have a cherry pitter, you can use a paper clip to pit the cherries (see below).

1 Preheat the oven to 400°. Coat an 8-inch square baking dish or a 9-inch pie plate with the butter or margarine and dust with 1 teaspoon of the granulated sugar.

2 In a blender or food processor (a blender works best), combine the remaining granulated sugar, the milk, flour, eggs, egg whites, vanilla and almond extract; blend or process until smooth.

3 Pour half of the batter into the prepared baking dish or pie plate. Add the cherries and pour in the remaining batter.

4 Bake for 20 to 30 minutes, or until the clafouti is puffed, browned and firm. Transfer to a wire rack to cool slightly.

5 To serve, place the confectioners' sugar in a small strainer and dust over the top of the clafouti. Cut the clafouti into 6 pieces.

Preparation time 20 minutes • **Total time** 50 minutes • **Per serving** 187 calories, 3.3 g. fat (16% of calories), 1.3 g. saturated fat, 74 mg. cholesterol, 60 mg. sodium, 1.1 g. dietary fiber, 68 mg. calcium, 1 mg. iron, 4 mg. vitamin C, 0.2 mg. beta-carotene • **Serves 6**

Place one cherry at a time in the pitter and squeeze the handles to pit.

Or, unfold one end of a large paper clip and use the "hook" to remove the pit.

COFFEE CUP SOUFFLÉS

- 1 tablespoon unsalted butter or margarine, at room temperature
- ¼ cup plus 1 tablespoon granulated sugar
- ¼ cup cornstarch
- 3 tablespoons packed light brown sugar
- 3 tablespoons unsweetened cocoa powder
- 1½ teaspoons instant espresso powder
- ¼ teaspoon ground cinnamon
- 1¼ cups evaporated skimmed milk
- 6 large egg whites
- ⅛ teaspoon salt
- 2 teaspoons vanilla extract
- Espresso beans, for garnish (optional)

What more appropriate servers for a mocha soufflé than coffee cups? They're just the right size, too. Use heavy porcelain cups—don't put your fine bone china in the oven.

1 Preheat the oven to 400°. Coat six 7-ounce ovenproof coffee cups, soufflé dishes or custard cups with the butter or margarine, and dust evenly using 2 tablespoons of the granulated sugar, turning the cups or dishes to coat the sides completely. Place the cups on a baking sheet.

2 In a medium, heavy saucepan, whisk together 2 tablespoons of the remaining granulated sugar, the cornstarch, brown sugar, cocoa powder, espresso powder and cinnamon. Gradually whisk in the evaporated milk until the mixture is smooth.

3 Place the pan over medium heat and cook, whisking frequently and then constantly as the milk mixture gets hotter, until it comes to a boil and thickens. Remove the pan from the heat. Place a sheet of plastic wrap directly onto the surface of the milk mixture to prevent a skin from forming; set aside.

4 In a large bowl, with an electric mixer at high speed, beat the egg whites and salt until foamy. Gradually beat in the remaining 1 tablespoon granulated sugar and continue beating until stiff peaks form.

5 Whisk the vanilla into the milk mixture. Stir a big spoonful of the beaten whites into the milk mixture to lighten it. Then pour the milk mixture into the beaten whites. With a large rubber spatula, fold the milk mixture into the whites until no white streaks remain. Divide the mixture evenly among the prepared cups or dishes.

6 Bake the soufflés for 13 to 15 minutes, or until puffed and firm to the touch. Remove from the oven and serve immediately, garnished with espresso beans, if desired.

Preparation time 10 minutes • **Total time** 45 minutes • **Per serving** 174 calories, 2.4 g. fat (12% of calories), 1.5 g. saturated fat, 7 mg. cholesterol, 166 mg. sodium, 0.8 g. dietary fiber, 168 mg. calcium, 1 mg. iron, 1 mg. vitamin C, 0.2 mg. beta-carotene • **Serves 6**

APPLE-CRANBERRY CRISP

¾ **cup old-fashioned rolled oats or rolled wheat**

⅓ **cup whole-wheat flour**

¼ **cup packed dark brown sugar**

⅛ **teaspoon salt**

⅛ **teaspoon ground allspice**

3 **tablespoons chilled unsalted butter or margarine, cut into small pieces**

3 **large Empire, Idared or Granny Smith apples, cored and sliced into ¼-inch-thick wedges**

½ **cup dried cranberries**

3 **tablespoons frozen apple juice concentrate**

1 **tablespoon granulated sugar**

A basic fruit-crisp topping is made with white flour, but this nicely crunchy version has rolled oats as its main ingredient, along with some whole-wheat flour. Rolled wheat, which is sold in health food stores, may be used in place of the oats. If you can't get dried cranberries, substitute other dried fruits, such as chopped prunes or apricots.

1 Preheat the oven to 425°.

2 In a medium bowl, combine the oats or wheat, flour, brown sugar, salt and allspice. Using your fingers or a pastry blender, lightly mix in the butter or margarine until the mixture is crumbly.

3 In an 8- or 9-inch square baking dish, toss together the apples, cranberries, apple juice concentrate and granulated sugar until well mixed. Sprinkle the oat or wheat mixture evenly over the top.

4 Cover with foil and bake for 20 minutes, or until the mixture is bubbly and the apples are tender. Uncover and bake for 5 to 10 minutes longer, or until the topping is lightly browned.

Preparation time 10 minutes • **Total time** 40 minutes • **Per serving** 188 calories, 5.2 g. fat (25% of calories), 2.8 g. saturated fat, 12 mg. cholesterol, 40 mg. sodium, 3.3 g. dietary fiber, 19 mg. calcium, 1 mg. iron, 10 mg. vitamin C, 0.1 mg. beta-carotene • **Serves 8**

The Empire, a tasty cross between a Delicious and a McIntosh, is firmer and crisper than either of its forebears.

The Idared is related to the Jonathan apple. Good for eating fresh, the Idared is also ideal for crisps and pies.

Granny Smith apples are quite hard, but not especially flavorful. Give them an extra pinch of spice and a squeeze of lemon.

BLUEBERRY-RASPBERRY BAKE

⅓ cup raspberry all-fruit preserves

1 tablespoon plus 1 teaspoon granulated sugar

1 tablespoon cornstarch

1½ teaspoons grated lemon zest

2 teaspoons fresh lemon juice

2 cups blueberries

2 cups raspberries

¾ cup all-purpose flour

¼ cup whole-wheat flour

3 tablespoons packed light brown sugar

1 teaspoon baking powder

¼ teaspoon baking soda

⅛ teaspoon salt

3 tablespoons chilled unsalted butter or margarine, cut up

¼ cup buttermilk or plain nonfat yogurt

Not quite a pie—nor a cobbler, a pandowdy or an upside-down cake—this homey dessert defies any label except "delicious." The sweetened berries are baked in a pie plate, then a scone-like dough is laid over the fruit and the mixture continues to bake until the topping is browned and crisp. Low-fat frozen lemon yogurt would make refreshing complement.

1 Preheat the oven to 425°.

2 In a medium bowl, combine the preserves, 1 tablespoon of the granulated sugar, the cornstarch, lemon zest and lemon juice. Add the blueberries and raspberries, and mix gently with a rubber spatula. Transfer the berry mixture to a 9 inch pie plate, cover with foil and bake for 20 minutes, or until the fruit is hot and bubbly. Remove from the oven and set aside, covered.

3 While the fruit is baking, in a food processor, combine the all-purpose flour, whole-wheat flour, brown sugar, baking powder, baking soda and salt. Pulse to mix and break up any lumps of sugar. Add the butter or margarine and pulse until very fine crumbs form. Add the buttermilk or yogurt and pulse just until a soft dough forms.

4 On a lightly floured surface, give the dough 5 kneads. With a lightly floured rolling pin, roll out the dough to a 7-inch circle. Uncover the fruit and place the dough on top. Sprinkle the surface with the remaining 1 teaspoon granulated sugar.

5 Place the pie plate on a baking sheet. Bake for about 15 minutes, or until the dough is lightly browned and crisp, and the fruit bubbles up along the sides. Transfer to a wire rack to cool briefly. Serve warm.

Preparation time 5 minutes • **Total time** 50 minutes • **Per serving** 195 calories, 4.8 g. fat (22% of calories), 2.7 g. saturated fat, 12 mg. cholesterol, 148 mg. sodium, 3.1 g. dietary fiber, 61 mg. calcium, 1 mg. iron, 14 mg. vitamin C, 0.2 mg. beta-carotene • **Serves 8**

SUBSTITUTION

This recipe can be prepared with frozen berries. After thawing the berries, drain them well and pat them dry. You can also use the berries without thawing them if you allow for a longer baking time.

ORANGE BASMATI RICE PUDDING

1½ cups water

¾ cup basmati rice, rinsed

¼ teaspoon salt

2 large eggs

1 large egg white

¼ cup plus 1 tablespoon no-sugar-added orange marmalade

¼ cup granulated sugar

1½ teaspoons grated orange zest

1 teaspoon vanilla extract

1 cup 1% low-fat milk

1 cup skim milk

3 juice oranges

1 tablespoon packed dark brown sugar

Basmati rice, with its toasty, nutlike fragrance, brings a new dimension to this old favorite. If you like, cook the rice the day before, or use rice left over from a meal (you'll need 2½ cups of cooked rice). Substitute regular rice if you can't get basmati.

1 In a medium, heavy saucepan, combine the water, rice and salt, and bring to a boil over high heat. Reduce the heat to low, cover and simmer for 15 minutes, or until the rice is tender and the liquid is absorbed.

2 Meanwhile, spray eight 6-ounce custard cups or ramekins with no-stick spray. Preheat the oven to 400°.

3 Spread the cooked rice in a jelly-roll pan and place it in the freezer for a few minutes to cool slightly while you prepare the custard.

4 In a large bowl, whisk together the eggs, egg white, ¼ cup of the marmalade, the granulated sugar, orange zest and vanilla. Whisk in the low-fat milk and skim milk. Stir in the cooked rice. Spoon about ⅔ cup of the mixture into each of the prepared custard cups or ramekins.

5 Place the custard cups or ramekins in a jelly-roll pan. Bake for 35 minutes, or until the puddings are lightly browned on the surface and set. Remove from the pan and place on a rack to cool briefly.

6 Meanwhile, with a knife, cut the peel and white pith from the oranges. Working over a bowl, cut the sections from between the membranes, letting the juice drip into the bowl. Squeeze the juice from the membranes into the bowl. (See pages 12–13 for more information on peeling and sectioning an orange.)

7 Whisk the brown sugar and remaining 1 tablespoon marmalade into the orange juice, then stir in the orange sections. Cover and chill until ready to serve. Just before serving, top the puddings with the orange sections and syrup.

Preparation time 5 minutes • **Total time** 1 hour • **Per serving** 195 calories, 3 g. fat (14% of calories), 0.6 g. saturated fat, 55 mg. cholesterol, 130 mg. sodium, 1.5 g. dietary fiber, 109 mg. calcium, 0 mg. iron, 27 mg. vitamin C, 0.2 mg. beta-carotene • **Serves 8**

APRICOT AND PLUM SLUMP

2¼ pounds ripe plums, cut into wedges (about 5½ cups)

⅔ cup dried apricot halves

¼ cup plus 3 tablespoons granulated sugar

⅓ cup white grape juice

2 tablespoons honey

1 tablespoon fresh lemon juice

1¾ cups all-purpose flour

1 teaspoon baking powder

½ teaspoon baking soda

⅛ teaspoon salt

3 tablespoons chilled unsalted butter or margarine, cut into small pieces

¾ cup buttermilk or plain nonfat yogurt

⅛ teaspoon ground cinnamon

Ground cinnamon, for garnish (optional)

Usually made with blueberries, a slump is an old New England dish with a less-than-elegant name that belies its luscious flavor. You'll appreciate this recipe in hot weather: No oven is needed because the slump cooks in a skillet on the stove. It's best to use a high-domed lid on the skillet to allow space for the dumplings to rise; if you don't have one, spray a regular lid with no-stick spray so the dumplings won't stick to it.

1 In a large, deep nonreactive skillet, combine the plums, apricots, ¼ cup of the sugar, the grape juice, honey and lemon juice. Bring to a boil over medium-high heat. Reduce the heat to medium-low, cover and simmer for 8 to 10 minutes, or until the fruit is fairly tender but not mushy. Remove the fruit mixture from the heat; set aside.

2 While the fruit mixture is cooking, in a food processor, combine the flour, baking powder, baking soda, salt and 2 tablespoons of the remaining sugar; process to blend.

3 Add the butter or margarine, and pulse until fine crumbs form. Add the buttermilk or yogurt, and pulse just until a soft dough forms.

4 In a cup, stir together the remaining 1 tablespoon sugar and the cinnamon.

5 Drop the dough by heaping tablespoons onto the hot fruit mixture. Sprinkle with the cinnamon sugar. Bring to a boil over medium heat, cover and immediately reduce the heat to medium-low. Simmer for 10 to 15 minutes, or until the dumplings are firm to the touch.

6 Remove the pan from the heat, uncover and let the slump cool briefly before serving. Sprinkle with a little ground cinnamon just before serving, if desired.

Preparation time 15 minutes • **Total time** 45 minutes • **Per serving** 305 calories, 5.6 g. fat (16% of calories), 2.9 g. saturated fat, 13 mg. cholesterol, 201 mg. sodium, 4.1 g. dietary fiber, 77 mg. calcium, 2 mg. iron, 14 mg. vitamin C, 0.8 mg. beta-carotene • **Serves 8**

CHOCOLATE BREAD PUDDING

1 cup skim milk

¾ cup 1% low-fat milk

1 ounce semisweet chocolate

⅓ cup granulated sugar

⅓ cup unsweetened cocoa powder

1 large egg

2 large egg whites

1½ teaspoons vanilla extract

½ teaspoon ground cinnamon

2½ cups cubed semolina bread or crusty white bread (½-inch cubes)

3 tablespoons currants

1 teaspoon confectioners' sugar

Fresh raspberries or other fresh fruit, for garnish (optional)

This pale golden, sesame-seeded bread is made from semolina flour, which is ground from the heart (endosperm) of durum wheat. Semolina bread flour is a finer-textured version of the flour used in all good brands of pasta.

Recipes like this one originated as thrifty solutions to leftovers—for example, as a way to use up a loaf that was going stale. Frugal housekeeping aside, it's a most delightful dessert, and it's hardly an extravagance to buy a loaf of golden semolina bread just for the occasion. You'll find the bread in Italian bakeries and many supermarkets. Challah or homestyle white bread (thick-sliced or unsliced) can be substituted.

1 Preheat the oven to 400°.

2 In a medium, heavy saucepan, combine the skim milk, low-fat milk and chocolate. Warm over medium heat, stirring frequently, until the chocolate is melted and the milk is hot. (The mixture does not need to be completely smooth.)

3 Meanwhile, in a large bowl, whisk together the granulated sugar, cocoa powder, egg, egg whites, vanilla and cinnamon. Gradually whisk in the hot milk mixture until smooth.

4 Spread the bread cubes evenly in an 8- or 9-inch square baking dish and sprinkle with the currants. Pour the milk mixture over the bread cubes, moistening them well. With a spoon, press the bread down into the milk.

5 Bake the pudding for 25 to 30 minutes, or until just set. Remove from the oven and transfer the baking dish to a rack to cool briefly.

6 To serve, place the confectioners' sugar in a small strainer and dust over the warm pudding. Garnish with fresh raspberries or other fresh fruit, if desired.

Preparation time 10 minutes • **Total time** 45 minutes • **Per serving** 261 calories, 5.6 g. fat (19% of calories), 2.7 g. saturated fat, 56 mg. cholesterol, 206 mg. sodium, 2.9 g. dietary fiber, 181 mg. calcium, 2 mg. iron, 1 mg. vitamin C, 0.2 mg. beta-carotene • **Serves 4**

ROASTED PEARS WITH GOAT CHEESE

2 tablespoons unsalted butter or margarine

¼ cup sugar

1 tablespoon fresh lemon juice

4 large ripe Bosc, Bartlett or Anjou pears

¼ cup seedless raspberry jam

¼ teaspoon coarsely ground black pepper

2 ounces goat cheese

Mint sprigs, for garnish (optional)

Here's a sophisticated finale that would not be out of place at a Parisian table, where fruit and cheese are the most popular desserts—served much more often than cakes or pastries. Truly ripe pears are delicious on their own (remember to allow a few days for ripening after buying them); baking them brings out their full "bouquet." Red Bartletts would look especially pretty topped with the ruby-colored raspberry sauce.

1 Preheat the oven to 450°.

2 While the oven is preheating, place the butter or margarine in a 13 x 9-inch baking dish. Place in the oven for about 5 minutes, or until the butter or margarine is melted. Remove from the oven and stir in the sugar and lemon juice.

3 While the butter or margarine is melting, halve the pears. Remove the cores with a melon baller or a grapefruit spoon and make a V-shaped cut at the bottom of each pear to remove each blossom end.

4 Transfer the pears to the prepared baking dish and turn to coat with the butter or margarine. Arrange the pears, cut-side up, making sure there is some butter or margarine in the cavities. Roast for 20 to 25 minutes, or until the pears are very tender. Remove from the oven and transfer the pears to 4 dessert plates, reserving the juices.

5 In a small saucepan, combine the raspberry jam and black pepper. Pour the juices from the baking dish into the pan and stir to combine. Bring to a boil over medium heat, stirring occasionally. Continue to boil for 2 to 3 minutes, or until the sauce is slightly thickened.

6 To serve, spoon some goat cheese into the cavity in each pear, then drizzle the raspberry sauce over the pears. Garnish with mint sprigs, if desired.

Preparation time 5 minutes • **Total time** 45 minutes • **Per serving** 353 calories, 11 g. fat (28% of calories), 6.5 g. saturated fat, 27 mg. cholesterol, 82 mg. sodium, 7.1 g. dietary fiber, 72 mg. calcium, 1 mg. iron, 14 mg. vitamin C, 0.2 mg. beta-carotene • **Serves 4**

PINEAPPLE CRUMBLE

One 4-pound fresh pineapple, peeled, cored and cut into ½-inch chunks (about 5 cups)

3 tablespoons honey

1½ teaspoons vanilla extract

¾ teaspoon ground coriander

1 cup all-purpose flour

¼ cup wheat germ

¼ cup packed dark brown sugar

2 tablespoons shredded coconut

⅛ teaspoon salt

3 tablespoons chilled unsalted butter, cut into small pieces

Supermarkets with exceptional produce departments have recently added a real convenience to the fruit aisle—a mechanical device that lets you core and peel a fresh pineapple with the pull of a lever. If this time-saver is not available where you shop, see pages 12–13 for information on how to peel and core a pineapple.

1 Preheat the oven to 425°.

2 In an 11 x 7-inch baking dish, combine the pineapple, honey, vanilla and ¼ teaspoon of the coriander.

3 In a medium bowl, combine the flour, wheat germ, brown sugar, coconut, salt and remaining ½ teaspoon coriander. Mix with a pastry blender or 2 knives to break up the lumps of sugar. Cut in the butter until the mixture forms fine crumbs.

4 Sprinkle the crumble over the pineapple mixture and bake for 25 to 30 minutes, or until the topping is browned, the pineapple tender and the juices bubbly.

Preparation time 10 minutes • **Total time** 50 minutes • **Per serving** 214 calories, 5.6 g. fat (24% of calories), 3.1 g. saturated fat, 12 mg. cholesterol, 43 mg. sodium, 2.1 g. dietary fiber, 19 mg. calcium, 2 mg. iron, 15 mg. vitamin C, 0.1 mg. beta-carotene • **Serves 8**

❧ ❧ ❧

A pastry blender, made of wires set into a handle, quickly combines the butter with the dry ingredients.

Two table knives (you don't need sharp blades) can also do the job; use them with a quick chopping motion.

WARM GINGERBREAD-PUMPKIN PUDDING

2 large eggs

2 large egg whites

¼ cup mild molasses

¼ cup sugar

1 cup solid-pack canned pumpkin

¾ cup skim milk

⅓ cup all-purpose flour

2 teaspoons ground ginger

1½ teaspoons ground cinnamon

1 teaspoon baking powder

½ teaspoon baking soda

¼ teaspoon ground allspice

⅛ teaspoon ground white pepper

1 teaspoon confectioners' sugar

Recipes for the steamed holiday puddings of Dickens's day make wonderful reading, but they required no end of time and effort, what with chopping the fruits, nuts and suet, mixing the batter in a mammoth bowl, steaming it in a cloth-wrapped basin for 9 to 12 hours and then aging the finished product for many months to blend the flavors to perfection. This spicy pumpkin pudding-cake—a flash in the pan by comparison—makes a terrific holiday dessert. Dress it up with a scoop of vanilla or lemon frozen yogurt.

1 Preheat the oven to 400°. Spray an 8- or 9-inch square baking dish with no-stick spray.

2 In a large bowl, combine the eggs, egg whites, molasses and sugar, and whisk until smooth. Whisk in the pumpkin and milk.

3 Add the flour, ginger, cinnamon, baking powder, baking soda, allspice and white pepper, and whisk just until smooth. Pour the batter into the prepared pan.

4 Bake for 25 minutes, or until the pudding is lightly browned and cracked around the edges but still a bit soft in the center. Transfer to a wire rack to cool briefly.

5 Just before serving, place the confectioners' sugar in a small strainer and dust over the warm pudding.

Preparation time 5 minutes • **Total time** 35 minutes • **Per serving** 156 calories, 2.1 g. fat (12% of calories), 0.6 g. saturated fat, 71 mg. cholesterol, 249 mg. sodium, 0.9 g. dietary fiber, 140 mg. calcium, 2 mg. iron, 2 mg. vitamin C, 5.5 mg. beta-carotene • **Serves 6**

KITCHEN TIP

White pepper might seem a bit out of place in the list of gingerbread spices, but it is actually a traditional ingredient in European recipes. Try a pinch of white pepper in your own recipes for ginger cookies or spice cakes.

MAKE AHEAD

Although this is a very quick recipe, you can shave off a few moments by measuring the dry ingredients in advance. Combine the flour, ginger, cinnamon, baking powder, baking soda, allspice and pepper in a container, stir well and cover.

BAKED APPLE FANS

1 tablespoon plus 1 teaspoon
unsalted butter or margarine

1½ tablespoons sliced unblanched
almonds

4 large Granny Smith apples

3 tablespoons apricot all-fruit
preserves

2 tablespoons sugar

1 tablespoon fresh lemon juice

Spread the apple slices with your fingers
as you would fan a hand of cards, then
lay them in the jelly-roll pan.

Baked apples become company fare when the fruit is sliced, fanned and graced with a lemon-butter glaze. Be sure to use apples that will hold their shape when cooked, rather than turning into sauce. The Granny Smith is one such apple; Golden Delicious and Cortlands are other options.

1 Preheat the oven to 450°. Coat a jelly-roll pan with ½ teaspoon of the butter or margarine.

2 Meanwhile, place the almonds in a small baking pan and toast in the oven while it is preheating for 3 to 5 minutes, or until lightly browned.

3 Peel the apples with a vegetable peeler and cut in half through the stem end. Remove the cores with a melon baller and cut a V-shape to remove the stem and blossom ends. Place each half, cut-side down, on a cutting board.

4 Slice the apples crosswise into ⅛-inch-thick slices, leaving the slices together. Fan out each sliced apple half and place in the prepared jelly-roll pan.

5 In a small saucepan, combine the preserves, sugar, lemon juice and remaining 1 tablespoon plus ½ teaspoon butter or margarine. Warm over medium-high heat, stirring frequently, until bubbly. Spoon the mixture over the apples, spreading it with the back of the spoon to coat the apples evenly.

6 Bake the apples for 10 to 12 minutes, or until tender. Turn the oven to broil. Broil the apples 4 to 6 inches from the heat for 1 to 2 minutes, or until the edges are lightly browned.

7 With a large metal spatula, transfer the apple fans to 4 warmed dessert plates. Sprinkle with the toasted almonds and serve.

Preparation time 5 minutes • **Total time** 40 minutes • **Per serving** 192 calories, 5.9 g. fat (28% of calories), 2.6 g. saturated fat, 10 mg. cholesterol, 1 mg. sodium, 3.1 g. dietary fiber, 15 mg. calcium, 0 mg. iron, 8 mg. vitamin C, 0.1 mg. beta-carotene • **Serves 4**

FRUIT GRATINS WITH ZABAGLIONE

1½ **cups blueberries**

1½ **cups pitted sweet cherries**

1½ **cups sliced strawberries**

¼ **cup sugar**

3 **tablespoons dry Marsala wine**

2 **large eggs**

It's easiest to whip the zabaglione with a portable electric mixer. Hold the double boiler handle to steady it as you mix.

You won't find grated cheese and breadcrumbs in the ingredient list: This is a different kind of gratin. Instead of a savory crust, the fruits are covered with zabaglione—a frothy egg custard that turns golden brown when broiled. Marsala is the traditional flavoring for zabaglione, but if you prefer to omit it, add 1 teaspoon of vanilla extract and a few drops of almond extract to the egg mixture. When cherries are out of season, use frozen ones, or simply increase the amounts of strawberries and blueberries. You can also use four 6-ounce gratin dishes instead of a large gratin dish.

1 Preheat the oven to 450°.

2 In a medium bowl, using a rubber spatula, combine the blueberries, cherries and strawberries with 1 tablespoon of the sugar and 1 tablespoon of the Marsala. Place the fruit mixture in a large (5-cup) gratin dish. Let stand for 10 to 15 minutes while you prepare the zabaglione.

3 In the top of a double boiler, off the heat, with a portable electric mixer at high speed, beat the eggs with the remaining 3 tablespoons sugar until light and lemon colored. Beat in the remaining 2 tablespoons Marsala.

4 Place the egg mixture over barely simmering water and continue to beat with the mixer at high for at least 10 minutes (to ensure the eggs are completely cooked), or until the mixture is glossy and thickened. Remove from the simmering water and set aside off the heat.

5 Cover the gratin dish with foil and place on a baking sheet. Bake the fruit mixture for 5 to 10 minutes, or just until heated through. Remove from the oven and uncover. Turn the oven to broil.

6 Spoon the zabaglione evenly over the gratin. Broil 4 to 6 inches from the heat for about 2 minutes, or until the zabaglione is warmed and lightly browned. Serve at once.

Preparation time 10 minutes • **Total time** 45 minutes • **Per serving** 187 calories, 3.4 g. fat (17% of calories), 0.9 g. saturated fat, 106 mg. cholesterol, 37 mg. sodium, 3.6 g. dietary fiber, 33 mg. calcium, 1 mg. iron, 43 mg. vitamin C, 0.2 mg. beta-carotene • **Serves 4**

Cookies & Bars

❧ ❧ ❧

LEMONY ICEBOX COOKIES, CHEWY
FRUIT BARS, LACY WAFERS, AIRY
MERINGUES—SOMETHING FOR EVERY
COOKIE JAR AND PARTY TABLE

LEMON DROP COOKIES

1 cup plus 2 tablespoons
all-purpose flour

⅛ teaspoon baking soda

⅛ teaspoon salt

2 tablespoons butter, softened

2 tablespoons reduced-calorie tub
margarine (6 grams fat per
tablespoon)

½ cup sugar

1 large egg white

1 teaspoon grated lemon zest

1 tablespoon fresh lemon juice

This simple gadget, called a citrus spigot,
is sold at kitchenware shops. It screws
into a lemon or lime, allowing you to pour
the juice right out. Roll and squeeze the
fruit to soften it before inserting the spigot.

These deceptively simple-looking drop cookies will surprise you with their buttery, melt-in-your-mouth texture and intense lemon taste. Although the lemon flavor is pure fruit, the butter flavor disguises the fact that half of the shortening is really reduced-calorie tub margarine, which has about half the fat of butter.

1 Preheat the oven to 350°. Spray 2 large baking sheets with no-stick spray; set aside.

2 In a medium bowl, combine the flour, baking soda and salt; set aside.

3 In a large bowl, with an electric mixer at medium speed, beat the butter and margarine until combined. Add the sugar and beat until light and fluffy. Add the egg white, lemon zest and lemon juice, and beat until well combined. (The mixture will appear curdled.)

4 With the mixer at low speed, gradually beat in the dry ingredients until well combined.

5 Drop the dough by rounded teaspoons, about 1 inch apart, onto the prepared baking sheets. Place both baking sheets in the oven and bake for 8 to 10 minutes (switching the position of the sheets halfway through baking), or until the edges of the cookies are lightly browned. Transfer the cookies to wire racks to cool.

Preparation time 5 minutes • **Total time** 30 minutes • **Per cookie** 34 calories, 1 g. fat (5% of calories), 0.4 g. saturated fat, 2 mg. cholesterol, 27 mg. sodium, 0.1 g. dietary fiber, 1 mg. calcium, 0 mg. iron, 0 mg. vitamin C, 0 mg. beta-carotene
Makes 3 dozen cookies

KITCHEN TIPS

If you forget to soften the butter, grate it on a hand grater, using the markings on the wrapper as your measuring guide. The grated butter will be soft enough to beat.

Insulated baking sheets are excellent for delicately browned cookies like these.

If you don't have these insulated double-bottom sheets, you can stack two baking sheets with similar results.

FOR A CHANGE

Equally delicious cookies can be made with orange juice and zest.

BANANA-CARROT SPICE BARS

- 2 large bananas (about 1 pound)
- 1 teaspoon fresh lemon juice
- ½ cup plus 2 tablespoons packed light brown sugar
- 2 cups cornflakes, crushed to make ½ cup
- ½ cup all-purpose flour
- ¼ cup whole-wheat flour
- 2 teaspoons baking powder
- 1 teaspoon ground cinnamon
- ½ teaspoon ground nutmeg
- 2 large egg whites
- 2 tablespoons canola oil
- 2 teaspoons grated orange zest
- 1 cup grated carrots
- ½ cup golden raisins

Cookies purchased at the health food store often make extravagant claims on their packaging about the low-fat, high-fiber, nutrient-rich goodies inside. But the cookies are, all too often, a disappointment—boring and dry as cardboard. Made with whole-wheat flour, bananas, carrots and raisins, these big, chewy bar cookies are good for you, and they're also temptingly moist, sweet and spicy.

1 Preheat the oven to 350°. Line a 13 x 9-inch baking pan with foil. Spray the foil with no-stick spray; set aside.

2 Peel the bananas and place them in a medium bowl. With a fork or potato masher, mash the bananas until smooth. Stir in the lemon juice; set the banana purée aside.

3 In a large bowl, combine the brown sugar, crushed cornflakes, all-purpose flour, whole-wheat flour, baking powder, cinnamon and nutmeg; set aside.

4 In another large bowl, with an electric mixer at medium speed, beat the banana purée, egg whites, oil and orange zest until well combined.

5 With the mixer at low speed, gradually beat in the dry ingredients until well combined. Stir in the carrots and raisins.

6 Spread the mixture in the prepared pan. Bake for 25 to 30 minutes, or until the edges pull away slightly from the sides of the pan. Transfer the pan to a wire rack to cool completely. Cut into 16 bars.

Preparation time 20 minutes • **Total time** 1 hour • **Per bar** 117 calories, 2 g. fat (15% of calories), 0.2 g. saturated fat, 0 mg. cholesterol, 110 mg. sodium, 1.1 g. dietary fiber, 50 mg. calcium, 1 mg. iron, 5 mg. vitamin C, 1.3 mg. beta-carotene
Makes 16 bars

KITCHEN TIP
Crush the cornflakes by placing them in a heavy-duty plastic bag and then squeezing them with your hands; or run a rolling pin over them.

MAKE AHEAD
Bar cookies freeze well. You can cut them up and wrap them individually; or, better still, remove the uncut cake from the pan and freeze it whole.

CHEWY OATMEAL-APRICOT COOKIES

1½ cups old-fashioned rolled oats

1¼ cups all-purpose flour

1 teaspoon baking soda

1 teaspoon ground cinnamon

½ teaspoon baking powder

½ teaspoon salt

¼ teaspoon ground nutmeg

¾ cup unsweetened applesauce

½ cup plus 2 tablespoons packed light brown sugar

2 large egg whites

2 tablespoons butter, melted

1 teaspoon vanilla extract

1 cup diced dried apricots

The concept of using fruit purée, such as applesauce or prune butter, instead of shortening has really taken the low-fat baking scene by storm. The fruit provides moisture and its fiber performs some of the same functions in a batter that fat does. In addition, fruit is naturally sweet, so many recipes can be made with less sugar. The fruit/fat substitution works best in simple drop and bar cookies; those that have a fruit or spice flavor are particularly well suited for this amazing fat-saving trick. So why is there still some butter in this recipe? Because of its inimitable taste.

1 Preheat the oven to 350°. Spray 2 large baking sheets with no-stick spray; set aside.

2 Spread the rolled oats on an ungreased baking sheet and toast for 8 to 10 minutes, or until lightly browned.

3 In a large mixing bowl, combine the toasted oats, flour, baking soda, cinnamon, baking powder, salt and nutmeg, and stir well; set aside.

4 In another large mixing bowl, with an electric mixer at medium speed, beat the applesauce, brown sugar, egg whites, butter and vanilla until well combined.

5 With the mixer at low speed, gradually beat in the dry ingredients until well combined. Stir in the apricots.

6 Drop the dough by level tablespoons, 1 inch apart, onto the prepared baking sheets. Place both baking sheets in the oven and bake for 10 to 12 minutes (switching the position of the sheets halfway through baking), or until the cookies are lightly browned. Transfer the cookies to wire racks to cool.

Preparation time 10 minutes • **Total time** 45 minutes • **Per cookie** 46 calories, 0.7 g. fat (14% of calories), 0.3 g. saturated fat, 1 mg. cholesterol, 63 mg. sodium, 0.6 g. dietary fiber, 9 mg. calcium, 0 mg. iron, 0 mg. vitamin C, 0.1 mg. beta-carotene
Makes 4 dozen cookies

❧ ❧ ❧

OATMEAL-PECAN LACE COOKIES

2 tablespoons pecans

1 cup old-fashioned rolled oats

½ cup packed light brown sugar

½ cup granulated sugar

2 tablespoons all-purpose flour

2 tablespoons reduced-calorie tub margarine (8 grams of fat per tablespoon), melted

1 tablespoon canola oil

2 large egg whites

2 tablespoons water

1 teaspoon vanilla extract

1 square (1 ounce) semisweet chocolate, chopped

Use a European style (one-piece) rolling pin to form the cookies into tuiles. A thick dowel could also serve the purpose.

Not your everyday lunch-box cookies, these rich but fragile wafers are worthy of an elegant afternoon tea. The lacy cookies can also be formed into *tuiles*—curved shapes so named because they resemble French roof tiles. To make tuiles, lay the still-warm cookies over a slender rolling pin to shape them. Remove the cookies from the rolling pin as soon as they are cool and firm.

1 Preheat the oven to 350°. Spray 2 large baking sheets with no-stick spray; set aside.

2 Place the pecans in a jelly-roll pan and toast for 8 to 10 minutes, or until lightly browned. Transfer to a cutting board and chop finely; set aside.

3 In a large bowl, combine the oats, brown sugar, granulated sugar and flour, and stir well. Add the margarine, oil, egg whites, water, vanilla and chopped pecans, and stir to combine.

4 For each cookie, spoon 2 level teaspoons of the batter onto one of the prepared baking sheets and smooth it into a 2½-inch circle. Leaving 1½ inches between cookies, repeat to make 18 cookies (9 per sheet).

5 Place both baking sheets in the oven and bake for 7 minutes (switching the sheets halfway through baking), or until the edges of the cookies are lightly browned. Let the cookies stand for about 2 minutes before removing them to wire racks to cool completely. Repeat with the remaining batter, spraying the baking sheets again, if necessary.

6 When the cookies have cooled completely, transfer them back to the baking sheets, working in batches if necessary. In a small saucepan, melt the chocolate over low heat. Place the melted chocolate in a plastic food storage bag. With scissors, snip a small piece from the corner of the bag. Drizzle some melted chocolate over each cookie. Freeze the cookies for 5 minutes, or until the chocolate hardens.

Preparation time 15 minutes • **Total time** 45 minutes • **Per cookie** 47 calories, 1.4 g. fat (27% of calories), 0.3 g. saturated fat, 0 mg. cholesterol, 9 mg. sodium, 0.3 g. dietary fiber, 4 mg. calcium, 0 mg. iron, 0 mg. vitamin C, 0.1 mg. beta-carotene
Makes 3 dozen cookies

Fruit and Nut Pinwheels

⅔ cup golden raisins

½ cup plus 2 tablespoons
    raspberry all-fruit preserves

3 tablespoons slivered blanched
    almonds

1 cup all-purpose flour

¼ cup sugar

2 ounces fat-free cream cheese,
    softened

2 ounces Neufchâtel cream cheese
    (⅓ less fat), softened

1 tablespoon plus 1 teaspoon
    reduced-calorie tub margarine
    (6 grams of fat per tablespoon)

1 teaspoon ground cinnamon

Old-world pastries like strudel are made by rolling dough around a filling, which can be a tricky task (strudel dough is paper-thin). Making these fruit and nut swirls is simpler, thanks to an easy-to-handle, firm-textured dough that is also low in fat. (Fat-free and Neufchâtel cream cheeses add texture and a rich taste without the fat.) Instead of forming each pinwheel individually, you roll the filling and dough, jelly-roll style, and then slice the roll crosswise.

1 Preheat the oven to 350°. Spray 2 large baking sheets with no-stick spray.

2 In a small bowl, combine the raisins, preserves and almonds; set aside.

3 In a large bowl, with an electric mixer at medium speed, beat the flour, 2 tablespoons of the sugar, the fat-free and Neufchâtel cream cheeses and margarine until well combined. Divide the dough in half and set aside.

4 In another small bowl, combine the remaining 2 tablespoons sugar and the cinnamon. Sprinkle a work surface with half the sugar-cinnamon mixture.

5 Place half the dough on top of the sugar mixture and, with a floured rolling pin, roll out the dough to an 11-inch round. Carefully spread half the raisin-almond mixture over the dough to the edge. Roll up the dough, jelly-roll style, around the filling. Slice the jelly roll into ¼-inch-thick slices, discarding the small end slices, if desired. Arrange the slices on one of the prepared baking sheets; repeat with the remaining sugar mixture, dough and filling.

6 Place both baking sheets in the oven and bake for 12 to 14 minutes (switching the position of the sheets halfway through baking), or until the cookies are golden. Transfer the cookies to wire racks to cool.

Preparation time 10 minutes • **Total time** 45 minutes • **Per cookie** 50 calories, 1 g. fat (19% of calories), 0.3 g. saturated fat, 1 mg. cholesterol, 19 mg. sodium, 0.3 g. dietary fiber, 10 mg. calcium, 0 mg. iron, 0 mg. vitamin C, 0 mg. beta-carotene
Makes 3 dozen cookies

❧ ❧ ❧

GINGER-GINGER COOKIES

2 cups all-purpose flour

1½ teaspoons ground ginger

½ teaspoon baking soda

¼ teaspoon ground allspice

¼ teaspoon ground cinnamon

¼ teaspoon ground cloves

¼ teaspoon salt

¼ cup reduced-calorie tub margarine (8 grams of fat per tablespoon)

½ cup packed dark brown sugar

2 large egg whites

1 teaspoon vanilla extract

1 tablespoon plus 1½ teaspoons minced crystallized ginger (1 ounce)

For round cookies, a drinking glass is a fine alternative to a cookie cutter.

G inger fans will be pleased to note that their favorite flavor is found in two forms in these rolled-and-cut cookies: There's the usual ground ginger, used as a spice, but the dough is also studded with tantalizing bits of crystallized ginger. With your favorite cookie cutters, match the shape to the holiday or occasion.

1 Spray 2 large baking sheets with no-stick spray; set aside.

2 In a medium bowl, combine the flour, ground ginger, baking soda, allspice, cinnamon, cloves and salt.

3 In a large bowl, with an electric mixer at medium speed, beat the margarine and brown sugar until light and fluffy, about 1 minute. Add the egg whites and vanilla, and beat until well combined.

4 With the mixer at low speed, gradually beat in the dry ingredients until well combined. Stir in the crystallized ginger.

5 Preheat the oven to 400°.

6 On a lightly floured surface, with a floured rolling pin, roll out half the dough to a ¼-inch-thick round. Using cookie cutters in any shapes you prefer, cut out the dough. Arrange the cookies, 1 inch apart, on the prepared baking sheets. Place both baking sheets in the oven and bake the cookies for 5 minutes (switching the position of the sheets halfway through baking), or until the edges of the cookies are lightly browned. Transfer the cookies to wire racks to cool. Repeat with the remaining dough and trimmings.

Preparation time 10 minutes • **Total time** 45 minutes • **Per cookie** 49 calories, 1 g. fat (18% of calories), 0.2 g. saturated fat, 0 mg. cholesterol, 47 mg. sodium, 0.2 g. dietary fiber, 6 mg. calcium, 1 mg. iron, 0 mg. vitamin C, 0 mg. beta-carotene
Makes 3 dozen cookies

KITCHEN TIP
If you dust the work surface and rolling pin too heavily with flour when rolling cookie dough, the cookies will turn out stiff and hard. So dust with a light hand, or use a pastry cloth and stockinette rolling-pin cover, which will keep the dough from sticking.

CHOCOLATE-ORANGE HAZELNUT BISCOTTI

¼ cup shelled hazelnuts

2½ cups all-purpose flour

¼ cup unsweetened cocoa powder

¾ teaspoon baking soda

¼ teaspoon salt

1 cup sugar

2 large eggs

1 large egg white

1½ teaspoons grated orange zest

1 teaspoon vanilla extract

The word *biscotti* means "twice baked," and these Italian specialties do go into the oven twice: The dough, formed into a log, is baked until firm, and then the logs are sliced and rebaked to produce crisp cookies that are traditionally served with a beverage for dunking.

1 Preheat the oven to 350°. Spray a baking sheet with no-stick spray; set aside.

2 Place the hazelnuts in a baking pan and toast for 8 to 10 minutes, or until the skins loosen and the nuts are lightly browned. Place the hazelnuts in a kitchen towel and rub to remove the skins. Finely chop the nuts; set aside. Reduce the oven temperature to 325°.

3 In a large bowl, combine the flour, cocoa powder, baking soda and salt; set aside.

4 In another large bowl, with an electric mixer at medium speed, beat the sugar, eggs, egg white, orange zest and vanilla until well combined. With the mixer at low speed, gradually add the dry ingredients and hazelnuts, and beat until well combined.

5 Turn the dough out onto a lightly floured surface. Shape the dough into two 12-inch-long logs.

6 Place the logs on the prepared baking sheet and bake for 20 to 25 minutes, or until the bottoms are lightly browned and the tops are set. Remove the logs to a wire rack to cool for about 10 minutes, then cut each log diagonally into ½-inch-thick slices. Return the slices to the baking sheet and bake for another 10 to 15 minutes (turning the biscotti once halfway through baking), or until lightly toasted all over. Transfer the biscotti to wire racks to cool completely.

Preparation time 10 minutes • **Total time** 50 minutes • **Per cookie** 59 calories, 0.9 g. fat (13% of calories), 0.2 g. saturated fat, 11 mg. cholesterol, 42 mg. sodium, 0.4 g. dietary fiber, 5 mg. calcium, 1 mg. iron, 0 mg. vitamin C, 0 mg. beta-carotene
Makes 40 cookies

MIXED DRIED FRUIT BARS

1½ **cups all-purpose flour**

⅓ **cup whole-wheat flour**

1 **teaspoon ground cinnamon**

¼ **teaspoon baking powder**

¼ **teaspoon baking soda**

¼ **teaspoon salt**

½ **cup packed light brown sugar**

½ **cup vanilla nonfat yogurt**

3 **tablespoons canola oil**

1 **large egg**

1 **large Granny Smith apple, peeled, cored and grated**

¾ **cup old-fashioned rolled oats**

½ **cup golden raisins**

2 **ounces dried cherries, chopped**

2 **ounces dried peaches or apricots, chopped**

2 **ounces pitted prunes, chopped**

Like fruit purées, yogurt can stand in for the fat (and the eggs) in some baked goods, such as muffins, quick breads and bar cookies. Here, vanilla nonfat yogurt adds flavor as it subtracts fat. Grated apple also contributes to the delectable moistness of these bars. As the old cookbooks used to say about cookies, "They'll keep well *if you hide them.*"

1 Preheat the oven to 350°. Coat a 13 x 9-inch pan with no-stick spray; set aside.

2 In a large bowl, combine the all-purpose flour, whole-wheat flour, cinnamon, baking powder, baking soda and salt.

3 In a medium bowl, whisk together the brown sugar, yogurt, oil and egg until well blended. Stir in the apples, oats, raisins, cherries, peaches or apricots and prunes. Add the yogurt-fruit mixture to the dry ingredients and stir to combine. Do not overmix.

4 Spread the batter evenly in the prepared pan. Bake for 25 to 30 minutes, or until the top is browned and firm to the touch. Transfer the pan to a wire rack to cool completely. Cut into 16 bars.

Preparation time 15 minutes • **Total time** 55 minutes • **Per bar** 170 calories, 3.3 g. fat (18% of calories), 0.3 g. saturated fat, 14 mg. cholesterol, 74 mg. sodium, 2 g. dietary fiber, 34 mg. calcium, 1 mg. iron, 1 mg. vitamin C, 0.3 mg. beta-carotene
Makes 16 bars

❧   ❧   ❧

To chop dried fruits quickly, first spray the blades of a pair of kitchen shears with no-stick spray.

After snipping the fruits into small pieces, you can wash the shears—something you shouldn't do with regular scissors.

Mocha Meringue Cookies

3 tablespoons blanched slivered almonds

2 tablespoons unsweetened cocoa powder

1 tablespoon all-purpose flour

¼ teaspoon ground cinnamon

¼ teaspoon instant espresso powder

2 large egg whites

⅛ teaspoon salt

½ cup sugar

Recipes for meringues often bristle with alarming admonitions—about everything from the size of the eggs and the shape of the bowl to the oven temperature and the state of the weather (meringues absorb moisture from the air, so it can be tricky to make them when it's extremely humid). But meringues are really very easy to prepare and are virtually fat free, since they contain no egg yolks or shortening: The small amount of fat in these cookies comes from the almonds.

1 Preheat the oven to 350°. Spray 2 large baking sheets with no-stick spray; set aside.

2 Place the almonds in a jelly-roll pan and toast for 5 to 8 minutes, or until lightly browned. Remove the pan from the oven and finely chop the almonds; leave the oven on.

3 In a small bowl, combine the chopped almonds, the cocoa powder, flour, cinnamon and espresso powder; set aside.

4 In a large bowl, with an electric mixer at medium speed, beat the egg whites and salt until foamy.

5 With the mixer at high speed, gradually beat in the sugar until stiff peaks form and the mixture is glossy. Stir in the almond-cocoa mixture until well combined.

6 Drop the meringues by rounded teaspoons onto the prepared baking sheets. Bake for 10 to 12 minutes, or until the meringues are set. Remove the meringues to wire racks to cool.

Preparation time 15 minutes • **Total time** 35 minutes • **Per cookie** 16 calories, 0.4 g. fat (23% of calories), 0.1 g. saturated fat, 0 mg. cholesterol, 10 mg. sodium, 0.1 g. dietary fiber, 2 mg. calcium, 0 mg. iron, 0 mg. vitamin C, 0 mg. beta-carotene
Makes 40 cookies

KITCHEN TIP
Eggs separate more easily when cold, but egg whites whip up to the greatest volume when at room temperature. So separate the eggs straight from the refrigerator, drop the whites into a cup and then let them come to room temperature while you prepare the other ingredients.

BLONDIES

1 cup packed dark brown sugar

½ cup unsweetened applesauce

2 tablespoons butter, melted

1 large egg

1 large egg white

1½ teaspoons vanilla extract

1¾ cups all-purpose flour

2 teaspoons baking powder

½ teaspoon salt

¼ cup chopped walnuts

Brown sugar stored in the box often turns lumpy and hard. To avoid this, transfer the sugar to a jar and add a slice of apple or a piece of fresh bread.

Blondies are un-chocolate brownies; in fact, they were originally called blond brownies. They're rich, chewy bar cookies made with brown sugar for a butterscotchy flavor. Of course, you can't have butterscotch without butter, but this recipe calls for just 2 tablespoons: Applesauce takes the place of most of the shortening. Compare this with standard blondie recipes, which commonly use ½ to ¾ cup of butter.

1 Preheat the oven to 350°. Spray a 13 x 9-inch baking pan with no-stick spray.

2 In a large bowl, with an electric mixer at medium speed, beat the brown sugar, applesauce, butter, egg, egg white and vanilla until well combined.

3 With the mixer at low speed, beat in the flour, baking powder and salt. Stir in the nuts. Spread the mixture evenly in the prepared pan. Bake for 15 to 20 minutes, or until a toothpick inserted in the center comes out clean. Remove the pan to a wire rack to cool completely. Cut into 24 bars.

Preparation time 15 minutes • **Total time** 30 minutes • **Per bar** 92 calories, 2 g. fat (20% of calories), 0.7 g. saturated fat, 11 mg. cholesterol, 105 mg. sodium, 0.4 g. dietary fiber, 35 mg. calcium, 1 mg. iron, 0 mg. vitamin C, 0 mg. beta-carotene
Makes 24 bars

FOR A CHANGE
Leave out the walnuts and add ½ cup of sweetened flaked coconut to the batter; if you do so, you can also substitute ½ tea-spoon of almond extract for ½ teaspoon of the vanilla. Or, try ½ cup of semisweet or milk chocolate chips or butterscotch chips instead of the walnuts.

SPICY MOLASSES COOKIES

2 cups all-purpose flour

2 teaspoons ground cinnamon

2 teaspoons ground ginger

1 teaspoon baking soda

½ teaspoon ground cloves

½ teaspoon salt

½ teaspoon freshly ground black pepper

1 cup sugar

¼ cup unsweetened applesauce

¼ cup canola oil

¼ cup molasses

2 large egg whites

You won't mind hearing the "clink" of the cookie-jar lid when that snack source is filled with these healthful treats. And you may hear it often, because the cookies are richly spiced, with a satisfyingly chewy texture. When trying this recipe for the first time, check the oven after about 8 minutes to see whether the cookies are done: Baked goods with molasses have a tendency to overbrown and the baking time may be shorter than what's suggested.

1 Preheat the oven to 350°. Spray 2 large baking sheets with no-stick spray.

2 In a large bowl, combine the flour, cinnamon, ginger, baking soda, cloves, salt and black pepper; set aside.

3 In another large bowl, with an electric mixer at medium speed, beat the sugar, applesauce, oil, molasses and egg whites for 1 minute, or until well combined.

4 With the mixer at low speed, gradually beat in the dry ingredients until well combined.

5 Working in batches, drop the dough by level tablespoons, 1 inch apart, onto the prepared baking sheets. Place both baking sheets in the oven and bake for 10 minutes (switching the position of the sheets halfway through baking), or until the cookies are lightly browned. Transfer the cookies to wire racks to cool. Repeat with the remaining dough, spraying the baking sheets again, if necessary.

Preparation time 5 minutes • **Total time** 40 minutes • **Per cookie** 59 calories, 1.4 g. fat (21% of calories), 0.1 g. saturated fat, 0 mg. cholesterol, 60 mg. sodium, 0.2 g. dietary fiber, 7 mg. calcium, 0 mg. iron, 0 mg. vitamin C, 0 mg. beta-carotene
Makes 3½ dozen cookies

NUTRITION NOTE
Molasses is the only sweetener that has any nutritional value aside from calories. As a by-product of sugar manufacturing, molasses ends up with the minerals that are removed when sugarcane or sugar beets are refined. Although we don't consume enough molasses to make it an important dietary mineral source, it does contain iron, calcium, magnesium and potassium. Blackstrap molasses, the least-refined type, contains the most minerals.

CHOCOLATE PEANUT BUTTER BALLS

1½ cups chocolate-wafer cookie crumbs (about twenty-five 2½-inch cookies, finely crushed)

1 cup plus 2 tablespoons sifted confectioners' sugar

⅓ cup honey

¼ cup plus 2 tablespoons reduced-fat creamy peanut butter

To make cookie crumbs without making a mess, place the chocolate wafers in a heavy-duty zip-seal bag and crush them with a rolling pin.

If you love to give homemade cookies as holiday gifts—but dread the thought of long hours of baking—here's your solution: Make a few batches of these no-bake peanut-butter-and-chocolate gems, which look like fancy chocolate truffles (but are far lower in fat), and pack them in pretty boxes.

1 In a large bowl, combine the cookie crumbs and 1 cup of the confectioners' sugar.

2 In a medium bowl, whisk together the honey and peanut butter until well combined. Add the honey mixture to the cookie crumb mixture and stir until well combined. (The mixture may be crumbly at this point.)

3 With your hands, shape the mixture into thirty-six 1-inch balls (the mixture should hold together as you shape it). Set the balls aside at room temperature until ready to serve or store them in an air-tight container at room temperature for 2 to 3 days. Just before serving, roll each ball in the remaining 2 tablespoons confectioners' sugar.

Preparation time 10 minutes • **Total time** 35 minutes • **Per ball** 56 calories, 1.6 g. fat (25% of calories), 0.3 g. saturated fat, 0 mg. cholesterol, 36 mg. sodium, 0.2 g. dietary fiber, 2 mg. calcium, 0 mg. iron, 0 mg. vitamin C, 0 mg. beta-carotene
Makes 3 dozen balls

KITCHEN TIP
For elegant gifts, pack the cookies as if they were fine chocolates: Fluted paper or foil candy cups are sold at cookware shops and baking-supply houses. You could also use the paper liners made for miniature muffin pans, which are available at most housewares stores and many supermarkets.

NUTRITION NOTE
Regular peanut butter, which consists mainly of ground peanuts, is a high-fat food. But reduced-fat peanut spreads, which incorporate lower-fat ingredients such as corn syrup solids and soy protein, offer a better option: They contain about 6 grams of fat per tablespoon, rather than the 8 grams in regular peanut butter.

Cakes, Pies & Tarts

❧ ❧ ❧

CITRUSY BUNDT CAKE, FROSTED
CHOCOLATE CAKE, PUMPKIN AND
BERRY PIES, LUSCIOUS TARTS—
ALL PREPARED THE HEALTHY WAY

LEMON-LIME CAKE WITH RASPBERRY SAUCE

2 teaspoons all-purpose flour

4 cups cake flour

2½ teaspoons baking powder

½ teaspoon salt

1⅓ cups plain nonfat yogurt

¼ cup fresh lemon juice

¼ cup fresh lime juice

2 teaspoons grated lemon zest

2 teaspoons grated lime zest

2 teaspoons vanilla extract

1½ cups sugar

¼ cup unsalted butter, softened

2 tablespoons canola oil

2 large eggs

2 large egg whites

1 cup bottled all-fruit raspberry sauce

Although this citrus-suffused cake is far less rich than a standard bundt cake, it is wonderfully moist and keeps well, thanks to the nonfat yogurt in the batter. You don't have to include both lemon and lime: If you prefer, choose one or the other, using a total of ½ cup of juice and 4 teaspoons (1 tablespoon plus 1 teaspoon) of zest.

1 Preheat the oven to 350°. Spray a 10-inch bundt pan with no-stick spray. Dust the pan with the all-purpose flour and tap out any excess.

2 Sift the cake flour, baking powder and salt together into a large bowl; set aside.

3 In a small bowl, stir together the yogurt, lemon juice, lime juice, lemon zest, lime zest and vanilla until well combined; set aside.

4 In another large bowl, with an electric mixer at medium speed, beat the sugar, butter and oil until combined. (It will have a grainy consistency.) Add the whole eggs and egg whites, and beat for about 2 minutes, or until the mixture is smooth and thick. With the mixer at low speed, beat in half the reserved flour mixture and all of the reserved yogurt mixture until well blended. Add the remaining flour mixture and beat until incorporated.

5 Pour the batter into the prepared pan and spread evenly. Bake for 30 to 35 minutes, or until a cake tester inserted into the thickest part of the cake comes out clean. Transfer the pan to a wire rack and let the cake cool in the pan for 10 minutes. Invert the cake and remove from the pan. Transfer to a serving plate to cool completely.

6 When the cake has cooled, cut it into 10 slices and serve with the Raspberry Sauce.

Preparation time 20 minutes • **Total Time** 1 hour plus cooling time • **Per serving with sauce** 416 calories, 10.1 g. fat (24% of calories), 3.5 g. saturated fat, 56 mg. cholesterol, 282 mg. sodium, 1.2 g. dietary fiber, 149 mg. calcium, 4 mg. iron, 12 mg. vitamin C, 0.2 mg. beta-carotene • **Serves 10**

❧ ❧ ❧

PEACH UPSIDE-DOWN CAKE

2½ **pounds large, ripe freestone peaches (5 or 6 peaches)**

⅔ **cup sugar**

2 **tablespoons unsalted butter**

1 **cup all-purpose flour**

1 **teaspoon baking powder**

½ **teaspoon baking soda**

½ **teaspoon ground cinnamon**

¼ **teaspoon salt**

1 **tablespoon canola oil**

1 **large egg**

1 **teaspoon vanilla extract**

1 **teaspoon almond extract**

½ **cup low-fat buttermilk**

A brief blanching in boiling water renders the peaches easy to peel. If you cut an "X" in the stem end before placing the peaches in the water, it makes the peeling process even easier.

Fresh peaches make a refreshing change from canned pineapple in this tempting cake. Half the small amount of butter in the cake is used where it has the greatest flavor impact: It is melted with sugar to form a caramel-like glaze on the peaches.

1 Preheat the oven to 375°. Bring a large saucepan of water to a boil. Score the stem end of each peach and place the peaches in the boiling water. Boil for about 1 minute, or until the skins soften. Transfer to a bowl of cold water to cool, then peel, halve and pit the peaches.

2 In a 9-inch cast-iron skillet, combine ⅓ cup of the sugar with 1 tablespoon of the butter. Cook over medium heat for 3 to 5 minutes, or until the sugar begins to melt. Add the peaches to the skillet, cut-side up, in one layer (the fruit should fit tightly). Remove the pan from the heat and set aside.

3 In a medium bowl, combine the flour, baking powder, baking soda, cinnamon and salt; set aside.

4 In a large bowl, with an electric mixer at medium speed, beat the remaining ⅓ cup sugar and 1 tablespoon butter with the oil until combined. Add the egg, beating until smooth, then beat in the vanilla and almond extract. With the mixer at low speed, add the buttermilk and the reserved flour mixture, beating until just incorporated.

5 Spoon the batter evenly over the peaches in the skillet, place the skillet in the oven and bake, uncovered, for 20 to 25 minutes, or until a cake tester inserted into the center of the cake comes out clean.

6 Transfer the skillet to a wire rack to cool for 3 to 4 minutes. Loosen the edges of the cake with a knife. Invert the cake onto a serving plate. If any of the peaches stick to the skillet, remove them with a knife and replace them on the cake.

Preparation time 10 minutes • **Total Time** 50 minutes • **Per serving** 230 calories, 5.7 g. fat (22% of calories), 2.3 g. saturated fat, 35 mg. cholesterol, 224 mg. sodium, 2.1 g. dietary fiber, 67 mg. calcium, 1 mg. iron, 7 mg. vitamin C, 0.5 mg. beta-carotene • **Serves 8**

❧ ❧ ❧

KIWI CUSTARD TART

Tart Shell

1 cup all-purpose flour

1 teaspoon sugar

½ teaspoon lemon zest

¼ teaspoon salt

2 tablespoons chilled unsalted butter, cut into small pieces

2 tablespoons canola oil

3 tablespoons nonfat sour cream

2 to 2½ teaspoons cold water

Custard

1¼ cups 1% low fat milk

1 vanilla bean, split

One 3-inch-long piece lemon zest

¼ cup sugar

2 tablespoons cornstarch

Pinch of salt

1 large egg plus 1 large egg white, lightly beaten

Fruit Topping

5 kiwifruits, peeled and sliced ¼ inch thick

B ake this gorgeous fruit-topped tart when you really want to impress someone. Keep an eye on the tart shell while it's baking; if the edge browns too quickly, cover it with strips of foil.

1 For the tart shell, in a food processor, combine the flour, sugar, lemon zest and salt, and pulse to mix. Add the butter and oil, and pulse until the mixture resembles coarse meal. Add the sour cream and 2 teaspoons of the water, and process until the dough comes together. (Add a few drops of water if the dough seems dry.) Flatten the dough into a disk, wrap in plastic wrap and refrigerate for 15 minutes.

2 Meanwhile, start the custard: In a small saucepan, bring the milk, vanilla bean and lemon zest to a simmer over medium-high heat. Remove the pan from the heat, cover and let the mixture steep while the dough chills.

3 Preheat the oven to 400°. On a lightly floured surface, roll out the dough to a 10-inch round about ⅛ inch thick. Place the dough in a 9-inch tart pan and gently press it into the bottom and sides of the pan. Trim the edges and prick the bottom with a fork. Place the pan in the freezer for 5 minutes, then line the tart shell with foil and fill it with pie weights. Bake the tart shell for 8 to 10 minutes, remove the weights and foil, and bake for another 5 minutes. Transfer to a rack to cool.

4 Meanwhile, for the custard, in a medium bowl, combine the sugar, cornstarch and salt. Add the beaten egg and egg white, and beat well with a wooden spoon. Remove the lemon zest from the reserved milk mixture and scrape the seeds from the vanilla bean into the milk. Slowly add the warm milk to the egg mixture, stirring constantly until well combined. Pour the custard into the cooled tart shell and bake for 15 minutes. Transfer to a wire rack to cool briefly.

5 For the topping, arrange the kiwifruit on top of the custard, starting from the outside edge. Serve the tart at room temperature.

Preparation time 15 minutes • **Total Time** 1 hour • **Per serving** 209 calories, 7.6 g. fat (33% of calories), 2.5 g. saturated fat, 36 mg. cholesterol, 125 mg. sodium, 2 g. dietary fiber, 74 mg. calcium, 1 mg. iron, 37 mg. vitamin C, 0.2 mg. beta-carotene
Serves 8

SPICED CARROT CAKE

Cake

- 2 cups finely shredded carrots
- ¼ cup fresh lemon juice
- 1 cup all-purpose flour
- 1 cup whole-wheat flour
- 2 teaspoons ground cinnamon
- 1 teaspoon baking soda
- ½ teaspoon baking powder
- ½ teaspoon ground ginger
- ½ teaspoon salt
- ¼ teaspoon ground cloves
- ¼ teaspoon ground nutmeg
- ⅛ teaspoon freshly ground black pepper
- ⅔ cup honey
- ⅓ cup plain nonfat yogurt
- ¼ cup canola or safflower oil
- 1 large egg
- 1 cup golden raisins

Topping

- 1 tablespoon confectioners' sugar
- ¼ teaspoon ground cinnamon
- ¼ teaspoon ground ginger

Carrot cake has an undeserved reputation as some sort of "health food," simply because it has carrots in it. But along with those carrots you usually get (at least) a cup of oil and 4 eggs—not to mention a half-pound of cream cheese and a stick of butter for the frosting. You'll find this delightfully spiced single-layer cake a refreshing change from the old-fashioned version. For an exceptionally pretty cake, dust the confectioners' sugar through a lacy doily, or place small paper cutouts (geometric shapes, hearts, stars or whatever you like) on top of the cake before sifting the sugar over it.

1 Preheat the oven to 350°. Spray a 9-inch round cake pan with no-stick spray. Line the bottom with a circle of wax paper and spray again.

2 For the cake, in a large bowl, combine the carrots and lemon juice.

3 In a medium bowl, combine the all-purpose flour, whole-wheat flour, cinnamon, baking soda, baking powder, ginger, salt, cloves, nutmeg and black pepper, and whisk until well blended.

4 In a small bowl, combine the honey, yogurt, oil and egg.

5 Add the honey mixture to the carrot mixture and stir well. Add the flour mixture and the raisins, and stir until well combined.

6 Pour the batter into the prepared cake pan and spread evenly. Bake for 40 to 45 minutes, or until a cake tester inserted in the center of the cake comes out clean. Transfer the pan to a wire rack and let the cake cool for 10 minutes. When cooled, transfer the cake to a serving plate.

7 For the topping, in a small bowl, combine the confectioners' sugar, cinnamon and ginger. Place the sugar mixture in a small strainer and sprinkle over the top of the cake (in a pattern, if desired).

Preparation time 15 minutes • **Total Time** 1 hour plus cooling time • **Per serving** 276 calories, 6.5 g. fat (21% of calories), 0.6 g. saturated fat, 21 mg. cholesterol, 283 mg. sodium, 3.3 g. dietary fiber, 60 mg. calcium, 2 mg. iron, 6 mg. vitamin C, 3.7 mg. beta-carotene • **Serves 10**

❧ ❧ ❧

STRAWBERRY MERINGUE TART

¼ **cup cornstarch, sifted**

¼ **cup finely ground blanched almonds**

¾ **cup sugar**

3 **large egg whites, at room temperature**

⅛ **teaspoon cream of tartar**

Pinch of salt

1 **teaspoon vanilla extract**

1½ **pints strawberries, hulled and left whole**

2 **tablespoons seedless raspberry all-fruit preserves**

2 **teaspoons water**

Mint sprigs, for garnish (optional)

To make a simple shell, first spread some of the meringue into a flat round, then spoon dollops of the remaining meringue around the edges.

This elegant confection has a meringue shell rather than a pastry crust. The chewy meringue bakes more quickly, and in a hotter oven, than traditional meringues, emerging a delicate tan rather than a pure white.

1 Preheat the oven to 300°. Line a baking sheet with foil and lightly spray with no-stick spray.

2 In a small bowl, combine the cornstarch, almonds and ¼ cup of the sugar; set aside.

3 In a large bowl, with an electric mixer at medium speed, beat the egg whites, cream of tartar and salt until soft peaks form. With the mixer at medium-high speed, slowly add the remaining ½ cup sugar, 1 tablespoon at a time, continuing to beat until the egg whites are stiff but not dry. With the mixer at high speed, beat in the vanilla. Gently fold in the almond mixture.

4 Using a large spoon, or a pastry bag without a tip, spread enough of the meringue on the baking sheet to form an 8- or 9-inch round about ¾-inch thick. With the spoon, drop spoonfuls of the remaining meringue around the edge to form a border about 1 inch high. Or, use a pastry bag fitted with a large rosette tip to pipe a fancier border.

5 Bake the meringue shell on the bottom rack of the oven for 30 minutes, or until light tan and crisp. Transfer the baking sheet to a wire rack and let the meringue cool on the baking sheet for 5 minutes. Carefully peel off the foil, then transfer the meringue shell to a serving plate. Fill the shell with the strawberries.

6 In a small saucepan, combine the preserves and water, and melt over low heat. Strain into a small bowl. Using a pastry brush, lightly glaze the strawberries with the melted preserves. Serve the tart at room temperature, garnished with mint sprigs, if desired.

Preparation time 20 minutes • **Total time** 1 hour 10 minutes • **Per serving**
143 calories, 1.9 g. fat (12% of calories), 0.2 g. saturated fat, 0 mg. cholesterol, 39 mg. sodium, 1.9 g. dietary fiber, 17 mg. calcium, 0 mg. iron, 34 mg. vitamin C, 0 mg. beta-carotene • **Serves 8**

DEVIL'S FOOD CAKE WITH RASPBERRIES

Cake

  1 cup unsweetened cocoa powder

  2 cups cake flour

  ¾ cup packed light brown sugar

  ½ cup granulated sugar

  1½ teaspoons baking powder

  ½ teaspoon baking soda

  ½ teaspoon salt

  1 cup strong black decaffeinated coffee

  1 cup low-fat buttermilk

  2 large egg whites, at room temperature

  ¼ cup canola or safflower oil

  1 teaspoon vanilla extract

Frosting

  1½ cups granulated sugar

  ¼ cup water

  1 tablespoon light corn syrup

  2 large egg whites

  ¼ teaspoon salt

  1 teaspoon vanilla extract

  2 squares (2 ounces) unsweetened chocolate, melted

Topping

  ½ pint fresh raspberries

  1 tablespoon confectioners' sugar

The icing for this chocolate cake should be made just before you plan to use it, or it may become too stiff to spread. If need be, warm it in a microwave for a few seconds to soften it.

1 Preheat the oven to 325°. Lightly spray two 8-inch round cake pans with no-stick spray. Lightly dust the pans with a small amount of the cocoa powder, tapping out the excess.

2 For the cake, in a large bowl, combine the remaining cocoa, the flour, brown sugar, granulated sugar, baking powder, baking soda and salt. In another large bowl, with an electric mixer at medium speed, beat the coffee, buttermilk, egg whites, oil and vanilla. With the mixer at low speed, add the cocoa mixture and beat until just combined. Divide the batter between the prepared pans and bake for 30 minutes, or until a tester inserted in each comes out clean. Transfer the pans to wire racks to cool for 10 minutes before turning the cakes out.

3 Make the frosting just before you plan to use it. In a medium saucepan, combine the sugar, water and corn syrup. Bring to a simmer over medium-high heat, then cover and simmer for 2 minutes. Uncover and simmer for 2 more minutes, or until the syrup reaches 245° on a candy thermometer. Remove the pan from the heat.

4 In a large bowl, with an electric mixer at medium speed, beat the egg whites with the salt for 1 to 2 minutes, or until soft peaks form. While you beat the egg whites, return the syrup mixture just to a boil. With the mixer at medium-high, pour the hot syrup into the egg whites, immediately increase the mixer speed to high and continue to beat until the mixture is stiff and glossy. Beat in the vanilla, then stir in the melted chocolate until the mixture is smooth.

5 Transfer one cake layer to a plate and frost with ½ cup of the frosting. Place the other layer on top and frost the rest of the cake. Arrange the raspberries on top of the cake. Dust with the confectioners' sugar.

Preparation time 15 minutes • **Total time** 1 hour plus cooling time • **Per serving** 360 calories, 8.8 g. fat (22% of calories), 2.7 g. saturated fat, 1 mg. cholesterol, 289 mg. sodium, 3.3 g. dietary fiber, 90 mg. calcium, 3 mg. iron, 3 mg. vitamin C, 0 mg. beta-carotene • **Serves 12**

ANGEL CAKE WITH CHOCOLATE SAUCE

Cake

  1 **cup cake flour, sifted 3 times**

1½ **cups sugar**

 12 **large egg whites, at room temperature**

  1 **tablespoon orange-flower water**

 ½ **teaspoon vanilla extract**

 ½ **teaspoon cream of tartar**

 ¼ **teaspoon salt**

  1 **tablespoon grated orange zest**

Chocolate Sauce

 ¼ **cup plus 1 tablespoon sugar**

 ¼ **cup fresh orange juice**

 ¼ **cup water**

 ½ **cup unsweetened cocoa powder**

Topping (optional)

  Orange slices

Fragrant with citrus, this cloud-light cake is flavored with orange zest and also with orange-flower water, which is made from orange blossoms. You can buy it at many liquor stores, at pharmacies and at Indian or Near Eastern grocery stores.

1 Preheat the oven to 350°.

2 For the cake, in a small bowl, whisk together the cake flour and ½ cup of the sugar; set aside.

3 In a large bowl, with an electric mixer at medium speed, beat the egg whites, orange-flower water, vanilla, cream of tartar and salt until soft peaks form. With the mixer at medium-high speed, slowly add the remaining 1 cup sugar, a tablespoon at a time, continuing to beat until the whites are stiff but not dry. Gently fold the reserved flour-sugar mixture into the egg whites, then fold in the orange zest.

4 Pour the batter into a 10-inch tube pan and run a knife through the batter to remove any air bubbles. Bake for 30 minutes, or until the top springs back when lightly touched and a cake tester or toothpick inserted in the center comes out clean.

5 Remove the cake from the oven and invert on a wire rack. Let cool in this position until the pan is no longer hot. To remove the cake, run a sharp, thin-bladed knife around the sides and inner tube of the pan. Lift the cake out of the pan then remove the bottom of the pan. Place the cake on a serving plate.

6 For the sauce, in small saucepan, combine the sugar, orange juice and water, and bring to a boil over medium-high heat. Reduce the heat to low and whisk in the cocoa powder until smooth.

7 If desired, top the whole cake with orange slices before cutting. Serve with the chocolate sauce.

Preparation time 15 minutes • **Total time** 55 minutes plus cooling time • **Per serving** 268 calories, 0.8 g. fat (3% of calories), 0.4 g. saturated fat, 0 mg. cholesterol, 152 mg. sodium, 1.6 g. dietary fiber, 15 mg. calcium, 2 mg. iron, 4 mg. vitamin C, 0 mg. beta-carotene • **Serves 8**

❧   ❧   ❧

ZUCCHINI CAKE WITH LEMON SYRUP

Cake

1½ cups cake flour

1 teaspoon baking soda

1 teaspoon ground cinnamon

½ teaspoon Chinese five-spice powder (optional)

¼ teaspoon salt

1½ cups firmly packed finely shredded zucchini

⅔ cup firmly packed light brown sugar

⅓ cup canola oil

½ cup golden raisins or dried cranberries

2 large egg whites

Lemon Syrup

½ cup granulated sugar

¼ cup water

3 tablespoons fresh lemon juice

You can use the shredding disk of your food processor to grate the zucchini quickly.

Cinnamon is a requisite for spicy cakes and cookies, but you've probably never tasted a dessert made with Chinese five-spice powder, a heady blend of cinnamon, anise, cloves, Szechuan peppercorns and, sometimes, cardamom. If you can't get this ingredient, try adding a pinch each of ground cloves and ground cardamom along with the cinnamon.

1 Preheat the oven to 350°. Spray an 8½ x 4½-inch loaf pan with no-stick spray.

2 For the cake, in a small bowl, combine the flour, baking soda, cinnamon, five-spice powder, if using, and salt; set aside.

3 In a medium bowl, combine the zucchini, sugar, oil and raisins or cranberries. Add the flour mixture and stir to combine. Set aside.

4 In a large bowl, with an electric mixer at medium speed, beat the egg whites until frothy. With the mixer at medium-high speed, beat until the whites stiffen. Gently fold the egg whites into the zucchini mixture.

5 Spoon the batter into the prepared pan, spread evenly and bake for 40 to 45 minutes, or until a cake tester inserted in the center of the cake comes out clean. Transfer the pan to a wire rack and allow the cake to cool in the pan for 10 minutes.

6 While the cake is cooling, make the syrup. In a small saucepan, combine the sugar and water, and bring to a boil over medium-high heat. Let the mixture boil for 8 to 10 minutes, or until it is a golden-amber color. Remove the pan from the heat and stir in the lemon juice.

7 Remove the cake from the pan and cut it into 10 slices. Serve each slice with some of the lemon syrup.

Preparation time 10 minutes • **Total time** 1 hour 5 minutes • **Per serving** 249 calories, 7.5 g. fat (27% of calories), 0.6 g. saturated fat, 0 mg. cholesterol, 200 mg. sodium, 0.6 g. dietary fiber, 28 mg. calcium, 2 mg. iron, 5 mg. vitamin C, 0.1 mg. beta-carotene • **Serves 10**

CHOCOLATE-BANANA TART

Tart Shell

See Kiwi Custard Tart, page 485, for tart shell ingredients

Pudding

3 cups 1% low-fat milk

¼ cup plus 1 tablespoon cornstarch

⅓ cup plus 2 tablespoons sugar

⅓ cup unsweetened cocoa powder

Pinch of salt

1 teaspoon vanilla extract

2 large bananas

Glaze

⅓ cup apricot all-fruit preserves

2 teaspoons water

The filling peeking out from under the spiral of sliced bananas is velvety-smooth and rich, with a deep chocolate flavor. All that's missing is the fat: Most chocolate cream pie recipes call for solid chocolate, whole milk, egg yolks and butter, but this one is made with low-fat milk and cocoa powder instead. If you don't want to bother with the tart shell, the filling is excellent on its own, served as a pudding with some crisp cookies on the side.

1 To make the tart shell, follow Step 1 and Step 3 on page 485, up to the point of baking. To bake, preheat the oven to 400°. Bake the tart shell for 10 minutes, remove the weights and foil, and bake for another 8 to 10 minutes, or until the shell is golden brown. Transfer to a wire rack and let cool completely before filling.

2 While the tart shell is baking, make the pudding. In a small bowl, stir together ½ cup of the milk and the cornstarch. In a medium saucepan, combine the remaining 2½ cups milk, the sugar, cocoa powder and salt. Warm over low heat, then whisk in the cornstarch mixture. Cook, stirring frequently, until the mixture thickens and comes to a boil; let boil for 1 minute. Remove the pan from the heat and pour the pudding into a medium bowl (strain if lumpy). Stir in the vanilla. Cover the pudding and refrigerate for about 10 minutes, or until chilled and slightly firm.

3 When the pudding is chilled, slice the bananas into ¼-inch-thick rounds. Pour the chilled pudding into the tart shell and arrange the banana slices on top.

4 To make the glaze, in a small saucepan, combine the preserves and water, and melt over low heat. Strain the melted preserves into a small bowl. Using a pastry brush, lightly glaze the bananas with the melted preserves. Chill the tart until ready to serve.

Preparation time 15 minutes • **Total time** 1 hour plus chilling time • **Per serving** 288 calories, 8 g. fat (25% of calories), 3 g. saturated fat, 11 mg. cholesterol, 136 mg. sodium, 2 g. dietary fiber, 130 mg. calcium, 1 mg. iron, 4 mg. vitamin C, 0.2 mg. beta-carotene • **Serves 8**

SHORTCAKE WITH PLUMS AND RICOTTA

Shortcake

1½ **cups all-purpose flour**

½ **cup yellow cornmeal, preferably stone-ground**

¼ **cup sugar**

1 **tablespoon plus 1 teaspoon baking powder**

1 **teaspoon grated lemon zest**

¼ **teaspoon salt**

¾ **cup low-fat buttermilk**

¼ **cup canola oil or light olive oil**

1 **large egg**

1 **teaspoon vanilla extract**

1 **tablespoon sugar, for topping (optional)**

Plum Filling

1 **pound red plums, pitted and thinly sliced (4 or 5 plums)**

1 **tablespoon fresh lemon juice**

2 **teaspoons sugar**

¼ **teaspoon ground cinnamon**

Ricotta Filling

1 **cup part-skim ricotta cheese**

2 **tablespoons honey**

1 **teaspoon almond extract**

Biscuits are the preferred "cake" for old-fashioned shortcakes. These cornmeal-buttermilk biscuit wedges are filled with a honey-almond ricotta mixture and, for a pleasant change, sliced plums instead of berries. You can prepare the ricotta filling a day ahead of time, but the biscuits should be used the same day they're made; in fact, the biscuits taste best when still slightly warm.

1 Preheat the oven to 425°. Lightly spray a baking sheet with no-stick spray; set aside.

2 For the shortcake, in a large bowl, combine the flour, cornmeal, sugar, baking powder, lemon zest and salt. Make a well in the center.

3 In a large measuring cup, combine the buttermilk, oil, egg and vanilla. Pour the buttermilk mixture into the well in the dry ingredients and stir with a fork just until the dough comes together. Gather the dough with your hands and place it on the prepared baking sheet. Pat the dough gently into a 7½-inch circle about ½ inch thick. Score the circle into 8 wedges (do not score all the way through). If desired, sprinkle the top of the dough with 1 tablespoon of sugar.

4 Bake the shortcake for about 15 minutes, or until golden brown. Transfer to a wire rack to cool for about 5 minutes.

5 While the shortcake is baking, make the plum and ricotta fillings. In a small bowl, combine the plums, lemon juice, sugar and cinnamon; set aside. In another small bowl, combine the ricotta, honey and almond extract; set aside.

6 When the shortcake has cooled, separate it into wedges, then slice each wedge in half horizontally. Spread the ricotta filling on the bottom half of each wedge. Spoon the plum mixture over the ricotta, then place the remaining wedge half on top.

Preparation time 10 minutes • **Total time** 40 minutes • **Per serving** 320 calories, 11 g. fat (31% of calories), 2.5 g. saturated fat, 38 mg. cholesterol, 370 mg. sodium, 2.2 g. dietary fiber, 258 mg. calcium, 2 mg. iron, 7 mg. vitamin C, 0.3 mg. beta-carotene • **Serves 8**

FOUR-BERRY PIE

Crust

- 2 cups all-purpose flour
- 2 teaspoons sugar
- ½ teaspoon salt
- 4 tablespoons chilled unsalted butter, cut into small pieces
- 4 tablespoons canola oil
- 6 tablespoons nonfat sour cream
- 1 tablespoon cold water, plus 1 additional teaspoon, if necessary
- ¼ teaspoon almond extract

Filling

- 2 cups halved fresh strawberries
- 2 cups fresh raspberries
- 1 cup fresh blackberries
- 1 cup fresh blueberries
- 3 tablespoons fresh lemon juice
- ¾ cup to 1 cup sugar, depending on sweetness of fruit
- 3 tablespoons cornstarch
- 3 tablespoons instant tapioca
- 1 tablespoon sugar, for topping (optional)

Here's ample incentive for a trip to a "pick-your-own" berry farm. The crisscross lattice topping is a simplified version of the traditional under-and-over weaving method.

1 For the crust, in a food processor, combine the flour, sugar and salt, and pulse briefly to mix. Add the butter and oil, and pulse until the mixture resembles coarse meal. Add the sour cream, 1 tablespoon of the cold water and the almond extract, and process until the mixture just comes together. (If the dough seems too dry, add a few more drops of cold water.) Gather the dough and shape it into two disks; wrap in plastic wrap and refrigerate for at least 15 minutes, or until ready to use. The dough can be refrigerated for up to a day.

2 Meanwhile, make the filling: In a large bowl, combine the fruit and lemon juice. In a small bowl, combine the sugar, cornstarch and tapioca. Stir the sugar mixture into the fruit; let sit for 15 minutes.

3 Preheat the oven to 400°. Adjust the oven rack to the bottom shelf. Line a baking sheet with foil.

4 While the oven is heating, on a well-floured surface, roll out the dough to two 10-inch rounds about ⅛ inch thick. Keeping one round covered, fit the other round into a 9- or 10-inch pie plate, leaving the overhang. Spoon the filling into the shell. Cut the remaining round into ¾-inch-wide strips. Place half the strips over the filling at a 45° angle, spacing them evenly. Place the remaining strips at an opposing angle to the first strips to form a lattice pattern. Trim the ends of the lattice strips and the bottom crust to a ½-inch overhang, then fold the bottom crust over the lattice ends and crimp or pinch the edge to seal.

5 Place the pie on the prepared baking sheet and bake for 45 to 50 minutes, or until the crust is golden brown and the juices begin to bubble. Transfer the pie to a wire rack and let cool for 15 minutes before serving.

Preparation time 10 minutes • **Total time** 1 hour 20 minutes plus cooling time
Per serving 394 calories, 13.3 g. fat (30% of calories), 4.1 g. saturated fat, 16 mg. cholesterol, 165 mg. sodium, 4.5 g. dietary fiber, 41 mg. calcium, 2 mg. iron, 38 mg. vitamin C, 0.2 mg. beta-carotene • **Serves 8**

❧ ❧ ❧

Zuccotto

1 container (32 ounces) vanilla low-fat yogurt

¼ cup blanched slivered almonds

One (13.6-ounce) fat-free pound cake

3 tablespoons fresh orange juice

2 tablespoons sweet Marsala wine

½ cup confectioners' sugar

1 square (1 ounce) semisweet chocolate, finely chopped

1 envelope unflavored gelatin

¼ cup cold water

Sliced strawberries, for topping (optional)

Arrange enough pieces of cake in the bowl so they line it snugly. This layer of cake will form the dome that holds the filling.

In Italian, *zuccotto* means "skullcap"; this impressive dessert was apparently named for its domed shape. Substitute orange juice for the Marsala if you prefer to omit the alcohol.

1 Line a strainer with a double layer of paper towels and place over a medium bowl. Spoon in the yogurt and let drain for 4 hours. Discard the whey and spoon the yogurt into the bowl; refrigerate until needed.

2 Preheat the oven to 350°. Place the almonds in a baking pan and toast for about 8 minutes, or until lightly browned. Chop the nuts.

3 Spray a deep 8-cup bowl with no-stick spray. Line the bowl with plastic wrap. Cut the pound cake into twenty ¼-inch-thick slices. Place one whole slice of cake in the center of the bottom of the bowl. Cut the remaining slices in half diagonally. Arrange enough cake triangles around the inside of the bowl to cover the bowl, overlapping to fit.

4 In a cup, combine the orange juice and Marsala. Brush the cake slices with some of the orange juice mixture; set the remainder aside.

5 Add the confectioners' sugar, chocolate and toasted almonds to the drained yogurt, stirring until well combined. In a small saucepan, sprinkle the gelatin over the cold water and let stand for 1 minute. Cook over low heat, stirring, for 2 to 3 minutes, or until the gelatin dissolves. Gradually whisk the gelatin mixture into the yogurt mixture, whisking constantly until it is completely incorporated.

6 Gently spoon the yogurt mixture into the bowl to cover the cake. Cover the yogurt mixture completely with the remaining cake slices. Brush the remaining orange juice mixture onto the cake slices. Cover with plastic wrap and chill for at least 3 hours, or overnight.

7 To serve, uncover and invert the zuccotto onto a platter. Remove the bowl and plastic wrap. Top with sliced strawberries, if desired.

Preparation time 5 minutes • **Total time** 35 minutes plus draining and chilling time
Per serving 183 calories, 3.4 g. fat (17% of calories), 0.6 g. saturated fat, 2 mg. cholesterol, 137 mg. sodium, 0.8 g. dietary fiber, 89 mg. calcium, 0 mg. iron, 2 mg. vitamin C, 0.1 mg. beta-carotene • **Serves 12**

PUMPKIN PIE

Crust

1½ cups graham cracker crumbs

1 tablespoon margarine, softened

1 tablespoon canola oil

1 teaspoon ground ginger

1 teaspoon grated orange zest

1 tablespoon light corn syrup

1 tablespoon cold water, plus
1 teaspoon, if necessary

Filling

2 large egg whites

1 large egg

¾ cup firmly packed dark brown
sugar

1 teaspoon ground cinnamon

½ teaspoon ground ginger

½ teaspoon ground nutmeg

¼ teaspoon mace

¼ teaspoon salt

2 cups solid-pack canned
pumpkin

1 can (12 ounces) evaporated
skimmed milk

1 teaspoon vanilla extract

Topping

½ cup nonfat sour cream

1 tablespoon confectioners' sugar

1 teaspoon vanilla extract or
½ vanilla bean, split and scraped

Ground nutmeg, for garnish
(optional)

What a dream come true: a pumpkin pie light enough to allow for guilt-free "seconds!" Even the creamy topping is low in fat (but the pie is delicious without it, too).

1 Preheat the oven to 400°. Spray a 9-inch pie plate with no-stick spray.

2 For the crust, in a food processor, combine the graham cracker crumbs, margarine, oil, ginger and orange zest, and pulse briefly.

3 In a cup, combine the corn syrup and cold water. Add it to the crumb mixture and process until the mixture begins to hold together. (If the mixture appears dry, add a few more drops of water.) Press the crumb mixture onto the bottom and sides of the prepared pie plate. Bake for about 8 minutes, or until the crust is firm to the touch. Transfer the pie plate to a wire rack and let the crust cool briefly.

4 Meanwhile, make the filling: In a small bowl, lightly beat the egg whites and egg; set aside. In a food processor, combine the brown sugar, cinnamon, ginger, nutmeg, mace and salt, and pulse until well combined. Add the pumpkin, evaporated milk, reserved eggs and vanilla. Pulse just until combined, then process just until smooth.

5 Pour the filling into the prepared pie shell and bake on the middle oven rack for 35 minutes, or until the crust is browned and the filling is just set in the center. Transfer the pie to a rack to cool completely at room temperature or chill in the refrigerator until ready to serve.

6 While the pie is baking, make the topping: In a small bowl, combine the sour cream, confectioners' sugar and vanilla extract or vanilla bean; cover and refrigerate until ready to use.

7 To serve, cut the pie into 8 slices and top each slice with some of the sour cream mixture. Sprinkle with a little nutmeg, if desired.

Preparation time 15 minutes • **Total time** 50 minutes • **Per serving** 296 calories, 5.7 g. fat (17% of calories), 0.7 g. saturated fat, 29 mg. cholesterol, 320 mg. sodium, 1.8 g. dietary fiber, 200 mg. calcium, 2 mg. iron, 4 mg. vitamin C, 8.3 mg. beta-carotene • **Serves 8**

❧ ❧ ❧

INDEX

❧ ❧ ❧

Note: **Boldface** references indicate photographs.

International Conversion Chart

These equivalents have been slightly rounded to make measuring easier.

VOLUME MEASUREMENTS

U.S.	Imperial	Metric
¼ tsp.	–	1.25 ml.
½ tsp.	–	2.5 ml.
1 tsp.	–	5 ml.
1 Tbsp.	–	15 ml.
2 Tbsp. (1 oz.)	1 fl. oz.	30 ml.
¼ cup (2 oz.)	2 fl. oz.	60 ml.
⅓ cup (3 oz.)	3 fl. oz.	80 ml.
½ cup (4 oz.)	4 fl. oz.	120 ml.
⅔ cup (5 oz.)	5 fl. oz.	160 ml.
¾ cup (6 oz.)	6 fl. oz.	180 ml.
1 cup (8 oz.)	8 fl. oz.	240 ml.

WEIGHT MEASUREMENTS

U.S.	Metric
1 oz.	30 g.
2 oz.	60 g.
4 oz. (¼ lb.)	115 g.
5 oz. (⅓ lb.)	145 g.
6 oz.	170 g.
7 oz.	200 g.
8 oz. (½ lb.)	230 g.
10 oz.	285 g.
12 oz. (¾ lb.)	340 g.
14 oz.	400 g.
16 oz. (1 lb.)	455 g.
2.2 lb.	1 kg.

LENGTH MEASUREMENTS

U.S.	Metric
¼"	0.6 cm.
½"	1.25 cm.
1"	2.5 cm.
2"	5 cm.
4"	11 cm.
6"	15 cm.
8"	20 cm.
10"	25 cm.
12" (1')	30 cm.

PAN SIZES

U.S.	Metric
8" cake pan	20 x 4-cm. sandwich or cake tin
9" cake pan	23 x 3.5-cm. sandwich or cake tin
11" x 7" baking pan	28 x 18-cm. baking pan
13" x 9" baking pan	32.5 x 23-cm. baking pan
2-qt. rectangular baking dish	30 x 19-cm. baking pan
15" x 10" baking pan	38 x 25.5-cm. baking pan (Swiss roll tin)
9" pie plate	22 x 4 or 23 x 4-cm. pie plate
7" or 8" springform pan	18 or 20-cm. springform or loose-bottom cake tin
9" x 5" loaf pan	23 x 13-cm. or 2-lb. narrow loaf pan or paté tin
1½-qt. casserole	1.5-liter casserole
2-qt. casserole	2-liter casserole

TEMPERATURES

Farenheit	Centigrade	Gas
140°	60°	–
160°	70°	–
180°	80°	–
225°	110°	–
250°	120°	½
300°	150°	2
325°	160°	3
350°	180°	4
375°	190°	5
400°	200°	6
450°	230°	8
500°	260°	–